Righting Educational Wrongs

Critical Perspectives on Disability
Steven J. Taylor, Beth A. Ferri, *and* Arlene S. Kanter, *Series Editors*

RIGHTING

Disability Studies

EDUCATIONAL

in Law and Education

WRONGS

Edited by Arlene S. Kanter and Beth A. Ferri

With a Foreword by Nancy Cantor

SU

Syracuse University Press

For a listing of books published and distributed by Syracuse University Press,
visit our website at SyracuseUniversityPress.syr.edu.

ISBN: 978-0-8156-3325-9 (cloth)   978-0-8156-5235-9 (e-book)

Library of Congress Cataloging-in-Publication Data

Second City Conference on Disability Studies in Education (9th : 2009 : Syracuse, New York)
Righting educational wrongs : disability studies in law and education / edited by
Arlene S. Kanter and Beth A. Ferri ; with a foreword by Nancy Cantor. — First edition.
pages cm. — (Critical perspectives on disability)
Includes bibliographical references and index.
ISBN 978-0-8156-3325-9 (cloth : alk. paper) 1. People with disabilities—Education—
Law and legislation—United States—Congresses. 2. Disability studies—
United States—Congresses.   I. Kanter, Arlene S., editor of compilation.
II. Ferri, Beth A., 1961– editor of compilation.   III. Title.
KF4209.3.A75S43 2009
371.90973—dc23   2013034302

Manufactured in the United States of America

For Steven, Rachel, and Ari.
A.S.K.

For Vivian and this great life we keep making every single day.
B.A.F.

Contents

Foreword

In May 2009, Syracuse University was delighted and honored to host the Disability Studies in Education Second City Conference. I am equally delighted that some of the conference presentations have been developed into this excellent collection of articles by experts in the fields of disability studies, law, and education. This book, like the conference that inspired it, builds on the legacy of Syracuse University as an international leader in the field of disability studies and, in particular, on the legacy of Burton Blatt, the pioneering disability rights scholar and activist who, as dean of the School of Education, founded the Center on Human Policy.

The Center on Human Policy was the first university-based research and policy center dedicated to the equal rights of people with disabilities. Today, as the university-wide Center on Human Policy, Law, and Disability Studies, it has expanded the original center's scope and vision in its academic programs, research, publications, and advocacy.

Seven years before the passage of the Americans with Disabilities Act in 1990, Burton Blatt urged his fellow citizens to believe that "as a human being each person is as valuable as any other person" and to understand "that people are people, we're all fragile, we're all mortal, we're all interdependent." To change the world, he wrote, "the first step is to change ourselves."

As a scholarly organization, Disability Studies in Education is committed to a rich understanding of disability, drawing upon perspectives from culture, society, history, philosophy, literature, the arts, and aesthetics to inform and challenge medical, scientific, and psychological models of disability. Syracuse University shares this mission.

Our School of Education houses the nation's first Graduate School Certificate Program in Disability Studies with a truly international student body, and we recently began a new undergraduate program in disability studies. We care about change on the broadest possible spectrum, and we care about change one life at a time. Our College of Law houses the Disability Law and Policy Program, which includes the first joint degree program in law and disability studies, a certificate program in law and disability policy, and a disability rights clinic.

Through such interdisciplinary programs at Syracuse University, we recognize that we are interdependent. We must change ourselves. Our academic programs join forces with the Beyond Compliance Coordinating Committee, our graduate student organization, to raise awareness about disability issues and to challenge assumptions about how our campus can be designed to include everyone.

We know, however, that legislation, compliance, and enforcement are not enough. Our University Task Force on Disability and our new Disability Cultural Center, the first of its kind, also look beyond the relatively easy tasks of building ramps and accessible classrooms to creating what the disability activist Norman Kunc has called a "community of belonging," a place of inclusion and acceptance that celebrates diversity and holds it dear.

I am proud to write the foreword to this volume, and I give a special thanks to Professor Arlene Kanter of the College of Law and Professor Beth Ferri of the School of Education for their work as its editors and for their leadership in the new and exciting multidisciplinary field of disability studies. Disability studies not only enriches Syracuse University and other university communities but also has the potential, as you will read here, to create a new world of inclusion, acceptance, and belonging for all.

Nancy Cantor, Chancellor
Syracuse University

Acknowledgments

We thank our colleagues in Disability Studies in Education who allowed us to host the ninth annual Second City Conference on Disability Studies in Education, which took place at Syracuse University in 2009. The theme for that conference was "righting educational wrongs," and the presenters who shared their work at the conference provided the initial impetus for this volume. The conference was a wonderful example for how to invite cross-disciplinary dialogues to promote the values of inclusion and acceptance of disability as part of diversity that should be, but is not always, the hallmark of any educational association and institution. We are fortunate to teach at Syracuse University, where, under the leadership of Chancellor and President Nancy Cantor (2004–13), who has lent her leadership skills and commitment to justice and equality to creating a more inclusive university community at Syracuse University.

In addition to offering our thanks to Nancy Cantor, we wish to thank two other outstanding Syracuse University colleagues, scholars, friends, and mentors—Professors Steve Taylor and Doug Biklen—for their unwavering support and leadership in establishing disability studies at Syracuse University. We thank Steve Taylor, Centennial Professor, codirector of the Center on Human Policy, Law, and Disability Studies, and coeditor of this series, for his leadership, vision, commitment, and ethical stance toward integration and inclusion. His words and actions continue to guide us and inspire us in untold ways. We also thank Dean Doug Biklen of the School of Education, whose dedication to inclusion and acceptance of *all* people, with and without all types of labels and differences, is a model for all of us. Of all of the many valued colleagues whom we have the good fortune to work with, Doug and Steve continue to provide a touchstone to what it means to do research that matters.

We thank, too, our many colleagues in the Disability Studies Program, including our faculty colleagues, Christine Ashby, James Bellini, Alan Foley, Wendy Harbour, Stephen Kuusisto, Nancy Mudrick, Michael Schwartz, and Diane Wiener, as well as Steve Simon, director of the Office of Disability Services. We have learned a great deal from each of these persons individually and collectively, and we are proud to be a part of such an impressive and caring group of people. Finally, we thank our families for their patience, sustenance, and good humor at the end of a long day.

We also would like to thank our College of Law student research assistants, Alessandra Baldini and Mary Bertelsmann for their help on the preparation of this manuscript and the Syracuse University Office of Research for its support in the final stages of this volume. We are most grateful to Chris Ramsdell for her tireless work in helping us to coordinate, finalize, and prepare this manuscript for publication. Finally, we thank the contributors to this volume, from the fields of disability studies, education, and law, whose scholarly contributions help to promote the changes in society that are necessary to correct the many wrongs within our educational system, and beyond. We are thrilled with the collective voice with which this manuscript speaks in support of the educational rights of all students.

Introduction

Righting Educational Wrongs—Disability
Studies in Law and Education

ARLENE S. KANTER and BETH A. FERRI

This book cultivates a critical conversation among scholars of disability studies in education and law about contemporary struggles around access to education and inclusion. Authors in this text draw from disability studies as the theoretical basis from which to examine disability-related policies and practices as they contribute to or undermine educational access and inclusion for individuals with disabilities.

Although much has been written about disability, education, and law, no volume has tackled the intersection of these fields of study from a disability studies framework. In fact, disability studies is relatively new to the fields of both law and education. Moreover, although legal and educational scholars have written much about disability, for the most part their work has not been informed by disability studies. Thus, this book stands in sharp contrast to previous collections related to disability law or special education law. At the same time, it also expands our understanding of legal studies' potential to inform work in disability studies in education and vice versa by introducing the field of disability legal studies.

The book is divided roughly into three parts. The first four chapters explore the intersections between disability studies, law, and education and attempt to forge a theoretical framework for thinking about educational access. Chapters 5 through 7 take a critical look at some of the histories of exclusion in education and ways that these exclusions have been upheld by a variety of educational policies and practices. The final five chapters reflect on the ways in which individuals and families have experienced the Individuals with Disabilities in Education Act of 1990 and the implication of these experiences for higher education.

In chapter 1, "The Relationship between Disability Studies and Law," Arlene Kanter introduces readers to the field of disability legal studies. As a subpart of the general field of disability studies, disability legal studies explores the relationship between disability studies and the law. In this chapter, Kanter argues for a disability studies–informed critique of the law, legal institutions, and legal education, similar to the ways that critical and feminist legal scholars have challenged the law's exclusion of other marginalized groups. According to Kanter, disability legal studies, as a new field of scholarship, provides new understanding about power, oppression, and privilege with respect to people with disabilities and the law. It also offers an opportunity to introduce disability law and cases throughout the traditional legal curriculum, which, she argues, will enhance the study of law, leading to better legal practice.

In chapter 2, "Universal Design in Education: Remaking All the Difference," Martha Minow builds on her landmark work *Making All the Difference* (1990), which examines ways in which "difference" gets assigned by law, custom, practice, or unconscious perception to some people even when "difference" is always a comparison, a relationship between people. In this chapter, she argues that in order to make a "real difference," we must go beyond mainstreaming and adopt inclusive practices that are based on principles of universal design. Only then, she believes, will we truly open our classrooms, workplaces, and the world to people with disabilities.

In chapter 3, "Rights, Needs, and Capabilities: Institutional and Political Barriers to Justice for Disabled People," Thomas M. Skrtic and J. Robert Kent explore various models for social justice in relation to disability. They specifically suggest that actualizing Martha Nussbaum's capabilities approach to social justice for disabled people will require embedding her understanding of human flourishing in a broader institutional theory of justice. This process will result in a notion of social justice that is centered in a developmental liberal conception of democracy.

In chapter 4, "Ending the Longing for Belonging: Teaching Disability Studies in the College Core Curriculum," Susan Baglieri and Linda Ware point to the need for disability studies to be thought of as an integral part of the college core curriculum rather than to be relegated to fields within the professional schools, such as special education and law. After providing an overview of the interdisciplinary approaches they take in teaching disability studies–related courses at two different universities, they examine student responses and offer their own reflections about infusing disability studies within the general college curriculum.

Chapter 5, "Treating the Incomplete Child: How the Science of Learning Disabilities Was Built for Exclusion," by Scot Danforth and Theodoto Ressa, traces the history of special education science that inadvertently paved the way for exclusion of students with disabilities. In this chapter, the authors unpack the intellectual and practical foundation of American special education policy and practice through a focused examination of the history of the science of learning disabilities between World War I and the landmark federal special education legislation of 1975.

In chapter 6, "The Present King of France Is Feeble-Minded: The Logic and History of the Continuum of Placements for People with Intellectual Disabilities," Philip M. Ferguson explores the historical context of the emergence of the continuum of the supports model in special education practice. Ferguson questions the underlying logic of matching the intensity of support with the restrictiveness of the educational setting and proposes an alternative to this foundational model of service delivery within special education.

Chapter 7, "Disabling Racial Repetition," by Zanita E. Fenton, examines the negative effects of disability classification systems in schools, especially on black males. In particular, Fenton explores the overrepresentation of black males in the categories "mentally retarded" and "emotionally disturbed" and compares the exclusion and marginalization of black males and of all children with disabilities to illustrate how these forms of exclusion resurface and repeat themselves. She argues convincingly that overrepresentation of students of color in special education must be remedied in order to avoid the perpetuation of disparities that begin in early education and continue later to all other areas of life.

In chapter 8, "Children with Disabilities, Parents without Disabilities, and Lawyers: Issues of Life Experience, Affinity, and Agency," Mark C. Weber explores the tension between the need of people with disabilities to claim power and autonomy for themselves. The reality is that parents or lawyers who are not themselves disabled are most often placed in the position of advocating on behalf of their children with disabilities. Weber looks at ways to ensure that individuals with disabilities are positioned as agents, not objects, in legal contexts.

Chapter 9, "The Tale of a Reluctant Expert Witness," by Alicia A. Broderick, presents an intimate look at the experience of an expert witness in two Individuals with Disabilities Education Act (IDEA) cases. Through the use of vignettes based on her own experience as an expert witness in IDEA cases, Professor Broderick illustrates the decision-making process for students with significant motor and communication impairments for whom educational decisions must often be made under conditions of profound uncertainty about what the student may or may not know, understand, need, or desire. Broderick also explores the ways in which educational wrongs may (or may not) be righted through the process of litigation under the IDEA.

In chapter 10, "The Case for Inclusive Eligibility under the Individuals with Disabilities Education Act," Wendy F. Hensel questions whether narrowing eligibility requirements under the IDEA would lead to greater integration of students with disabilities or ultimately reinforce stigma and result in greater inequality. Although acknowledging the burgeoning number of children who receive services under the IDEA, she draws lessons from the Americans with Disabilities Act to caution against narrowing eligibility requirements.

In chapter 11, "Disability, Vulnerability, and Fragmented Protections: Accessing Education, Work, and Health Care," Ani B. Satz argues that disability laws fragment disability protections by including only certain impaired individuals in the protected class and by providing only limited and situation-specific accommodations. She suggests a more universal approach to ensuring access to education as well as to employment and health care.

In chapter 12, "Inclusion in K–12 and Higher Education," Wendy S. Harbour expands the conversation to consider inclusion in higher education settings. She insightfully argues that the more inclusive K–12 becomes, the more expectations will rise for higher education to be equally inclusive. She likewise notes that the more inclusive higher education becomes, the more expectations will rise for inclusion in the workplace and the community. She also suggests that universally designed and inclusive higher education contexts can also inform inclusion efforts in K–12 settings.

Finally, in the epilogue, Beth A. Ferri concludes the book with a critical retelling of the origin story of disability studies and a call for more cross-disciplinary dialogues.

For ease of reading, in the chapters we have used a shortened citation system for legal cases, statutes, and regulations, giving only a name and a year as a general reference, but including details if a specific citation is warranted. Full reference information for all cases, statutes, and regulations is included in the second section of the references at the back of the book.

Righting Educational Wrongs

1

The Relationship between Disability Studies and Law

ARLENE S. KANTER

What Is Disability Studies?

Disability studies is not one discipline, nor does it profess to subscribe to one particular theory, perspective, or approach to the study and teaching of disability. However, as a new academic field it does offer a new way to approach and view the production and perpetuation of disability as a social identity.

First, disability studies is a multidisciplinary field of study. As such, it borrows from the scholarship of many disciplines and occupies its own place between and among different disciplines. Thus, scholars in disability studies do not simply add to existing disciplines; they also create new scholarship by posing traditionally ignored questions about the place of disability in society. Second, disability studies scholars critically explore the place of disability in society. Not satisfied with accepting the invisibility and inequality of people with disabilities in society, they examine disability as a social, cultural, and political phenomenon and perceive disability as the result of sociocultural dynamics that occur in interactions

Portions of this chapter are a revised excerpt from an article published as "The Law: What's Disability Studies Got to Do with It, Or An Introduction to Disability Legal Studies," *Columbia Human Rights Law Review* 42, no. 2 (2011): 403–79, reprinted with permission.

between society and people with disabilities. By viewing disability in this way, they reject the view that disability is solely a medical problem or a personal tragedy that involves an inherent, immutable trait located in a person. Instead, within disability studies, disability is positioned as a social construct, thereby putting the responsibility for reexamining and repositioning the place of disability on society itself.

Disability studies scholars, therefore, see people with disabilities not as patients or charitable "cases," but rather as human beings who exist as an important part of the social fabric (Kudlick 2003, 775). The term *disabled* is to be defined subjectively because, in the final analysis, disability is "a political or a moral judgment, based not on anything about the individual in question so much as on the viewer's own perception and attitudes about the way society should function" (M. Johnson 2003, 46). When disability is defined as a social category rather than as an individual characteristic, it is no longer the exclusive domain of medicine, rehabilitation, special education, physical or occupational therapy, and other professions oriented toward the cure, prevention, or treatment of disease, injury, or physical or mental impairment. In this way, disability studies stands in sharp contrast to the clinical, medical, or therapeutic perspectives of disability, which focus on the person and render disability a series of medical, physiological, anatomical, psychological, and functional pathologies that originate in the person's body or mind (Linton 1998b, 529–31). In short, disability studies embodies values that are based on viewing the person with a disability not as a victim or as a "defective" person, but as someone who is limited by social attitudes and environmental barriers. In asserting that disability is a social construct derived from a history of stigmatization and exclusion, disability studies recognizes that knowledge of disability is to be found among people with disabilities themselves. It thus uses the perspectives and experiences of people with disabilities as foundations for research and training.

What Disability Studies Is Not

As discussed so far, disability studies differs from traditional disability-related fields such as occupational therapy, physical therapy, rehabilitation counseling, and social work, which generally train people to work with people with disabilities as patients or clients. It is also different from the research conducted in these fields, which focuses more on the study of disability itself than on the study of the society that perpetuates the stigma and exclusion of people with disabilities. Disability studies accordingly differs from the study *of* disability in several significant ways.

First, a disability studies research paradigm differs from the paradigm used in traditional disability-related fields by perceiving disability as a natural part of the human condition, not a as defect in the person that needs to be eliminated, treated, or cured. It therefore shifts the emphasis away from a prevention/treatment/remediation paradigm to a social/cultural/political paradigm. Disability studies rejects the perception of disability as a functional impairment that limits a person's activities and instead challenges society to reimagine the place of disability within society. A disability studies paradigm therefore examines the question of "fixing" systems so that they are accessible to and usable by people with disabilities rather than focusing on "fixing" the individual so that he or she can better fit into the existing systems, as in the traditional paradigm.

A second way in which disability studies research differs from the traditional paradigm for understanding disability is that it seeks to portray people with disabilities as individuals with dignity who are capable of contributing to society, even if they do so in "different" ways. Disability studies research, therefore, is not limited to empirical research or to statistics about people with disabilities. In fact, empirical studies that seek to count and categorize people with disabilities for the purpose of research related to such issues as benefits eligibility, census counts, and service delivery are for the most part not considered disability studies research at all. If such empirical research challenges what disability means, who is making that decision, and how society creates and perpetuates the category of disability, then it can be considered disability studies research. However, if it focuses only on the person with a disability as an object of study, without seeking also to bring forth that person's voice and viewpoint, then it will not likely be considered disability studies research. When research on disability uses disability as a category for comparison that focuses on people with disabilities in their particularity, and their particularity becomes the subject of the research, it is not considered empowering to people with disabilities and is therefore not disability studies research (Linton 1998a, 134–35). Of course, related problems are created when research on the general population excludes disability altogether because it considers people with disabilities to be too particular to be relevant (Longmore and Umansky 2001, 7).

Either way, traditional studies *of* disability generally position the researcher as the expert, with authority, but people with disabilities only as objects of such research. The field of disability studies research challenges this paradigm by viewing people with disabilities themselves as experts in addition to professionals who also know about various medical, legal, sociological, and educational conditions that have historically defined disabilities. It is for this reason that emancipatory or participatory research has found a comfortable home within disability studies (Oliver 1997, 15).[1]

A third way that disability studies differs from more traditional research *on* disability is that it challenges the view of disability as "tragedy." People who work with people who are blind, deaf, autistic, developmentally disabled, and physically disabled often see their clients' or patients' impairments as a personal tragedy. For example, recent quality-of-life studies have revealed that physicians generally have a much lower view of the quality of life of a person with a disability than does the person himself or herself. In one study for example, only 17 percent of medical providers said that the quality of life of a person with quadriplegia is at most average,

---

1. It is important to mention here that just calling a certain type of disability research "disability studies research" does not end the analysis of whether it is consistent with the goals of the new field of disability studies. For example, my coeditor, Beth Ferri, and I have discussed the fact that simply because research is qualitative does not mean that it is any more empowering and less objectifying of people with disabilities than empirical research. In fact, qualitative research that involves interviews, personal stories, and data can treat people with disabilities as objects just as much as quantitative research. Qualitative research may, in fact, feel intrusive and more like a violation of the dignity of a person with a disability than, say, anonymous test scores or other kinds of empirical data that are not personally revealing.

whereas 86 percent of the people who are quadriplegic rated the quality of their lives as average or higher. In the same study, only 18 percent of emergency care providers imagined they would be glad to be alive if they were paralyzed, whereas 92 percent of the people who are quadriplegics reported that they were glad to be alive (Basnett 2001, 7). Such discordant views between service providers and those whom they serve can have serious results, particularly for the person with a disability in the context of making decisions, especially end-of-life decisions. Indeed, such different perspectives about quality-of-life issues have given rise to the "not dead yet" movement, which challenges the notion that professionals know better than a person with a disability whether that person should continue to live or die (Not Dead Yet.org 2013).

Disability studies also affirms the value of life with a disability. It embodies values based on viewing the person with a disability not as a victim, but as a participant in the world and as one who is limited only by social, legal, environmental, and attitudinal barriers. In contrast to others, in particular medical professionals, people with impairments do not generally see themselves or their lives as tragic and not worth living. For example, Liat Ben-Moshe, a recent PhD recipient at Syracuse University, uses a wheelchair and has written that her real lived experience—including using a wheelchair—can be enriching and empowering. She explains that a student told her once that "she felt confused and did not know what to do; that she felt *paralyzed*." Ben-Moshe responded (to herself), "That's funny; I am paralyzed, and I know just what to do" (Ben-Moshe 2005, 111).

A fourth way in which disability studies differs from studies *of* disability is the background of the scholars and their audiences in the two areas. Disability research historically involved doctors, nurses, rehabilitation counselors, physical therapists, occupational therapists, psychologists, psychiatrists, teachers, social workers, and other members of what are considered the "helping professions." Disability studies includes those fields, but it also includes disciplines that previously had not addressed the issue of disability as a social construct, such as architecture, journalism, film, philosophy, policy, art, choreography, literature, poetry, history, anthropology, sociology, and law. Moreover, the audience of disability studies scholarship includes not only members of the so-called helping professions, but also people with disabilities themselves and other social justice advocates seeking to challenge the creation of hierarchies in society that result in the overall exclusion and marginalization of people with disabilities. The scope and breadth of disability studies research and its audience are accordingly far more expansive and interdisciplinary than the scope and breadth of traditional disability scholarship.

Finally, the outcomes of disabilities studies research are different from those of traditional research about disability. Studies *about* disability generally focus on the number of people with disabilities participating in certain programs or activities or an understanding of issues related to diagnosis, prevention, rehabilitation, treatment, and cure of a given impairment. By contrast, disability studies may involve similar findings, but from the perspective of the person with a disability. More commonly, however, the outcome of this research focuses on other issues, such as an understanding of history, politics, economics, culture, and civil and human rights. The overarching purpose of disability studies research, therefore, is to offer alternative ways in which society may view both disability as a category and the people with disabilities themselves, as a group and in their particularity (Linton 1998a, 9).

In short, at the risk of reducing either disability studies or traditional approaches to the study of disability into an oppositional binary, it may be safe to say that disability studies recasts disability as a set of relations that determines a person's place in society and reframes the study of disability by focusing on it as a social phenomenon, social construct, metaphor, and culture (Linton 1998a, 10). The fundamental issue, then, becomes "not one of [the] individual's inabilities or limitations, but rather, [of] a hostile and unadaptive society" (Swain 2003, ii). But even within disability studies there is little agreement about the models of disability or the correct or preferred language to use, as explained in the next section.

Models of Disability and Disability Studies

In addition to the theoretical challenges posed by disability studies, several different models of disability have emerged. Some scholars see these models as part of the same overall view of disability and believe that naming the different models is less important than the critical viewpoint they espouse. Other scholars see certain models as limiting and unresponsive to the real, lived experiences of people with disabilities. But what most disabilities studies scholars agree on is that viewing disability solely through the medical model is no longer acceptable.

According to the medical model, people with disabilities are generally seen as sick and in need of treatment, rehabilitation, or a cure. Because the medical model places responsibility on the individual to change or to be "cured," society itself is under no obligation to change or to adjust itself to the needs of people with disabilities. Indeed, as a result of viewing disability through the lens of the medical model, societies have erected large institutions to care for people with disabilities and to protect them from society (or vice versa) rather than to facilitate their inclusion within society. Today, disability studies scholars and disability rights activists alike reject the medical model and its pathologization of certain behaviors that looks to the medical establishment for solutions. As Paul Longmore and Lauri Umansky have written, the medical model "personalizes disability, casting it as deficit located within individuals that requires rehabilitation to correct the physiological defect or to amend the social deficiency" (2001, 7).

One result of relying solely on a medical model of disability is that it relieves society of any obligation other than to care, treat, or cure the person. Society itself has no obligation to look at how it is structured, how it creates barriers to inclusion, and how it shares in the responsibility to eliminate barriers in order to invite people with disabilities into its schools, workplaces, and neighborhoods. As a result, disability studies scholars have generally dismissed the medical model of disability in favor of the minority or social model of disability, which instead places responsibility for reexamining and repositioning the place of disability not on the individual (and on his or her doctor or treating professional), but on society. Beyond that, great variation exists regarding how disability studies scholars approach the study of disability itself. Some of them see disability as a label and a social construct, whereas others view it in terms of group status, identity, and culture or a combination of all of these things.

The Minority-Group Model of Disability

The minority-group model of disability views people with disabilities as an oppressed and "disadvantaged" group (Hahn 1985, 94). According to this model, people with disabilities are victims of indignities, discrimination, and exclusion from society in much the same way people of color, women, homosexuals, and other marginalized groups are. The disability rights movement (like the civil, women's, and gay rights movements before it) focuses on issues of identity and power relationships. The minority model supports this rights-based view of disability. It "provides the collective context for political identification . . . and involves processes which challenge views of disabled people as incapable, powerless and passive; and it establishes disabled people as the experts on disability and disabled people's definitions as the most appropriate approaches to disability, rather than the traditional domination of professionals" (Shakespeare 1996, 102). However, membership in the group of people with disabilities in society necessarily imposes a nonmajority, second-class, "other" status that necessarily shapes its members' life experiences.

It is undeniable that people with various disabilities have been treated as "the other" throughout history. As a group, they have been denied the right to vote (Kanter 2011, 422; Waterstone 2005) and have been locked away in remote institutions, excluded from society, and subjected to neglect and abuse (Blatt and Kaplan 1974; Kanter 2003, 243). History is replete with numerous incidents of assault, rape, and even murder of people simply because they were considered disabled (Barnes 1997). People with disabilities continue to face widespread discrimination today. As a result of such discrimination, they, as a group, are less wealthy, less educated, less often employed, and more often underemployed than their nondisabled peers, including those in other minority groups.

In the United States, for example, 46 percent of adults with disabilities live in households with a total income of less than $25,000, and 25 percent report that they receive all of their personal income from benefits and insurance programs (National Organization on Disability 2004, 22, 13). In the area of employment, two-thirds of working-age Americans with disabilities are not working, yet eight out of ten of those individuals say they want to work; only one in five working-age adults with disabilities works full-time, and only 11 percent work part-time (National Organization on Disability 2004, 7–8). Work disincentives also may play a role in keeping people with disabilities unemployed, although recent changes have made it possible for people to work and still retain their health benefits under Medicaid, a policy that kept many people at home for decades. Fifty-seven percent of people with disabilities fear they will lose vital benefits and supports if they secure a job; 50 percent of current students and trainees with disabilities expect to encounter job discrimination; and 30 percent of disabled workers report discrimination owing to their disability (National Organization on Disability 2004, 7). For example, in 1988, workers with disabilities earned only 64 percent of what their nondisabled coworkers earned (National Organization on Disability 2004, 22). Those individuals with the most stigmatized type of impairments, such as cognitive disabilities or mental illness, as well as women, people of color, and gay, bisexual, or transgendered people with disabilities fare even worse.

From an education perspective, people with disabilities have made some advances that have put them in a position slightly better than in the past. But they still remain far behind their nondisabled peers in access to education in the United States and in most countries throughout the world. Many more students with a range of disabilities have not completed high school in the United States than their peers without disabilities. Moreover, even since the enactment of the Americans with Disabilities Act in 1990 (ADA), approximately 40 percent of Americans with disabilities believe that things have not gotten much better for them (M. Russell 1998, 111).

In order to change this situation and improve the lives of people with disabilities within society, disability studies scholars who subscribe to the minority view seek to bring forward the voices of people with disabilities in the same way that scholars have provided venues for the voices of other oppressed and unrepresented minorities to be heard. A tension exists, however, between the minority-group model and other models of disability.

Under the minority-group model, the goal of disability-related scholarship (and activism) is to provide people with disabilities the same rights, privileges, and benefits enjoyed by other groups in society. In the United

States (and in other countries as well), we now have laws that provide accommodations in the workplace, increased benefits for people with disabilities who cannot work, and civil rights laws guaranteeing equal access to services, education, public accommodations, housing, and employment (Kanter 2011, 425). The tension grows, however, as claims for equal treatment reinforce the notion of the "deserving" person with a disability, which in turn perpetuates the location of disability within the person rather than in society. Although the minority-group model seeks to provide greater political legitimacy to people with disabilities as a group, it also runs the risk of failing to challenge the "existing structures and values of a disabling society" (Barnes 1999, 72). As such, the minority-group model may "accord disabled people's demand a degree of political legitimacy they do not have at present, but without eradicating the causes of their disablement" (Barnes 1999, 72).

The Social Model of Disability

Some scholars consider the social model and minority model interchangeable. Lennard Davis (2002) regards the social model as the US version of the British minority-group model. Other scholars see the social model as expanding upon the minority-group model (e.g., Barnes 2003). For these scholars, the social model, like the minority model, sees disability as part of the human experience and offers "a strategy of barrier removal, and education to remove prejudice, with the goal of inclusion" (Barnes 1999, 72). But unlike the minority-group model, the social model focuses less on the relationship between the group of people considered disabled and other groups and "more on disability as a relationship between people with impairments and a discriminatory society" (Barnes 1999, 72).

The social model places the responsibility squarely on society and not on the individual with a disability to remove the physical and attitudinal barriers that "disable" people with various impairments and prevent them from exercising their rights and fully integrating into society. In other words, a person's impairment does not diminish that person's right to exert choice and control in his or her life or to participate fully in and contribute to his or her community through full integration into the economic,

political, social, cultural, and educational mainstream of society. According to the social model of disability, it is impossible to say that any person
is "unable" or "unqualified" to exercise his or her rights or to participate
fully in society. Instead, it is affirmatively society's obligation to change or
adapt its services, programs, facilities, and systems so that *all* people can
exercise their rights, regardless of whether they have particular impairment or not.

But if disability itself is socially constructed, as the social model proposes, what is the value of the real, lived experiences of people with disabilities? Where do the pain and suffering of people with certain disabilities fit
in? This question is commonly posed to proponents of the social model of
disability. The response to this question is that although the social model
of disability views disability as socially constructed, it does not go so far as
to negate the existence of the impairment, nor does it deny the person's
pain, suffering, or need for treatment, rehabilitation, and support. Instead,
the social model sees the social meaning of the impairment as the source
of the person's oppression rather than the person's impairment itself. Harlan Hahn (1988), a noted sociologist, has labeled this phenomenon "exis-
tential anxiety"—when we obscure "our" own deviations from the norm
(cited in Macurdy 1995, 450).

The Cultural Model of Disability

Related to the social model of disability is the cultural model. The latter
incorporates a range of critical and postmodern theory in its analyses. By
drawing on Michel Foucault (1965), for example, it understands disability
as a category of social control emerging in a process of "subjection." This
approach shifts our attention from the person with an impairment to the
statutory, regulatory, and political processes that construct him or her as
disabled (Barnes 1999). It also offers an alternative, postmodern framework and a fragmented, decentered sense of self made intelligible via multiple, conflicting identities. The application of critical and postmodern
theory to disability results in the view that the definition of disability itself
is "unstable and open to contestation" and should be replaced with the
view that disability "occurs alongside multiple other identities (such as

sexuality, race and ethnicity, socioeconomic status, etc.)" (Sherry 2008, 75). According to Deborah Stone, whose writings rely heavily on Foucault, disability became a separate social category that, beginning with the enactment of the nation's poor laws, drew a distinction between deserving and undeserving poor (1984, 55). To her, such categorization continues to permeate social policy today.

Writers such as Susan Sontag, Adrienne Rich, Simi Linton, Rosemary Garland-Thomson, Sharon Snyder and David Mitchell, Marion Corker, Robert McClure, and others have used disability as part of their notion of cultural representation, drawing on Foucault's concept of discursive formations. This critique of disability as a cultural category challenges popular representations of people with disabilities as inferior, abnormal, and worthless by unpacking the cultural patterns that produce those images. As Elspeth Morrison and Vic Finkelstein have observed, "To encourage the growth of a disability culture is no less than to begin the radical task of transforming ourselves from passive and dependent beings into active and creative agents for social change" (1991, quoted in Barnes and Mercer 2010, 207).

Film and literature have been used as a medium through which to analyze cultural representations of disability. In Neil Marcus's illuminating words, "Disability is not a 'brave struggle' or 'courage in the face of adversity[.]' . . . [D]isability is an art. It's an ingenious way to live" (1996, 23). Linda Ware, a disability studies educator, has written: "When disability is considered through a cultural lens, ability is interrogated in much the same way that gender is interrogated by feminist studies scholars and Whiteness is interrogated by ethnic studies scholars" (2001, 110). Ware suggests that if educators accept the challenge of reimagining disability in society, "[it] will necessitate new alliances with colleagues in the humanities" (120) and, it should be added, throughout the university community.

The Human Rights Model of Disability

A recent variant of the social model is the human rights model of disability that has gained recognition since the adoption of the Convention on the Rights of Persons with Disabilities (CRPD). The United Nations adopted the CRPD in 2006, and it is the first binding international treaty that approaches disability as a human rights issue (Kanter 2007). The CRPD refuses to define disability according to a medical model and instead affirms the basic human rights of all people with disabilities and guarantees that they enjoy the same rights and protections as people without disabilities. It goes one step further than any other previous international human rights instrument by also guaranteeing all persons with disabilities their right to legal capacity. No person with a disability, including a person with a cognitive or psychosocial disability, may be deprived of his or her legal capacity owing to a diagnosis or label of disability (Kanter 2007). Thus, this new convention makes clear that it is no longer permissible under international human rights law to view people with disabilities as only objects of charity or in need of medical intervention; they must now be viewed and valued as subjects of their own lives and holders of international human rights (Kanter 2007).

As disability studies develops in and among different fields of study, these models will overlap and expand. Just as the definition of *disability* can be seen as flexible, so too can the analytic models followed in disability studies as well as the language it uses.

The Language of Disability Studies

In addition to various theories and models of disability that have developed within the field of disability studies, most scholars also have explored the use of language to describe disability as part of the disability studies paradigm. A society's view of people with disabilities and the words it uses to describe them tell a great deal about its values (Jones and Basser Marks 2000b). Disability studies provides us with the tools to understand the connection between language, power, societal attitudes, and beliefs (Kudlick 2003, 768–69).

The law in particular relies heavily on the written and spoken word. Indeed, language is one of the most important tools of the legal profession. Lawyers use oral and written language to negotiate, interview clients, cross-examine witnesses, present arguments in court, and form briefs and judicial opinions. Understanding language and the power of language is as important to law students as it is to practicing lawyers and judges. Not only do we strive for our students to use language well in writing (as seen in highly coveted law review editing positions), but most law schools now prominently feature new programs in legal writing and oral advocacy. In a profession that relies so much on the written and spoken word, those of us who are legal scholars need to invite our students to think about how we refer to other people. Who has the right to decide what any given group of people should be called? Which words hurt and should be avoided, and which bring pride and should be used? What does one's word choice generally reveal about one's values and point of view? Similarly, in the field of education students are regularly given disability-related labels, many of which have histories of insult and derision. In both the law and education, we must be mindful of how our ways of talking and writing about other people's lives can be oppressive and disrespectful.

In his often-cited article "Violence and the Word," former Yale law professor Robert Cover brought into public scrutiny, perhaps for the first time, the relationship between law, language, and violence. He acknowledged that words alone can bring violence to and delegitimize the individual when he wrote: "Legal interpretive acts signal and occasion the imposition of violence upon others: A judge articulates her understanding of a text, and as a result, somebody loses his freedom, his property, his children, even his life. . . . When interpreters have finished their work, they frequently leave behind victims whose lives have been torn apart by these organized, social practices of violence. Neither legal interpretation nor the violence it occasions may be properly understood apart from one another" (1986, 1601).

The power of language is particularly controversial with respect to words that describe people with disabilities. Word choice can reveal values that reflect the speaker's beliefs about disability as well as about human worth in general (Cohen 1954, 545). Demeaning and degrading language that detracts from the value of people with disabilities in society is everywhere. Newborns are labeled as "defective" and so may receive substandard care; adults are called "incompetent" and so risk losing their autonomy; children with "special needs" may face isolation from their peers (Macurdy 1995, 443). Terms such as *mentally retarded* have accordingly been replaced with the description "a person with a cognitive (or intellectual or developmental) disability"; *cripple* has been replaced with the description "a person with a spinal cord injury"; and *nut* or *lunatic* has been replaced with the description "a person with a psychiatric disorder or a consumer (or survivor) of mental health services." Such changes in the language of disability are not merely about political correctness. They reflect an overdue recognition of the respect owed to people with different impairments who are no less part of our society and who are no longer willing to accept labels of exclusion and stigmatization.

Language also has unintended consequences in that disability has come to denote deficiency. Used as a metaphor, disability connotes what is not "normal." Examples such as "dumb luck," "lame idea," "falling on deaf ears," "blind rage," and "stand up for yourself" are significant for the images they present (Ben-Moshe et al. 2005). A "crazy" or "retarded" idea is a bad idea; "blind to the fact" means lacking knowledge or having no understanding; and someone who is "crazy" means someone who is out of control and not someone you would want to get to know. In other words, disability studies scholars have critiqued the use of disability as a metaphor "to denote a deficiency, a lack or an ill-conceived notion [for] reproduce[ing] the oppression of people with disabilities" and for ignoring the fact that the actual experience of living with a disability "can be quite enriching and empowering" (Ben-Moshe 2005, 109, 108).

Within disability studies, however, there is no agreement regarding which language should be used to refer to the people at the center of inquiry. Disability studies scholars use country-specific language. In the United States, it is common to refer to "a person with a disability," a phrase that relies on "people first" language to convey the idea that having a disability is secondary to a person's primary identity as a "person" or "human being." Similarly, the phrase "labeled as disabled" or "labeled as mentally ill" focuses on how disability, mental illness in particular, is a socially constructed definition imposed on a person who may or may not agree with the classification or even the existence of the condition known as mental illness. Other scholars, particularly in the United Kingdom, refer to "a disabled person" to draw attention to the centrality of disability in the individual's identity. Many disabled activists in the United States also prefer this terminology. Similarly, the terms *deaf* and *Deaf* may mean different things when referring to a person. The former includes deafness as one of many adjectives that might be used to describe the person, whereas the latter emphasizes the person's membership in a culturally defined linguistic minority.

It is also important to note that each of these examples ignores entirely other aspects of the person's identity, including the person's race, gender, sexuality, age, ethnic, cultural or religious background, and even physical traits or personality characteristics. Seldom do we hear "a person with a disability" described instead as "the attractive man" or the "friendly woman" or "the bright young student." Once a person becomes disabled, the disability itself becomes not only the person's primary identity as seen by others, but more often than not the person's only socially relevant identity. All other physical, sexual, gender, intellectual, emotional, or personality characteristics of the person seem to disappear.

In addition to examining how we use language, disability studies helps us to describe the large, diverse, and growing number of people with disabilities. In the United States, more than 50 million people are considered "disabled"; the estimate for the world is now more than one billion people (World Health Organization 2011). Disability studies raises the question of what so many people from so many parts of the world with so many different abilities and impairments may possibly have in common with each other that the label *disabled* implies.

For example, a twenty-three-year-old white male law student from New York City who is blind and attends Syracuse University may have little in common with a seventy-eight-year-old African American woman who is blind and works as a teacher in Chicago or even with a twenty-three-year-old Deaf white male law student at Syracuse University. A child with autism in Egypt may have little in common with a child with spina bifida in Canada; and a twenty-five-year-old mother in Ghana who is HIV positive may have little in common with a twenty-five-year-old young woman in Turkey who is confined to a mental hospital. People who use wheelchairs or who have chronic pain or students who learn or write at a slower pace than other students may have vastly different experiences and perspectives from one another and from other people who do not use wheelchairs, who do not live in chronic pain, or who are considered to have higher measured intelligence. Yet people with these different experiences share one important and salient feature: they all are perceived by society as disabled, regardless of whether they see themselves or each other that way. People who have vision or hearing impairments or who have physical or cognitive impairments or are labeled mentally ill are considered "disabled" and therefore not "normal." From the "feel good" stories about the poor "crippled" children featured in fund-raising materials to the media's idealization of youth and vigor, perfection of body and mind is the desired (but unattainable) norm from which people with disabilities differ (Kudlick 2003, 8–9).

Indeed, disability studies challenges us to reexamine our assumptions about the universality of the concept of the norm. As the disability studies scholar Lennard Davis has observed, "normal" itself is a fiction and evolved as a category during the mid–nineteenth century's occupation with human sciences and the rise of statistics. The concept of an "average person" emerged and became the "normal person"—the standard against which human deviation was measured. Prior to that time, the standard was a "divine body," an "ideal body [that] . . . was recognized as not attainable by a human" (2006, 4–5).

Even some very progressive and popular thinkers throughout history used the concept of "normal" and "average." Karl Marx's notion of labor theory of value and average wages was based on the idea of the average worker (Davis 2006, 5–6). Despite Marx's significant contribution to modern social thought, one may examine his complicity in enforcing normalcy by seeking to minimize certain deviations from the norm in society in terms of the distribution of wealth. Psychologists and psychiatrists, too, are implicated. Sigmund Freud's work could not have been done without the idea of the normal (Davis 2006, 10). With this concept of the norm, of course, came the concept of deviation from the norm, and people with disabilities became the deviants.

As disability became conflated with deviance, the eugenics movement was born (Burleigh 1995, 18–24). The early-twentieth-century eugenics movement was social, political, scientific, and racist. Although we usually think of eugenics as being associated with Nazism, it was also practiced in the United States and not just by a fringe group. Historians of disability policy have written persuasively about how eugenics was part of the work of thinkers who were considered enlightened at the time and was even included on socialist platforms (Davis 2006; Selden 2000). Emma Goldman, for example, wrote that unless birth control were encouraged, the state would "legally encourage an increase in paupers, epileptics, cripples, and degenerates" (quoted in Kevles 1985, cited in Davis 2006, 8).

The eugenics movement emerged from a belief that "normal" (white) people were becoming outnumbered by genetically defective nonwhite, "feeble-minded" epileptics, criminals, and insane individuals who had to be institutionalized and stopped from reproducing because of the danger they posed to society (Mazumdar 2006). By the 1900s, eugenics began to define all people with disabilities as deviants based on the concern that individual differences and "defects" would permeate the national identity. This view led to eugenics laws and forced sterilization. By 1941, thirty-three US states had endorsed sterilization policies (Mazumdar 2006). Even today, sterilization of women with cognitive disabilities continues in many countries of the world.

Thus, regardless of how people with disabilities see themselves or each other, for centuries they have been referred to as "not normal" by a majority who view themselves as strong, intelligent, sighted, hearing, ambulatory, in control, able-bodied, nondisabled, and therefore "normal." Given this situation, one of the tasks for disability studies scholars today, in Lennard Davis's words, is "to reverse the hegemony of the normal and to institute alternative ways of thinking about the abnormal" (2006, 15).

Disability Legal Studies:
Where Law and Disability Studies Meet

It is now well accepted that disability studies has emerged as a new and exciting field of academic inquiry. Many academic institutions now offer courses or programs in it,[2] and most professional academic organizations

---

2. In 1993, the Society for Disability Studies developed the following working guidelines for any program that describes itself as "disability studies": (1) It should be

now have sections devoted to the study of disability within their respective disciplines. Among the most recent fields to begin to explore its relationship with disability studies is law.

Why should those of us who teach and study law care about including disability-related topics or, better yet, a disability studies perspective within our research agenda or our law school curriculum? Why would we want to consider introducing a disability studies perspective into a course on evidence, property, family law, or even tax? What can the emerging field of disability studies teach us and our students within the field of legal education? How will the inclusion of a disability studies perspective within the legal academy help our students to become better lawyers and, perhaps more important, help to promote fairness and justice in society?

My response to these questions is relatively straightforward. Disability studies infuses into the legal academy the perspective of those who are

---

interdisciplinary and multidisciplinary. Programs in disability studies should encourage a curriculum that allows students, activists, teachers, artists, practitioners, and researchers to engage the subject matter from various disciplinary perspectives. (2) It should challenge the view of disability as an individual deficit or defect that can be remedied solely through medical intervention or rehabilitation by "experts" and other service providers. Rather, a program in disability studies should explore models and theories that examine social, political, cultural, and economic factors that define disability and help determine personal and collective responses to difference. At the same time, disability studies should work to destigmatize disease, illness, and impairment, including those that cannot be measured or explained by biological science. And although acknowledging that medical research and intervention can be useful, disability studies should interrogate the connections between medical practice and stigmatizing disability. (3) It should study national and international perspectives, policies, literature, culture, and history with the aim of placing current ideas about disability within their broadest possible context. Because attitudes toward disability have not been the same across times and places, much can be gained by learning from these other experiences. (4) It should actively encourage participation by disabled students and faculty and should ensure physical and intellectual access. And (5) it should make it a priority to have leadership positions held by disabled people; at the same time, it is important to create an environment where contributions from anyone who shares all these goals is welcome.

routinely made invisible and marginalized, just as feminist legal studies before it did for women (Abrams 1997; Dowd and Jacobs 2003; Frug 1992; Karst 1984; Levit and Verchik 2006; Silvers 1998) and critical race theory (Ball 1990; D. Bell 1980b, 1995; Brewer 2005; Crenshaw et al. 1996; Delgado 1995; Delgado and Stefancic 1993, 2001) did for people of color.

Disability studies helps us to see disability as part of the human experience and to understand how the law and society in general view difference as a deviation from an "unstated norm" (Minow 1990, 51). When the issue involves race, for example, whites are treated but never acknowledged as the norm, whereas blacks are considered the deviation. Similarly, when the issue is gender, men are treated but never acknowledged as the norm, whereas women are considered the deviation. When the issue is disability, the able-bodied, seeing, hearing, mentally "healthy" person with a certain score on an intelligence test is treated but never acknowledged as the norm, whereas people who communicate through sign language, use wheelchairs, or speak, think, or hear differently are considered the deviation. Disability studies helps us to understand the implications, including the legal implications, of the preferences given to the able-bodied person.

Disability studies therefore offers the law and legal education the opportunity to critically examine the role of "normalcy" within the law specifically and within society generally. It challenges us to examine our unstated assumptions and requires us to recognize, appreciate, and, most important, value differences among us. Because law itself is in the business of deciding how to recognize, legitimate, and allocate differences (different rights, responsibilities, and resources), disability legal studies offers an appropriate lens through which we can view the legal profession and the meaning of difference within the legal system and society. Conversely, the field of law may inform the field of disabilities studies by providing a context in which to examine the meaning of differences within our legal and extrajudicial systems. It also may help us to see issues of power, privilege, and participation more clearly.

In order to discuss what the law can learn from disability studies, we must first define what we mean by "the law." According to tradition, laws are written by legislators, interpreted by courts, and enforced by governments. As such, "the law" is a collection of rules imposed by authority; a legal document setting forth rules governing a particular kind of activity; a rule or body of rules of conduct inherent in human nature and essential to or binding upon a society; a generalization that describes recurring facts or events in nature. The law also encompasses jurisprudence, the branch of philosophy concerned with the principles that lead courts to make the decisions they do as well as the profession that is mastered by graduate study in a law school and that is responsible for the judicial system.

Although the role of law has been viewed differently over time, throughout most of history the law has been seen as the ultimate authority in any given society. Writing in 350 BCE, for example, the Greek philosopher Aristotle declared that "it is more proper that law should govern than any one of the citizens" (1987, 3.16). Societies enact laws to maintain order and to protect persons and property from harm. Laws also serve to mediate relations between people. But, above all, to the extent that law is generally viewed as a system of rules that shape politics, power, and society, it becomes the vehicle with which the status quo and existing power relationships are maintained. Indeed, laws are designed to conserve and preserve the rule of law. But do they? And on whose behalf and for whose benefit? These are some of the questions that critical legal theorists as well as law and society scholars have raised (Altman 1993, 11; Bauman 2002; Brown 2003; Finnis 1985; Halley 2001; Kairys 1998; Kelman 1987; Duncan Kennedy 1997, 2004; Kennedy and Fisher 2006; Unger 1983; Ward 2004). They are also questions posed by disability legal studies scholars today.

The law governs a wide variety of social activities and human interactions. But law can mean many different things depending on its context. Our legal system elaborates rights and responsibilities in a variety of ways that raise important and complex issues concerning equality, fairness, liberty, justice, and power relations.

Contract law regulates everything from hiring a new employee to renting an apartment. Property law defines rights and obligations related to the transfer and title of your car or home or related to a woman's womb; tort law provides remedies for persons who have been injured or whose property has been harmed. If the injury or harm is outlawed in the penal code, criminal law offers the means by which the state can prosecute the perpetrator. Constitutional law provides a framework for the creation of laws, the allocation of powers of the branches of government within society, the protection of civil rights, and the election of political representatives; administrative law is used to review the decisions of government agencies; and international law governs affairs between sovereign nation states in activities ranging from trade to environmental regulation to international conventions such as the CRPD.

Law is also a profession and an academic discipline. The academic study of law, both as a science (jurisprudence) and as coursework by students preparing to become licensed to practice law, is taught in the United States at specialized postgraduate law schools. In other countries, students take law as their first degree or as a one-year course after majoring in another discipline. Yet in the United States and in most other countries throughout the world today, legal education focuses on the doctrine of law as well as on the skills and procedures necessary for the practice of law as a profession. Legal education seeks to equip soon-to-be lawyers with knowledge and skills pertaining to the law, the legal process, and the legal system as well as the fundamental principles, theories, and values on which these things are based. It seeks to foster not only the knowledge and skills, but also the values that students need to function effectively in a pluralistic, democratic society based on the rule of law. Although legal education in the United States has evolved in the past century, its structure and format remain strikingly similar to the days of Christopher Columbus Langdell and the founding of the nation's first law school in the late nineteenth century (Sheppard 1999).

Over the decades, many legal scholars have begun to explore the relationship between law and society and to ask critical questions about the role of law in society. What is the proper function of law? What sorts of acts should be subject to punishment, and what sorts of punishment should be permitted? What is justice? What rights do "we" have? Who are "we," and who bestows which rights on others? Who makes the laws, and who defines who breaks the laws? To the extent that law governs relations between people and between the state and individuals, how does law facilitate or impede access to power, justice, fairness, and responsibility?

Indeed, legal issues related to difference and power have been studied for at least three decades within the legal academy. Throughout the 1960s and into the 1990s, law and society in general as well as the critical legal studies movement, critical race theories, feminist legal scholarship, queer legal studies, and postmodernism challenged the academy to look at how decisions are made and for whose benefit.

Early law-and-society scholars drew on social sciences "to provide insights about both the ways that prevailing legal norms tend to legitimate social hierarchy and the complex manifestations of legal claims and tactics by groups aiming to challenge those hierarchies and injustices" (McCann 2006, 18). Indeed, sociolegal scholars contributed research on such topics as the effect of the judiciary, interest-group litigation, cause lawyering, and the politics of rights—to name just a few—that are highly relevant to understanding the relationships between law and social movements.

Critical legal studies, building on the realists' critiques of law, exposed the relationships between law and power, claiming that the law is not neutral or value free, but rather an active participant in power dynamics. Critical legal theorists have accordingly characterized the law as a set of rules used by the powerful to oppress the powerless and have focused their inquiry on questions related to access to power (D. Bell 1987; Haney Lopez 1996; Matsuda 1991; Williams 1991). To them, law *is* politics.

Feminist legal theorists have constructed their criticism of law by asking such questions as, How does law exclude women? How can law be reformulated to incorporate women's experiences? How can feminist legal theory reconfigure existing law? And with regard to disability, feminists may ask, How can existent feminist legal scholarships in family, labor, caretaking, reproduction, and sexuality be reformulated to incorporate the experiences and perspectives of women with disabilities? (See, e.g., Abrams 1997; Frug 1992; Silvers 1998.)

By contrast, the role of disability in law has been less studied (Kanter 2011, 443; Mor 2006, 77–78). Yet disability studies has enormous potential within the legal academy because scholars are now beginning to present such inquiries as, Which legal theories inform the transforming and reconceptualizing of both law and disability? Disability studies presents a new lens through which to examine the place of law in society and to pose certain questions: How do legal definitions of disability regulate, exclude, and/or protect marginalized populations based on their physical and mental differences, gender, economic status, race, ethnicity, and sexual orientation? What are the respective roles of human rights, formal equality, and antidiscrimination legislation in various approaches to disability? What can people with disabilities offer to reconfigure existing law?[3] By infusing a disability studies perspective into the law, we may shed light on complex lessons about our culture, society, minority rights, power, authority, and the role of law in changing society just as the study of the law's relationship to issues of race, ethnicity, gender, and sexual identity has informed our understanding of society and power.

Why Teach Law from a Disability Studies Perspective?

Only recently have legal scholars begun to explore the intersection of law and disability studies. This new field, which I call "disability legal studies," refers to scholarship that seeks to apply a disability studies perspective to law (Mor 2006). As Sagit Mor has written, "Although disability studies' critique is not altogether new to some legal scholars, it has not yet gained adequate recognition in legal discourse. I maintain that the time has come to identify, introduce, and label the field of DLS [disability legal studies], bring it to light, attend to its premises, and incorporate its lessons into legal theory and practice. I further suggest that attending to DLS would bring a shift in writing on disability and the law from a focus on doctrinal analysis or policy advocacy, to a research regarding the constitutive role of law in the production of disability" (2006, 64).

Legal scholars, law students, and lawyers are generally familiar with disability as a legal issue. Through the disability rights movement and

3. These questions are based on a call-for-papers announcement for the Workshop on Feminist Legal Theory and Disability Studies at Emory University, fall 2009. Available at http://disabilitystudiescfp.blogspot.com/2009/10/call-for-papers-feminist-disability .html (last visited June 22, 2010).

the enactment of various disability rights laws—in particular the ADA and the Individuals with Disabilities in Education Act of 1990 (IDEA) as well as their provisions regarding "special education," antidiscrimination, accommodations, and accessibility—lawyers, Congress, and the courts have become familiar with disability as a legal issue. But the new field of disability legal studies looks beyond the traditional view of antidiscrimination laws to promote equality, as in the Lockean and Millsian sense that each person has the right to be treated like anyone else. Instead, it seeks to challenge the way disability is constructed by law in our social environment locally, nationally, and globally. It adopts the social model of disability that sees disability as a social construct shaped by social systems of domination. As such, a study of disability in law, particularly in a global context, provides law teachers and their students the opportunity to discuss how to bridge this gap between civil rights and human rights as well as between formal and substantive equality.

Yet the question remains: What does a disability studies perspective have to do with what law teachers do in their classrooms? How would a disability studies perspective help law students or lawyers understand contracts, torts, evidence, or tax regulations, to name a few areas of law? Or, put another way, why would law faculty choose to integrate disability studies into the law school curriculum?

We may begin to answer this question by recognizing that because law reflects society's norms, values, and intolerances, it is an arbiter of power relations. Thus, the law itself can become part of the problem by creating social barriers and classifications based on competency or abilities. It can be "implicated in subordinating and oppressing people with disabilities, through express rules, the application of exclusionary values in judicial decision making, or simply by failing to take action to ensure that people with disabilities have access to justice" (Jones and Basser Marks 2000a, 3). But the "law can also be seen to offer a path to equality—to be part of the solution as well as part of the problem" (Jones and Basser Marks 2000a, 3). Stated differently, the legal system can be a source of social change through the enactment and implementation of progressive laws and inclusive interpretation of laws by legislators, attorneys, and the courts. In other words, the law provides a framework with which to assess the infusion of disability studies values within society. Disability studies, then, can provide the tools to explore such regenerative aspects of law. One positive example of the law's regenerative aspect is the United Nations' recent adoption of the CRPD. The CRPD creates, for the first time, affirmative obligations on state parties to recognize and ensure equality of people with disabilities throughout all aspects of society. Although the implementation of the specific mandates in the CRPD will vary from country to country and even within a given country, the CPRD's role in potentially changing the view of people with disabilities by advancing their cause worldwide cannot be ignored (Kanter 2007).

Within the law, a shift has already begun to take place from the traditional doctrinal analysis that adopted the view that discrimination on the basis of disability is forbidden to a more textured understanding of people with disabilities as a minority group and growing attention to disability as a social construct (Crossley 2004; Diller 2000; Drimmer 1993; Kanter 2007; Mor 2006). As we continue now to examine law through the disability studies lens, the focus will become how exclusion of people with disabilities in the law appears in the first place and how inclusion may occur. As Colin Barnes, Geof Mercer, and Tom Shakespeare have written,

> While the voice of disabled people and their organizations is being heard more often and more distinctly than before, the struggle for improved socio-economic conditions, for a better quality of life, and for citizenship rights generally goes on. Recent policy debates ranging across welfare benefits and services to abortion and euthanasia have increased the suspicions of disabled people. There is generally a much changed political rhetoric responding to disabled people's claims, and in considering research evidence and making policy proposals, but promised improvements all too often fail to materialize. (2005, 227)

From a practical view, however, even with this change in discourse, most people with disabilities in the United States do not believe that things have improved for them over the past twenty years (Bagenstos 2009, 1117–19). Why is this so, especially in a country that has dedicated itself to equal rights and opportunities for all? What are the root causes of this problem? And, most important, what can we do to alter this situation? Such questions are (or should be) central to the study of law. They raise important issues regarding the concepts of justice, power, equality, and liberty. Indeed, the relationship between citizen and society is essential to legal education, although different law schools give priority to different subject areas or skills.

In most law schools today, some courses focus primarily on the laws that affect the daily lives of all people, including criminal and civil law. Other courses focus on fundamental legal concepts and principles, including their origin and contemporary influence and impact. Yet other courses stress the application of legal principles and skills in specific real-world situations through clinics and externships. Still other courses examine law as an institution that provides the government with power and authority that can bring both order and the risk of abuse and look at the relationship between power and law, as was the focus of the critical legal studies movement. In so doing, legal education has the potential to understand how law can and has promoted inclusion, social cohesion, and social change. Let me suggest several additional reasons why disability studies is relevant to our law school curriculum and the legal academy in general (Bryen and Shapiro 1996; Linton 1998b; Syracuse University Center on Human Policy 2004).

Disability Is "Us"

The first reason why a disability studies perspective is relevant to the study of law (and to all disciplines, for that matter) is that disability itself directly or indirectly affects almost everyone in any given society throughout the world. As noted earlier, the estimate of the number of people with disabilities throughout the world is now more than one billion (World Health Organization 2011). In the United States alone, 15 to 20 percent of the population, or approximately 56.7 million people, are considered disabled (US Bureau of the Census 2010). In addition to people with disabilities themselves, their family members, friends, teachers, and neighbors are also affected by disability, so that perhaps as many as half or more of the US population is directly affected by disability. Therefore, it is beyond dispute that people with disabilities are "too large [a minority] to ignore" (Davis 1997b, 4).

Moreover, if not now, then at some point in the future many more law students, lawyers, judges, and law faculty will either experience disability directly or have a family member, classmate, student, professor, client, colleague, or friend with a mental or physical impairment. It may accordingly be said that we all are "temporarily able-bodied" because sooner or later most of us will be disabled at some point in our lives. Whether it comes sooner or later depends on one's circumstances. As Susan Wendell explains, according to Catherine Kudlick, factors "such as race, class, gender, nationality, and age can have a significant impact on the experience of living with an impairment and its disabling consequences" (2003, 768). But the fact remains that anyone can become disabled at any time.

People with disabilities also are the fastest-growing minority in the world (Wendell 1996, 18). As more people live longer owing to advances in medical research and technology, more may be expected to acquire impairments and become disabled in old age (Fagan 2002; Kanter 2009). In 1980, it was estimated that in the United States 370 million people were older than sixty (Chen 1987). Today one in ten people is now sixty years of age or older (Fagan 2002, 331). In Italy, Germany, and Japan, more than 20 percent of their respective populations are now older than sixty-five (McNicoll 2009). By 2025, there will be 1.1 billion elderly people worldwide (Chen 1987, 175).

Not only is the population of people with disabilities and those affected by it increasing, but people with disabilities themselves have become more visible within society. The increased visibility is owing in large part to the changing view of disability brought about by the enactment of such laws as the Rehabilitation Act of 1973, the Fair Housing Amendments Act of 1988, the ADA, and the IDEA.

One can just look at the list of the original supporters of the ADA, for example, to see that literally each one of them is disabled or has a family member with a disability: Tony Coelho, a Congressman from Maryland who sponsored the original ADA bill in the House, uses a wheelchair; Steny Hoyer's wife has epilepsy; Senator Lowell Weicker has a son with

Down syndrome; Senator Bob Dole and Senator Bob Kerry are disabled war veterans; Senator Tom Harkin had a deaf brother; Senator Edward Kennedy had a son who lost a leg and a sister with a developmental disability; Senator Orrin Hatch has a brother-in-law with postpolio syndrome (Stein 2004, 627n201).

Further, within the legal profession, one can assume that more lawyers with disabilities are working, although the exact number is difficult to ascertain because only three of fifty-four American jurisdictions that license attorneys collect information on lawyers with disabilities (American Bar Association Commission on Mental and Physical Disability 2010).[4] In addition, more students with disabilities are attending our universities and law schools (National Center on Education Statistics 2010).[5] In US law schools today, it is estimated that at least 10 percent of law

4. The American Bar Association (ABA) compiles disability-related statistics on the legal profession based on its annual census. The 2010 *Disability Statistics Report*, prepared by the ABA Commission on Disability, gives the following data according to the ABA's 2009 annual census. Only 1,658, or 6.76 percent, of the ABA's 383,000 members in 2009 answered affirmatively to the question, "Do you have a disability?" That percentage is a slight increase from the number in the 2008 census, 6.69 percent, but a decrease from the number in the 2007 census, 7.18 percent. Douglas Kruse of Rutgers University and the National Bureau of Economic Research, using 2007 American Community Survey microdata, reports an even lower number, indicating that out of the 1.08 million Americans who are lawyers or judges, magistrates, and other judicial workers, only 3.8 percent have a reported disability. The US Bureau of Labor Statistics has its own figure, reporting that for the third quarter of 2009 (July, August, and September), 2.6 percent of those employed in the legal occupation (e.g., lawyers, judges, magistrates, law clerks, court reporters, paralegals) had a disability (American Bar Association Commission on Mental and Physical Disability 2011).

5. According to the National Center for Education Statistics (2006), 11 percent of undergraduates reported having a disability in 2003–4. The enrollment of people with disabilities in two- or four-year-degree institutions has increased steadily (Gerald and Hussar 2002). College enrollment includes close to half a million students with disabilities (Wagner et al. 2005, 4-7.). However, the rate of people with disabilities attending postsecondary school is less than half that of their peers in the general population (Wagner et al. 2005, 3-1; see also Bruder and Mogro-Wilson 2010, 4).

students have a disability (K. Smith 1999, 2; Donald Stone 2000, 26). Such numbers are not completely accurate, however, because they may not include students with invisible disabilities (such as learning disabilities or neurological or psychosocial impairments), nor do they include those students who refuse to be "counted" owing to the stigma that still attaches to most disabilities today.

Attending schools with nondisabled peers is not new for most law students. The IDEA has facilitated the graduation from high school of many students with disabilities, and they go on to attend colleges and graduate schools in law, among other fields. Most law students today thus attended primary and secondary schools along with students with disabilities as a result of the IDEA, which has mandated mainstreaming for more than three decades. As a result of the IDEA, literally millions of students with disabilities—approximately 6.7 million children and youth, or about 9 percent of all children and youth between the ages of three and twenty-one—have received IDEA services (as of 2006–7) (National Center for Education Statistics 2006). Most law students, therefore, are used to being in classes with people with different types of disabilities and are likely to expect such diversity within their law school classes. One would hope that the more law students learn about disability and get to know fellow students with disabilities, the more likely they will reject stereotypes and traditional ways of thinking about the role of disability in society as solely a medical problem and thereby become more welcoming to clients with disabilities when they eventually practice law.

Although law students with and without disabilities may be used to classrooms inclusive of students with a range of impairments, for those faculty who have not grown up with people with disabilities, teaching students with disabilities might be an unwelcome challenge. Based either on a lack of knowledge or on their own prejudices or fears, these law faculty may relate to students with disabilities in a way that creates barriers to their acceptance as competent law students (see Bruder and Mogro-Wilson 2010). The inclusion of students with disabilities in our law school classrooms may accordingly challenge both the concept and the constituency of disability (Ware 2001, 108).

Disability Is Inclusive

In addition to the prevalence of disability within society in general and within law schools in particular, a second reason to teach law or other disciplines from a disability studies perspective is that disability itself is inclusive. Disability crosses all lines of race, ethnicity, gender, sexuality, religions, nationalities, and generations. And, like race, gender, and sexuality, it teaches about inclusion, exclusion, and the diversity of the human experience. Despite the number of people with disabilities in our neighborhoods, workplaces, and schools, stereotypical ideas and negative views of people with disabilities remain. Disability continues "to carry a negative social charge still supported by dominant cultural assumptions across the economic, political and intellectual spectrum" (M. Johnson 2003, 44). As a result, on college campuses and in law school hiring committee meetings, disability is noticeably absent from diversity discussions. Many faculty who are progressive on issues of race, gender, and lesbian, gay, bisexual, and transgender issues, for example, may be resistant to promoting affirmative action based on disability—even though people with disabilities are grossly underrepresented in the academy, especially on law school faculties. As one disability studies scholar has observed, "While race has become in the past 10 years a more than acceptable modality from which to theorize in the classroom and in print, as a discourse, a critique, . . . disability continues to be relegated to hospital hallways, physical therapy tables, and remedial (special) classrooms" (Davis 1997b, 1–2).

Furthermore, although most college campuses today value diversity, disability is often excluded from conversations about diversity. In diversity-training programs for students, for example, students with disabilities have described how they have to "push their way" into the planning process. Not only is disability not generally part of diversity discussions, but when disability does come up, it is often focused on an immediate need—for instance, to install a ramp to a building or grab bars in restrooms—not on the importance of including people with disabilities as a group that faces discrimination and exclusion on a daily basis.

Disability in the Legal System

A third reason to teach law from a disability studies perspective is that disability can shed light on the history and values of our legal system (Syracuse University Center on Human Policy, Law, and Disability Studies 2004). Although people with disabilities (and their accomplishments) have remained largely invisible throughout our history, further research reveals that disability, in fact, has been "present in penumbra if not in print, on virtually every page of American history" (Longmore and Umansky 2001, 2). People with disabilities, for example, have for a long time figured prominently (but negatively) in popular culture, beginning with the freak shows of the 1930s and followed by the Barnum and Bailey Circus (Bogdan 1988, vii–x).

Disability historians also have revealed that during the Great Depression the League of the Physically Handicapped staged actions in protest of job discrimination resulting from the medical model of disability that had begun to shape policy, professional practices, and social arrangements of the early twentieth century (Longmore and Goldberger 2000, 889–90). In addition, stories of veterans returning from World War II and the annihilation of people with disabilities in concentration camps entered our collective consciousness in the postwar years. More recently, stories of soldiers returning from Vietnam, Iraq, and Afghanistan with post-traumatic stress syndrome also have challenged us as a society to consider the price of war. A less known but powerful story is the account of a group of conscientious objectors to World War II who, after refusing to serve based on their religious views as pacifists, were required to work at state mental institutions. Horrified by what they saw, these individuals helped to expose the abuses and atrocities of mental institutions in the 1940s, which led later to the politics of deinstitutionalization and to today's scholarly study of disability (Taylor 2009).

More recently, protests by activists in the disability rights movement provided the backdrop against which President George H. W. Bush signed one of the country's most comprehensive civil rights laws, the ADA (Switzer 2003, 68–89). Such action also provides the backdrop to the historic role of people with disabilities from all over the world in drafting the new United Nations CRPD (Kanter 2007, 294).

Disability issues are also prominent in the history of American jurisprudence. Numerous landmark cases involve people with disabilities,
including *Buck v. Bell* (1927), in which the Supreme Court upheld as constitutional forced sterilization of women with mental disabilities; *City of
Cleburne v. Cleburne Living Center* (1985), in which the court upheld the
right of a group home to open in a residential area and by breathing new
life into the rational basis test of the Equal Protection Clause of the Fourteenth Amendment; *Youngberg v. Romeo* (1982) and *O'Connor v. Donaldson* (1975), in which the Supreme Court upheld the right to treatment as
a quid pro quo for institutionalization; and *Atkins v. Virginia* (2002), in
which the Supreme Court held that the execution of a man considered
"mentally retarded" constituted cruel and unusual punishment under the
Eighth Amendment. These cases are landmark cases not only in the area
of disability law, but in American constitutional history as well. Further,
the Terry Schiavo case (*Schiavo ex rel. Schindler v. Schiavo* 2005) will certainly go down in legal history as the case that required an emergency session of Congress after the Supreme Court rejected an emergency appeal
just eighteen hours before Terry Schaivo's life-sustaining feeding tube was
to be removed in a Florida hospital.

In fact, as further evidence of the role of disability in the legal sphere,
it is worth noting that the Supreme Court decided perhaps more cases
under the ADA during the first ten years of its enactment than under most
other statutes (Kanter 2003). Most of these cases addressed fundamental
issues of law such as the role of the federal government vis-à-vis the states,
the nature and meaning of due process under the Fourteenth Amendment, and the contours of the rights protected by the Bill of Rights. For
example, in *Board of Trustees of University of Alabama v. Garrett* (2001),
the Supreme Court held that Title I of the ADA was unconstitutional inso-
far as it allowed states to be sued by private citizens for money damages.
In *United States v. Georgia* (2006), the Supreme Court ruled that Title
II of the ADA abrogates sovereign immunity in cases involving alleged
violations of the Eighth Amendment. In *Tennessee v. Lane* (2004), the
Supreme Court held that people with disabilities had been denied their
right to access the courts, a fundamental right protected by the Due Process Clause of the Fourteenth Amendment.

Further, the Supreme Court's 1999 "trilogy" of decisions in which the Court addressed the definition of disability under the ADA[6] is significant not only for scholars of disability law, but also for scholars of the Supreme Court and Congress. These three cases brought into focus the jurisprudential philosophy of the Court's individual members. In each, the Court's decision rested on which justices adopted the majority textualist view of judicial decision making, which required them to disregard the agency regulations that defined disability differently from what the majority of the Court ultimately decided. These cases, all of which were eventually overturned by Congress's decision to amend the ADA in 2008, are important to scholars interested in the relationship between Congress and the Court.

In addition to Supreme Court jurisprudence, other aspects of our legal system are deeply entwined in disability issues of all kinds: the guardian laws that afford courts the power to decide who is and is not competent to make decisions about their own lives; the insanity defense, which involves an inquiry into whether an individual is culpable or exonerated based on what experts tell the court about the person's state of mind; the best interest of the child, which is the standard used by courts to judge custody decisions and which might result in termination of rights based on a parent's disability, depending on the judge's knowledge of and prejudice about parents with disabilities; insurance laws, which offer different levels of coverage for treatment of physical or mental impairments in many states; and others. In each of these areas, disability is embedded with social and cultural meanings in our legal system. As the late disability rights advocate and law professor Alan Macurdy observed,

> As advocates, we deal every day with the ways in which legal power is used against individuals with disabilities, so the idea that disability bias is embedded in the structure of law is built into how we do our jobs. We see how rigid conceptions of competency are manipulated to deny people with disabilities control over their property, their living

6. *Sutton v. United Air Lines, Inc.* (1999); *Murphy v. United Parcel Service, Inc.* (1999); *Albertson's, Inc. v. Kirkinburg* (1999).

arrangements, and their bodies. We have learned that core values of individual autonomy, equality, and due process are left behind by "treatment" models and paternalism. We no longer question, though we each might express the point differently, that the law proceeds as if there were an identifiable standard of "ableness" that describes most of us, and justifies different treatment of everyone else, and that such a standard is myth. (1995, 443–44)

Disability studies therefore provides a vehicle with which to explore questions about our rights and responsibilities and the general role of the government in promoting and protecting the welfare of all citizens. Just as discussions of gender and race have had an impact well beyond women and people of color, so too can disability force the legal academy to reconsider the economic, social, political, cultural, religious, legal, philosophical, artistic, moral, creative, and medical aspects of almost everything "we have taken for granted" (Kudlick 2003, 5–6).

Conclusion

Disability studies has emerged within the academy as a new multidisciplinary field. It requires us to (re)consider how society excludes people with disabilities not because of their limitations, but because of the way in which society itself is structured and operates. From this viewpoint, it is not as if there are no differences among people who are Deaf or blind or have other impairments, nor does this view deny the suffering, pain, and lack of needed support that many people with disabilities experience. Instead, disability studies allows us to explore how to mitigate or even eliminate the social outcomes of differences with an awareness of the role that power plays in shaping the development of laws and legal rights.

Disability legal studies presents to the law and legal education both challenges and opportunities. It challenges legal scholars to view critically the place of disability within the legal system and the legal academy as well as within society generally. Viewing law through the lens of disability studies challenges us to examine disability—like race, gender, class, and sexuality—as a social and political construct derived from a history of stigmatization and exclusion. It also challenges us to consider the complex ways in which our system of laws, government, social structures, institutions, culture, and customs contributes to the disablement of persons in our own society and in societies throughout the world.

Disability legal studies also presents opportunities. As part of the larger field of disability studies, disability legal studies provides legal scholars the tools to develop a critique of the law with respect to disability and to explore the role and manifestations of ableism in social practices and institutions that "portray people with disabilities as useless, marginal, abnormal, a burden on society, and perhaps most offensively, as living a life that is not worth living" (Mor 2006, 69). It also provides the context in which to deconstruct and reconstruct the meaning of disability through investigating the social construction of disability as well as the power structure that supports and enhances ableism.

Disability legal studies does not seek to maintain the status quo. It is "a radical move as it seeks to transform mainstream legal education" (Mor 2006, 64n4). It provides theoretical tools as well as advocacy strategies to challenge our cultural norms that have resulted in the creation of legal, physical, and attitudinal barriers to inclusion of people with disabilities in society. As such, it has the potential to expose legal scholars, our students, and the legal academy to new areas of academic inquiry beyond what disability studies itself offers. It adds to the questions posed by disability studies, including: What does it mean to be "normal" for the purpose of legal decision making? How does and should the law respond to differences among us? How can we challenge the privilege afforded to the able-bodied norm within the legal system?

A first step in responding to these questions is to increase the visibility of people with disabilities within law schools and within the academy itself. In recent years, more students with disabilities are demanding their place in law schools, but few faculty with disabilities are visible in most law faculties. Further, when students and faculty with disabilities are noticed or discussed on campuses, they are often portrayed as threats or vulnerable victims, but not as valued members of the academic community.

Syracuse University has taken steps to change this situation by recruiting and retaining more students, faculty, and staff with disabilities; by nurturing the development of disability studies programs; and by improving access and accommodations with the goal of creating a community of inclusion for all. Although we still have a long way to go, such efforts are well worth it. With such changes, our universities, legal institutions, and society as a whole will benefit from the participation of people with disabilities in our classrooms, our neighborhoods, and our lives.

2

Universal Design in Education

Remaking All the Difference

MARTHA MINOW

In *Making All the Difference: Inclusion, Exclusion, and American Law* (1990), which I wrote more than twenty years ago, I worked to examine the ways in which we assign "difference" through laws, customs, practices, or unconscious perceptions. The notion of a "difference" is so often assigned to and located in some people even when "difference" is a comparison, describing a relationship between people. I worked with the then-emerging idea of the "social construction" of difference. Particularly for persons with disabilities, societal attitudes and practices determine the degree to which their "differences" pose obstacles in their daily lives and life aspirations. Although it seems easy to assume that the "difference" lies in the person who uses a wheelchair, it is the stairway that makes a building inaccessible to the wheelchair user; it is the widespread ignorance of sign language that places the student who uses it outside the mainstream; it is constantly being "discount[ed] in advance," not a disability itself, that, as Randolph Bourne once said, puts people "at cross-grains with the world," needing to guard against growing up "with a bad temper and a hateful disposition," becoming "cynical and bitter against" those who turn them

This chapter was originally presented at "Righting Educational Wrongs: Disability Studies in Education, Policy, and Law," the Ninth Annual Second City Conference on Disability Studies in Education in partnership with the Syracuse University Center on Human Policy, Law, and Disability Studies and the College of Law's Disability Law and Policy Program, May 1–3, 2009, Syracuse University.

away (quoted in Miller and Longmore 2006, 68). The predictable objections come quickly: "But there are REAL differences, don't deny them"; some people cannot hear; some people have a neurobiological disorder associated with dopamine neurotransmitter systems in the brain that produce motor restlessness, impulsive behaviors, and difficulties maintaining attention over a sustained time period; or, in one of the more provocative recent scholarly statements, people with mental disabilities impose "hedonic costs" through "emotional contagions" affecting those who have to work with them (Emens 2006, 399, 401).[1]

Over the past two decades, I have worried about these kinds of questions while also reveling at the enactment of the Americans with Disabilities Act. Even as judicial decisions have curbed its scope, advocates have pressed for regulatory and statutory reforms, and federal and state agencies have helped in the struggles to shape a nondiscriminatory, inclusive society.

Along the way, I have noticed a paradoxical development. On the one hand, the term *disability*—meaning people with disabilities and the concept of disability—has increasingly entered the mainstream. On the other hand, the goal of social integration is now newly up for debate. So although the academic and policy focus on disability becomes increasingly integrated, the aspiration of integration for people with disabilities to join in schooling and to work with people without disabilities faces renewed debate and dispute. I explore both sides of this paradox—the mainstreaming of disability and the renewed questions about the integration ideal—and conclude with an argument for the ideal of "universal design," which approaches physical and virtual environments with the full range of human beings already in mind.

Disability Law as the Mainstream

In many ways, disability has become mainstreamed. For example, widely read and beloved books among the elementary and middle school set

---

1. Despite these pejorative phrases, Elizabeth Emens largely defends accommodations and integration in another article (Emens 2008), emphasizing the benefits to "third parties" from employer accommodations for persons with disabilities.

notably feature children with disabilities. *Joey Pigza Swallowed the Key* by Jack Gantos (1998) features a character with attention deficit hyperactivity disorder; he learns ways to manage his condition even as each page brings humor to his situation. In *Yours Turly, Shirley* by Ann M. Martin (1998), the main character has dyslexia and, perhaps even more challenging, a little sister who is a high academic achiever. Janet Tashjian's *Multiple Choice* (1999) involves a girl with obsessive-compulsive disorder. Lois Lowry's *Gathering Blue* (2000), a sequel to her award-winning book *The Giver* (1993), has a main character who is visually impaired and also a talented artist. In *Rules* (2006) by Cynthia Lord, a sister of a boy with autism tries to teach him social rules while learning herself about times to break the rules. A favorite in my household is *Freak the Mighty* (1993) by Redman Philbrick, in which a boy with learning disabilities befriends a physically disabled genius who happens to have a father in trouble with the law.

Less colorfully, legal scholars now treat disability as a frequent topic. Whether as an example or central focus, disability law and related issues occupy leading scholars who work on law and economics, statutory interpretation, antidiscrimination law, intersectionality, constitutional law, employment law, property law, and human rights (Jolls 2004; Kanter 2011; Singer 2006). Growing attention to international human rights contributes to and reflects the United Nations Convention on the Rights of Persons with Disabilities (Kanter 2007). This development in turn has catapulted from the margins to the mainstream new conceptions relating political, civil, economic, and social rights, just as the focus on disability has prompted new analyses of civil rights costs and benefits, access to legal services, and the right to counsel (Nussbaum 2006a; Stein 2007). The Americans with Disabilities Act draws a focus in employment and discrimination law scholarship. Jurisprudence scholars—affectionately known as "jurisprudes"—turn to disability issues in developing the conception of human dignity that some advance as a core concept for constitutional law and international human rights (O'Connell 2008; Reaume 2003).

Perhaps more surprisingly, disability law is central to the Supreme Court's shifting jurisprudence governing the scope of congressional power under the Commerce Clause and under section 5 of the Fourteenth Amendment (*Board of Trustees v. Garrett* 2001; *Tennessee v. Lane* 2004).

In the litigation battles over both separation of powers and federalism, the Court has addressed access of disabled persons to court and their treatment in prisons. The litigators and the judiciary have thereby shined a spotlight on the assumptions built into public institutions that in turn produce disadvantage and pain for persons with disabilities. In these developments, it is intriguing to consider whether disability law has been merely mainstreamed or has emerged as a model of inclusion. Educators increasingly distinguish the two concepts in the context of K–12 educational settings. "Mainstreaming" in this context means "the selective placement of special education students in one or more 'regular' education classes" to the extent that these students can "keep up" with the work assigned by the regular classroom teacher utilizing the relevant educational and related services (Higbee, Katz, and Schultz 2010). "Inclusion" means structuring the educational environment to the extent possible to include students with special needs in general classrooms where they can benefit from related services brought within the classroom (Causton-Theoharis and Theoharis 2008).

The distinction between the two contexts can be put more simply: mainstreaming brings children with special needs into the regular classroom and supports them in trying to fit into the existing classroom methods and goals, whereas the inclusionary approach calls for changing the status quo to provide education that is responsive to all students' needs and promotes the success of each individual student and of the community of students as a whole (Perles 2012). By analogy, adding the Americans with Disabilities Act to employment law courses and its scholarship is mainstreaming; inclusion, however, is exemplified when scholars look to disability law to reimagine the relationships between political and civil rights, on the one hand, and social and economic rights, on the other, in order to suggest ways to change the field for all.

It is precisely the contrast between mainstreaming and inclusionary education in actual school practices that has triggered backlash against the presumption of integration in the concrete context of public education. The practical problems with inclusion as a practice inside of classrooms are large. To make inclusionary classrooms work, all teachers need to learn to assess individual students' educational needs, work with differentiated instruction in mainstream classrooms, and revamp their classrooms to permit more individualized and small-group work. These approaches are difficult. Pursuing them can seem in tension with the push toward accountability standards and boosting test-score results—standards that now govern so many classrooms, schools, and teachers.

Unlike mainstreaming, inclusionary efforts call upon general and special education teachers to collaborate by bringing the supports to the child rather than moving the child to the supports. When done well, inclusionary classrooms can offer benefits in differentiated instruction, smaller instructional units, responsiveness to varied learning styles, and access to more teachers and helpers for all students. When done poorly, however, inclusion can leave children with special needs stranded without adequate supports, produce resentment among other students and parents, and exceed the capacity of even well-motivated teachers.

Jancy Corner, a student at Central Missouri State University, captures common concerns posed by inclusionary initiatives when she writes: "I believe that inclusionary practices are not meeting the needs of all parties involved. There are still too many children with disabilities that are not getting the education that they deserve. The main factor contributing to this is the lack of teacher training and support. . . . Many schools do not have the money to pay for a paraprofessional to assist each child with special needs" (2002, 12). Her solution is to train students to be peer helpers, which can offer real benefits to them, but not all parents are sold on that option as a solution.

Anyone who suggests that mainstreaming or inclusion is cheaper than running two separate general and special education systems should be severely questioned. Done well, both require a continuum of placements, with experts and aids. Training in "special education" remains a specialty in this country, with distinct certification requirements in all fifty states and a robust prediction of strong demand for more special training, consistent with the labor demand in other fields (US Bureau of Labor Statistics 2012). The stimulus package enacted early in President Barack Obama's administration included aid directly for state special education programs and in fact represents the largest federal expenditure on special education since the 1975 enactment of the predecessor bill to the Individuals with

Disabilities Education Act (IDEA) (Converge Staff 2012).[2] These funding streams—combined with distinct administrative structures, certification processes, and institutionalized interests—tilt toward continuing to distinguish "special" and "regular" education.

The contrast between inclusion and mainstreaming is subtle. They ultimately share more than they diverge, however; they are two versions of the big shift away from the earlier segregative framework. As *Education Week* reported around the fiftieth anniversary of *Brown v. Board of Education* (1954), "[M]ost students with disabilities spend the majority of their time in the regular classroom" ("Special Education" 2004).[3] More than 95 percent of all students ages six to twenty-one who have identified disabilities attend school with their nondisabled peers ("Special Education" 2012). In this context, the US Bureau of Labor describes the impact on teachers:

> As schools become more inclusive, special education teachers and general education teachers increasingly work together in general education classrooms. Special education teachers help general educators adapt curriculum materials and teaching techniques to meet the needs of students with disabilities. They coordinate the work of teachers, teacher assistants, and related personnel, such as therapists and social workers, to meet the individualized needs of the student within inclusive special

2. Stimulus funds include the $39 billion State Fiscal Stabilization Fund for local school districts and public colleges and universities, distributed through existing state and federal formulas, as well as the Title I $12.4 billion to help close the achievement gap and enable disadvantaged students to reach their potential.

3. Today, according to US Department of Education estimates, nearly 6 million of the nation's schoolchildren ages six to twenty-one receive special education services under IDEA Part B. Sixty-seven percent of those students have specific learning disabilities or speech or language impairments. Fewer than 12 percent are diagnosed with significant cognitive disabilities, such as mental retardation or traumatic brain injury. Most students with disabilities spend the majority of their time in the regular classroom, a testament to the implementation of the IDEA. The size of that group of students—along with their inclusion in the general education classroom—has raised a host of concerns about academic expectations, teacher preparedness, and cost.

education programs. A large part of a special education teacher's job involves communicating and coordinating with others involved in the child's well being, including parents, social workers, school psychologists, occupational and physical therapists, school administrators, and other teachers. (2012)

Integration that joins students with disabilities and students without disabilities, whether through mainstreaming or inclusion, requires work, retraining, and resources.

Questioning the Integration Presumption

Perhaps, given the challenges for teachers posed by combining students with disabilities and nondisabled students, it is not surprising that real debate has recently erupted over the integration presumption. Integration has never been fully achieved: the institutional and funding mechanisms thus far preserve a distinctive identity for special education. Resistance to integration mounts from varied quarters. Parents of children with special needs and parents of "typical" children understandably resist expansive forms of inclusion done badly, for those forms deny meaningful educational opportunities for all children. Even when done well, inclusionary education may seem too expensive or too difficult to sustain—or may appear to reduce attention to one or another kind of student. Teachers are themselves often torn about or even opposed to mainstreaming or inclusion or variations of each.

These varied sentiments in the field did not receive much attention among legal scholars until Professor Ruth Colker threw down the gauntlet in 2006 and questioned what she calls "the disability presumption"—that children with disabilities be educated to the maximum extent with children without disabilities. The regulatory language implementing the 2004 revisions of the IDEA states that "to the maximum extent appropriate, children with disabilities[,] including children in public or private institutions or care facilities, are educated with children who are nondisabled; and special classes, separate schooling or other removal of children with disabilities from regular educational environment occurs only if the nature or severity of the disability is such that education in regular classes with the use of supplementary aids and services cannot be achieved satisfactorily" (34 C.F.R. Assistance to States for the Education of Children with Disabilities, Least Restrictive Environment Requirements, §300.114(a)(2)). Colker makes the case against this integration presumption and argues that facts, not ideology, ought to guide us. She tries to assemble facts to demonstrate that integration is not working. She points to a 1983 case and a 1989 case that resulted in integration even where the children involved did not make progress in the settings where they were placed; she cites studies trying to assess the impact of different settings on the educational attainment of students with mental retardation, behavioral disorders, and learning disabilities. These elements of her argument are, however, brief and limited. I consider responses to this legal analysis in her argument before turning to her broader policy concerns.

Leading disability law scholars, including Professors Sam Bagenstos and Mark Weber, offer thoughtful responses to Colker's challenge. They argue that her position rests on a faulty view of the IDEA's historical purpose as restricted to deinstitutionalization, a distorted selection of old cases to manufacture a controversy over integration, and neglect of what they identify as the real issue. Critical is not whether integration is a presumption, but instead "the presence or absence of related services for the child in the integrated setting" (Weber 2007b, 182). They further argue that Colker overemphasizes the costs of integration and underplays the benefits (Bagenstos 2007). Finally, they emphasize that as a *presumption* the statutory call for integration is and has always been subject to specific fact finding. Individual children who are not best served by integrated settings should be given placements and services appropriate to their circumstances. The problem, these critics would emphasize, is improving the implementation of this standard on a case-by-case basis and the existence of viable options. The likely solution is actually remarkably close to an element of Colker's own approach: ensuring a real continuum of services within each school district. For Colker, the presence of such a continuum is sufficient to replace the presumption for integration. For her critics, the presumption is still needed to guard against the long-standing and still-existing pressures and biases that push kids who are "different" away from their classmates into segregated and most likely inferior educational settings.

For example, Weber concludes that the presumption for integration should remain in place but notes that it has never been absolute; it produces success where services are provided to facilitate success. Schools that resist integration should be examined to ensure that the practices serve the child at issue rather than the status quo. In the absence of this pressure, there are simply too many financial and attitudinal reasons to accept removal of children with disabilities from other students' sight and side.

I count myself among the defenders of the integration presumption, but I take Colker's point that we should put students and their needs at the center and not simply enforce a reflexive attachment to an old idea. In giving her argument a close look, I was struck by how much it tracks revisionist thinking about racial integration in the wake of the nation's difficult reactions to *Brown v. Board of Education* and its progeny.

Hence, a considerable portion of Professor Colker's argument against the integration presumption for students with disabilities is a policy argument stemming from and explicitly relying upon the analogy to racial integration and the disillusionment and frustration with the racial integration project. Colker turns to studies raising questions about potential harm to the self-esteem of black students when they are placed in racially mixed environments where the white students are largely of higher socioeconomic classes than the students of color. She also cites studies showing injuries to students of color associated with hostile reception by white students (Colker 2006). She suggests that similar harms face children with disabilities, and so she questions whether being surrounded by students who attain higher achievement levels will raise the achievement levels or the frustration of those with disabilities.

It is difficult to disentangle these arguments and even the social science research from the complex backlash against racial desegregation that has washed over this country, especially in the past thirty years. This backlash deserves close attention, but it also raises issues quite different from those involved in the integration of disabled and nondisabled students. When it comes to the backlash against racial desegregation, demographic shifts and the alteration of the issues from state-mandated rules to private choices complicate the analysis. White flight from urban areas and violent confrontations over busing helped to fuel the rise of Republican leadership, which in turn altered the judicial and administrative approaches to implementation of *Brown v. Board of Education*'s directive to end official racial segregation of schools. Yet for the period when federal courts and agencies actually enforced the Supreme Court's landmark decision, racial integration produced good results for both black and white students. Between 1964 and the early 1980s, black students' high school graduation rates escalated, and their performance on standardized tests emerged much closer to the performance of white students (Hochschild and Scovronick 2003; Minow 2010). The major study of equal educational opportunities commissioned by Congress in 1964 reported that the "[a]ttributes of other students account for far more variation in the achievement of minority group children than do any attributes of school facilities and slightly more than do attributes of staff" (Coleman et al. 1966, 318–19).[4] Notably and inadequately publicized, the graduation and test performance of white high school students also increased during the same period (Hochschild and Scovronick 2003).

This high-water mark was short-lived, however. A majority of whites told opinion pollsters that the Johnson administration had pursued civil rights too aggressively (Klarman 2007). Opponents renamed desegregation "forced busing" and protested it in many regions. In Boston, the protests turned violent, building on an antibusing movement that was launched even before the court-ordered desegregation plan started (Formisano 1991). White families with sufficient resources fled to the suburbs or private schools (Clotfelter 2004). The conservative appointees to the Supreme Court in 1973 rejected a challenge to interdistrict disparities

---

4. The report went on: "The higher achievement of all racial and ethnic groups in schools with greater proportions of white students is largely, perhaps wholly, related to effects associated with the student body's educational background and aspirations. This means that the apparent beneficial effect of a student body with a high proportion of white students comes not from racial composition *per se*, but from the better educational background and higher educational aspirations that are, on the average, found among white students" (307).

in school expenditures in Texas (*Moose Lodge No. 107 v. Irvis* 1972; *San Antonio Independent School District v. Rodriguez* 1973).[5] In 1974, the Court announced a decision that fueled white flight and set back the cause of integration. In *Milliken v. Bradley*, the Court confined desegregation orders to the lines of Detroit District in which intentional official segregation had been demonstrated and forbade the inclusion of the neighboring suburbs to rectify urban segregation—despite the evidence in that very case that the state government in Michigan was responsible for the policies producing the city's racial segregation.

One scholar, writing in 1976, captured familiar perceptions from that time while describing persistent racial segregation in California: "The fact remains that most California white parents do not want their children transported to schools with predominantly poor minority student bodies located in black or brown neighborhoods. The parents fear that such schools will be educationally inferior and that their children will be victims of violence and reverse discrimination. Certainly none of these fears are without foundation, but it is possible that they are exaggerated by underlying racist feelings" (Wollenberg 1976, 182–83). White families with financial means on the whole have preferred predominantly white communities and white schools, which they associate with better opportunities for their children (Hochschild and Scovronick 2003).

However described or understood, the confluence of public actions and private decisions jeopardized the possibility of actual racial integration in schools around this country. With little attention to the actual history, courts and commentators recast the project of racial integration of the schools as a failed policy. Justice Louis Powell treated residential segregation as a product of economic and social forces beyond both school board action and legitimate judicial remedy when he dissented from the Court's approval of desegregation plans in 1979 (*Columbus Board of Education v. Penick* 1979).

5. In *Moose Lodge* (1972), the Court also allowed private discrimination to proceed outside equal-protection guarantees even when the private group received public support through a state liquor license.

Yet the recent history is better understood as failed politics than as failed policies. Resistance to desegregation was egged on by inadequate leadership, fueled electoral politics, and influenced judicial appointments. White parents predominantly and repeatedly demonstrated a preference for mainly white schools (Clotfelter 2004)—often simply as a proxy for "good" schools—but their movement to almost exclusively white suburbs and to private schools became understood as a protected, private choice. Yet it is government policies that shape the possibility of residential separation by race—and the association of "good" schools with white schools. Given historic residential patterns, legacies of racially restrictive covenants, and the convergence of race and economic class, most whites over the past forty years could choose largely white schools by moving to the suburbs, selecting private schools, or arranging placement of their children in high academic tracks (Clotfelter 2004).[6] That these movements further isolated the most impoverished and nonwhite students reflected the confluence of zoning policies and rulings about the limitations on school desegregation as well as the rules of school finance. When the courts began to treat racial segregation as the result of private residential choices, they placed it beyond state action and beyond constitutional purview—using government action, of course, to do so. Over time, the Supreme Court drew sharp lines between official and intentional governmental segregation that would warrant a desegregation remedy and "de facto" segregation resulting from individual choices or social practices and thus exempt from judicial remedy. De facto segregation in many communities emerged as society embraced a norm against de jure racial classification—and neglected race-based subordination (Siegel 2004).

The ideal of integration no longer currently motivates many people of any race. Richard Kallenberg recently surveyed national attitudes and concluded that there is a consensus that integrated schools seem like a good idea, but "we shouldn't do anything to promote them" (2001, 42).

6. From *Brown* on, the Court rejected official segregation. The question, then and now, is about unofficial segregation: What does it communicate when it involves whites resisting education with nonwhites?

Equal opportunity remains the established goal of schooling at least since *Brown v. Board of Education*, but racial mixing and the aspiration to build an inclusive and collaborative multiracial community prompt resistance from many quarters.

Resistance is not confined to whites (Glen 2006; Heise 2005; Powell 2005, 281, 294).[7] Justice Clarence Thomas's resistance to desegregation efforts resonates with many African Americans who are insulted by the suggestion that educational excellence cannot occur in an entirely or predominantly black or black and Hispanic school (*Missouri v. Jenkins* 1995, at 70, 114). For them, the betrayal of Brown's promise lies not in finding students of color in schools largely with other students of color, but instead in low expectations and low achievement levels widely found among these students (*Grutter v. Bollinger* 2003; Tatum 2007). The aspiration of integration might even be seen as a problematic tool of condescension or even cultural oppression. In the context of education for Native Americans, contemporary critics blame segregated boarding schools for stripping Indian children of their familial and cultural ties, but critics also attack early attempts to educate American Indian children in California alongside white children, which produced alienating and frustrating experiences and high drop-out rates for the Indian children (Spring 2012; Wollenberg 1976). Culturally oriented claims similarly appear among some advocates of "Afro-centric" education, elevating a focus on African and

---

7. When W. E. B. Du Bois raised concerns in the 1930s that the desegregation focus could leave black children worse off than they would be in segregated schools, he had to resign from his post as editor for the National Association for the Advancement of Colored People's (NAACP) *Crisis* magazine, but advocates and scholars devoted to redressing racial oppression have followed Du Bois in defending separate educational institutions for students of color where these institutions are more likely to raise expectations and achievement than experiments in racial mixing. Like the NAACP lawyers who debated in the 1940s whether attacking segregated schools would undermine progress toward equalizing educational resources available to black students, advocates in this new century explore whether financial and programmatic solutions will work better than the disappointing desegregation initiatives (see Glen 2006, describing how districts with adequacy remedies narrowed the racial gap in student achievement; Heise 2005; Powell 2005).

African American history and culture to root African American students, enhance their self-esteem, and preserve their distinctiveness.

One does not have to embrace such cultural claims to conclude that mixing students of different backgrounds by itself does not produce equality if the adults and students replicate stereotypes and stratification based on race. Claude Steele's (1997, 2010; Murphy, Steele, and Gross 2007) research documents how through unwelcoming settings schools can create a sense of threat to students around their racial identities, which in turn undermines their academic performance (see also Rubenstein 2007). Many students' experience confirm his research.

Casting aside the integration presumption for children with disabilities is especially unwarranted given the overrepresentation of minority students in special education for students with learning or emotional disabilities. This persistent overrepresentation raises questions about how negative racial attitudes persist long after they are legally ruled out of bounds in student assignments (Harry and Klinger 2006; Losen and Orfield 2002b). Increased uses of alternative education for students who have been disciplined may present real questions about new yet hidden modes of racial segregation.[8] Resurging racial segregation may be proceeding through these means, whether they are simply by-products of faulty sorting measures or the results of unconscious bias.

Doubt about the commitment and capacity of racially mixed schools to ensure that the minority students are valued, well taught, and prepared for a still-prejudiced society is underscored by research findings about contemporary schooling (Markus 2008; Steele 1997). Renewed interest in the accomplishments of all-black schools during segregation and the commitment of teachers and communities to these schools and their students underscore historic paths to individual success outside of the integrationist ideal (J. Anderson 1988; V. Walker 1996).

8. Thanks to Deborah Gordon Klehr of Pennsylvania's Education Law Center, who has pointed out new forms of segregation after *Brown*, as children are pushed out of regular school for disciplinary reasons, with disproportionate results affecting communities of color. On issues arising from one state's use of alternative education as discipline, see Education Law Center 2010–11.

All of these developments, though, suggest that what failed after *Brown* was societal commitment to alter the assumption of racial hierarchy that produced segregation and that persists even in schools where racial mixing occurs. African American and Hispanic students who live in areas of concentrated poverty are most hurt by the decline of desegregation efforts, given their consignment to disproportionately inadequate and poorly performing public schools and their lost access to other social networks. White students in predominantly white schools have in general better educational opportunities and participate in the life of higher-performing schools. Yet students of all backgrounds lose the benefits offered by the integrationist project when that project itself fails: the benefits of working with diverse groups and building a sense of "we" through common goals and experiences, overcoming the distortion of stereotypes, and developing the capacity to work with others unlike oneself. Given the importance that employers place on working with diverse teams and the relevance of a sense of "we" to democratic governance, the entire nation loses as well.

There is something very similar at risk if the presumption of integration fades away in the context of students with disabilities. Here, the fundamental benefits from integration stem not only from terminating the predominant and easy use of isolating and segregating institutions, but also from renovating the assumption of radical difference that continues to fuel stigma, harassment, and dehumanization of people with disabilities. Mark Weber's powerful book *Disability Harassment* (2007a) provides sober insights into the devastating effects of harassment and bullying experienced by people with disabilities. Here the analogy to race and to sex is well taken; hostile environments have palpable psychological and sociological costs that jeopardize people's well-being and even their lives. Integration in the context of disability also holds promise of enhancing social understandings and the sense of "we" among all students. Integration can give occasions for students who are not identified as disabled to gain life lessons in patience and appreciation for what they can do and for what others surmount. Another lesson comes with the happiness earned from helping others. Further, improving the educational experiences of all children, those with and those without disabilities, is the great promise of the integration presumption, for it draws teachers and students alike into recognizing how each student learns differently from others. Prompting and equipping teachers to learn to reach a variety of students and encouraging students to develop self-awareness of their own learning needs and accomplishments, integration across the disability line can generate changes in the mainstream classroom itself in pursuit of better learning for all.

Revisiting Integration through Universal Design

Rather than perpetuate debates over the integration presumption, the next period of disability advocacy might take a more productive turn inspired by the concept of universal design. Initially developed in architecture and design of products and environments, universal design calls for building spaces and products to be usable by the widest array of people regardless of age, ability, or situation (Preiser and Smith 2011). The same idea can inform the construction of classrooms and teaching materials; in this case, it is the concept of universal design for learning, developed by people at the Center for Applied Special Technology (CAST) (CAST 2010; Council for Exceptional Children 2005; Meyer and Rose 1998; Rose and Meyer 2002, 2006; Rose, Meyer, and Hitchcock 2005; Stahl 2002). Architects using universal design anticipate the wide range of people who should be able to use a building and then build it to be accessible to all. The building that has only a staircase excludes people who use wheelchairs and hence can be retrofitted to include a ramp. But universal designers build in access from the beginning, incorporating ramps into the architectural design. Similarly, universal design for learning anticipates all the different kinds of individuals who will be students and ensures that the means of teaching and conveying material are accessible to all. A physical book excludes people who are visually impaired, who have physical impairments preventing the use of the book, or who have learning or attention problems that make the book ineffective. In accordance with the universal design principle, however, educational materials instead can be digitized and then connected with software that enables a user to turn them into Braille or to have them read aloud or to integrate them with interactive materials that attend to attention or learning problems. The stroke of a key can render the material available in sign language, and the user can select the appearance and clothing of the animated character doing the signing.

Universal design for learning has been especially helpful in realizing the requirements of the 1997 amendments to the IDEA that seek to improve outcomes for children with disabilities by including them in standards, methods, and accountability and by requiring access to the general curriculum for them. Teachers working alone often have real trouble opening up this kind of access. Technological innovations, rendering material into flexible digital formats, offer many exciting possibilities that reach students with disabilities and that—it turns out—also assist students without disabilities.[9] Appropriate supports and challenges can be provided, and so can resources for self-expression, interest, and engagement—again through multimedia formats. Emerging over time is the concept of "print disability," expansive enough to include persons with learning disabilities, quadriplegia, and other conditions that make it difficult or impossible to read and learn through conventional print.

I had the privilege to work with CAST and the US Department of Education in a partnership to enhance access to the general curriculum. CAST pointed out the barrier posed by the usual hard-bound textbook. Major adoption states, including Texas, Georgia, and Kentucky, started to require publishers to provide the files of their adopted texts in digitized formats to enable access for students with disabilities, but different states required different formats. The federal government started to consider legislation for a nationally required format. The major textbook companies disliked the regulation but disliked inconsistent and competing regulations even more. With the help of CAST, I first explored the possibility of developing contracts through which the textbook publishers would waive copyright to enable adaptation of their materials for students with disabilities. Yet the publishers indicated their fears of being sued by the authors of materials included in their texts who had not waived their rights.

9. Any such "copy" in digital formats would violate the copyright law, although there is an exception for materials for persons with visual and related impairments (see Perl 2003).

So with the help of friends at Harvard Law School Berkman Center for the Study of Law, Internet, and Society, we brought together representatives of the textbook industry, tech experts, lawyers, and experts on learning and disability (CAST 2010). We explored together how the world would be better if textbooks were from the start designed to be accessible rather than produced and then later just retrofitted to become accessible. We also identified ways that interactive texts with supports could be attractive and effective for a wide range of students, including English-language learners, kids who do not like school, and "digital natives"—students born into a world that is already digital and multimedia (Palfrey 2008). This vision now guides many publishers who work to develop texts that are digitized and that include images, sounds, and scaffolding for students who would benefit from interactions while reading and learning, from glossaries, and from capacities to generate expressive materials. As we sketched these possibilities, the publishers began to realize that it makes no sense to imagine a core group of homogeneous learners and a marginal group with disabilities. Common sense and recent research in neuroscience reveal that learners are diverse in many dimensions, including the feelings they have about learning, how they process information, and what makes them feel motivated. Finding ways to engage all students in learning is as important a challenge as devising access for students who are visually impaired.

Universal design for learning calls for multiple means of representation to allow learners alternative avenues for acquiring information and knowledge, multiple means of expression to provide learners ways to demonstrate what they know, and multiple means of engagement that tap into their interests and offer appropriate challenges and increase motivation (Hitchcock et al. 2002). Just as a curb cut originally designed to help people who use wheelchairs to negotiate sidewalk curbs ends up easing travel for people pushing strollers, riding skateboards, using canes, or simply walking, digitized textbooks can benefit a wide range of students. Television captioning is a powerful precedent. When captions first appeared, they were aimed at people with hearing impairments. Close-captioning initially required the purchase of expensive decoder boxes and the retrofitting of televisions to access those captions. Later, decoder chips were built into every television, making it possible for all kinds of people to access the captions. Captioned television is currently popular among people using exercise machines in health clubs, diners in noisy restaurants and bars, individuals learning English, and couples who go to sleep at different times while the television is on in the bedroom. When it is built into the front end of the broadcast and television hardware, captioning costs a few cents compared to the thousands of dollars it costs when done after the show and the television are produced. Universal design not only is cheaper but also extends benefits beyond the initial target group.

Working with universal designs for learning is empowering and invigorating. The US Department of Education was so impressed by the progress we made with the textbook publishers that it funded the creation of a panel to address the intermediate step of shared standards for digitizing current texts to enable connections with software-enabling access for persons with disabilities. The panel devised voluntary standards for digitizing instructional materials responsive to the needs and interests of a variety of competing and contrasting disability groups (National Center on Accessible Instructional Materials n.d.). Congress in turn saw the power of the voluntary standards and directed use of them to comply with federal law. CAST currently leads two federally funded centers to advance the implementation of these standards. Universal design for learning has recently informed the congressional standards for higher education materials.

Universal design for learning also can shed light on the debate over mainstreaming and inclusion and put the argument over the integration presumption in a new light. Instead of asking where we place the wall between the conventional and special classrooms, universal design starts with the variety of students that exist and directs the development of learning opportunities with all of them in mind. The result creates supports for people previously unidentified as potentially benefiting from such help. Multiple forms of representation, multiple forms of expression, and multiple means of engagement work for many kinds of students. For example, CAST now has software that allows anyone to build an interactive book.[10] This software benefits many students, including those who are not

10. For this software, see http://bookbuilder.cast.org/.

identified as having any disability but who are also engaged by interactive materials. A focus on those students who were once at the margin can help those who have historically been at the center.

Universal design for learning makes the goals of education more transparent. Teachers and students alike can work with it to become more self-conscious about learning and to see this self-consciousness itself as a gain. Books featuring students with disabilities aimed at the elementary and middle school crowds (see the titles at the beginning of the first section) are popular not only because they are funny and well written, but also because they offer every student insight into the varied ways in which people learn, the emotional contexts that affect learning, and the rewards in seeing the world from another's perspective.

Benjamin Disraeli once said that the greatest good you can do for another is not just to share your riches, but to reveal to him his own. Making schools inclusive places is a way that we can reveal to one another the talents and gifts each of us has. That is really making all the difference.

3

Rights, Needs, and Capabilities

Institutional and Political Barriers to Justice for Disabled People

THOMAS M. SKRTIC and J. ROBERT KENT

In *Frontiers of Justice,* Martha Nussbaum (2006a) addresses disability and disability law from the perspective of what justice requires. Her understanding of these requirements builds upon sympathetic criticism of John Rawls's theory of justice and her own construction of an alternative *capabilities* approach. Nussbaum's critique centers on the deficiencies of the social contract tradition to which Rawls aligns himself. Although we find Nussbaum's criticism of Rawls and her application of the capabilities approach to disability insightful and philosophically important, we also believe her analysis is unsatisfactory with respect to the institutional and political requirements of and barriers to social justice for disabled people.

The chapter is organized in four parts. The first part reviews Nussbaum's criticism of Rawls's contractarian theory of justice and outlines her alternative-capabilities approach. The second reviews and criticizes her analysis of the Individuals with Disabilities Education Act (IDEA), which she considers an important exemplar of the capabilities approach. The third part treats the shortcomings as well as the strengths of legal rights discourse, or "rights talk," as a political strategy and argues that a more appropriate strategy requires an institutional understanding of rights and injustice as well as, ultimately, an idiomatic move to *"needs* talk." Our aim in this part is to show that Nussbaum's approach to what justice requires for disabled people rings hollow without some theorization of the institutional context in which capabilities needs-claims are adjudicated. In fairness to

Nussbaum, she recognizes the ambiguities (and continuing importance) of rights talk, and the capabilities approach does contain a conception of needs and needs-claims. However, in the absence of some theorization of the institutional context in which needs-claims are adjudicated—Nussbaum's treatment of IDEA notwithstanding—her approach to what justice requires for disabled people is truncated and too abstract.[1] In the concluding part, we suggest that the capabilities approach has a crucial role to play in an *institutional* theory of justice centered in a substantive conception of democracy. This broader understanding of justice, we assert, resonates with developmental liberalism, the strain of American liberalism that historically has stood in sharp contrast to the more dominant strains of market and managerial liberalism that are implicated in institutionalized injustice.

Capabilities Approach to Social Justice

In his pioneering work on international gender justice, development economist Amartya Sen (e.g., 1992, 1999) rejected the resource model of economic growth (based on gross domestic product) as a poor indicator of a nation's quality of life because it occludes women's distributional inequities. Instead, he proposed a human-development model based on human capabilities—a far superior approach to gender justice, according to Nussbaum, because it is based not merely on what people have but on "what people are actually able to do and be" (2003, 33). Although she endorses Sen's idea of human capabilities, she criticizes him for his reluctance to say which capabilities are most important for societies to pursue and to specify the required minimum level of capability development for a just society. Over the past two decades, Nussbaum has developed such a list of essential capabilities, the latest version of which appears in *Frontiers of Justice* (2006a, 76–81), wherein she also argues that justice requires that every society

---

1. We are not suggesting that Nussbaum is unconcerned about injustice of one kind or another, but rather that her writings lack sustained discussion of various forms of institutionalized injustice in particular social contexts, which is what an institutional understanding of rights, needs, and injustice is designed to remedy.

provide for the cultivation of all these capabilities to a level where individuals can assume major responsibility for their own self-development.[2] In extending the capabilities approach to people with intellectual and physical impairments and associated disabilities,[3] Nussbaum criticizes Rawls's (1971) theory of justice because, like all social contract theories, it excludes people whom it considers incapable of the kind of political bargaining for mutual advantage that is the hallmark of the social contract tradition.

The Social Contract Tradition

The social contract is a thought experiment for identifying just political principles upon which to structure society—principles that in turn serve as benchmarks of political legitimacy. In the experiment, what Rawls calls the "original position," rational people join together for mutual advantage, leaving a fictional "state of nature" (1971, 121, 12) in which all humans are imagined to be, in Locke's terms, "free, equal, and independent" (quoted

---

2. This list and the list in Nussbaum's most recent relevant book, *Creating Capabilities* (2011, 33–34), are identical.

3. Nussbaum's use of the term *disability* and related terms is based on the following definitions: *impairment,* "a loss of normal bodily function"; *disability,* "something you cannot do in your environment as a result"; and *handicap,* "the resulting competitive disadvantage" (2006a, 423–24n5, 96–100). Although she refers to the source of this usage simply as "the disability literature" (423n5), in effect she is using the World Health Organization's (WHO, 1980) distinction among impairment, disability, and handicap (see also Bury 1996, 19). Nussbaum is not using the impairment/disability distinction of the social model of disability, in which impairment is roughly the same as in her usage, but disability is "culturally produced and socially structured" (Oliver 1990, 22; see also Oliver 1996), or even the more recent WHO (2001) model in which disability is an interaction between impairment and environmental and personal contextual factors. Finally, Nussbaum discusses "physical and mental impairments" but focuses on the latter because they challenge the theories in question more fundamentally (2006a, 99). Although she includes in mental impairments both "mental illness" and "'cognitive impairments' or 'intellectual disabilities'" (2006a, 424n5), her disability arguments and exemplars (see note 11) primarily involve the latter (see Nussbaum 2009, 332). Thus, unless quoting Nussbaum, we use the term *intellectual impairments* instead of *mental impairments.*

in Nussbaum 2006a, 9) to govern themselves by law premised on a social contract. According to the theory, the political principles reflected in such a contract are just because they are the result of a fair process and a fair starting point. The process is fair because it follows a procedure that divests participants of the artificial advantages that some people have in actual societies. The starting point—the original position—is fair because the "circumstances of justice" in which the contract is developed entail "the normal conditions under which human cooperation is both possible and necessary" (Rawls 1971, 126), conditions that include, among other things, participants who are roughly similar in terms of needs and interests, knowledge and judgment, and physical strength and intelligence—the latter "native endowments" stipulated by Rawls to fall "within the normal range" ([1993] 1996, 25).

Using this approach in A *Theory of Justice*, Rawls arrived at his two famous principles of justice and a list of primary goods to be distributed according to the two principles (1971, 60–61, 75–83, 302–3). The first principle prioritizes a set of basic liberties for each citizen, and the second, the "difference principle" (76), proposes to deal with social and economic inequalities by permitting only those that are "to the greatest benefit of the least advantaged" (83). Rawls focused on primary goods because the utilitarian theory of justice he sought to improve upon tends to reduce all human ends to one ultimate good (pleasure). In opposition to this tendency, he posited that justice should be concerned only with the distribution of primary goods—that is, those goods necessary for pursuing any human end, thus leaving the question of what constitutes the ultimate human good to "the plurality of distinct persons with separate systems of ends" (29). As such, Rawls's primary goods are a mix of material and nonmaterial social goods that he considers basic to the pursuit of any "rational plan of life," including "rights and liberties, powers and opportunities, income and wealth . . . [and] self-respect" (62), but focusing most prominently on wealth and income.[4]

---

4. Rawls's use of wealth and income as indices of well-being is a key point of criticism for Nussbaum because of their inadequacy as indices of people's well-being, including

Problems with Rawls's Contractarian Distributive Justice

For Nussbaum, contractarian theory, especially Rawls's, is "the strongest theory of basic social justice we have so far" (2006a, 161). In fact, despite different starting points (a crucial difference taken up later in this essay), the capabilities approach arrives at principles that converge with Rawls's two principles, given that both sets of principles attempt "to capture and render politically concrete the idea of a life in accordance with human dignity" (Nussbaum 2006a, 177). Nevertheless, Nussbaum notes that no contractarian approach can adequately address three unresolved problems of social justice—that is, achieving justice for people with physical and intellectual impairments and for those who care for them, the focus of this chapter, as well as extending justice to all world citizens and addressing unjust treatment of nonhuman animals (2006a, 1). Although Rawls recognized these problems as especially difficult for his theory and worked on the second one for the rest of his career, he referred to the first and third problems as "problems on which justice as fairness may fail" ([1993] 1996, 21).

Nussbaum identifies two related problems with social contract theories of justice for people with impairments and associated disabilities, both of which problems are forms of exclusion from the original position.[5] First, quoting Locke and Rawls, Nussbaum notes that social contract theories conceive of the contracting agents who choose the political principles by

---

those with disabilities (2006a, 164). Also, Rawls's idea of distributing primary goods for pursuit of any human end follows directly from his "political liberalism" ([1993] 1996, 13), which is broadly compatible with *multiple* conceptions of valued human ends, as opposed to "comprehensive" liberalisms, which adhere to a *particular* conception. Nussbaum agrees on the necessity of a political liberalism with abstract principles of justice to protect and respect a plurality of diverse perspectives on human ends (2006a, 86, 182). Also see Nussbaum 2000b, 77, and notes 6, 7, and 35 in this chapter.

5. Although Nussbaum criticizes these and other problematic features of Rawls's contractarianism, she doesn't reject contractarian theory completely, noting more recently that "a different type of contractarian theory might yet be developed to handle [the issue of justice for disabled people]" (2006b, 491).

which to design the basic structure of society as "free, equal, and independent," the citizens whose interests they represent as "fully cooperating members of society over a complete life" (Rawls [1993] 1996, 20), and both groups as in possession of "a rather idealized rationality" (Nussbaum 2006a, 98). As a result, the first problem with such theories of justice is that they don't include people with significant intellectual impairments in the group of contracting agents who choose basic political principles (Nussbaum 2006a, 14–15). Nussbaum finds the exclusion of people with impairments and disabilities who are fully capable of participating in political choice to be particularly galling. For her, their omission is a defect of justice because they are not being treated as fully equal citizens, which is even more egregious because many of the factors that exclude them from participation are social and not inevitable. In contrast, the failure to include people with significant intellectual impairments in the group of political choosers is not an injustice to Nussbaum, "so long as there is some other way to take their interests into account" (2006a, 15).

But this is the second problem with contractarian theories for Nussbaum (2006a, 98–99, 110–12, 120–24): they fail to adequately take the interests and needs of citizens with impairments and disabilities into account because the political principles derived from such theories are the result of a contract for mutual benefit. That is, she explains, the social contract tradition "conflates two questions that are in principle distinct: 'By whom are society's principles designed?' and 'For whom are society's principles designed?'" (2006a, 16). According to the tradition's core moral idea of mutual advantage and reciprocity among those who create such a contract, the contracting parties and the citizens who will live by its principles are one and the same people. As such, although the interests of other persons—women, children, and elderly people, historically, and people with impairments and disabilities currently—may be included either indirectly, through the contracting parties' own concern for them, or at a later stage, after the political principles are chosen, the primary subjects of justice are those who chose the principles. The implication for people with significant intellectual impairments and disabilities is that by not being included in the group of choosers, they are not included (except indirectly or at a later stage) among those for whom principles are chosen.

It is clear, Nussbaum concludes, that the failure of contractarian theories of justice to address significant intellectual impairments and related disabilities except as an afterthought, "after the basic institutions of society are already designed," means that "people with mental impairments are not among those for whom and in reciprocity with whom society's basic institutions are structured" (2006a, 98). In effect, as Rawls makes clear ([1993] 1996, 20–21, 184), their interests will be considered "out of charity . . . not out of basic justice" (Nussbaum 2006a, 123), which Nussbaum finds totally unsatisfactory (61, 118, 123, 137, 148).

Nussbaum's answer to this injustice in contractarian theories of justice is to decouple the "by whom" and "for whom" questions. That is, she says, one might have "a theory that held that many living beings, human and even nonhuman, are primary subjects of justice, even though they are not capable of participating in the procedure through which political principles are chosen" (2006a, 17). Moreover, one would have good reason to seek such a theory if one starts from the idea that "many different lives have dignity and are worthy of respect. If one thinks that way, one would acknowledge from the start that the capacity to make a contract, and the possession of those abilities that make for mutual advantage in the resulting society, are not necessary conditions for being a citizen who has dignity and deserves to be treated with respect on the basis of equality with others" (2006a, 17). The normative idea of human dignity is the starting point of the capabilities approach. What Nussbaum is after—what her approach provides by way of a list of capabilities—is the substance of "a life worthy of human dignity" (2006a, 82). We cannot know what justice requires until we have some idea of what a good human life, a flourishing life, entails. The fact that she starts from a conception of a good life is the "deepest difference" (81) between the capabilities approach and Rawlsian contractarianism. Rawls's theory is procedural. If the procedure in the original position is fair and impartial, then it can be relied upon to yield a just outcome. By contrast, Nussbaum's approach is outcome oriented; that is, it starts with a conception of the multivalent quality of life people should enjoy and then designs a procedure that achieves this result. However elegantly a procedure may be designed, if it doesn't result in a life that corresponds with our sense of dignity and fairness, it should be rejected.

The Capabilities Approach: Nussbaum's Alternative

Given her normative starting point of human dignity, Nussbaum substitutes for Rawls's list of primary goods a list of "central human capabilities" whose social cultivation all people need in order to flourish in society (2006a, 76). She considers the list open to revision, and it has been revised several times to include the capabilities of life (being able to live a human life of normal length); bodily health (being able to have good health, adequate nourishment, and shelter); bodily integrity (being able to move freely and be secure against assault); senses, imagination, and thought (being able to use the senses, to imagine, to think, and to reason); emotions (being able to have attachments to things and other people); practical reason (being able to conceptualize the good and plan one's life); affiliation (living with and toward others and having the social bases of self-respect); other species (being able to live with concern for other species and nature); play (being able to laugh, play, and enjoy recreating); and control over one's environment (being able to participate in political choices, to have equal property rights, and to work as a human being) (2000b, 70–86; 2006a, 76–78). For Nussbaum, these ten capabilities represent the core entitlements of a just society, a threshold of social support for human flourishing and living life with dignity.[6] Thus, she encourages us to think of the capabilities list as a set of constitutionally guaranteed rights embodied in something analogous to the Fundamental Rights Section of the Indian Constitution or the Bill of Rights in the US Constitution

---

6. Nussbaum's capabilities capture, in high abstraction, what people are able to do and able to be relative to living a flourishing life (2006a, 70). Given her political liberalism (see notes 4 and 7 in this chapter), however, she respects a plurality of ways of living such a life by differentiating capabilities and "functioning," wherein developing the former enables functioning in multiple ways based on individual choice (79–80). For adults, capabilities are the basic entitlement, not the social functioning they make possible, except for self-respect and dignity, in which case functioning is the entitlement and policy aim (172). However, for children and "people with severe mental impairments" (172), functioning, not capabilities, is the aim because they can't make the necessary choices in vital areas of care and safety.

(2006a, 155–56). Securing these rights entails the state's overseeing development of all of these capabilities to a level where individuals can function adequately in all the dimensions of human life that the capabilities separately define. Rights are not truly effective, Nussbaum recognizes, unless there is "affirmative material and institutional support" that enables their exercise (2003, 38).

Nussbaum draws her notion of human flourishing from Aristotle's conception of the person as a political and social animal, both needy and dignified, who seeks social engagement, shares social ends, and finds deep fulfillment in political relations with others (2006a, 85–87). For her, as for Aristotle, human flourishing is inconceivable "outside a network of such relations" (86).[7] As such, her capabilities approach begins to resolve the contractarian problem of exclusion of people with impairments and associated disabilities by introducing an Aristotelian conception of the person "as a social animal, whose dignity does not derive entirely from an idealized rationality," thereby proffering a broader conception of "the full and equal citizenship of people with mental impairments" (92). She then extends the notion of dignity by combining Aristotle's conception of humans as political animals with Marx's idea that they are creatures "in need of a plurality of life-activities" (quoted in Nussbaum 2006a, 159), creating a view that "sees the rational as simply one aspect of the animal, and, at that, not the only one that is pertinent to a notion of truly human functioning" (159). As Nussbaum explains,

> The capabilities approach sees the world as containing many different types of animal dignity, all of which deserve respect and even awe. The

---

7. Given her political liberalism (see note 4), Nussbaum is not arguing for a comprehensive conception of the good as in Aristotle's normative theory. Instead, like Rawls's primary goods, capabilities in Nussbaum's view are "prerequisites" of multiple conceptions of human flourishing (2006a, 182). Limited space precludes full consideration of Nussbaum's version of political liberalism, but her commitment to it is a key barrier to a capabilities approach to deliberative democracy, which we argue requires a capabilities conception of human flourishing and compatible developmental liberal social and political institutions. See the conclusion and note 35.

specifically human kind is indeed characterized, usually, by a kind of rationality, but rationality is not idealized and set in opposition to animality; it is just garden-variety practical reasoning, which is one way animals have of functioning. Sociability, moreover, is equally fundamental and equally pervasive. And bodily need, *including the need for care*, is a feature of our rationality and our sociability; it is one aspect of our dignity, then, rather than something to be contrasted with it. (159–60, emphasis added)

Recognizing the human dignity of bodily need, including the need for care, leads Nussbaum to focus on "the importance of care as a primary social entitlement" (2006a, 178). In turn, such a focus leads to a socialized and moralized redefinition of the basis of social cooperation, one that moves away from the contractarian motivation of gaining mutual benefit. Social cooperation is socialized in the capabilities approach because, as noted, it uses Aristotle's conception of the person as a political and social animal who "seeks a [social] good . . . and who shares complex ends with others at many levels" (158). It is moralized because it envisages human beings as cooperating out of a wide range of motives, including "love of justice itself" and prominently "compassion for those who have less than they need to lead decent and dignified lives" (156–57). Crucially in this regard, Nussbaum stresses that there is no assumption that justice is relevant only in situations of rough equality where people are motivated to make a deal for mutual advantage. She argues that, in addition to ties of advantage, human beings are joined by "ties of love and compassion . . . by the love of justice as well as the need for justice" (157). Such a moralized account of social cooperation views human beings as held together by many altruistic ties in addition to that of mutual advantage, and it treats justice and inclusiveness as intrinsic ends from the outset.

For Nussbaum, the advantage of grounding the capabilities approach in the idea of human dignity is that it is already basic to many nations' constitutions. Moreover, because human dignity, if not the social cooperation to ensure it as a matter of justice, has a long record of judicial interpretation, we may assess its practical potential by considering "what creative jurisprudence has been able to make of [the idea of human dignity] in various areas of human life" (Nussbaum 2006a, 156). One area of creative jurisprudence that Nussbaum holds up as exemplifying the capabilities approach with regard to both human dignity and social cooperation is that associated with the IDEA.[8]

The IDEA as Exemplar of the Capabilities Approach

Nussbaum identifies education both as a central concern in her list of human capabilities and as a key area of injustice toward children with impairments and disabilities in all modern societies (2006a, 199–200). She then reviews the litigation that challenged these inequities in US public schools and led to passage of the Education for All Handicapped Children Act of 1975 (EAHCA) and its reauthorization as the IDEA. In this review, she highlights two disability rights cases—*Mills v. Board of Education* (1972), an access-to-education case that resulted in the EAHCA, and *City of Cleburne v. Cleburne Living Center* (1985), a zoning case brought under the Fourteenth Amendment's Equal Protection Clause—as well as a welfare rights case brought under the Fourteenth Amendment, *Goldberg v. Kelly* (1970). Together, these cases articulate conceptions of social cooperation and the purposes of political principles that run completely counter to those embodied in mutual-advantage contractarianism, while supporting the principles of the capabilities approach, according to Nussbaum (2006a, 200–204). In *Mills*, the US District Court for the District of Columbia drew expressly on the *Brown v. Board of Education* (1954) decision that

8. Associating "truly human functioning" (Nussbaum 2000b, 76) with capability development raises questions about people who lack capabilities, and Nussbaum has been criticized for statements judging persons lacking a vital capability as "not really a human being at all" (73) (for such criticism, see, e.g., Baylies 2002; Stein 2007). She modifies such statements in *Frontiers of Justice* (2006a, 181), admitting that some statements made in her articles published in the 1980s and 1990s "might have been read to suggest that if any one of the capabilities is totally cut off, the life is no longer a human life" (2006a, 432n18). As we have seen, this is not the position she takes in *Frontiers of Justice*, in which she defends the dignity of individuals with significant intellectual impairments and argues for an inclusive conception of justice.

prohibited racial segregation in schools in order to rule that the District of Columbia public schools' exclusion of children with disabilities was a violation of the Equal Protection Clause. Moreover, Nussbaum (2006a) notes that by citing *Goldberg,* in which the Supreme Court ruled that the state's interest in the welfare of its citizens clearly outweighs any competing concern for an increase in fiscal and administrative burdens, the District Court ruled that the violation of the equal-protection principle in *Mills* could not be reasoned away on the grounds that the school system had insufficient funds and that these children might be expensive to educate.

In terms of social cooperation, Nussbaum takes from *Goldberg* that its goal is not to gain an advantage, but "to foster the dignity and well-being of each and every citizen[,] . . . [which] is interpreted to mean that expenditures on poverty, though they may be costly, are required by the very nature of our social commitment" (2006a, 202). Although Rawls would agree with such expenditures for the poor, "he refuses to commit the state to full support for people with physical and mental impairments in the basic political principles themselves, deferring that issue until a time when basic principles will already have been fixed" (202). However, she notes, the *Mills* decision makes Rawls's distinction unacceptable: "we must support these citizens as equals," she says, "in and through our basic principles" (202). *Goldberg,* Nussbaum concludes, requires a level of support based on the principle of equality, even if providing it is costly. *Mills* adds that justice requires such support because our fundamental constitutional principle of equal protection requires it.

The articulation of this fundamental insight in *Mills* set the stage for the national debate that resulted in the EAHCA, which "[gave] disabled children enforceable rights to free suitable public education, and [made] funds available to states to help them meet their constitutional obligation" (Nussbaum 2006a, 203). The EAHCA was modified and expanded in its 1990 reauthorization as the IDEA and modified and expanded again in that act's 1997 and 2004 reauthorizations.[9] Prior to these reauthorizations,

---

9. Nussbaum confuses the substance and significance of the 1990 and 1997 IDEA reauthorizations, claiming that the EAHCA was reauthorized as the IDEA in 1997

however, Nussbaum notes, the Supreme Court decision in *Cleburne* also played an important role in establishing the political justification for the IDEA by revising further the conception of social cooperation in the direction of the capabilities approach with regard to the idea of equal respect for human dignity.

Cleburne concerned the denial of a city permit for a group home for persons labeled with mental retardation because the denial was prompted by local property owners' expressed fear of and negative attitudes toward such people. In a "very surprising ruling" (Nussbaum 2006a, 204), the Court held that the denial had no rational basis and instead rested on blatant discrimination as well as irrational prejudice and fear. What was significant in this ruling was that whereas until then the standard for judging the rational basis of an enacted law was extremely low, the Court in *Cleburne* "endowed the standard with meaningful teeth" (Nussbaum 2006a, 204), precluding mere stigma and the desire to exclude an unpopular minority from counting as a legally justifiable reason for legislative classifications. In effect, the Court articulated the idea of "equal respect for dignity" (Nussbaum 2006a, 204) at the heart of the capabilities approach in a way that again represented a major break with the values of mutual-advantage contractarianism, from whose perspective the town of Cleburne's residents had good reasons to deny the permit—ostensibly to protect their property values and emotional well-being by keeping people with intellectual impairments marginalized, which in a contractarian sense added up to good economic sense.

Nussbaum traces the manifestation of these noncontractarian conceptions of social cooperation and the purpose of political principles in the IDEA, which she considers an important exemplar of the capabilities approach in two respects (2006a, 205–8). First, it is premised on the

---

rather than in 1990 and, more important, asserting that the 1997 reauthorization only "slightly modified and elaborated" the law (2006a, 203). Although the 1990 reauthorization largely can be characterized as such, the 1997 reauthorization was a watershed move away from the principle of appropriate *individualized* education (see Skrtic, Harris, and Shriner 2005, 2–5).

"simple yet profound idea . . . of human individuality," which, for her, is a core liberal idea that should be retained while criticizing the social contract tradition (205). As she explains, "[R]espect for individuality has to be paramount, if the goals in the capabilities approach are to be realized" (207). In this regard, she commends the IDEA for assuming that "disabled persons . . . are in fact individuals, with varying needs, and that therefore all prescription for groups of them would be inappropriate" (205). She thus identifies the "guiding idea of the act [as] the Individualized Education Program (IEP), 'a written statement for each child with a disability that is developed, reviewed, and revised'" (205). With regard to its development, review, and revision, she further highlights IDEA's procedural safeguard requirements, which give parents a voice in IEP decisions as well as due process rights when they disagree with those decisions. Finally, she relates a fourth IDEA requirement to the capabilities approach: the "least restrictive environment," or the regulatory preference for serving students covered under the statute in integrated mainstream or regular classrooms. However, she also interprets this requirement in terms of respect for individuality, noting that here, too, "the underlying recognition of individuality is paramount: thus, when a child seems to profit more from special education [i.e., a more restrictive placement] than mainstreaming, the state is required to support such a special placement" (206).[10]

The second sense in which Nussbaum considers the IDEA to be exemplary with respect to the capabilities approach to justice is that the statute's "respect for citizens is *equal respect* in a very strong sense," a virtue embodied in its "zero reject" requirement, another policy she places at the core of the act (2006a, 207, emphasis in original). The statute is exemplary for her in this sense because there is no entry requirement of specific skills and abilities in order to be entitled to education as is any other citizen. "The underlying recognition of human dignity (in [the capabilities]

10. Nussbaum bifurcates special education placement options into these two (the regular classroom or a more restrictive separate, special education classroom) and doesn't appear to be aware of the full continuum of allowable placements of which they are a part (see note 14 in this chapter).

sense, where dignity is not seen as based on a specific set of skills) is the touchstone" (208).

Nussbaum recognizes that the IDEA is not perfect in theory or practice (2006a, 208–11). In practice, it is "rarely as individualized as it ought to be," and it is "often unequal, giving better results to parents who are well-read about their child's disorder and energetic in prodding the local school system" (208). She also identifies two serious theoretical problems with the law. The first is that the law also includes, in addition to individuals with "pervasive cognitive disabilities,"[11] those individuals with "a wide variety of 'specific learning disabilities' whose etiology and nature are poorly understood" (208), the presence of which leads to three additional implementation problems. First, given the difficulty of distinguishing a student with a learning disability from one "who is simply slow or less talented than many" (209), IDEA funding encourages districts to overidentify students as learning disabled. Second, the classification may not benefit the student instructionally while stigmatizing her socially (209). Third, the learning disability classification tends to be unfair to children who have difficulties in school but who can't be classified as such, a problem that is mitigated somewhat by "the looseness of the classificatory system, as school districts seek to include as many children as possible in the funding eligible pool" (209).[12]

11. Here, she is referring to three individuals with disabilities that she uses as exemplars in *Frontiers of Justice* (also see Nussbaum 2001): Sesha, the twenty-something daughter of philosopher Eva Kittay, has "congenital cerebral palsy and severe mental retardation" (2006a, 98) and is cared for at home (see Kittay 1999); Arthur, the ten-year-old son of Nussbaum's sister, has Asperger's and Tourette syndromes and receives IDEA funding to attend a private special education day school; and Jamie, the three-year-old son of literary critics Michael Bérubé and Janet Lyon, has Down syndrome and attends his local district's inclusive preschool (see Bérubé 1996).

12. Nussbaum's sole source for this problem is Kelman and Lester 1997, which argues that students labeled with learning disabilities neither constitute an objective disability type nor a historical, sociocultural group beset by stereotypes or prejudice and thus that their interests do not represent valid civil rights claims. For a critical review of this argument, see Weis 1998.

The second and, for Nussbaum, most significant theoretical problem with the IDEA is that it "still single[s] out children with mental impairments as a class apart, and say[s] [that] for them education should be individualized and aimed at fostering capabilities" (2006a, 209). Real progress for Nussbaum would be acknowledging that "there is really no such thing as 'the normal child': instead, there are *children* with varying capabilities and varying impediments, all of whom need individualized attention as their capabilities are developed" (210). In spite of this problem, Nussbaum defends the law by returning to its significance with regard to individuality. Following Erving Goffman (1963), she argues that, as a stigmatized class, children with impairments and associated disabilities are subject to human encounters in which the entire interaction is with the stigmatized trait. And because "stigma tends to submerge individuality" in such encounters, the IDEA rightly focuses on "protecting what most urgently needs protection: the claim of stigmatized children to be seen, and educated, as individuals" (2006a, 210).[13]

Problems with Nussbaum's Interpretation of the IDEA and Its Principles

The IDEA rests on six principles: zero reject, nondiscriminatory evaluation, appropriate education, least restrictive environment (LRE), procedural due process, and parent participation (Turnbull, Stowe, and Huerta 2007). The first four govern the processes that school districts follow in order to "confer on each IDEA-covered student the benefit of a free appropriate education in the least restrictive environment," and the last two represent procedural safeguards that covered students and their parents use "to hold the [school district] accountable for complying with the first four principles and to be partners with the schools in the student's education" (Turnbull, Stowe,

---

13. Nussbaum treats, in addition to education, the policy implications of her approach for guardianship and the problem of care. In the interest of space, we forego a discussion of these areas except to say that, with regard to care, she sees the capabilities as a set of social benchmarks for policy design for both the cared-for person and the caregiver.

and Huerta 2007, 44). In making her case for the IDEA as exemplar of the capabilities approach to justice, Nussbaum (2006a) considers the two procedural safeguard principles and three of the four process principles. She emphasizes the significance of the act's zero-reject policy—especially appropriate education, which she identifies as the IDEA's touchstone, reflecting its underlying respect for human dignity, and individualized education (including the IEP), which she sees as the statute's guiding idea, reflecting its respect for human individuality.[14] Although she recognizes the value of the LRE principle, she considers it secondary to that of appropriate education, and she does not address the nondiscriminatory evaluation principle—a significant oversight, we believe.

In this section, we use insights from institutional theory and Martha Minow's (1990) relational understanding of disability to highlight problems with IDEA implementation and Nussbaum's (2006a) interpretation of the statute and its principles. Together, these problems call into question her claim about the statute's respect for human individuality and human dignity and thus her characterization of it as an exemplar of the capabilities approach. In the next section, we reconsider the design and institutional interpretation of the IDEA with respect to the same claim and characterization from the perspectives of "institutionalized injustice" and "needs politics." Our larger aim in raising these questions is to show that Nussbaum's approach to what justice requires for disabled people is an empty proposition without adequate theorization of the institutional context in which capabilities needs-claims are adjudicated.

Minow's relational understanding of disability views human differences as "features of relationships rather than [as] traits that reside in the 'different' person" (1990, 86). As such, she is concerned with power relations in disability classification processes and the way institutions employ

14. Although Nussbaum emphasizes "zero reject" in this regard, she doesn't comment further on it, so we will not discuss it except to note her higher regard for "inclusion" in the zero-reject sense of access to education than in the LRE sense of access to regular classrooms. Her lesser regard for inclusion in the latter sense may stem from her focus on more significant impairments, for which she apparently prefers separate placements over more inclusive ones (see notes 10 and 11 in this chapter).

these processes to "construct and utilize difference to justify and enforce exclusions" (86), ultimately implicating them in the oppression and domination of difference as disability. Institutional theory is concerned with the institutionalization of such processes in organizations, emphasizing the social construction of rules, myths, and beliefs (Powell and DiMaggio 1991) and their effects on how organizations respond to their environments, especially with respect to their structural characteristics (e.g., DiMaggio and Powell 1983) and how they change (e.g., Meyer 1979).

Institutional theory posits that schools' survival depends on their ability to maintain legitimacy and stability (Rowan 1982). To maintain legitimacy, they must be responsive to the often conflicting demands and constraints of four environmental entities: the social state (including governmental agencies, regulatory structures, laws, and courts), the education profession, influential interest groups, and public opinion in general (DiMaggio and Powell 1983, 147; Scott 1987a, 498, 1987b, 114). Schools react to these demands by reproducing or imitating organizational structures, activities, and routines to respond to legal and regulatory requirements and cultural expectations, to model similar organizations perceived to be more legitimate or successful, and/or to conform to the expectations of the profession (DiMaggio and Powell 1983, 150–54). Over time, the resulting structures, activities, and routines become calcified because imitation involves conformity, habit, and ritualized activity rather than reflective strategic choice, leading to unquestioned acceptance of institutionalized structures, classifications, and practices (DiMaggio 1988; Tolbert and Zucker 1983). As such, schools come to define and structure their activities around functions—for example, general, special, and compensatory education—that reflect institutionalized or "ritual" classifications of students, personnel, and programs rather than technical assessments of effectiveness and efficiency (Meyer and Rowan 1977, 1983). Although ritualization fosters stability in schools, it makes changing in response to evolving environmental expectations and especially to more punctuated change mandates that require substantially different structures and activities more difficult for them. Schools cope with this potential threat to legitimacy by using various types of "ceremonial activity" and "decoupling" devices (Meyer and Rowan 1977, 355, 357) to signal the environment that they have changed when in fact they remain largely the same (Meyer 1979; Zucker 1981). Special education in general and the IDEA, as implemented, in particular are archetypical cases of such symbolic change in public education (see Skrtic 1991b; Skrtic and McCall 2010).

Appropriate Education and the IEP

With regard to the principle of appropriate or individualized education, Nussbaum rightly notes that IEPs are rarely as individualized as they should be in that "formulas are typically found for common disorders" (2006a, 208). However, she does not pursue this implementation problem beyond providing a counterexample of the tendency toward formulaic IEPs in which she locates the problem in teachers' unwillingness to individualize instruction for particular students. Had she pursued the problem in more depth, she would have found that for most IDEA-covered students, the IEP is largely symbolic, serving more to signal compliance with the appropriate-education requirement than actually to specify and guide an individualized education for each covered student (Pretti-Frontczak and Bricker 2000; S. Smith 1990; Smith and Kotering 1996; Ysseldyke et al. 1983). In fact, questions of IEP quality and function gave way in the 1980s to concern for "reducing the cost and time necessary to complete [them]" and eventually to the development of computer software that did so by "using formulas" rather than individualized planning (S. Smith 1990, 11, 10).

Moreover, although Nussbaum (2006a) doesn't address this issue, the 1997 IDEA reauthorization shifted the focus and mechanism of accountability from procedural compliance with the statute's provisions to student performance on state and local standardized achievement tests (McLaughlin and Tilstone 2000). In the interest of improving academic outcomes for IDEA-covered students, special education policy was aligned with the standards-based reform model that was introduced in the 1994 reauthorization of the Elementary and Secondary Education Act of 1965 and subsequently consolidated, in extreme bureaucratic form, in its 2001 reauthorization as the No Child Left Behind Act (NCLB)

(Kleinhammer-Tramill and Gallagher 2002).[15] Despite concerns that this alignment would narrow the curriculum for students with disabilities (Wehmeyer and Schalock 2001) and standardize their instruction (Skrtic, Harris, and Shriner 2005, 2–5), by 1999 states already had begun using "standards-based IEPs" to align instructional goals for students with disabilities with general education curriculum standards (Ahearn 2006, 4), and today two-thirds of the states have instituted or are implementing this type of IEP (Ahearn 2010). Whereas "IDEA and good practice dictate that, for a student's education to be appropriate, it must be individually tailored to fit that student" (Turnbull, Stowe, and Huerta 2007, 161), standards-based IEPs are premised on students' attainment of state "academic standards for [their] enrolled grade" (Ahearn 2010, 2).[16] Although the goal of increasing the academic achievement of students with disabilities is laudable, as in symbolic IEP implementation, an overemphasis on academic achievement defined narrowly as attainment of state standards contradicts the IDEA's original emphasis on appropriate individualized education, turning the principle of individualization into standardization of curriculum and instruction. Although Nussbaum's claim that the appropriate-education principle reflects an underlying respect for human individuality may be true in principle, it is not the case in practice, given the prevalence of symbolic compliance with IEP provisions and the erosion of the principle itself under standards-based reform.

LRE and Inclusion

Although IDEA contains a regulatory preference for inclusive general education or regular classroom placements, the LRE principle is a rebuttable

15. Standards-based reform is an outcomes-based approach to accountability that uses student achievement to publicly evaluate professional and system performance, with the school as the unit of accountability (Elmore, Abelmann, and Fuhrman 1996). On its extreme bureaucratic form in NCLB, see O'Day 2002.

16. Another indication of a move away from individualization in the 2004 reauthorization is the elimination of benchmarks and short-term objectives in the IEP for all IDEA-covered students except those with the most significant impairments.

presumption; an inclusive placement "is not an absolute right but is secondary to the primary purpose of [appropriate] education" (Turnbull 1993, 159). Nussbaum recognizes the value of the LRE principle for disabled and nondisabled students but notes that, for purposes of the law and realization of the goals of the capabilities approach, appropriate education and thus respect for individuality take precedence over the LRE principle when a child may profit from a more restrictive placement (2006a, 205–6).

From the perspective of institutional theory, schools use separate, decoupled classrooms and programs to signal compliance with environmental demands for change while minimizing disruption to their conventional activities and practices, thereby helping them maintain legitimacy and stability simultaneously (Meyer and Rowan 1977, 1978). The segregated special classroom, a key example of this form of decoupling, was created in the early twentieth century to separate and contain student diversity resulting from compulsory-attendance legislation (Lazerson 1983, 16–21), thereby maintaining public schools' legitimacy and stability by signaling their compliance with the demand for universal public education (Skrtic 1995, 214–16). Criticism of these classrooms in the 1960s as racially biased, instructionally ineffective, and psychologically and socially damaging (e.g., Dunn 1968; Mercer 1973) added force to EAHCA proponents' campaign against exclusion, but schools often exploit the ambiguity created by the statute's dual commitment to the appropriate-education and LRE principles by using arguments for the former to defeat the latter. "After all," Minow explains, "the commitment to the least restrictive alternative was devised in part to combat [the] very reluctance of the classroom teacher to deal with the unusual or more difficult child." As such, the ambiguity preserved by IDEA's commitment to both principles permits "the incentives of teachers . . . to give content to the law" (1985, 178).

Moreover, to be consistent with Nussbaum's (2006a) Aristotelian/Marxian ideal of sociability and the human dignity of bodily need, inclusive placements can't simply locate the problem of difference in the student to be included "while making the unimpaired students—and the classroom designed for them—the norm" (Minow 1990, 84). Nussbaum provides two illustrations of when the state is required to support a more restrictive placement, one in which the student's "cognitive level is so out of step with those of other children . . . that more progress can be made [in a separate setting]" and one in which the student's "behavioral difficulties . . . are likely to lead to stigmatizing and ostracism . . . [and to be] disturbing to the other children" (2006a, 206). In both cases, she makes the unimpaired students and the regular classroom the norm, assuming its existing instructional and management practices to be what Minow calls "natural and necessary" (1990, 83–86). Drawing on the concept of "universal design," a framework for structuring inclusive human settings so that they benefit everyone in them, Minow provides an alternative illustration in which a regular classroom teacher includes a student with a profound hearing impairment by teaching all students to use sign language and presenting instruction in spoken and sign language simultaneously, thereby treating difference as "embedded in the relationships among all the students, making all of them part of the problem" (84). Among the advantages of such an approach, Minow notes that, rather than making the trait of hearing impairment "signify stigma or isolation," it responds to that trait "as an issue for the entire community" (84). Moreover, she argues that by focusing on the individual child, individualized planning ignores the child's relationships with others and "the construction of difference in those relationships" (86). An individualized plan would not have conceived of a class of students fluent in sign language because it would leave existing classroom practices in place and expect the included student to adjust to that structure. This illustration disrupts the relative merit of the two IDEA principles, in effect rendering the LRE principle as primary as that of appropriate education and relegating the conventional regular classroom to a rebuttable presumption.

Building on the civil rights movement and the *Brown* decision, the EAHCA framers conceptualized the LRE principle as a way to address "the stigma of separate treatment" (Minow 1985, 168). Although Nussbaum recognizes disabled children as a stigmatized class, she emphasizes the effect of stigma on their individuality at the expense of the role that separate treatment, or exclusion, plays in their stigmatization. The important thing about stigma for her is that it submerges individuality, and though she acknowledges that inclusive placements minimize stigma and teach appreciation for diversity, what makes the IDEA an exemplar of the capabilities approach for her is that it protects the claim of stigma-tized children "to be seen, and educated, as individuals" (2006a, 210). By elevating individuality over inclusion, however, Nussbaum contradicts the emphasis upon "affiliation" in her list of capabilities. Individual flourish-ing presupposes individuality, but it also presupposes affiliation, which in part means "being able to live with and toward others, to recognize and show concern for other human beings, to engage in various forms of social interaction; to be able to imagine the situation of another" (2006a, 77). Protecting this capability, she adds, requires protecting institutions that constitute and nourish it. As such, an inclusively ordered public education is an institution that deserves our protection as much as the claim to be seen and educated as individuals because inclusion, or participation, is essential to human flourishing; inclusive placements are both a form of affiliation and a means to its cultivation and thereby a defense against stig-matization and exclusion, especially as children who participate in them "discover that differences are features of relationships rather than traits that reside in the 'different' person" (Minow 1990, 86).[17]

Nondiscriminatory Evaluation and Disproportionality

Although Nussbaum (2006a) doesn't include the nondiscriminatory eval-uation principle in her analysis of the IDEA, it is a critically important component of the statute that addresses the most obdurate problem in spe-cial education: the misclassification and disproportionate representation of poor, working-class, and racial and ethnic minority students in special education.[18] Drawing once again upon the civil rights movement and the

---

17. Nussbaum's concern for individuality in interpreting the IDEA is understand-able given that the capabilities approach remains a liberal theory of justice in which respect for individuality is a core idea. Also, the IDEA's individualized focus is character-istic of American disability law in general, which reflects the liberal preoccupation with individuality in much of US law as well as the coveted shift from charity to rights as the appropriate legal framework for disabled people (Minow 2008, 2–8).

18. Nussbaum's omission of this principle is puzzling because Kelman and Lester 1997, 75–82, her primary source on IDEA implementation, highlights the issue of racial/

Brown decision as well as on the research on racial/ethnic and social class discrimination in segregated special classroom placements noted earlier, EAHCA framers and, later, disability advocates conceptualized the non-discriminatory evaluation principle to address "the risks of misclassification and labeling in creating stigma and low self-esteem, and the abusive use of separate classes to perpetuate discrimination against racial and ethnic minorities" (Minow 1985, 168). It seeks to protect students by requiring that classification and placement decisions are made by an evaluation team, including parents, that conforms to specified evaluation standards, including use of nondiscriminatory tests and administration procedures (Turnbull, Stowe, and Huerta 2007). The problem, however, is that over the history of the EAHCA and more recently of the IDEA, the disproportionate representation of economically disadvantaged and racial/ethnic minority students in special education and, especially African American students, in more restrictive special education placements has continued largely unabated (National Research Council 1982, 2002; Skiba, Poloni-Staudinger, et al. 2006; Skiba, Simmons, et al. 2008).[19]

Disproportionate representation was formally recognized as a policy problem over the course of the 1960s, when in the context of resistance to the *Brown* decision, including various forms of "resegregation within desegregated schools" (D. Bell 1980a, 531), the disproportionate identification of African American students as "educable mentally retarded" attracted increasing attention. Although Derrick Bell didn't connect special education programs to this form of resistance in his 1980 analysis,

---

ethnic and class bias. Her apparent unfamiliarity with the issue may stem from omitting cases focusing on such biases in her review of IDEA-related litigation (e.g., *Hobson v. Hansen* [1967], which also was cited in the *Mills* decision that she highlights) or from her focus on objective impairments (see note 11 in this chapter) rather than on the subjective or judgmental disabilities implicated in racial/ethnic and class bias or from both.

19. Disproportionate representation is most pronounced for African American and American Indian/Alaska Native students who, respectively, are 1.42 to 2.84 and 1.24 to 1.79 times more likely to be labeled with intellectual disabilities, emotional disturbance, and learning disabilities (US Department of Education 2009). Latino students are not overrepresented nationally, but they are in some states and districts (Artiles et al. 2005).

others have implicated them in the resegregation process (e.g., Ferri and Connor 2005a, 2005b; Skrtic 1991b; see also Fenton, chapter 7, in this text). From an institutional perspective, the disproportionality problem can be understood as another form of decoupling in which schools use an existing decoupling device—selected special education programs—to maintain their legitimacy and stability while failing to meet the needs of disproportionate numbers of African American students in purportedly desegregated schools (Skrtic 2003). This is possible because, like implementation of IEP provisions, compliance with nondiscriminatory evaluation provisions for these and other economically disadvantaged and racial/ethnic minority students is ceremonialized within team evaluation processes. In the same way that the IDEA's dual commitment to appropriate education and LRE permits teachers' incentives to give content to the law, the availability of special education programs has permitted resistant administrators in the decades following *Brown* and reluctant teachers then and now to give content to the *Brown* decision. Moreover, symbolic compliance with nondiscriminatory evaluation provisions legitimates the IDEA identification and placement process, which by justifying discriminatory classification and placement decisions continues the abusive use of special education to perpetuate racial/ethnic and class discrimination (Skrtic and McCall 2010).

Prior to 1975, misclassified economically disadvantaged and racial/ethnic minority students were identified primarily as "educable mentally retarded," whereas when the learning disabilities classification emerged in the 1960s, it was used virtually exclusively for failing white middle-class students (Carrier 1983; Sleeter 1986). Beginning in the 1970s and 1980s, however, economically disadvantaged and racial/ethnic minority students were increasingly identified as learning disabled (McLesky, Waldron, and Wornhoff 1990; J. Tucker 1980), and by the 1990s they were disproportionately identified in this classification (Reid and Valle 2004). This shift in identification patterns can be understood in terms of another institutional phenomenon referred to recently as the "high-road/low-road hypothesis" (Ong-Dean 2009, 74), which explains the career of a disability classification in terms of an early "high-road" phase in which privileged parents create it to benefit their children exclusively and a subsequent "low-road" phase in which it comes to serve the institutional needs of schools as a way to remove socially and economically disadvantaged students from regular classrooms. Nussbaum considers the IDEA's learning disabilities classification a serious theoretical problem (2006a, 208–9), but she recognizes only that its classificatory looseness has resulted in the overidentification of students as disabled, not that it has become a mechanism in the over-representation of economically disadvantaged and racial/ethnic minority students among those overidentified. Not recognizing this problem and the IDEA's failure to resolve it further undercuts Nussbaum's case for the IDEA as an exemplar of the capabilities approach to justice. We argue here that the IDEA, a law intended to stop injustice toward disabled students, has done little to stop the use of disability as an instrument in the perpetuation of racial/ethnic and class injustice.

Parent Participation and Procedural Due Process

Although Nussbaum considers the procedural safeguards of parent participation and procedural due process essential to actualizing the IDEA's respect for individuality, she recognizes that parent participation in the IEP process is often unequal, resulting in better outcomes for parents who are "well-read about their child's disorder and energetic in prodding the local school system" (2006a, 208). Referring to the professional occupations and advanced degrees of the parents of IDEA-covered children that she uses as exemplars, she notes that "it is no accident that [these parents] have succeeded in using the system to their advantage, while many other parents have not" (208). Although Nussbaum apparently recognizes class bias in special education, by not pursuing the matter her analysis fails to capture the extent and pernicious effects of class and racial/ethnic discrimination in the IEP process. Such discrimination has been recognized and studied extensively for some time (e.g., Harry 1992; Kalyanpur, Harry, and Skrtic 2000); more recently, however, the influence of parent privilege in special education has begun to receive more critical attention (e.g., Ginsburg and Rapp 2010; McCall and Skrtic 2009; Ong-Dean 2009). As an extension of research on the influence of privilege in education (Lareau 2003), the argument is that parents with the most cultural and economic capital—that is, "white, middle- to high-income, English-speaking, professional, and college educated" parents (Ong-Dean 2009, 3)—are best equipped to advocate for their children in the IEP process and thereby more likely to secure better outcomes for them. Moreover, in terms of challenging IEP decisions, cultural and economic capital also affect the nature and distribution of due process hearing requests and cases, both of which are more prevalent in more privileged districts, as well as the nature of the challenges put forth, even the most typical of which "presuppose a fair degree of parental privilege" (Ong-Dean 2009, 132). Thus, privileged parents' incentives give content to the two IDEA procedural safeguard provisions.

Approaching the problem of discrimination in special education from the vantage point of cultural capital also enhances our understanding of the nature and effects of disproportionate representation. Bias in the IEP process favoring privilege puts poor, working-class, and racial/ethnic/linguistic minority parents at a disadvantage relative to professionals and to more privileged parents in resisting inappropriate disability diagnoses, accommodations, and placements for their children or, when called for, in recognizing and claiming the most advantageous ones for them (McCall and Skrtic 2009, 14–15). As such, the unfair influence of economic and cultural capital in special education perpetuates the disproportionality problem, and the IDEA's parent-participation and procedural due process provisions legitimate their unjust outcomes (discussed in the next section), thereby muting broader social concern for the long-standing problems of ineffectiveness, exclusion, and disproportionate representation in special education. Moreover, this problem is not merely one of implementation; the injustice is built into the structure of the law itself, into the procedural safeguards that Nussbaum (2006a) believes are essential to actualizing the core liberal idea of respect for individuality and thus to realizing the goals of the capabilities approach.

Rights, Needs, and Relationships

These design and implementation problems constitute a disjunction between the rights conferred by the IDEA and their realization; they are injustices that the statute either has not been able to overcome or has perpetuated or created. Nussbaum's claim that the IDEA gives disabled children enforceable rights to an appropriate individualized education (2006a, 203) is true only in a formal sense; the rights conferred by the statute are not fully realized in the institutional context that it seeks to change. Such disjunctions are a central concern in the critique of liberal legal consciousness, the framework that underwrites the IDEA and other disability and civil rights legislation, which holds that legal rights discourse or "rights talk," as a political strategy, is both indeterminate and legitimating. It is indeterminate because the value of a right in eliminating injustice is determined by the structure and political commitments of its institutional context, not by the right itself. Rights talk is legitimating because by appearing to confer rights in such contexts, it legitimates the injustice it seeks to eliminate, in effect legitimating the continued exercise of political power over the disempowered (Crenshaw 1988, 1351–54; Kelman 1987, 262–68). In response to this "postrights" critique, however, legal scholars of color defend rights talk as a political strategy, both crediting it for rights achieved in the civil rights movement and, with the recognition of the idiom's indeterminate and legitimating effects, calling for a "jurisprudence of reconstruction" (A. Harris 1994, 744) to fully actualize those rights by reconstructing them to reflect the real needs and political commitments of communities of color (Crenshaw 1988, 1349–69; Williams 1991, 146–65).

The disability rights movement[20] today is in a position similar to that of the broader civil rights movement. It has used the rights idiom successfully to establish disability rights in law, but the material realization of those rights is at best indeterminate, institutionally mediated, and disempowering, especially for individuals and families subject to the intersecting oppressions of race/ethnicity, class, gender, language, and disability (Connor 2008, 42–51; McCall and Skrtic 2009). In terms of a direction for

20. Here "disability rights movement" refers both to the larger social movement of the 1960s and 1970s that ran parallel to the women's and civil rights movements and over time in the United States won legislation such as Section 504 of the Rehabilitation Act of 1973 and the Americans with Disabilities Act and to that portion of it led by parent and professional groups that lobbied for and won the EAHCA.

remedial action, the one proposed by civil rights scholars makes sense as far as it goes; that is, current indeterminate and legitimating disability rights must be reconstructed to reflect the disability community's real needs and political commitments. The advantage of the capabilities approach in this regard is that, as a model of social justice, it replaces the contractarian sense of justice with values such as human dignity, care, inclusion, and human flourishing, all backed by a set of morally and politically entitled capabilities.[21] However, reconstructing disability rights to reflect the disability community's real needs and political commitments requires more than a jurisprudence of reconstruction that establishes human capabilities as fundamental entitlements. It also requires overcoming two additional problems, a theoretical problem that we discuss in the next paragraph and a political problem addressed in the concluding section.

The theoretical problem is the one illustrated in our analysis of the IDEA: the need to theorize the institutional context in which reconstructed rights and capabilities needs-claims are adjudicated. Although Nussbaum recognizes that institutions are crucially important in implementing capabilities, she admits that her account of the capabilities approach "does not say enough about [them]" (2006b, 502).[22] Moreover, it is not enough merely to recognize the role of institutions in creating just conditions for the cultivation of capabilities. As illustrated in the analysis of IDEA principles, we also need detailed analyses of how institutionalized organizations can obstruct capability cultivation and produce unjust outcomes with relative impunity. The question for us is what a more complete theory of justice—one that puts institutional analysis in the foreground—would entail. Beyond recognizing that institutions can

21. Concerning the shortcomings of rights talk and its continuing importance, Nussbaum has argued, and we agree, that rights discourse is valuable because it represents "urgent claims"—for example, needs-claims—"based upon justice" (2003, 39).

22. In works preceding *Frontiers of Justice* (e.g., Nussbaum 1988, 1990, 2000a, 2000b, 2003), Nussbaum consistently recognizes the role of institutions in the cultivation of capabilities, but in them, too, she doesn't say much more about them than that they provide "the requisite affirmative support" (2003, 55) for cultivating capabilities.

be carriers of injustice or, appropriately transformed, instruments of social justice, such a theory requires clarity about what injustice entails and how it is sustained. Although Nussbaum has dealt minimally with this topic, political philosophers Iris Marion Young (1990) and Nancy Fraser (1989a, 2008) as well as legal scholar Martha Minow (1990) have done exemplary scholarship on it.

Institutionalized Injustice

Iris Young (1990) criticizes Rawls and the distributive paradigm generally for ignoring and presupposing the given institutional context that determines material distribution as well as for misrepresenting nonmaterial goods—including rights, opportunities, self-respect, and, we would add, capabilities—as things. They are not things, she argues, but relationships based on processes that are mediated by social institutions that have been implicated historically in the construction, oppression, and domination of difference. Despite significant conceptual disagreements between Fraser and Young (see Fraser 1995; Young 2008), their writings converge on the scope and substance of theories of such "institutionalized injustice" (Fraser 2008, 327). They also converge in centering their own theories in a robust conception of democracy, both arguing that we cannot know what justice requires in particular social situations until we listen, albeit critically, to individuals and groups who are suffering various forms of institutionalized domination or oppression (Fraser and Honneth 2003, 10–15, 207–10; Young 1990, 5–7, 2000, 71–77, 103, 105). In addition to producing unacceptable levels of political and material inequality, such institutionalized injustices weaken and corrupt existing democratic policies by marginalizing or excluding whole classes of citizens in diverse decision-making fora—the state, economy, and civil society—that directly affect their lives (Fraser 2008, 332, 345, 2009, 16–18; Fraser and Honneth 2003, 8–9, 15–16, 31–34, 91–95; Young 2000, 121–24). As critical theorists, both Fraser and Young make the critique of institutionalized injustice a priority in pursuing their emancipatory interest in unmasking domination or, as Fraser puts it, in formulating a "critical theory of (in)justice" (2008, 336).

Like Nussbaum, Minow criticizes Rawls's contractarian theory of justice for excluding people it considers incapable of the political bargaining
for mutual advantage (1990, 149–55). She also criticizes rights analysis
for creating the "dilemma of difference" (20), in which analysts "face
the dilemma of attempting to justify both equal and special treatment"
(216), as well as for leading to incremental reforms that leave institutional
sources of injustice intact. As an alternative to an exclusively rights-focused
approach to justice, she proposes a "social-relations approach to the legal
treatment of difference" (172), as we have seen. Like Young in her relational interpretation of nonmaterial goods and Nussbaum in her notion
of networks of social relations required for human flourishing, Minow
locates "rights *in* relationship" (282). In addition, like Young's (1990, 2000)
and Fraser's (1989a, 2008) approaches, Minow's social relations approach
treats existing institutional arrangements as "a conceivable source of the
problem of difference rather than as an unproblematic background"
(1990, 112).

Finally, Minow links the source of these unjust disciplinary practices
to early-twentieth-century progressive reformers (1990, 257–66). Although
she commends them for articulating "visions of mutual support" and associated policies to care for and protect dependent and vulnerable citizens,
she explains that the institutions they created to actualize these visions
and policies were problematic because they "avoided participatory processes that could have challenged their biases, imposed their interests
on those they claimed to help, and perpetuated a world distinguishing
'us' from 'them' while expanding bureaucratic power" (266). By "avoided
participatory processes," Minow means that these reformers' institutions
excluded the perspectives and participation of those who were supposed
to benefit from them. That is, absent from these institutional settings was
genuine deliberative democracy "through which people would share decisions about their collective future" (264). As such, Minow concludes, one
legacy of the Progressive Era is another version of the dilemma of difference: "collective neglect of individual need denies relationships and
oppresses individuals, but so may efforts to acknowledge need and responsibility toward others" (266).

Needs Politics

Whereas Young (1990, 2000) and Minow (1990) theorize the nature of rights and injustice in social institutions, Fraser (1989a) theorizes how injustice is enacted and sustained in them, focusing on the political and institutional processes for making and adjudicating the needs-claims that rights are established to recognize and satisfy.[23] This focus requires an understanding of the political career of such claims in liberal welfare state societies, for which Fraser introduces the concept of "needs talk" (1989a, 161), a political idiom involving disputes about people's needs and whether and how government should provide for them. Arguing that needs talk is the dominant form of political discourse in such societies, coexisting with talk about rights and interests, she is concerned with the barriers and opportunities it poses for social movements that want to make these political cultures more just and equitable. Her research is an institutional analysis of power in which "needs politics" is the medium of struggle among unequal groups, a process through which the relationship between oppression and activism is enacted in social institutions.

Key among Fraser's insights on needs politics are two axes of needs struggle (1989a, 171–81). The first is the struggle between what she calls "oppositional" and "reprivatization" discourses (171). Oppositional discourses are those of social movements that attempt to "politicize" their needs by reinterpreting them in ways that make them a matter of public concern and provision, such as the oppositional discourse that produced the EAHCA. Moreover, by politicizing their needs, members of oppositional discourses contest their subordinate identities and invent new discursive forms and vehicles for interpreting and disseminating their alternative need interpretations. As such, oppositional needs talk is "a moment in the self-constitution of new collective [political] agents" (171). Reprivatization discourses arise in resistance to oppositional discourses. They reflect the

---

23. This section draws on prior treatments of needs politics in Skrtic 2000 and McCall and Skrtic 2009.

entrenched need interpretations of those who oppose state provision for reinterpreted needs and thus try to "depoliticize them" (172) or to keep government from accepting responsibility for them.

The second, largely veiled axis of needs struggle pits successful oppositional discourses against expert discourses in government human-service agencies. As the vehicle for translating state-recognized needs into objects of state intervention, expert discourses emerge when politicized needs become candidates for state provision. The central issue here, Fraser explains, is politics versus administration (1989a, 174). Administratively, expert discourses translate successfully reinterpreted oppositional needs into "administrable needs" by recasting them in ways that tacitly presuppose the prerogatives of the service agency and its professionals, typically redefining them as needs already covered by an existing service or program or by a service or program that can be established with the least increment of disruption to the system. Politically, expert discourses simultaneously recast members of successful oppositional movements as individual "cases," thereby turning political activists into "individualized victims" (176). As such, expert discourses are also depoliticizing. In the end, those who have collectively secured the political status of their needs are atomized and pathologized, recast as individual victims rather than as members of a political movement, thereby positioning them as passive recipients of predefined services rather than as agents involved in interpreting their own needs and shaping their own life chances.

Finally, Fraser notes three possible relationships between oppositional and expert discourses in needs politics (1989a, 175–81). The first type, noted earlier, is the tendency for expert needs discourses to depoliticize oppositional groups by redefining their needs in terms of an administrable service and, moreover, by atomizing and pathologizing their members, turning political activists into individualized victims. The second type of relationship is what Fraser calls the "countertendency" in needs politics that "runs from administration to client resistance and potentially back to politics" (177), a process in which, despite the atomizing and depoliticizing dimensions of an administrable service, the recipients of that service share common grievances and join together to repoliticize and thereby redress them. The third type of relationship is when social movements manage to co-opt or create critical oppositional segments within an expert discourse, which allows them to disseminate oppositional need interpretations to a wider audience of discourse publics and thus increase their perceived legitimacy. In the next section, we apply Fraser's conception of needs politics to four episodes of disability needs politics over the past fifty years to highlight the role of expert discourses in the disjunction between established and realized disability rights under the IDEA as well as in the institutional practices that Young (1990) and Minow (1990) implicate in the oppression and domination of difference.

Expert Depoliticization of Oppositional Needs

The segment of the US disability movement concerned with public education has been very successful historically in terms of politicizing their needs. Legislation passed in the 1950s and early 1960s that funded research, teacher education and doctoral programs, as well as federal administration and oversight represented major victories in the struggle to establish the educational needs of children with disabilities as a legitimate concern for state provision.[24] The problem was that in the 1960s the expert education discourse translated these needs into a bureaucratically administrable need satisfaction, an educational service premised on segregated special education classrooms and virtually no individualized planning or parent participation. As such, the needs whose political legitimacy had been secured were tacitly stripped of their oppositional meanings and reinterpreted in ways that presupposed the prerogatives and perspectives of the expert discourse. Moreover, children labeled with disabilities and their

24. This legislation includes the Education of Mentally Retarded Children Act of 1958, the Mental Retardation Facilities and Community Health Centers Construction Act of 1963, and the Elementary and Secondary Education Amendments of 1966, the latter of which among other things created the US Bureau of Education for the Handicapped (now the Office of Special Education and Rehabilitative Services) and the National Advisory Council (now the National Council on Disability).

parents were recast as individualized victims, thus repositioning them as passive recipients of predefined services rather than as political agents and thereby stripping them of their human dignity.[25]

The depoliticization of disability needs politics in the 1960s gave rise to the countertendency running from administration back to politics. This time aligning themselves with the broader civil rights movement and drawing upon the *Brown* decision, disability advocates of the late 1960s and early 1970s resisted the segregated-services model by repoliticizing their needs-claims, a resistance that, with help from the courts and a co-opted expert discourse critical of the special-classroom model (e.g., Dunn 1968; Mercer 1973), led to enactment of the EAHCA. As significant as the statute was, however, in the late 1970s and 1980s it was undercut by symbolic compliance, which, though more subtle than the blatant need translations of the 1960s, nonetheless stripped the oppositional meaning of needs whose political legitimacy had been secured in the EAHCA, in effect reinterpreting those needs in ways that preserved the prerogatives and practices of the expert discourse, thereby allowing schools to respond to the law with the least increment of change. And here, too, children labeled with disabilities and their parents were atomized, recast as individualized victims rather than as self-determined political agents engaged in interpreting their own needs and shaping their own life conditions. Although the principles of the EAHCA appeared to create an ideal framework for such a self-determined process, symbolic compliance repositioned these children and their parents as passive recipients of expert-defined services, once again stripping them of their dignity and only symbolically respecting their individuality.

These and other implementation problems led to a third round of resistance and repoliticization in the late 1980s and early 1990s in which the central issue was "inclusive education," a more aggressive form of integration

---

25. The same analysis holds for the segment of the civil rights movement that successfully politicized the needs of poor and minority children and their parents in the 1960s with enactment of the Elementary and Secondary Education Act. See McCall and Skrtic 2009, 12–13.

than mainstreaming in which the primary placement for most students labeled with disabilities is the general education classroom (for a review, see Skrtic 1991a). This round of needs politics followed the same pattern of expert translation of politicized needs into administrable needs, beginning with the reinterpretation of the idea of inclusive education when the IDEA was aligned with NCLB's extreme bureaucratic version of standards-based reform, under which the need for "inclusion in [regular] classrooms" became the need for "access to the [regular] curriculum" and "inclusion in state and local standardized testing" (Skrtic, Harris, and Shriner 2005, 2–5). Although one can argue as we have against the wisdom of such an alignment, it was undertaken justifiably to improve the academic achievement and school and postschool attainment of IDEA-covered students by making schools more accountable for their performance as an identifiable student subgroup (see Hehir 1994; Riley 1995). In implementation, however, the reinterpreted meaning of "inclusive education" was further compromised by NCLB provisions and regulations that by the 2008–9 school year were permitting states to exclude more than 40 percent of their students with disabilities from consideration in local accountability systems (Harr-Robins et al. 2012).[26] Moreover, school administrators have reinterpreted the need for access to the general curriculum as the need for instruction in "special regular classrooms" (McCall and Skrtic 2009, 14), in which a special educator teaches a general education subject-area class exclusively to students labeled as disabled and at risk (see Schumaker et al. 2002), which is a throwback to segregated special classrooms and thus

26. In an IDEA-mandated study of the inclusion of students with disabilities in school accountability systems under NCLB, Jenifer Harr-Robins and her colleagues found that the statute's provisions and regulations—on things such as minimum subgroup size for accountability purposes and methods for measuring student progress—make it "challenging to determine exactly how well [students with disabilities] have been performing" (2012, 10), in part because of permissible state variation in "how [students with disabilities] are included or excluded from school accountability systems" (10). In addition, for school years 2005–6 through 2008–9, Harr-Robins and her colleagues found that "[t]he majority (55 percent) of the public schools in 32 states with relevant data were not accountable for the [students with disabilities] subgroup in any of the 4 years examined" (32).

a return to the egregious conditions that gave rise to the oppositional discourse that won the enactment of the IDEA in the first place.

Atomization of Needs Politics

In addition to a return to the conditions that led to the IDEA, perhaps the most egregious injustice of all is built into the design of the law's provisions with respect to parent participation and due process and is a product of needs politics during the framing of the original EAHCA. The "egalitarian and democratic impulses" (Ong-Dean 2009, 12) of the oppositional discourse that fought for the EAHCA led its members to target the systemic special education problems that had been identified during repoliticization, especially exclusion and racial/ethnic and class inequality, and to seek democratic solutions to them. In this regard, they saw great potential in parent participation and due process rights as a means of addressing these problems.[27] EAHCA proponents in Congress assumed that due process procedures would be substantively oriented and thereby lead to "systematic pressure on school systems to improve special education practice" (Ong-Dean 2009, 25). Moreover, disability advocates called for a precedent-based system in which the results in individual cases would be "followed across the board, producing a general pattern of compliance" (Clune and Van Pelt 1985, 13; see also Kirp, Buss, and Kuriloff 1974), and for due process hearings to be open to the public, allowing for "a steady improvement of special education practices through the expansion of common norms . . . [and structured so that] nonprofit organizations could advocate for children collectively" (Ong-Dean 2009, 25).

As we know, however, the system created by the parent-participation and due process provisions that ultimately were enacted is individualized and closed, which, by reducing problems of special education practice to isolated cases, creates "an individualized and competitive environment"

---

27. With regard to racial/ethnic inequality, the EAHCA parent-participation and due process provisions were valued more highly than its nondiscriminatory evaluation provision (Ong-Dean 2009, 23–24).

(Ong-Dean 2009, 14) that advantages parents who have the most cultural and economic capital in both the IEP and due process hearing processes.[28] This closed, individualized system not only precludes systemic reform but, by atomizing and depoliticizing advocacy and activism, perpetuates racial/ethnic and class inequality in three interrelated ways. First, the design of these provisions atomized the oppositional discourse that had produced the statute by individualizing activism within IEP meetings and due process hearings focused on individual children and families. Rather than parents acting as collective agents of a political movement, under IDEA parents advocate for their children individually in direct, solo encounters with professionals (McCall and Skrtic 2009), interactions in which they are at a distinct disadvantage (Mehan, Hertweck, and Meihls 1986), especially if they are poor, working class, and/or members of a racial or ethnic minority group (Harry 1992). Second, the design and legal interpretation of these provisions undercut the egalitarian and democratic motivations of the social movement that fought for and won the statute. Rather than providing democratic solutions to recognized systemic problems, including race and class inequities, the law merely enables individual parents to mount "individualized, technical disputes" (Ong-Dean 2009, 10) over their child's diagnosis and accommodations. Finally, in addition to muting broader social concerns about problems in special education, reducing them to individualized cases in a competitive environment, the law has supplanted the solidarity of collective agents involved in a political movement and institutionalized a class divide in the special education process (McCall and Skrtic 2009). That is, although the parent-participation and procedural due process provisions atomized advocacy and depoliticized the oppositional discourse, the degree to which parents are reduced to

28. Technically, parents can request an open due process hearing, but few do (Ong-Dean 2009), and though redacted hearing decisions are accessible to the public, they typically are not used by parents individually or collectively through advocacy groups in the precedent-setting way envisioned by pre-1975 EAHCA proponents. Moreover, the courts, especially since the Supreme Court decision in *Board of Education v. Rowley* (1982), "now review due process hearing decisions primarily to question their legal reasoning . . . while deferring to the hearing officer's findings of fact" (Ong-Dean 2009, 115).

passive cases in the special education process depends on their economic and cultural capital (Skrtic 2010). And because privileged parents are in a far better position to secure better educational outcomes for their children, the individualized and competitive school environment created by the IDEA also "perpetuate[s] the hierarchies from which [these parents'] own privileges come" (Ong-Dean 2009, 3). As such, these IDEA provisions do more than put poor, working-class, and racial/ethnic/linguistic minority parents at a disadvantage in advocating for their children in school. By legitimating racial, ethnic, and class inequalities in special education, they perpetuate the racial/ethnic and social class hierarchies that sustain them (McCall and Skrtic 2009).[29]

Justice and Democracy

The effects of nearly four decades of implementation of the IDEA challenges Nussbaum's (2006a) claim that it is an exemplar of the capabilities approach to justice. Given the nature and functioning of schools as institutionalized organizations, the statute merely ceremonializes respect for individuality while perpetuating and even creating racial/ethnic and class inequalities. Given the nature and effects of needs politics in and around these organizations, expert discourses reinterpret the needs-claims of the disability rights movement in ways that strip away rather than respect human dignity, especially for less-privileged families, thus perpetuating the class and cultural hierarchies that sustain racial/ethnic, class, and disability inequalities in school and society. Although in practice the IDEA is not an exemplar of the capabilities approach, the half-century of needs politics surrounding the statute and its implementation is both a striking example of the indeterminate and legitimating effects of rights talk as a political strategy and strong support for the necessity of a strategy

29. Although privileged parents' advantageous position suggests that cultural and economic capital can overpower the interests of schools as institutionalized organizations, this is true only to a point. Colin Ong-Dean's (2009) high-road/low-road hypothesis shows that even the considerable advantages of privilege are transitory relative to school organizations' institutional interests (see Skrtic 2010).

that combines rights talk and needs talk within a broader institutional approach to justice. We believe that entitling human capabilities—human flourishing—is the right approach to justice for disabled people (and other oppressed groups), but if we are to reconstruct indeterminate and legitimating disability rights and establish new ones with regard to human flourishing, our activism must be guided by this broader understanding of justice. Moreover, the political problem is that this broader institutional theory of justice must be centered in a substantive conception of democracy.

As noted, because an institutional theory of justice recognizes that institutions can be carriers of injustice or potentially transformed into instruments of justice, it must be clear about what institutional injustice entails, how it is sustained, and the means and ends of transformation. Surveying forms of injustice, Fraser differentiates three distinct but overlapping types (1997, 13–16; 2009, 16–18). The structure of the economy can maldistribute resources necessary for self-development; hierarchies of cultural values and discriminatory discursive practices can produce demeaning status inequalities in major institutional spheres; and these economic and cultural injustices can result in a political structure that misrepresents individuals and groups with diminished status by silencing their voices in legislative bodies and civic life. Fraser groups just remedies for these types of injustice under the labels *redistribution, recognition,* and *representation* (2009, 1–29, 100–115; also see Young 2000, 121–53), and for both Fraser and Young justice requires transforming (or eliminating) institutions that produce these types of injustice—with the proviso that transformations be the result of fair, deliberative democratic procedures (see Fraser 2008, 344, 336–37, 339; Young 1990, 10, 23, 67, 91–95, and 2000, 17, 27–31). For both writers, justice is covalent with deliberative democracy: Fraser treats justice as "participatory parity" (2008, 327), and Young considers "democracy . . . an element and condition of justice" (1990, 10; also see Shapiro 1999, 19, 231).

For our purposes, Young's treatment (2000, 18–26) is especially important because she contrasts deliberative democracy and "aggregative" democracy, the differences between which are profound (18). Whereas the latter views democracy as a marketlike mechanism for aggregating preferences and protecting private rights and interests, the former views it as more intrinsically valuable because it promotes social cooperation and collective problem solving while contributing to individual self-development, providing "the best political means for confronting injustice," and determining what justice requires (26). Whereas aggregative democracy restricts the scope of politics to elections and what political elites and experts do in their public roles, the deliberative model treats democracy and justice as "coextensive with the political" (Young 1990, 9), broadly construed as politics concerning "all aspects of institutional organization, public action, social practices and habits, and cultural meanings" that are subject to collective evaluation and decision making (Young 2000, 27).[30]

Although Young (2000) doesn't make the connection, the aggregative model is the form of democracy definitive of *managerial* liberalism, the strain of liberalism that rose to prominence in the Progressive Era, during which emerged, as Minow notes (1990, 241–47), the oppressive institutional arrangements that Minow (along with Young and Fraser) criticizes. Minow locates the essence of progressivism in white, middle-class reformers' respect for the efficiency of bureaucratic organization and science-based, professional expertise—both of which she claims (and we agree) are incompatible with the substantive democracy she prefers. However, this view of progressivism captures only the track of progressive reform informed by managerial liberalism. The second, politically less powerful track was informed by the *developmental* strain of liberalism, which includes the voices of progressives that Minow (182–84, 241–47) clearly admires—Jane Addams, George Herbert Mead, and John Dewey.[31]

30. Fraser concurs and, especially important for us, adds that this broader conception of politics includes "struggles over cultural meanings . . . [that is, struggles] for the power to construct authoritative definitions of social situations and legitimate interpretations of social needs" (1989b, 66).

31. Limited space precludes an extended argument for our own interpretation of progressivism, but we believe that Minow's interpretation of it as conflicted by dual motives of justice and social control through "managerial efficiency" (1990, 245), with which we agree, underestimates the influence of its developmental liberal track. On this track's influence, see Robin Muncy, who calls it progressivism's "social justice wing" (1991, 164).

Whatever blind spots and naïveté we may find among these early developmental liberals, they for the most part respected cultural differences, defended communicative reciprocity across differences, and argued for strong, deliberative democracy (Furner 1993; Kent 2007; Muncy 1991).[32]

Both of these Progressive Era strains of liberalism arose in opposition to the classical or market liberalism of the nineteenth century (Foner 1998, 152–61). With intellectual roots in classical political economy, market liberals argue for minimal government, the expansion of free markets, and laissez-faire economic and social policies, yielding a weak form of democracy in which citizens are individual competitors for political goods and in which government is merely a protector of economic markets and private rights (Held 1996, 94–100; Macpherson 1977, 77–92).[33] Market liberals embrace this thin model of aggregative democracy, insisting on a restricted role for citizens (and democracy itself) to prevent government interference in the economy (Foner 1998, 204–5; Ryan 1972). The managerial alternative was inspired by positivism, utilitarianism, technocratic professionalization, and empirical social science. It argues for an expanded government capacity to regulate the economy and distribute social services, a capacity premised on the promise of technocratic efficiency made possible by science and bureaucratic administration (D. Price 1974, 1663–68). Managerial liberals are also weak democrats; like market liberals, they, too, want limited citizen participation, in their case to insulate official policymaking fora and expert discourses in public bureaucracies from lay citizen interference.

An institutional theory of justice inclusive of the imperatives of economic redistribution, appropriate forms of recognition and representation,

32. Nussbaum also calls for "a new form of liberalism" (2006a, 221). Expressed in terms of its differences from Rawls's liberalism, this liberalism has an affinity with development liberalism, but it is not equivalent to the Deweyan form discussed later in this essay.

33. Neoliberalism, the dominant form of liberalism in contemporary Western political culture (see Harvey 2005; Mirowski and Plehwe 2009), is an extreme form of market liberalism.

and a deliberative model of democracy is a recipe for social democracy.[34] Although such a theory is anathema to market liberals early and late, managerial liberals can be and developmental liberals generally are social democrats. As such, both strains embrace an egalitarian conception of positive liberty entailing notions of social and economic rights. Despite a common embrace of social democracy, however, the differences between managerial liberalism and developmental liberalism are insurmountable with respect to the aim and scope of democracy, wherein the aggregative model is definitive of the former, as noted, and a robust form of deliberative democracy is definitive of the latter (Hanson 1985, 80–86). For managerial liberals, democracy is a procedural method of preventing tyranny through periodic elections, but for developmental liberals democracy is a way of life that requires the cultivation of skills, habits, judgment, and other traits of character necessary for constructive participation in all spheres of society. For John Dewey—the quintessential developmental liberal with roots in the same neo-Aristotelianism that underwrites Nussbaum's capabilities approach—democracy so construed was linked to a belief in equal opportunities for self-development or self-realization "independent of the quantity or range of [an individual's] personal endowment" ([1939] 1991a, 226). Early managerial liberals doubted the political wisdom of citizens and sought to minimize their influence, placing their faith instead in bureaucracy and technical expertise. But Dewey ([1927] 1988, 351–72) and fellow developmental liberal progressives Jane Addams (1902) and Herbert Croly ([1909] 1965) sought to create deliberative institutional conditions—including nonbureaucratic, collaborative, problem-solving organizations—for an informed, self-conscious, inclusive, and participatory public to work in partnership with government facilitated by a new breed of socially committed and community-oriented professionals (Sullivan 2005, 99–115, 179–87). This type of "civic" (Sullivan 2005,

---

34. Although Nussbaum (1990, 2000a, 2003, 2006a) expresses strong democratic sentiments, she doesn't associate them with any specific form of democracy (see note 35 in this chapter). Absent a theory of democracy, she provides no sustained discussion of how democracy and social justice are linked. On deficiencies in Nussbaum's scattered references to democratic processes, also see Crocker 2008.

185) or "democratic" (Dzur 2008, 101) professionalism is premised on the cultural sensibility of the strong democrat, the practical reasoning of pragmatism, and the traditional idea of a profession as a calling, and the developmental liberal progressives saw it as a way to restore a sense of collective social purpose in the professions, one based on recognition of the professions' responsibility to the community and especially to those most negatively affected by social inequities.[35]

However, the principal difference that sets developmental liberalism apart from the other two strains of liberalism lies in the ideal of self-development, of human flourishing, in diverse contexts of work, leisure, and citizenship, which is what makes developmental liberalism—or what Dewey alternately called "renascent," "radical," or "democratic" liberalism ([1935] 1991b, 41, 45, 64)—and its strong, deliberative model of democracy an ideal political grounding for the capabilities approach to justice.[36] Paraphrasing Aristotle, Nussbaum writes, "[W]hat all citizens must have is *some* sort of deliberative and judicial functioning, [recognizing that] . . . concrete institutional realization of this varies with the city" (1988, 178, emphasis in original). What is missing from her capabilities approach in this regard is consideration of the scope of democratic citizenship and how the political practice of citizens so construed might be institutionalized in a *just* modern society. What justice requires for disabled people, we believe, is this kind of society: a strong, deliberative democracy with participatory social institutions and civic professionals committed to realizing the developmental liberal ideal of human flourishing for one and all.

35. See Skrtic 1991b, 170–71, 174–82, and 2005, 151–52, on the place of deliberative schools and civic professionalism in education and special education reform, as well as Skrtic 2012 and McCall and Skrtic 2009, 15–18, on their role in redesigning the IDEA.

36. With human flourishing as the core of Nussbaum's theory of justice, we believe her liberalism is best construed as developmental, and there are many indicators in *Frontiers of Justice* and elsewhere (e.g., 1990, 238–39, 232–33; 2000a, 110–12; 2000b, 104) that she has social democratic sympathies. However, what prevents Nussbaum from fully embracing these ideals is a selective reading of Rawls's *Political Liberalism* ([1993] 1996) that ignores the linkage between justice and democracy in that book (see notes 4 and 7 in this chapter).

4

Ending the Longing for Belonging

Teaching Disability Studies in the College Core Curriculum

SUSAN BAGLIERI and LINDA WARE

In this chapter, we recount our experiences as two education professors who have the dual responsibility of teaching disability studies content in the college core curriculum at our respective universities, Long Island University (LIU, Baglieri) and State University of New York (SUNY) at Geneseo (Ware). As scholars and teachers of disability studies in education (DSE) assigned to special education programs, we have for the most part successfully embedded disability studies content into our special education teacher-preparation programs. Like many of our DSE colleagues, we have experienced some success in "corrupting" teacher education curricula in our home institutions to more critically conceptualize disability and schooling as topics that are separate and distinct from those taken up in special education (Baglieri and Moses 2010; Danforth and Rhodes 1997; Ferri 2006; Ware 2006a, 2006b, 2006c). However, our embeddedness in schools of education, which reflect systems insistent on medicalizing and pathologizing disability, too often limits a broader exploration of disability studies, especially its art and perspective in critique and interpretation, its conversation with popular culture, and its activism (Ware 2008, 2010, 2011).

It is a sad reality that the disciplinary space for such coursework in teacher education is not available—an irony that compounds the DSE curriculum problem. At a time when adding courses (and tuition costs) to programs of study is unlikely to be fruitful and when reframing and reconfiguring the coursework of schools of education are complicated (K.

Young 2008), we contribute a set of teaching experiences, student work, and our reflections on both to highlight the positive impact of taking disability studies into the undergraduate general/core curriculum. The benefits for students, teaching faculty, and their institutions are seemingly endless when disability is presented as more than affliction, misfortune, freakery, and a fate worse than death. Moreover, if we desire students studying law, education, and other disciplines to practice their professions with perspectives that reflect disability studies, then we must offer opportunities to engage in the field early in their undergraduate experience. We hope to encourage educators to seek out similar opportunities on their campuses in an effort to broaden their own experience teaching others besides education majors as well as to encourage new audiences for disability studies throughout higher education (Broderick, Reid, and Valle 2006; Ferri 2006; Gallagher 2005; Valle and Connor 2011; Ware 2001, 2010; Ware and Valle 2010).

Part I of this chapter begins with an overview of our semester-long courses "The Idea of the Human" (Baglieri), offered at LIU's Brooklyn campus, and "Disability in America" (Ware), offered each semester at SUNY Geneseo. Part II follows with Baglieri's description of the approach she takes in teaching disability-related content, including her discussion of student work samples, and part III includes Ware's similar overview of her course. We conclude in part IV with a reflection that summarizes the strongly held belief that DSE faculty consider teaching similar courses on their campuses in an effort to disturb the disciplinary borders and to incite disruption of the exclusively medicalized view of disability within schools of education. Were students to experience exposure to disability studies content early in their college experience, they might be poised to build on this framework in their education coursework.

Part I: An Overview of Our Courses

Yes! We Dare

The ideal of the undergraduate general or "core" curriculum in university/postsecondary educational study is most often characterized as a set of disciplined engagements with varied topics in the liberal arts and sciences. In addition to delving further into the "Western canon" through the curriculum offered by most American universities, learners increasingly gain opportunities to consider various perspectives on race, gender, and sexuality through fulfilling "diversity course" requirements (Linton, Mello, and O'Neill 1995). Students may take interdisciplinary seminars and coursework in the political sciences or various "studies" departments and programs on campuses—for example, American studies, women's studies, African American studies, queer studies, and so on. Disability studies, as Simi Linton, Susan Mello, and John O'Neill reported in 1995, arrived controversially but has since found faculty and students answering Linda Ware's (2001) question "Dare we do disability studies?" with a resounding "Yes! We dare."

Our courses, "The Idea of the Human" and "Disability in America," share many structural similarities: both are offered as part of the college core requirements for all freshmen at our respective institutions; both are designed to develop research-informed persuasive-writing and critical-reading skills that foster understanding through writing activities rather than through examinations; and both value an interdisciplinary approach to the topic of study. Our courses are organized in a seminar format that assumes student engagement with the content and with one another in a more intimate setting than students find in the large lecture format of many of their first-year courses.

The Idea of the Human

The LIU Core Seminar became a part of the general curriculum in 2003 with the purpose to foster interactive learning among students and faculty through a seminar rather than lecture format. The Core Seminar's goals include:

- To develop dispositions and skills that allow us to effectively and professionally gain from and contribute to academic discourse with others.
- To learn how to examine a general topic from a number of perspectives.
- To engage in careful analysis and critical interpretation of reading materials.

- To develop skills to engage in disciplined and efficient research, including selecting an area of interest appropriate for inquiry, developing a thesis statement, planning an efficient and appropriate course of inquiry, and choosing relevant and scholarly supporting materials.
- To develop an academic style of persuasive writing and argumentation.

In addition to better utilizing a seminar format in undergraduate curriculum, the Core Seminar is also designed to blur disciplinary boundaries in the general liberal arts and sciences curriculum. To facilitate inquiry across academic disciplines, the theme "the idea of the human" is a fluid, "big" idea, and faculty from many departments and areas of study are encouraged to teach the course. In so doing, instructors are able to craft the curriculum and the thrust of content to suit their discipline and interests. Collaboration among teams of instructors from different disciplines is encouraged and supported in planning the curriculum each semester.

An administrative office is dedicated to organizing and assessing the Core Seminar and supporting faculty teaching it, and approximately sixteen sections of twenty-two students each run every semester. An open invitation to information sessions for interested faculty is sent out twice a year, and an orientation seminar series is offered for those who are interested in teaching the Core Seminar. Instructors are then divided into teams composed of all those teaching the seminar at the same time, which facilitates one of three common experiences that all students are intended to have. First, all seminars include a minimum of two joint sessions in which all students and instructors who have class at the same time meet for cross-discipline activities; second, all seminars incorporate at least one field activity in which students are to engage in a shared experience related to the seminar, but outside of the classroom; third, all students must engage in a process of research, leading to the writing of a paper.

Disability in America

The SUNY Geneseo writing seminars aim for similar interdisciplinarity in the design of course offerings in that faculty members from across the college are invited to propose a seminar determined by their own interests.

Course proposals are reviewed by a committee of interdisciplinary faculty for initial approval of the content, and, once approved, the seminar remains an active offering at the discretion of the assigned faculty member. Recent writing seminar offerings include "Affluence in America," "Metafiction," "Philosophical Paradoxes," "Arthur Miller—Legacy & Heritage," "Splitsville—Divorce in America," and "Identity in Multicultural Literature." In addition, the seminar's interdisciplinarity is enhanced by the composition of the class, which includes those who have declared a variety of majors as well as those who have yet to declare a major course of study. What typically follows is a healthy mix of perspectives across institutionally rigid disciplines that would otherwise exclude disability-related discussion through a cultural lens.

Part II: The Idea of the Human (Susan Baglieri)

The theme of the Core Seminar, the idea of the human, offers many ways to cultivate a broadened view of human experiences by posing as natural all kinds of experiences, bodies, and minds across the human tapestry. Designed to be cross-disciplinary, the seminar course uses an annotated anthology developed specifically for the course and organized into three themes: scientific, political, and imaginative/creative perspectives on human experience. The idea of the human put forth by the readings provides several writings and perspectives from a variety of thinkers and artists but—not surprisingly—offers few materials to launch discussion about disability experiences. For example, a selection from Stephen Jay Gould's *The Mismeasure of Man* ([1981] 1996) could be used to discuss the construction of cognitive disability, but other works lending themselves to the study of disability and disabled experience are absent.

"Cripping" Core Seminar

In developing a "cripped" curriculum when I first began to teach the Core Seminar, my aim was not to marginalize disability-related work as a separate unit of study, but to position inquiry related to disability alongside thematic approaches to the study of the idea of the human.

The Core Seminar's existing framework of studying scientific, political, and imaginative/creative ideas of the human offered three points of intersection with disability studies. First, considering the use of prosthetics indicated one way to explore a facet of the impact of science and technology on human experience; second, expanding our study of creative and imaginative expressions of human experiences told in poetry and literature was easily accomplished by using a wider variety of work; third, the political perspective that highlighted the study of human rights was a clear fit with disability rights. Bringing disability and disability studies into the Core Seminar curriculum thus primarily involved an expansion of course materials.

The new "cripped" set of materials encompassed experiences of disability in order to spark students' thoughts about the construct of normality and its influence on human rights and perceptions of difference. In one joint session related to scientific perspectives, instructors were able to cultivate thought and discussion about disability and biotechnology through a class related to Oscar Pistorius, the South African sprinter whose prosthetics ignited controversy in the International Olympic Committee in 2007 (see Longman 2007). My students and I read the United Nations Convention on the Rights of Persons with Disabilities (2007) alongside the declarations on human rights and women's rights (which are included in the course reader). We studied the poems "I Am Not One of the" by Cheryl Marie Wade (2002) and "The Magic Wand" by Lynn Manning (1997) alongside Langston Hughes's and Maya Angelou's work. A reading of Kurt Vonnegut's story "Harrison Bergeron" ([1961] 1998) and a viewing of Billy Golfus and Doug Simpson's 1995 documentary *When Billy Broke His Head . . . and Other Tales of Wonder* further added to the study of creative and political works and posed normality as a contestable construct to query.

Teaching Experience

The addition of disability-related materials contributed to students' learning of the broad course themes and alerted them to the often underrepresented perspectives and experiences of disabled persons. Each semester more than a few students reflected on our work as being the first time they had considered the inclusion of disability as a facet of human experience; many more noted their surprise and newfound appreciation for the lives and contributions of the disabled writers and activists included in the course. This section highlights an activity that used poetry to offer students insight into the idea of human empowerment and the slipperiness of perception and stereotype.

Maya Angelou's poem "Caged Bird" ([1983] 1994) and Langston Hughes's work "Theme for English B" ([1951] 1990) are featured in the course anthology. Both poems can be read and analyzed against the backdrop of African American experiences. Angelou's highly popular figure of the caged bird who has clipped wings and tied feet but who "opens his throat to sing" is contrasted with the "free bird" who "dares to claim the sky" in alternating verses. The caged bird's song symbolizes the cry for freedom within American enslavement and oppression. The comparison of the free bird and the caged bird is a readily interpretable metaphor for the free and enslaved positionalities of white Americans and those of African descent, respectively.

Hughes's theme is the complexity of American racial identities set in 1920s Harlem as expressed through the voice of a black student in response to his white instructor's assignment to write: "And let that page come out of you— / Then it will be true" ([1951] 1990, 247). Writing one's identity is hardly a simple task, David Jarraway notes, so the poem "explodes the notion of a racially pure self" (1996, 833). Hughes describes the whole of an American culture that is the result of intersubjective experiences and positions—separate, perhaps, but mutually constitutive.

Angelou's poem describes the contrasting, mutually constitutive positions of enslavement and domination, which emphasize divergent perspectives born of hierarchical relationships. Hughes synthesizes racially stereotyped subjectivities into an American whole, acknowledging the complexity and discomfort therein. Read together, these two works allow for interpretations and insights into the possibilities for poetic expression: the possibility for self-expression; the possibility to resist attributed identities and positions; and, thematically, the possibility to reveal the architecture of position and hierarchy in relation to identity.

Disability poetry, or "crip" poetry, as Jim Ferris (2007) describes it, often features themes similar to those under study in the Core Seminar's use of Hughes's and Angelou's works. According to Ferris, "[C]rip poetry rejects views of disability as a shameful, pitiable, tragic and individual phenomenon. Fundamental to crip poetry is an understanding that disability is a made thing, a social construction. . . . [C]rip poetry is also sharply aware that a major part of the impact disabilities have on lives results from the ways those human differences are interpreted and responded to by society, so often with prejudice, marginalization, and discrimination" (2007, para. 4). One characteristic of disability poetry, Ferris continues, is its "challenge to stereotypes and an insistence on self-definition" (para. 6).

Two poems—both noted in Ferris's essay—were readily available to incorporate and enliven our study. Cheryl Marie Wade, writer, performer, and activist, is author of the poem "I Am Not One of the" (2002), which has been anthologized in a variety of collections. Ferris highlights Wade's work as an expression of resistance to stereotype that "finds value and strength within disability experience, not in spite of impairments but because of and through them" (2007, para 5).

I am not one of the physically challenged—

I'm a sock in the eye with gnarled fist
I'm a French kiss with cleft tongue
I'm orthopedic shoes sewn on a last of your fears

I am not one of the differently abled—

I'm an epitaph for a million imperfect babies left untreated
I'm an ikon carved from bones in a mass grave at Tiergarten, Germany
I'm withered legs hidden with a blanket

I am not one of the able disabled—

I'm a black panther with green eyes and scars like a picket fence
I'm pink lace panties teasing a stub of milk white thigh
I'm the Evil Eye

I'm the first cell divided
I'm mud that talks
I'm Eve I'm Kali
I'm The Mountain That Never Moves
I've been forever I'll be here forever
I'm the Gimp
I'm the Cripple
I'm the Crazy Lady
I'm The Woman With Juice[1]

Wade's work is an assertion of self-definition, which resists labels attributed to disabled identities in favor of claiming a more complicated self and positionality. Her power and sensuality are not possessed in spite of the "gnarled fist" or "cleft tongue," but embodied through them. Conjuring the histories and positionalities of disabled persons before her, Wade's sense of self and affirmation of identity embraces the denial of care and genocide of disabled children across time, a denial marked by the Third Reich's massacre at Tiergarten. She recalls the subjugation and hiding of disabled bodies—both acts of shameful disguise and polite nods to ease public reception. Wade's declaration that she is "not one of the" paternalized disabled women known by the euphemistic labels "physically challenged," "differently abled," or "abled disabled" is resistance to others' desires to describe her gnarled form in more palatable terms. She rails against the linguistic simulacra imposed on disabled positionalities and identities. Wade claims and embraces her identity as a "Gimp" and "Cripple" as one of many powerful, enduring images and personas of womanhood.

A second poem featured in my version of the Core Seminar was one of actor and playwright Lynn Manning's works, "The Magic Wand" (1997).[2] "The Magic Wand" is featured in Kenny Fries's anthology of disability

---

1. "I Am Not One of the" first appeared in *Sinister Wisdom* 35 (1987) and also appeared in *Ms.* 12, no. 3 (1995): 77. It is reprinted with permission from Cheryl Marie Wade.

2. Excerpts from "The Magic Wand" are reprinted with permission from Lynn Manning and come from *Staring Back: The Disability Experience from the Inside Out*, edited by Kenny Fries, 165–66 (New York: Plume, 1997).

writing *Staring Back: The Disability Experience from the Inside Out* (1997), in Manning's live performance *Weights,* and on Manning's 1994 spoken-word album *Clarity.* "The Magic Wand" captures the interplay and power of stereotype as the narrator is transformed from "black man to blind man / with a flick of [his] wrist" as he whips out his folded cane.

> It is a profound metamorphosis—
> From God gifted wizard of roundball
> dominating backboards across America,
> To God-gifted idiot savant composer
> pounding out chart-busters on a cockeyed whim;
> From sociopathic gangbanger with death for eyes
> to all-seeing soul with saintly spirit. (Manning 1997, 165)

Alternating stereotypes of black men and blind men in America, Manning captures the struggle for identity. He ends his verse with a comment on perception and power:

> My final form is never of my choosing;
> I only wield the wand;
> You are the magicians. (165)

Jim Ferris (2007) highlights Manning's "The Magic Wand" as an example of crip poetry's attention to society's responses to disability, often with prejudice, marginalization, and discrimination. Beth Ferri interprets Manning's work as revealing ways in which "dis/ability and race are socially constructed and maintained through relations of power" (2008, 497). Manning meditates on the power held by others—the magicians—to "wield the wand" and determine his "final form."

In having seminar students read the four poems alongside each other, my purpose was to put forth the possibility of creative and imaginative forums through which writers express themes of political struggle that are embodied in the struggle for self-expression and identity. In particular, these poems highlight historically marginalized positionalities relevant to race, disability, and gender.

Student Work Samples

In reading "I Am Not One of the," students are often puzzled by what the poem might be about. I have yet to encounter a student familiar with Wade prior to the course or who has had any experiences with disability culture or expressions of disability pride and identity. Usually one or two savvy readers cautiously ask, "Is there something wrong with her?" or "Is she in a wheelchair?" in response to the self-declaration "I'm the Cripple" (line 19). Expressions of embarrassment tend to wash over the group at the reading of the line "I'm pink lace panties teasing a stub of milk white thigh" (line 11). Their hesitant surprise at the revelation that Wade is a disabled woman who wears pink lace panties (!) usually gives way to understanding grins and chuckles when we discover that "The Woman With Juice" (line 21) has power in her power chair. The mood lightens as we listen to the inevitable story about a student impressed or terrorized by someone they encountered motoring faster than he or she could move out of the way. I have found that our reading of Wade and sharing of stories of encounters with disability center our experiences of disability. Students who are stymied during the reading become more comfortable and can understand Wade as less alien.

A frequent theme students take up in their later writing with regard to Wade's poem is that of personal empowerment. Regine, for example, commented:

> Wade wrote the poem, "I Am Not One of the" to empower other physi-
> cally disabled people. With her choice of words, she shows other physi-
> cally disabled people to not view themselves as disabled. She shows this
> when she writes, "I am not one of the physically challenged— . . . / I am
> not one of the differently abled— . . . / I am not one of the able disabled—
> . . . / I'm the Gimp / I'm the Cripple" (Wade 1995, lines 1, 5, 9, 18, 19). In
> these lines, I feel that Wade tells other physically disabled people to not
> accept the "politically correct" terms of physically challenged and such;
> rather they should embrace the words of gimp and cripple.

Another student, Ariana, described that the "message I received from [Wade] is that being different is not always less empowering. The poet creates an image [of a woman] that has a higher self-image than some 'normal' women who are seen to be perfect." A third response, Ahn's reading, was that "[Wade] knows that she is different and accepts that fact. Her refusal of euphemisms [is] justified, for such phrases do not succinctly describe her for whom and what she is."

Both Regine and Ahn focused on Wade's play with language as acts of self-definition. All three read Wade's work as a declaration of self-empowerment, and another student, Ariana, believed the author's purpose is also to empower other disabled people. The range of responses to "I Am Not One of the" include general consensus on the theme of empowerment: Wade is read as powerful, sexual, and resistant to stereotype and "politically correct" terminology.

Responding to Manning: The Problem with Perception

Because LIU is located in Brooklyn, New York, the students in any given section of the Core Seminar generally appear to represent the richness of the city's racial and cultural range. LIU Brooklyn's institutional mission is to cater to first-generation college-goers and nontraditional undergraduates, and to embrace the diversity that characterizes its geographic locale. Students in the seminar have usually completed at least a semester of study at LIU and have already gained familiarity—through lived experience or through prior coursework—with thought about racial stereotyping and prejudice. In reading Lynn Manning's "The Magic Wand," students are generally quick to identify the racial stereotypes in response to lines 6–9:

> From God gifted wizard of roundball
> dominating backboards across America,
> To God-gifted idiot savant composer
> pounding out chart-busters on a cockeyed whim[.] (1997, 165)

Small-group conversations have yielded exclamations such as "Oh yeah! He's talking about Stevie Wonder" and the sometimes sarcastic, sometimes declarative "Of course black men play basketball." In small groups, some students struggle to figure out whether Manning is declaring his identities or just talking about stereotypes. It is a fruitful struggle that allows them to consider the relationships between one's own identity and the stereotypes attributed to an individual according to appearance.

Students' written responses to "The Magic Wand" typically refer to society's ignorance and the pitfalls of stereotyping. Marko wrote: "Manning shows how his two different physical appearances can help him understand how it's up to society to label him differently. With his folding cane, society describes him as a 'poor motherless child' but as soon as that cane goes away he becomes a 'sociopathic gangbanger with death for eyes.' His interesting 'metamorphosis' helps show how ignorant society can be." Lakeisha similarly referred to the role of societal perception but further described the interpretive act as disempowering: "He describes this transformation as his, 'change from black man to blind man with a flick of the wrist' (Manning). With that, we can see how the simple accessory of a cane can change how a person is seen by others. With the addition of a cane, our poet is in some ways stripped of all his other traits like his color and socioeconomic status." She noted the problem of attributing a single, master identity to a poet undoubtedly more complex. In reading Lynn Manning's work, students may gain insight into racial and disability stereotyping and the influence of it on the perception of an individual's selfhood or into what stereotyping signifies for the "magicians" in society. Like Lakeisha, others may press the complexities of identity, of not being described as "either/or"—as Langston Hughes did. As Beth Ferri (2008) and Jim Ferris (2007) discuss, Manning's work serves as a useful starting point for students to begin to consider social constructions of race and disability.

By positioning the work of Cheryl Marie Wade and Lynn Manning alongside Maya Angelou and Langston Hughes, who were already included in the Core Seminar curriculum, our study of disability perspectives does not emerge as ancillary to the otherwise "normal" curriculum, but contributes to it. Criticisms of disability studies—including fears that "scholarship on disability will 'water down' the diversity requirement" or accusations that the field is "parochial, and will further atomize the curriculum" (Linton, Mello, and O'Neill 1995, 9)—are unfounded, as evidenced by this example of the inclusion of material focusing on disability.

Disability poetry, or crip poetry, offers many themes that easily comple- ment and invigorate many existing courses of study.

Part III: "Disability in America" (Linda Ware)

Whereas Baglieri's approach in the Core Seminar "The Idea of the Human" is one that embeds disability content into a course with an eye to establishing a clear fit with the existing canonical works and preexist- ing course objectives, the course "Disability in America" represents an immersion approach focused on the introduction of disability studies in a required course for all incoming freshmen and transfer students, and yet it is an independent course that is fully at the discretion of the instruc- tor's design. I begin the course with the acknowledgment that although disability is ubiquitous in history, culture, and the arts, the study of dis- ability as a cultural phenomenon has yet to be integrated into the cur- riculum in higher education. In this way, the motif for our course as "uncharted territory" serves to "hook" the students who, with the excep- tion of a few education majors, claim little or no prior knowledge about disability. My introduction to the course and to disability studies outlines the following aims:

- To probe the enduring reality of the cultural locations of disability (Snyder and Mitchell 2006).
- To interrogate the impulse to cast disability as an "unlivable life" (Garland- Thomson 2009).
- To deconstruct the multilayered construct of the ideology of ability (Siebers 2008).

These objectives then organize a broad array of course content over a fifteen-week semester in a manageable yet flexible structure that allows for the integration of additional content culled by students from vari- ous media sources. At the beginning of the semester, I survey students about their rationale in selecting to take "Disability in America." Most simply cite a good "fit" with their schedule; others believe the seminar will inform their major course of study (pre-med, education, etc.); and one or two may cite personal experience with disability. However, it is often the case that with time students grow more comfortable with the content and the course structure to reveal personal experience with disability that drew them to the course.

Teaching Experience

In keeping with the frame for the course as "uncharted territory," we begin with a short essay by Michael Bérubé, who proposes the need for a college curriculum "makeover" that would include disability-related topics ranging from "genomics to prenatal testing to special education to employment discrimination to mental illness to advance directives to Alzheimer's [because] disability is integral to how humans define the parameters of the human" (2005, 16). Working in small groups, students consider the veracity of his argument by reflecting on their own prior K–12 educational experience, only to discover the common experience of the absence of disability-related content in both their elementary and secondary curriculum. They then set about to identify current SUNY Geneseo curriculum offerings that might be related to disability as more than a marginal subject. At the close of the first class meeting, students have a clearer understanding of the need to reconceptualize and reconstitute disability through an interdisciplinary lens that makes disability visible in the context of their college experience.

Depending on the semester, our readings have included *Disability Theory* (Siebers 2008); *Cultural Locations of Disability* (Snyder and Mitchell 2006); *Claiming Disability* (Linton 1998a); and *Nothing about Us without Us* (Charlton 1998). Excerpted works by Michael Bérubé (2003), Douglas Baynton (2001), Ann Fox (2002), Robert McRuer (2002), Carrie Sandahl and Philip Auslander (2005), Susan Schweik (2009), and Rosemary Garland-Thomson (2002, 2009) are but a few of the texts taken up in the course and most are then purposefully linked to disciplinary fields of study. For example, the historical analyses offered by Baynton and Schweik have been assigned along with the documentary *A World without Bodies* (Snyder and Mitchell 2001) to promote discussion that might potentially surface in subsequent history coursework relative to citizenship, eugenics, the Holocaust, or civil rights policy. During one semester in 2010, the theater analyses of Fox's and Sandahl and Auslander's work were taken up in advance of a campus visit by Fox, who directed theater and education students in a staged reading of excerpts from *P.H.*reaks: The Hidden History of People with Disabilities* (Baizley and Lewis 1997).

During our annual multicultural and diversity week in 2010, Geneseo invited the poet and disability activist Eli Clare, whose readings on identity at the intersection of queerness, transgender, class, and disability were then integrated into the course in advance of her presentation in October. Most recently (2011), Students Educating Against Ableism, a student advocacy organization I sponsor, in cooperation with the Student Association and the Center for Multicultural programs, sponsored Bill Shannon, the New York City–based performance artist. Such campus events were not offered prior to "Disability in America" because much of the interest on campus generated by disability studies could be tied to former students who assumed and sustained a leadership role in Students Educating Against Ableism. In addition, support from the college through increased funding for special events and learning opportunities for faculty and students in a variety of formats has revealed that the potential exists to grow disability studies across the college in various pockets that might otherwise consider its exclusive fit within a school of education (Ware 2010). Purposeful links to these campus-sponsored events have broadened the reach of the classes I teach and have created the possibility of sustaining students' interest well after the seminar concludes.

Finally, in addition to the texts, readings, and college-sponsored events, the seminar includes a required library instructional module that infuses disability studies content with research activities linked to the five-volume *Encyclopedia of Disability* (Albrecht 2006). The students find multiple strands of content to explore because they, too, are required to locate media, including newspapers, film, and Web-based resources, throughout the semester that will extend our disability theorizing. Their work is discussed in the next section.

Student Work Samples

The photograph of Liu Yan in the *New York Times* article "Still Danc-ing in Her Dreams" (Barboza 2009) is introduced to students early in the semester.[3] They work in small groups to respond to the image by consider-ing these questions: What do you notice? What is compelling? What looks familiar? What is unfamiliar? Some recognized the famous "Birds Nest" National Stadium in Beijing, which then signals others to the possibility of an Olympics-related event or, as one group conjectured, "perhaps the Special Olympics." For the most part, each group offers a variation of the "overcoming" narrative in which Liu Yan "appears" to have overcome great obstacles to have "finally made it to the Olympics" or that she was expressing her "gratitude for the opportunity to participate" or perhaps "celebrating that she had led her team to victory." Because we have yet to consider the well-rehearsed "overcoming narrative" that many in class offer as they describe the photograph, I do not cringe in response. My pedagogy when teaching about disability is lodged in the belief that stu-dents profit from the experience of building their own knowledge when-ever possible. When our disability-related conversations begin, I am less concerned about what is right or wrong; rather, my intention is to engage students with the content as they name it and to dig deep to find a place for the content within their lives (Ware 2006a).

An assigned reading of Rosemarie Garland-Thomson's "The Politics of Staring" (2002) follows the photo of Liu Yan rather than preceding our discussion of it. In that way, I can build on the perceptions and observa-tions that students bring to our class in advance of scholars theorizing dis-ability. This strategy serves on several levels, chief among them providing the opportunity to unseat the perception that we must deploy "PC" atti-tudes and language when discussing disability content. By encouraging students to grow comfortable with the freedom to express their initial reac-tions free of instructor or peer judgment, the possibility of reconsidering

3. To see this photo, go to http://www.nytimes.com/2009/04/19/arts/dance/19barb .html?pagewanted=all&_r=0.

their perceptions can readily follow. Working from the image of Liu Yan against the analysis of Garland-Thomson's more layered insights and discussion of her index of visual rhetorics, students return to class with a vocabulary that supports a more richly textured understanding of disability representations as "mediations" between disabled and nondisabled people (Garland-Thomson 2002). This utilization of the media serves to allow the practice space for students to theorize disability representations through a social political lens in advance of writing papers that would require them to unpack many of the seemingly "dense" arguments made by the disability studies scholars we would read. The class discussion, the students' insights, and new understandings are made more obvious when scaffolded to visual and pop culture.

It bears mention that for the majority of students who enroll in the seminar, most claim limited prior experience with disabled people. This fact is distinct from the students who enroll in my education course that includes an introduction to disability studies. Among the education students, many arrive in class poised to recite categories of human difference using the labels previously learned in their special education coursework. They have worked in summer camps or volunteered for Special Olympics and possess a résumé reflective of a clear investment in "helping" children with disabilities. In contrast, my writing seminar students report limited or no knowledge about disability; their point of reference is typically informed by representations of disability rather than "real-time" human interactions. And yet as the course progresses, many gain the confidence to share personal experiences with disability—shared for the first time in a class and even in public. I attribute this growing openness to pedagogical decisions that all but ensure that the students will grow comfortable accessing prior knowledge and experience, which then informs our collective exploration of the content. New meanings are made through the self rather than through mastery by rote memorization of definitions, dates, diagnoses, or other typical approaches to understanding disability noted, and in this way students begin to unpack the ideology of ability (Siebers 2008). According to Tobin Siebers, "Disability is the invisible center around which our contradictory ideology about human ability revolves. For the ideology of ability makes us fear disability, requiring that we imagine that our bodies are of no consequence while dreaming at the same time that we might perfect them. . . . [I]t describes disability as what we flee in the past and hope to defeat in the future" (2008, 8–9).

Among the central themes posited by Siebers in *Disability Theory* is the argument that to understand disability as part of the human condition warrants understanding of "ability" as an ideology that privileges able-bod-iedness. At its most "radical," he notes, the ideology of ability defines the "baseline by which humanness is determined, setting the measure of body and mind that gives or denies human status to individual persons" (2008, 8). On the face of this claim, students nod with wonder, unable to understand how "ability" can be constructed as anything but a positive and naturally worthy ideology. Small-group discussion invites deeper understanding of the contention that the ideology of ability affects nearly all of our "judg-ments, definitions, and values about human beings" (Siebers 2008, 8), and in dialogue they summon examples from their own lives and patterns of behavior that expose the power of unconscious thought. That ability serves to mark that the "other" in society is no longer refuted as something that happens only among those who bully. With reference to the local context, they are quick to observe that Geneseo admits noticeably fewer visibly disabled students than they saw enrolled in their K–12 school experience (Ware 2009). Their own exclusionary education at Geneseo, when theo-rized as informed by Sharon Snyder and David Mitchell's (2006) analy-sis of the "cultural locations of disability," gains exponential meaning too powerful to dismiss. What initially began as an illogical critique of ability gives way to recognition of their own able-bodied cachet in higher educa-tion. In discussion of the content, many make important connections to institutional ableism in higher education specific to its exclusive focus on ability and attainment for some, not all. In subsequent courses designed to expose the mechanisms of privilege through the work of Peggy McIntosh (1988) and others, students who took my seminar have reported the impact of introducing ableism to their peers and their professors, augmented by the analysis offered by McIntosh. Through such exchanges, the students become an informal source educating the campus by multiples greater than one class in any given semester and importing their learning to wholly new contexts. The examples given here provide but a glimpse into this phenomenon spread across various semesters.

Importing Student Learning to New Contexts

In the Example of Righteous Anger. Following the screening of the disability studies classic *When Billy Broke His Head and other Tales of Wonder* (Golfus and Simpson 1994), Cara, a communications major, took an early interest in understanding disability through Ed Roberts's claim that "anger is one of the best things disabled people have going for us" (in Golfus and Simpson 1994). Throughout the semester, she was troubled by the notion of anger as a good and necessary feature of social movements, although not so good at the individual level. Righteous anger in her first essay then evolved to a lengthier research paper on the topic of anger management and its overuse in special education with boys who need to be "fixed." She researched primary source materials (images and documents) imported from the Disability History Museum website (www.disabilitymuseum .org), which included early descriptions of ill-behaved children in religious tracts that were popular in the eighteenth century along with the reports issued by institutions. Borrowing language from Snyder and Mitchell's (2006) description of the cultural locations of disability as sites where disabled people are held against their will, Cara recounted the stress her family experienced when her brother was initially placed in special education. Several years later her mother was still negotiating his "release" from special education and the removal of the label of emotionally disturbed so that he could attempt to join the military. Although her brother's experience was not the initial motivation for her research inquiry, she readily connected the dots spurred from the anger her brother expressed for years, "first [for] being held against his will in the classroom for dummies and second, [for being] stamped with a label he felt he did not deserve."

Cara moved from her brother's individual experience to more recent images taken from the same website depicting protests over delays in the signing of the Americans with Disabilities Act (ADA). In discussing the 1990 demonstration photographs by Tom Olin (see Olin 1990), she described the power of collective anger that propelled the protestors to ditch their wheelchairs and crawl up the steps to the Capitol building. That some media venues opted to cover the protest without the footage of the massive crawl episode suggested that the visage of angry disabled people even in the face of injustice was considered "indelicate." Cara continued to develop disability-related themes in her ongoing communications coursework at Geneseo. She emailed to me various episodes that evidenced the enduring impact of the content of my course upon her. In the course "Cultural Diversity and the U.S. Media," she prepared a paper and presentation titled: "Is It Easier for Those Living with Disabilities Today to Simply Live post ADA?" which was informed by Kevin Connolly's photographs[4] and Bill Shannon's performance work. Cara returned to an essay from our class by Ann Millet (2008), who was troubled by the "gaze" in an example of Connolly's work, and discussions about why people stare taken from essays by Garland-Thomson (2002, 2009). Later, in an email to me Cara wrote, "[T]he questions I have about disability are not at all like the ones I had when I started your class—it's like Bill Shannon says about the 'reverse assumptions' people with disabilities make about able-bodied people, and those we make about non-disabled people—there's so many issues that come out of these interactions which I have only begun to realize—especially when I speak to my friends or present my work in my classes" (October 2008).

In the Example of Eugenics. Students frequently gravitate to the topic of eugenics during my writing seminar, and their interest is often revisited in later coursework. Rafe began with a research assignment linked to the *Encyclopedia of Disability* (Albrecht 2006), which was then broadened to include the work of Stephen J. Gould's *The Mismeasure of Man* ([1981] 1996) and Douglas Baynton's (2001) analysis of immigration and the use of IQ to advance his discussion of biological determinism and eugenics in modern society. Rafe, a sociology major, hoped to demonstrate how ableism operated to cast disability as an "'unlivable' life" in the development of technology that would ensure the normalization of "designer babies." He

---

4. For these photographs, go to http://therollingexhibition.com.

concluded his second-year sociology paper with the call to "appreciate the value of all human life as a good place for us to start."

Another student, a budding animal rights activist, tackled the work of the Australian philosopher Peter Singer in her final paper. Although prior to the seminar she had been a fan of Peter Singer, given his support of animal rights, new questions emerged for her following the assigned reading of his exchange with Harriet McBryde Johnson (2003). The student's nascent experience with disability studies scholarship left her with the belief that Singer's work was contradictory and difficult to reconcile with her own sense of social justice and humanity.

Institutional Inequality and Exclusion. In this final example, a seminar student who planned to become a physical therapist realized numerous contradictions in the practice of service provision for children with disabilities when completing a college service-learning activity associated with her major. Here I quote at length because the material clearly sums up the deeper meaning I hope students will acquire when they recognize the pernicious workings of the ideology of ability sanctioned within the institutions purportedly designed in the best interests of disabled people. She explained:

> I shadow physical and occupational therapists at the campus preschool where students through age eight are pulled out of their classroom for physical, occupational, and speech therapy as well as other remedial services. I see this service as a benefit, but also inhibitory. It is wonderful that these children can get the assistance they need while they are at school and do not need to be taken to other facilities each week for such care. However, they continuously miss out on the social aspect of their class and the classroom activities. Elle, a five year old at the school, constantly missed the dance lesson for the day because she was getting physical therapy in a separate room away from her classmates. This situation seems backwards because, in this case, dance would have actually helped her muscle strengthening just as in her physical therapy session. A similar situation occurs for the speech therapy that some of the children receive; much of this social engagement actually occurs in the classroom. When the students are taken out of the room for speech therapy, they are missing the social interaction with the other students

that actually could help them in social situations and communication with other children.

These examples suggest the importance of exploring disability studies early in the undergraduate experience, especially at Geneseo, where students have only three options for coursework that considers content through a disability studies lens. In addition to "Disability in America," I teach a second-year women's studies course, "Gender & Disability," and a third-year course restricted to education majors—in effect, this amounts to only two disability studies courses. The majority of Geneseo students are likely to complete their undergraduate experience with little or no awareness of disability as part of the larger scheme of living in a diverse society. And yet with limited exposure to disability-related content, many have made meaningful connections to subsequent coursework in their declared majors. Although no data exist to support what amounts to anecdotal evidence, my colleagues across the campus often ask my former students if their disability critique followed enrollment in one of my classes. To be sure, this progress is slow but significant.

⛝

In the next section, we offer a discussion that summarizes our belief that DSE scholars would provide an incredible service to their institutions, their students, and the field if they were to find ways to support disability studies outside of schools of education.

Part IV: Where We Dare End the Longing for Belonging

Attempting to "crip" our courses, we began our projects in search of curricular space in which disability studies might "belong" within our respective institutions. Our motivation differed given the somewhat different contexts of our home institutions; however, several characteristics of "The Idea of the Human" and the "Disability in America" writing seminars make them ideal spaces to introduce students to disability studies. The emphasis on critical reading and writing ushers in the kinds of thinking demanded by reimagining the meaning of ability and possibility in the human form. The gathering of instructors with varied disciplines alerts students to the likelihood of learning something unexpected or outside of their major course of study, which may make them amenable to new and challenging ideas. Finally, because students take these courses as part of the general curriculum, they are poised to revisit disability themes in their ongoing coursework (as noted in the section by Ware). Offering disability studies to first- and second-year college students can lay important groundwork on which more in-depth examinations of social experience and identity can be based and that is crucial to the academic mission of liberal arts institutions.

The courses "The Idea of the Human" and "Disability in America" provide extremely satisfying teaching experiences, and yet as we wrote this chapter, it became apparent to both of us that our teaching offers a study in contrasts when considered against teacher-preparation coursework. Our students' interest in the content we offer has far exceeded our initial expectations. Had we ourselves come to a narrow sphere of expectation, restricted by standards imposed upon us by state and national benchmarks and standards? Had our conformance to the norm of "over"defining the assignments we developed in teacher education courses to comply with mandatory course outlines muted our own sensibilities? The freedom our students enjoy as they work in an open-ended fashion to consider disability as other than pathology and problem has been equally challenging to us as their instructors.

In contrast, although it is certain that educators have embraced disability studies content at both the pre-service and in-service levels (Danforth and Gabel 2006; Valle and Connor 2010; Ware 2001, 2003a, 2003b, 2008), the challenge remains for educators to translate their enthusiasm for a disability studies perspective on teaching while working in the throes of unyielding systems that demand the medicalization of disability (Ashton 2011; Brantlinger 2006; Reid and Valle 2004; Ware 2006b; K. Young 2008). Certainly, teachers engage disability studies in productive ways whenever possible, but they are tethered to belief structures that cannot be easily reconciled with more humane considerations of disability (Ware 2006a, 2010). There is too little curricular space for coursework in teacher education that advances disability studies, with the notable exception of

City College and Syracuse University. This reality is compounded by P–12 educational structures that have yet to recognize the need to seriously "rethink" inclusion informed by disability studies (Valle and Connor 2010; Ware 2001; Ware and Valle 2010).

In closing, it is our hope that the DSE curriculum will be unencumbered by a need to "fit" within education in the same ways that it has been free to make some headway in medicine, rehabilitation, literary studies, and law. This process will certainly be difficult, but we believe it will be aided by students in those disciplines who come to new understanding early in their undergraduate experience. We close with a riff on something that Michael Bérubé notes in his afterword to *Disability Studies: Enabling the Humanities* (Snyder, Brueggemann, and Garland-Thomson 2002): in order to "do justice" to disability studies, it must be recognized that the project will "last many lifetimes" (2002, 343). His hope is that he will live long enough to realize disability studies widely understood as one of the "normal—but not normalizing—aspects of study in the humanities, central to any adequate understanding of the human record" (343). Should teacher education likewise recognize the value of disability studies—widely understood—as central to the long overdue reconceptualization of schooling for all, then we, too, should live so long.

5

Treating the Incomplete Child

How the Science of Learning Disabilities Was Built for Exclusion

SCOT DANFORTH and THEODOTO RESSA

From Fictional to Factual

In October 1963, President John F. Kennedy signed legislation that provided funds for research and personnel preparation to educate children with a variety of disabilities. This law, Public Law 88-164, also created the first federal office devoted to the education of disabled children, the Bureau of Handicapped Children in the US Office of Education. In his statement, Kennedy appointed Samuel Kirk, a University of Illinois professor and national leader in the growth of the field of special education, to direct the new office. Kirk took a pay cut to accept the post.[1]

At this point, we temporarily step aside from the facts in order to play at historical fiction by imagining that Kirk, after attending the signing ceremony in the White House, met with President Kennedy in the Oval Office to discuss the work that Kirk would undertake in the bureau. Let us imagine a scene that went something like this.

Professor Kirk shuffled his feet nervously and took quick sips of coffee as he waited alone in the Oval Office. His eyes landed on a pair of small black-and-white photographs of the president and his daughter

---

1. Samuel A. Kirk briefly held this position in order to launch the office, and then he returned to the University of Illinois (J. Gallagher 1998; Kirk 1976, 1984).

127

Caroline. She was perhaps four years old, smiling broadly in her striped dress, and in her hand she held a half-eaten apple.

The president suddenly burst into the room, walking quickly and motioning for Kirk not to stand up. He sat down next to Kirk on the couch. "I want you to hit the ground running, Sam. There's no time to waste," he said.

"Yes, sir. I agree," Kirk replied.

"Well, where are we? What is the state of research? What do educators know how to do for handicapped kids?"

"Well, Mr. President, we have made a good start. Even before I started up the Institute for Research on Exceptional Children, we had a few decades of research about children as social beings, as members of microcommunities of learning and friendship. At Illinois, we've built on that knowledge base—a very practical foundation of science—that examines how educational contexts provide social support and appropriate instruction for all students, the handicapped students and the normal students. Our goal has been to understand how classrooms and schools can enact the principles of American democracy, how all students can be viewed as valuable contributors to the common community."

"Terrific. That's just dandy, Sam," the president commented. "But what does your research tell us about this kind of equal classroom . . . what do you call it? Democratic?"

"I've been calling it 'inclusive.'" Kirk replied with a small grin.

"Inclusive?" The president smiled and looked up, as if envisioning something grand. "Oh, I like the sound of that."

"Yes, well, everyone is included. All in."

The president nodded. "Yes, yes. So what is your research telling us? And where do we go from here?"

"Although we have a good empirical foundation, we've really just begun the practical, school-based work, sir." Kirk took a deep drink of his coffee and thought about how to sum up nearly a decade of his own research, the contributions of his colleagues at other universities, as well as the many years of important prior scientific work. So much had been done, but Kirk knew, too, that so much was left to do.

"We have been focusing primarily on preschools. We developed training modules for the teachers. Some of those have to do with understanding various handicaps and the needs of handicapped children.

But most of them have to do with instructional practices, classroom management, ways of interacting with and relating to the children. We trained teachers in five preschools, and we've been carefully studying how the education provided in those five programs impacts the growth and development of the students. We have developed a number of—"

"Of the handicapped kids?" asked the president.

"Sir?"

"The growth and development of the handicapped kids?"

"Well, yes, sir. But even more. This is really about all of the children. So we track all of them."

"And what are the results?" The president pressed the hesitant researcher to jump to the last page of the mystery, skipping all the chapters to get to the final climactic scene, where the detective reveals everything. "What can we conclude about this inclusive education?"

"Sir, I don't believe we can make firm conclusions yet. I don't believe we know enough about the practice, the pedagogy of inclusive work. But our results so far have been very good, very positive."

"OK, OK," the president turned away and nodded to a young assistant who rushed in and handed him a folder. The meeting seemed to be wrapping up. The assistant scurried off. The president clasped his hands together and smiled, "So where do we go from here?"

"I think, Mr. President, that our first step is to expand this research. The new federal funding will help get researchers and teachers going in many sites around the country. Not just in Illinois and not just at the preschool level. We need to develop inclusive education at all grade levels and explore how to implement it in the most effective way."

"You have the vision, Sam. Put it into action. I want to see results." The president grasped the professor's hand, slapped him on the shoulder, and the two men shook triumphantly.

Although we do know that President Kennedy in truth had high hopes for what Professor Kirk might accomplish in his new role as chief of the new Bureau of Handicapped Children, and it is certain that the two discussed how educational research might benefit students with disabilities, we obviously have no record of any conversation like this ever happening. In creating this fictitious scene, we have taken the relatively recent term *inclusion* and forced it back into a historical scene before inclusive education was even widely discussed as a possibility. Our reason for injecting a current education term, concept, and goal into a historical scene is to give dramatic emphasis to exactly what did *not* happen.

As the Bureau of Handicapped Children opened in 1964, signaling the start to what would be a dramatic expansion of federal power in relationship to the education of disabled students, special education research and practice in the United States was *not* built on a foundation of decades of scientific work examining how children of differing abilities might be educated together in the same classrooms. The scientific foundation that supported the creation of the federally mandated field of special education in 1975 did not involve any significant theory or research contributing to the goal of inclusive education. More dramatically, that foundation was built solely of intellectual ingredients—of assumptions about the nature of humanity, community, and schooling—that all but precluded the imagination or development of inclusive educational practices. If we are to stick to the historical facts, we must tell a story of the development of a special education science that worked quite distinctly toward the creation of segregated classrooms and programs for students with disabilities in the United States.

This chapter explores a history of special education science that, to put it succinctly, prepared for exclusion. We illuminate the central conceptual elements of the intellectual and practical foundation of American special education through a focused examination of the history of the science of learning disabilities between World War I and the landmark federal legislation of 1975.

Our reasons for looking at the science of learning disabilities as the central plank of the developing field of special education research are twofold. First, nearly half of all public-school students served today by the special education system have an identified learning disability. It is the largest category of disability qualification in the American schools. By sheer numbers, learning disability is the keystone of special education. Second, the political victory and appropriation of the science of learning disabilities was pivotal to passage of the Education for All Handicapped Children Act of 1975, or Public Law 94-142. The political rise of the learning disabilities movement, spearheaded by parent advocacy groups during the 1960s, was vital to the legal creation of the current system of special education. The science of learning disabilities, as a tradition of concepts, theories, assumptions, and practices, arguably became the knowledge centerpiece of the modern professional culture of special education research.

Our approach in this chapter is to provide relatively brief profiles of four important researchers who contributed to the development of the learning disability construct through their scientific investigations. Our goal is to understand how a succession of influential researchers between World War I and the early 1970s contributed to a science that ultimately framed the child with a learning disability as requiring educational instruction conducted in physical isolation from general education peers. We begin with Kurt Goldstein, a German neurologist who treated and studied soldiers who had suffered traumatic brain injuries during World War I. Our chronology will continue with the work of Alfred Strauss, a physician who was deeply influenced by Goldstein. Strauss conducted research on children with brain injuries along with his colleagues Heinz Werner and Laura Lehtinen at the Wayne County Training School in Detroit in the 1930s and 1940s. He transplanted Goldstein's ideas about the effects of brain injury from Germany to America and, perhaps more important, from soldiers with evident head injuries to children who had not been struck on the skull. Our case profiles will culminate with examinations of two prominent figures in the "birth" of the learning disability construct in the early 1960s: Samuel Kirk, the so-called father of learning disabilities, and Newell Kephart, a psychologist who worked in the highly prominent area of sensorimotor and perceptual treatment.

By exploring how a series of leading researchers built a science of learning disabilities in the decades leading up to the parent advocacy movement, this chapter provides insight into how the intellectual foundation of American special education developed toward what we are calling a "counterinclusive" tradition of theory and practice. We use the term *counterinclusive* specifically to describe the political and practical dimensions of the science of learning disabilities that developed between World War I and the early 1960s. We are pointing to the fact that the science of learning disabilities conceptualized learning and teaching in a manner that did not provide researchers and teachers with concepts and practices conducive to the development of inclusive practices.

Quite clearly, as the historical profiles in this chapter demonstrate, the scientific foundations of the modern field of learning disabilities steered educational researchers and practitioners *away from* the development of concepts and practices of inclusive education. When President Kennedy and Sam Kirk discussed the work of the new Bureau of Handicapped Children in 1963, and, indeed, when the federal government leaped into a greatly enlarged role in the education of children with disabilities in 1975, the predominant discourse—the language and ideas used by both professionals and policymakers—concerned the corrective treatment of "handicapping" conditions. There was no discourse about how children with disabilities might be valued as equal school citizens in classrooms of diverse abilities. President Kennedy, Sam Kirk, and others had no such storehouse of cultural concepts and scientific research available to fuel their thinking about the future of special education. This chapter is an attempt to tell the story of why the fictitious "inclusion" discussion between Sam Kirk and President Kennedy could never have taken place.

Kurt Goldstein

During World War I, a German physician named Kurt Goldstein founded and directed the Institute for Research into the Consequences of Brain Injury, a rehabilitation facility in Frankfurt for brain-injured soldiers. A neurologist and psychiatrist by training, Goldstein teamed up with Adhemar Gelb, a Gestalt-oriented psychologist, on the development of a holistic approach to brain injury research. Their most famous case was a twenty-three-year-old former German soldier named Schneider who had suffered a serious traumatic wound to his brain. Clinical investigations of Schneider's unusual sensory perceptions indicated a particular form of dysfunction in the nervous system (Ash 1995; Goldstein 1967; Harrington 1996).

In one of the tests, Goldstein and Gelb discovered that Schneider could not identify a word flashed by a tachistoscope for one or two seconds but could identify the same word when the display was lengthened to ten seconds. They also observed that when Schneider read words aloud, his hand "wrote" the letters one over the other without moving across the page. He simultaneously traced the letters with head movements (Gelb and Goldstein [1918] 1997). However, Schneider was unable to read the same words when he was required to "trace" the letters in a different direction or when he was not allowed to trace.

When the researchers put strike marks across a word, Schneider's tracing behavior was disrupted, and his reading behavior halted. The researchers reasoned that the strike marks interfered with the soldier's ability to visually track the words in a line. Furthermore, they found that Schneider was not aware that he was physically "tracing" the letters as he read them aloud. Gelb and Goldstein ([1918] 1997) concluded that Schneider suffered from "psychical blindness" or word blindness, a neurological inability to perceive and make sense of written words.

Further investigation examined Schneider's capacity to interpret visual shapes formed out of arrangements of dots, a standard gestalt task involving the perception of whole figures built of parts. When presented with an equidistant arrangement of four dots, the corners of a square, the patient could not apprehend any order or grouping of the dots. He did not see a square.

It was also found that although Schneider was able to perceive still objects, he could not identify the same objects in motion. He perceived an arm moving between a straightened and a bent position not as movement, but only as an arm in two successive positions. If the researchers slowed down the arm motion, the patient could perceive the arm at various places in space, like catching still movie frames in isolation, but he could not see the arm's entire swinging motion (Gelb and Goldstein [1918] 1997, 317–22).

The researchers concluded that Schneider's perception captured parts while excluding wholes, focusing on isolated units while failing to comprehend how those units were situated within larger structures. His sensory perception of the world was limited to isolated segments while missing the entire configuration of letters, words, objects, and shapes.

The holistic interpretation of patient behavior that Goldstein and Gelb offered was unusual in the context of early-twentieth-century German neurology. At the time, medical researchers typically linked learning and behavioral anomalies with particular locations within the brain.

The well-known research of Goldstein's mentor Karl Wernicke served as a strong example of this tradition. Wernicke theorized three different types of aphasia, each with a different list of symptoms, each linked to a lesion in a certain area of the brain (Wernicke [1874] 1977).

Goldstein and Gelb set aside this tradition of functional localization to ask how the entire human organism interacted with the surrounding environment. Their holistic interpretation of Schneider's behavior rejected atomistic reflexology, which viewed thought and language as complex reflexes involving transmission of information from the brain's sensory center to its motor center. Instead, they globalized understanding of the operation of brain and body, holding that Schneider's brain injury had left him with a general nervous system failure to experience visual phenomena in complete wholeness (Gelb and Goldstein [1918] 1997; Goldstein 1967; Noppeney 2001).

An important example of Goldstein's science of brain injury was his notion of "catastrophic reaction" (Goldstein [1934] 1939, 35), a profound state of sickness and failure, a performative incongruity between human behavior and the environment. It could occur whenever the organism failed to meet the demands of the environment or when it experienced a temporary state of emotional confusion and cognitive disorganization—as when a brain-injured patient tried to solve a mathematics problem or when a recovered soldier attempted to rejoin his unit and return to battle. In the most severe form, it took the guise of an acute anxiety state, with confusion, excitement, dilated pupils, cold sweating, trembling, changes in pulse and breathing, and other bodily symptoms corresponding to dysfunction of the nervous system. In milder forms, it appeared as an inclination to faint; stuporlike inactivity; hypersensitivity to stimuli of all kinds; disturbances of sleep, pulse, and breathing; and asocial behavior (Goldstein [1934] 1939, 1940). In Goldstein's holistic thinking, these physiological reactions arose in the unhealthy interaction of brain-injured organism and environment.

Goldstein's holistic science undoubtedly represented a shift from the older style of atomistic analysis, the nineteenth-century neurology that yielded the discovery of Wernicke's Area, the hub of speech-comprehension activity, and Broca's Area, the center of speech production.

Goldstein's research focused on how the entire organism, body and mind, attempted to act in effective ways in response to the environment's numerous demands. He viewed concepts such as health and illness less in terms of the biological organization of internal physiology than in terms of the harmonic relationship between the functioning organism and the environment. Health was the effective coordination achieved by an organism with the environment, a state of effective equilibrium between the biology of man and the requirements of the environment. Illness, conversely, was the state of disorganization, of functional disjuncture, between organism and environment.

Despite Goldstein's holism, his theory emphasized only one side of the organism–environment equation. He offered no substantive theory of the environment—its constitution, nature, elements, dynamic activity, or development. He instead flattened and merged the social and political world of human interaction with the physical and architectural landscape under the loose and broad term *environment*. Lacking a complex articulation of the social and physical world that surrounds and influences the individual, Goldstein remained dedicated to the idea that learning and behavior were only outward reflections of individual personality. Failures of action, including difficulties in learning, ultimately reflected states of internal illness traced back to the patient's original brain injury. No matter how fully Goldstein theorized the equilibratory dance of personality and environment, he was unable to escape the assumption that his patient's brain damage was the undeniable basis of the person's struggles and suffering. Difficulties in learning, memory, and social interaction were outward expressions of the individual's mental impairment.

Alfred A. Strauss and the Wayne County Training School

Alfred Strauss, a neuropsychiatrist, and Heinz Werner, a psychologist, fled Germany during Hitler's reign. By the late 1930s, both had migrated to the United States and the Wayne County Training School outside Detroit. There they teamed up to apply central elements of Goldstein's science of brain-injured soldiers to the learning and behavior of institutionalized children with mental retardation (Cruickshank and Hallahan 1973).

At Wayne County, Strauss and Werner divided the institutionalized boys for their studies into two groups: exogenous and endogenous.
The exogenous group was believed to have a brain disease or injury of
some kind, whereas the endogenous group was presumed to have mental
retardation because of heredity or a poor learning environment. The first
study that Strauss and Werner conducted with five hundred children led
them to believe that the brain-injured child had untapped residual ability.
Their survey focused on the influence of the institutional environment
on general intelligence. It revealed that the exogenous group experienced
intellectual loss in the institution environment, whereas the endogenous
group experienced intellectual gain there. Further investigation of those
children whose intelligence could be traced back prior to institutionalization revealed that the exogenous group showed a steady decline before
and after institutionalization, but the endogenous group showed a decline
in intelligence until admittance, whereupon the trend was reversed, and
their intelligence improved (Kephart and Strauss 1940; Strauss and Kephart 1939). Until this time, mental retardation was perceived as a relatively
homogenous state. Strauss and Werner's construct contrasted with the
then presumption that considered all children at the Wayne School as
homogenous—uneducable mental defectives—and that a one-size-fits-all
teaching technique was applicable to whole school population.

Although Werner noted that IQ tests were deficient in measuring
abilities (because they quantified children's abilities by omitting aspects
that mathematics could not represent), the duo still used such tests to
conclude that the standard curriculum for children with mental retardation was ineffective for the brain-injured child. The environment per se
never became their pivotal area of investigation although it appeared in
undertheorized form in this investigation. Thus, their use of IQ tests to
evaluate the boys' responsiveness in different environment only advanced
the eugenics theory of classifying individuals according to their mental
competence. Incidentally, this notion influenced Kephart and Marianne
Frosting's reasoning, which later interpreted the child's environment in a
variety of ways. They related nurturing of behavior and intelligence to parents, their social class, their race, the community, and the physical characteristics of the school classroom. Conceptualization of these as fields

of immediate sensory inputs advanced the environment theory and the linking of children living in poverty with mental deficiency.

IQ tests, with their own inherent challenges, soon fell out of favor with the researchers. As a consequence, tracing children's abnormalities turned from using inference only to observing the children's behavior. Although the boys at Wayne County Training School had low IQ and were considered mentally retarded, Strauss and Werner wanted to identify a group within the population that would benefit from improved methods of educational treatment (Strauss and Werner 1939). They created a thirteen-item battery of finger schema tasks to analyze students' competency in arithmetic among other skills. The battery component was to identify finger agnosia, a condition caused by brain lesion in the parietal-occipital area. It led to a conscious lack of spatial configuration of one's own hand, including number and arrangement of fingers (Strauss and Werner 1938, 1939). Through a series of tests on a boy named JB, Strauss and Werner confirmed the coexistence of finger schema defect and low arithmetic achievement. Unsure of a neuropsychological relationship between functional deficiencies and spatial perception and configuration, the researchers conducted visual perception tests. They gave JB a series of basic shapes to copy. JB found it difficult to copy complicated figures that combined lines and figures. He also struggled on repeated trials to draw the remaining portions of a piece of paper with parts cut off of it. His performance on the tests, which involved counting his fingers or a researcher's fingers or both, demonstrated his impairment in spatial construction (Strauss and Werner 1939). This deficit in perceptual functioning was a psychological disability to construct an effective orientation to physical space.

Having found finger schema defect in JB and guided by Goldstein's work and gestalt psychology research on perception, specifically figure–ground concept, Strauss and Werner shifted their study to a bigger group of mentally deficient boys. They prepared a series of tasks to investigate the psychological relationships of finger agnosia and counting difficulties. In one task, they touched a finger on the boy's hand and then asked how many fingers had been touched. In another task, the researcher touched one of the boy's fingers and then asked him to locate the corresponding finger on a hand drawn on a blackboard. In 130 total trials, boys in the high arithmetic ability group made only sixteen errors, whereas each of the boys in the arithmetic disability group made on average thirty-six finger schema errors (Werner and Strauss 1939). The results showed the relationship between the boys' deficits in basic arithmetic skills and their inability "to recognize, indicate on request, name, or choose with open eyes, individual fingers either of their own hands or the hands of others" (Strauss and Werner 1938, 719)—in other words, a developmental failure to translate concrete, motoric operations into abstract, mental number concepts. To Strauss and Werner, injury in the parietal-occipital area of the left hemisphere caused disturbance of body schema—a lack of consciousness of the spatial configuration of one's own hand (ground) as well as of the number and arrangement of own fingers (figure). This confirmation of the coexistence of finger schema defect and low arithmetic achievement led to identification of Strauss syndrome. Thus, Strauss and Werner framed the disorder as a neurosensory "disturbance of the foreground–background relation" (Werner and Strauss 1941, 247).

Although Strauss and Werner located the disorder in the brain, they were unsure if the relationship between finger agnosia and arithmetic difficulties might indicate the prevalence of functional impairment. They accordingly conducted three types of visual perception tests: tachistoscopic, visuomotor, and tactual-motor (Werner and Strauss 1941). Having dealt with visual perception, they designed further experiments to investigate general central nervous system and other sensory input. These experiments led to tests on auditory-motor functions, verbal intellectual functions, cognition, and thinking. For example, in the multiple-choice test conducted with two groups made up of twenty-seven mentally deficient children in each group, Strauss and Werner presented "a geometrical figure constructed of heavy circular dots embedded in a configuration of small dots" (Werner and Strauss 1941, 239). After the card with this figure was flashed, the children were shown three choice cards: card B contained only the background of the original card; card DF showed the original background with a different figure; and card F showed the original figure on a different background. The children were then asked to choose the card similar to the test card. The brain-injured (exogenous) children chose card B in 52 percent of the trials (reacting more to the background), whereas the endogenous children chose card B in 27.5 percent of the trials. The visuomotor and tactual-motor stimuli tests found the exogenous group to exhibit more forced responsiveness than the endogenous group. The researchers concluded that this result demonstrated a disturbance in the differentiation of figure and background (Werner and Strauss 1941, 240).

Strauss and Werner's science of concussion and brain injury involved both close analyses of individual cases and mathematical comparisons of group measures (Lehtinen and Strauss 1944; Werner and Strauss 1938, 1939). For example, a study on the exogenous children's verbal intellectual functions showed that they were verbose, fluent, and full of neologism and that they used language affectively, characteristics that were different from the endogenous and normal groups, who were found to be direct, plain, and realistic in addressing a difficulty (Lehtinen and Strauss 1944; Strauss and Kephart 1940; Strauss and Werner 1941). Because the exogenous children's cognitive understanding of the world was distorted, Strauss and Werner reasoned that the exogenous child's memory was disconnected and fragmentary (Strauss and Werner 1938, 1939; Werner and Strauss 1939). Further analysis of the thought process of the exogenous child revealed malformed thinking, a discovery that led Strauss to summarize the brain injury syndrome as "a thinking disturbance" (Werner and Strauss 1943, 295). This discovery extended earlier work on cognition, in particular Gestalt notions of perception and Goldstein's organismic attitude (Strauss 1944).

Strauss and Werner conceived children's minds as going through qualitative psychological change over time and that mastery of specific tasks depended on differentiation and development of the brain (Werner 1937, 1948). This conception regarded psychopathological persons as likely to reach the highest level of psychophysiological functioning once "[t]he activities at the motor, sensory, or emotional levels are subjected to the dominance of the higher functions of mentality" (Werner 1948, 55). Werner and Strauss found consistent behavioral differences conceptually between the exogenous group and the endogenous group. Based on the same idea, Strauss and Lehtinen reconceptualized the Strauss syndrome by ultimately isolating the brain injury syndrome from mental retardation. They recommended an educational environment that would help such students cope with their distractibility and hyperactivity by attenuating inessential stimuli and accentuating essential stimuli (Strauss, Lehtinen, and Kephart 1947).

Strauss, Werner, and Lehtinen framed learning as a neurological process that took place inside the brain. They discovered a neuroperceptual disorder involving the brain's ability to effectively manage input from multiple sensory fields. Consistent with this reasoning, a child who struggled to learn had a neurological dysfunction that could be remedied through appropriate pedagogical methods. Such pedagogical practices compensated neuropsychological deficit and nurtured the capable portion of the brain-injured child's brain (Kephart and Strauss 1940; Werner and Strauss 1938, 1939).

Like Strauss's mentor Kurt Goldstein, the Wayne County Training School researchers located learning and learning problems within the human mind while ignoring notions of learning as a social activity that involves patterns of interaction and communication. By not focusing on how social milieu shapes the mind through negotiation and collaboration, they neglected the importance of teacher–student relationships as well as the rich social environments that allow peers to co-create cultural meaning. Although the solutions Strauss and his colleagues sought quite understandably focused on education (remediating or compensating areas of mental deficit), their scientific conceptualization of neuropsychology excluded social aspects, making their conclusion on neuropathology incomplete.

Newell C. Kephart

Newell Kephart believed that a young child's early experiences in the family and home had a profound, formative effect on mental development and that a child's central nervous system was to some extent a malleable system developed in interaction with early environments. He argued that children raised in confined urban homes and neighborhoods ended up living in small and restricted mental universes. However, he believed that carefully designed programs of training based on psychological knowledge could effectively ameliorate cases of lagging neuropsychological development. His belief in the significance of social and environmental factors in children's learning saw him theorize three alternative specific etiologies for a learning disability: brain injury, emotional disturbance, or lack of rich experiential content (Kephart 1968). During the 1950s and 1960s, Kephart was a leading figure in the field of "movement education," which offered curricula of physical activity and perceptual training as remediation for neurologically based delays in development and learning. Movement educators (Wapner and Kaplan 1964)—a group that included Marianne Frostig, Gerald Getman, and Ray Barsch—used a "holistic psychology within a liberatory framework" (Danforth 2009, 67) to address the needs of children relative to their environment.

In one case example, Kephart described the treatment of perceptual disorder with Jim, a young boy who had problems with the development of "laterality" (Radler and Kephart 1960, 8), the ability to recognize and coordinate the two symmetrical halves of the body. Jim had a normal intelligence, personality, and visual acuity but experienced reading problems. At grade three, he was overwhelmed and frustrated by academic work, and his behavior and attitude had degenerated (Radler and Kephart 1960). Experiences with many children like Jim convinced movement educators such as Kephart that missing or malfunctioning neurons in the brain were responsible for the interference with physiological and psychological processes. The interference led to mental disorganization. In turn, the disorganized mind created a disruption for physiological and psychological growth. According to Kephart, great "pressures for organization" (Kephart 1968, 7) incapacitated the child to organize and integrate perceptual and conceptual information.

Kephart's perceptual-motor theory relied on two assumptions: (1) motor development precedes visual development, and (2) kinesthetic sensations from motor movement provide feedback on visual-motor activities. Based on these assumptions, Kephart recommended that motor training precede visual perceptual training. He contrived four bases of motor learning: posture, laterality, directionality, and body image. Through posture, children develop movement patterns necessary to learn complicated motor tasks. Laterality enables children to distinguish two different sides of their body, which allows them to keep their balance when attempting difficult motor tasks. Locomotion and directionality are necessary for spatial exploration; they allow understanding of the relative position of two objects. Kephart viewed body image as knowledge of different body parts in reference to the child's midline as well as to one another. Through body image, the child relates to objects in space. According to Kephart, the achievement of these four bases enabled the child to manipulate his environment meaningfully, and lack of the achievement led to neurological failure, specifically mental disorganization. He therefore viewed children who had difficulties with reversals—for example, problems discriminating the letter *b* from *d* or *p* from *q*—as needing training in laterality (Radler and Kephart 1960).

Kephart's early research after World War II focused on the relationship between visual skills and successful work experiences among employed adults. In a series of studies, he demonstrated a correlation between good vision and effective work among workers in textile factories and corporate offices (Getman and Kephart 1956; Kephart 1948). When he transplanted this experience into the field of education, he found that school achievements among children increased when visual problems were corrected (Kephart 1947, 1948, 1951, 1953). As he advanced in his educational studies, however, he became less interested in common psychological analyses of groups involving statistical means and standard deviations. Instead, he embraced "the clinical results on one patient at a time" (Getman 1976, 215) because direct communication between a patient and practitioner revealed individual abilities and needs.

Kephart thought that a disorganized mind, a brain incapable of effectively managing and interpreting multiple strands of sensory input, could be aligned with the physical world through perceptual-motor training. He believed that a properly developed motor system and adequate perceptual skills led to complex mental processes. He also believed that development of most behaviors arose from a hierarchy of motor achievements. His neuropsychological "hierarchy of readiness skills" (Kephart 1968, 13) included (in order of complexity) movement control, systematic exploration, perception, intersensory integration, and concept formation (Gesell et al. 1949; Getman 1976). He reasoned that a child with well-developed motor skills learned by moving through the environment. Thus, perceptual systems allowed the child to extract information from the environment through the sense organs. As such, motor activity and behavioral development were complementary.

Kephart's version of movement education, developed with optometrist Gerald N. Getman, offered a treatment of childhood learning and behavioral problems through perceptual and sensory-motor activities (Getman and Kephart 1956). The treatment involved physical activities such as jumping, bouncing balls to rhythm, being blindfolded and identifying objects, balancing, drawing, listening, and reciting (Barsch 1965, 1968). Movement educators assumed that (1) learning standard academic skills such as reading depends wholly on adequate physiological and developmental perceptual skills (especially visual); (2) motor development during early years determines attainment of adequate neuropsychological skills of sensory perception; and (3) physiological development of children depends on interplay of conjoined motor activity and sensory perception (Danforth 2009, 105).

Kephart applied neurological holism and functional psychology within a clinical orientation to treat learning problems that movement educators located in the fields of education, neurology, psychology, and optometry. By looking into the development of sensory-motor integration, Kephart ultimately incorporated neurological networks into his theory of development. The perceptual-motor and movement education aimed at addressing multisensory areas of a brain-injured child, and this approach is evidenced in the Purdue Perceptual-Motor Survey, a test battery that Kephart developed to evaluate a particular child's perceptual-motor development. It emphasized building on visual-auditory, auditory-visual, auditory-kinesthetic, and kinesthetic-visual linkages. Learning disabilities were accordingly the demonstration of a glitch or delay in early motor development, and therefore appropriate motor training, the basis for learning, could be developed for brain-injured children.

Building a theory of how children learn and how to address learning problems on the foundation laid by Goldstein and Strauss, with additional input from functional psychology and optometry, Kephart broadened the location of learning difficulty from the brain to the entire human body. Remediation required activities not only mental, but also physical. Healing learning disabilities involved confronting the entirety of the developing neurological apparatus through bodily movement (Kephart 1968; Radler and Kephart 1960).[2]

Despite this comprehensive understanding of brain injury (and what was called "learning disabilities" by the early 1960s), Kephart crafted his theory based on the assumption that learning was wholly an individual affair, not social.

For Kephart, learning did not occur between and among people, but rather solely in the neurological body. Thus, like his predecessors Goldstein and Strauss, he conceived of learning problems as an individual psychopathology that appropriate measures or strategies could correct or ameliorate for an individual with disability to effectively adapt or conform to the dominant social norms. This theory omits social, historical, and cultural aspects as well as the importance of interaction, negotiation, and collaboration in meaning making. Physical spaces such as classrooms, schools, and opportunities that children and adults create not only are important in themselves but allow for physical-psychological growth and development.

Samuel Kirk

In 1929, when Samuel Kirk was a young graduate student in psychology at the University of Chicago, he applied a rudimentary pedagogy on a ten-year-old mentally deficient boy who was not able to read to help him develop reading skills (Kirk 1976, 1984).[3] Kirk was working at a time when

2. See also Kephart Center Series Videotape 1, circa 1968–73, Newell C. Kephart Special Collection, Archival Services, Univ. of Northern Colorado, Greeley.

3. See also Samuel A. Kirk, "Lecture—Final Report, Advanced Institute for Leadership Personnel in Learning Disabilities, Department of Special Education, University of Arizona," typescript, p. 5, Box 10, Samuel A. Kirk Papers, Archives Research Center, Univ. of Illinois, Urbana.

such children were generally viewed as incapable of learning to read, so his first student made substantial progress (Kirk 1963a, 1963b; Kirk and Kirk 1971).[4]

This single achievement stands as the symbolic and practical beginning of Kirk's long and storied career. Behind many decades of exhaustive work in the fields of policy, research, and practice, Kirk was concerned with teaching young children with disabilities how to read. He arguably became the most influential person during the growth of special education as a scientific and professional field from 1950 to 1980. He was called the "father of special education" (Mather 1998; Minskoff 1998)—the man who fashioned "the basic format of the IEP [Individualized Education Plan 8/4/13]" (Danforth, Slocum, and Dunkle 2010; Minskoff 1998), the standard scheme of psychoeducational assessment (Minskoff 1998), the federal definition of learning disabilities (Bos and Vaughn 1998; Danforth 2009), and the common framework and content of the university special education textbook (Brantlinger 2006; Kirk 1962).

During the 1930s, Kirk spent four years working with Thorleif Hegge, research director of the Wayne County Training School, creating a remedial reading program for children with mental retardation. Psychologists and educators widely believed "that special reading disability in cases of lower IQ is an aspect of mental deficiency and that the case therefore is untrainable" (Hegge 1934, 298). Kirk shared Hegge's worry that the "problem of reading disability has hardly been touched upon in connection with the mentally retarded" (Hegge, Sears, and Kirk 1932, 152). Hegge and Kirk embraced "a more optimistic attitude" (Hegge 1934, 298) toward the treatment of reading problems among mentally deficient children, especially those with IQs higher than 60.

After World War II, working at the Institute for Research on Exceptional Children at the University of Illinois, Kirk investigated the influence of early preschool programs on intellectual development for both

---

4. See also Samuel A. Kirk, "Are We Confused?" (version 2), typescript, pp. 1–2, Box 2, Kirk Papers, Univ. of Illinois.

children with mental retardation living in institutions and those living with their families. Four groups of young children (three to six years old) with low IQs (between 45 and 80) were compared over the course of three to five years regardless of whether the low intellectual functioning had an organic or an environmental cause. In the four groups, twenty-eight children lived at home and were in preschool programs; twenty-six children lived at home and did not attend preschool programs; fifteen children lived in institutions and attended preschool programs; and twelve children lived in institutions and did not attend preschool programs. The children were tested at the beginning of the experiment, during the preschool period, prior to leaving preschool, and then at regular intervals for up to five years. Kirk used IQ tests and case study methodology to evaluate the groups. The institution experiment group that attended preschool coincidentally improved in intelligence (Kirk and Karnes 1958).

This research, in combination with Harold Skeels's empirical findings concerning the influence of environment on IQ (Skeels 1938, 1940; Skeels and Dye 1939) persuaded Kirk that untapped potential residing in the brains of handicapped young children could be greatly enhanced by suitable instruction and specialized educational environments (Kirk 1936, 1940, 1952). He thus recommended designing educational programs to match individual children's needs (Kirk and Kirk 1978).

In the 1950s, dissatisfied with the educational utility of IQ testing, Kirk built the Illinois Test of Psycholinguistic Abilities (ITPA), a multifaceted test of language capacity (Kirk 1976, 1984; Kirk and McCarthy 1961). It identified specific areas of visual- and auditory-based language deficit needing professional remediation. It consisted of twelve multifaceted conduit systems involving (*a*) two primary channels of communication flow, (*b*) three psycholinguistic processes, and (*c*) two levels of overall organization. Channels were the modalities, auditory-vocal or visual-motor, through which sensory information is received and then expressed (Kirk and Kirk 1971). Psycholinguistic processes included reception, expression, and organization (Kirk 1966). Organization was the internal manipulation of information of concepts and linguistic skills. The twelve subtests were for visual reception, auditory reception, visual association, auditory association, verbal expression, motor expression, visual sequential memory, auditory sequential memory, visual closure, auditory closure, grammatical closure, and sound blending. The instrument identified specific psycholinguistic weaknesses, thereby merging diagnosis and instruction, assessment and treatment (Kirk and Kirk 1971).

Although Kirk viewed learning as simultaneously biophysical and psychological, he emphasized a psychology of mental activity and behavior over Strauss and Kephart's medical neuroscience. He wanted to articulate learning issues in terms and concepts that were useful to educators, the professional group that he viewed as the key to treating learning disabilities. Kirk used the ITPA to diagnose children with psycholinguistic disabilities, employing the results within in-depth case analysis of individual abilities and disabilities. Although classificatory diagnosis distinguished inter-individual differences—how children differed from mathematical group norms—Kirk's ITPA also examined the intra-individual differences, or the internal psychological discrepancies between performances across a child's different psychological abilities (Kirk 1966). As a consequence, the ITPA played a significant role in reinforcing the notion that children with learning disabilities had psychological profiles involving intra-individual differences. Moreover, as an assessment instrument, it directly led to education treatment of a disorder (Kirk 1976; Kirk and Kirk 1971, 1983). Kirk ultimately viewed the ITPA and his practice of complex case analysis as the proper professional basis for public-school remedial instruction of learning disabled students as well as the foundation for research on childhood learning issues.

Kirk's psycholinguistic science embraced Goldstein and Strauss's neuroscience of brain dysfunction; at the same time, it moved the instructional management and treatment of the disorder from a medical orientation to an educational practice. Thus, clinical approaches could be used to diagnose psychological dysfunction, whereas one-to-one intensive instructional regimen activities could be used to stimulate recovery of psychological processes. Because educational regimens could rehabilitate the defective child, Kirk advocated for a special education rather than a medical regimen—for teachers instead of doctors to tackle learning disabilities (Kirk and Kirk 1971). In the midst of Kirk's conceptualization of learning disability as far from stable and unambiguous, he tended to maintain four definitional elements throughout the 1960s and 1970s. He held that a learning disability is: (1) intrinsic to the child's psychology; (2) heterogeneous—that is, it can vary greatly in content from child to child; (3) marked by a significant discrepancy between learning potential (measured intelligence) and academic performance (measured skills in reading, writing, mathematics, and oral language); and (4) not caused by cultural, educational, environmental, or economic factors or by other disabilities (such as mental deficiency, visual or hearing impairments, or emotional disturbance). Kirk conceived learning disability as affecting a person's attention, memory, coordination, social skills, and emotional maturity. Equally important, these children had differing capabilities, with difficulties in certain academic areas, but not in others. Unlike other students with academic learning difficulties who could learn adequately with minimal guidance, learning disabled children required a special education program consisting primarily of one-to-one diagnostic-remedial tutoring (Kirk 1963a, 1963b; Kirk and Kirk 1971).

Although Kirk's thinking about children and education changed greatly over his long career, his first experience teaching an institutionalized ten-year-old boy how to read foreshadowed his approach to understanding learning difficulties over that career. Even as a young graduate student, Kirk already believed that understanding the learner's learning deficits and strengths needed an intensive focus and that a comprehensive knowledge of the learner's psychoeducational profile was necessary and important in analyzing learning difficulties and instituting appropriate remedial processes. Thus, despite shifting theories and terminology from medicine to educational psychology, Kirk's orientation in effect concurred with Goldstein, Strauss, and Kephart's theory of childhood learning difficulty as indicative of individual defect needing remediation. Kirk's innovation was in his psycholinguistic framing of the practical educational diagnosis of learning disability. But his imagination failed to examine how the social environments constituted by children and professionals might either support or fail to support the educational success of a diversity of children. His psycholinguistic science was completely individualized and pathological, seeking both failure and improvement within the limited landscape of the individual child's mind (Benjamin 2007; Kingsbury 1946; Kirk 1966, 1976; Kirk and Kirk 1983; McKinney 1978).[5]

Conclusion: Methodological Individualism and Inclusion

The science of learning disabilities, as built by important figures such as Kurt Goldstein, Alfred Strauss, Newell Kephart, and Samuel Kirk, began with a central assumption about the nature of scientific inquiry that rendered that science incapable of asking serious questions about how children of differing abilities, interests, and cultural backgrounds might share classrooms and schools. Lars Udehn has used the term *methodological individualism* to describe an orientation to the scientific analysis of human behavior through which the "actions of individuals are seen as resulting from (*a*) her/his psychology, (*b*) the physical surrounding, and (*c*) the actions of other individuals" (2002, 483). The researchers who contributed to the historical development of the learning disability construct employed a narrow version of methodological individualism that severely discounted the relevance of the latter two categories. They routinely assumed that childhood learning difficulties were solely the outward expressions of internal psychological and/or neurological defects.

There is an oft-stated truism that if one views human problems as nails, then quite understandably one will utilize a hammer as a primary mode of solving those problems. Beneath this mantra's trite superficiality is the crucial observation that the scientific framing of problems predisposes one to a limited range of corresponding solutions. In the case of the history of learning disabilities, the assumption of methodological individualism carried within the researchers' scientific orientation and practices logically paved a circumscribed array of solution pathways. Newell Kephart once wrote that the child with a learning disability is an "incomplete organism" (Godfrey and Kephart 1969, 12). The field of learning disabilities in the 1960s and 1970s took it as incontrovertible that problems in learning

---

5. See also Kirk, "Are We Confused?" (version 2).

existed within the individual child's material substance and required specialized instructional approaches to correct. This diagnostic–remediation ethos was central to the field of learning disabilities and quickly became a vital element of special educators' professional philosophy. Optimistic and hopeful educational practice necessarily consisted of finding individual defects and working to fix them.

Quite reasonably, such specialized instruction was understood in 1963, just as it is often understood today, as taking place in "special" classrooms and schools operated by educational professionals who have the necessary "special" training. Over the many decades of debate—from mainstreaming in the 1970s to the Regular Education Initiative in the 1980s, inclusion in the 1980s, and beyond—the assumption that the educational problems faced by students with disabilities inhere primarily to their own physiological and psychological constitution has remained a standard assumption of the field of special education. The profession's very identity has been built on the notion that special educators have an expertise in understanding and remediating those defective aspects of individual physiology and psychology. Closely related is the widespread practice of operating isolated special education classrooms and schools for the provision of educational services of diagnosis and correction.

The history of the science of learning disabilities provides insight into how a particular form of methodological individualism came to pervade the profession of special education such that inclusive education has seemed like both the wrong problem definition and the wrong solution to what ails children with disabilities. If the thoughts and words of national leaders such as Sam Kirk and President Kennedy had been fortified by decades of inclusive education research, then it is likely that the educational segregation of students with disabilities would be rare today. However, as we have attempted to demonstrate in this chapter, that was undoubtedly far from the case.

6

The Present King of France
Is Feeble-Minded

*The Logic and History of the Continuum of Placements
for People with Intellectual Disabilities*

PHILIP M. FERGUSON

In 1905, the philosopher Bertrand Russell published what has become a well-known paper titled "On Denoting" (1905). In that paper, he created and examined a simple declarative sentence: "The present king of France is bald." He then asked whether the statement was true or false. The problem, of course, is that the sentence seems to make a clear, sensible assertion but leads to contradictory results. On the one hand, the sentence is clearly not true because there is no present king of France. On the other hand, if we say the sentence is false, we seem to be implying that it is true to say that "the present King of France is not bald." We are left with a situation that seems to violate the "law of the excluded middle," whereby an assertion of fact is either true or not true; p or $\sim p$ in the language of symbolic logic.

For those who think philosophers should be arguing about the meaning of reality, the quest for Truth, the nature of goodness and beauty, this debate about whether a nonexistent king has hair or not may be a little underwhelming. And, indeed, a century of analytic philosophy has left much of what passes for academic philosophy these days a rather esoteric exercise. Moreover, I do not want my discussion of this sentence, esoteric or not, to be taken as an endorsement of Russell's larger agenda or that of the analytic philosophers generally. However, I refer to Russell's sentence because I think that his proposed solution to the problem is actually helpful to debates within special education and disability services. There are lessons here to help us understand the persistence of the status quo and the resistance to change among educators and adult service providers dealing with folks with intellectual disabilities.

With apologies in advance to analytic philosophers everywhere, let me try briefly to summarize Russell's solution to the king of France problem. For much of the twentieth century, a key piece of the analytic enterprise was to demonstrate that seemingly intractable philosophical debates were little more than linguistic confusion. One of these debates had to do with the nature of existence and theories of meaning. A central question for positivists at the turn of the twentieth century was how a correspondence theory of meaning could account for sensible statements that refer to nonexistent objects (e.g., round squares, present kings of France). In dealing with the issue, Russell was trying to improve on the work of Alexius Meinong and Gottlob Frege in solving this problem. It seems obvious to us now, perhaps, but Russell simply argued that the grammatical structure of the sentence obscured the underlying logic of what was being asserted. In what is now called his "theory of description" or "theory of definite description," Russell translated the sentence into its logical form and revealed a hidden conjunction that was actually being asserted. The new sentence becomes: "There is an X such that X is the present king of France, and X is bald," or in its symbolic notation: $\exists(x)\ P(x) \wedge Q(x)$. The falsity of the first part of the conjunction (X is the present king of France) falsifies the entire statement without implying the truth or falsity of the other part of the conjunction (X is bald). Logical order is restored. That messy middle between p and $\sim p$ remains excluded for all who would seek the truth of the world.

I want to move, now, from this introduction to argue two main points in this chapter. First, the language with which the continuum of services and placements for people with intellectual disabilities is defended is often similar to Russell's king of France sentence in that this language obscures a conjunction of assumptions that are too easily left unchallenged. We end up with a discussion where the specific choices of placement may be challenged, but the underlying logic of the options remains hidden. As a result, too many of our debates in special education about the least restrictive environment or residential or vocational services are really pointless squabbles about whether the present king is bald.

My second point is to argue that there is a history to the policy that lies behind this language. Moreover, that history goes back further than most discussions of the principle of least restrictive environments follow. We can, I think, look to developments in the Progressive Era in the United States—roughly the same period Russell was obsessing over bald monarchs—to find a time when professionals in education and human services first elaborated the assumptions underlying a continuum of placements. Understanding this history and how a conjunction of assumptions first emerged can also help us identify how thoroughly those assumptions are now hidden in a rhetoric of individualized support.

The Logic of the Continuum

A continuum of placements is the dominant model with which the array of services and supports for children and adults with intellectual disabilities is arranged. In our schools, this continuum ranges from the most segregated, self-contained school to something close to full-time placement in a regular classroom. Indeed, this range of placement options is enshrined in regulations, endorsed in policy, and defended by professionals, families, and many individuals with intellectual disabilities themselves. The federal special education statute is somewhat vague, saying that "removal of students from the regular educational environment" occurs only when made necessary by the "nature or severity" of a child's disability (Individuals with Disabilities Education Improvement Act [IDEA] [1990] 2004, §1412(a) (5) (A)). However, as one recent textbook summarizes the regulations and case law that have interpreted this passage, the legal definition of "least restrictive environment," or LRE, is clear about what school districts must offer. "To ensure that students with disabilities are educated in the LRE that is most appropriate for their individual needs, the IDEA requires that school districts have a range or continuum of alternative placement options to meet their needs. The continuum represents an entire spectrum of placements where a student's special education program can be implemented" (Yell 2006, 312).

For most students with intellectual disabilities, this focus on the continuum has meant, in practice, a continued exclusion from the regular classroom. According to the *29th Annual Report to Congress* by the US Department of Education (2010), students with the label of either *mental retardation* or *multiple disabilities* have the lowest rate of inclusive placement of any of the thirteen categories of eligible disabilities. Compared to an overall rate of almost 53 percent for all students with disabilities, less than 14 percent of students with a mental retardation label spend 80 percent or more of their school day in the regular classroom. Moreover, that rate of inclusive placement—between 10 percent and 15 percent—has remained more or less constant for more than twenty years. Half of these students with intellectual disabilities remain in self-contained classes for all or most of each day. More than 6 percent of those remain housed in totally "separate environments" (US Department of Education 2010, 1:75). Of course, the national rates disguise the range of the placement patterns across the various states. Some states rely very little on separate public schools (West Virginia's rate is the lowest, at 0.14 percent), whereas some of our most populous states greatly exceed the national average for such placements (New York, 14.95 percent; Michigan, 15.67 percent) (US Department of Education 2010, 2:167). However, all of the states, by policy, use the full range of educational placements to some degree or other.

The situation we are left with in our schools in both policy and pronouncement is one where the "the present king of France" becomes the "appropriately segregated child" and "baldness" becomes "intellectual disability." The special education version of Russell's sentence goes, "The appropriately segregated child is the one with a significant intellectual disability." Of course, in reality the assertion is never worded in exactly this way. The syntax is improved, the assumptions obscured, but the basic assertion remains: there are some people with intellectual disabilities so severe that they "belong" in self-contained settings. If we argue the truth of the statement, we seem to be quibbling over categories: whether intellectual disability is the only or most appropriate category for separate placement. Or we seem to be arguing over a specific child: this child may or may not belong in separate placement, but some children do.

However, using Russell's formula, we can easily find the hidden conjunction being asserted: "There is an X such that X is an appropriately segregated child, and X has a significant intellectual disability." In this clumsy but logical formulation, we can identify and challenge the hidden assertion that there is any child who is necessarily segregated.

The situation—and the language defending it—is similar when one looks at residential services. Although in this case there has been more movement than in our schools, the model for residential support arrangements in most states is this familiar continuum of placements, running from the most segregated to the most integrated. At one end, we have about thirty-five thousand individuals with intellectual and developmental disabilities still living in large state institutions (Lakin et al. 2010, 4) and another twenty-seven thousand living in large, private facilities (Lakin et al. 2010, 48). At the other end of the continuum, however, there are a growing number of individuals living in a variety of small, community-based residential arrangements.

Here again the continuum has been enshrined in law, this time notably by the Supreme Court in any number of cases. In one of the most important recent decisions, *Olmstead v. L.C.* (1999), the Court laid out the argument for LREs by saying that states have to place individuals with intellectual disabilities in community settings if they so desire and if "the State's treatment professionals have determined that community placement is appropriate" (at 582). However, even after granting "treatment professionals" the power to veto community placement, the majority of the Court went on to be clear about the need for states to maintain the full continuum of placements: "The ADA [Americans with Disabilities Act] is not reasonably read to impel States to phase out institutions, placing patients [*sic*] in need of close care at risk. . . . Some individuals . . . may need institutional care from time to time. . . . For others, no placement outside the institution may ever be appropriate" (at 584).

So we are left with thousands of individuals and family members hearing the king of France argument once again. These days the sentence usually becomes some version of the following in policy debates around the country: "The well-run institution has fewer than 300 residents." Opposition then easily falls into a numbers game, some saying that 200 should be the maximum, others wanting 150, a few saying 400 or 500 should be possible. As a result, the concept of the "well-run institution" is easily left unchallenged. With Russell's help, we can translate the assertion into the following formula: "There is an X such that X is a well-run institution, and X has fewer than 300 residents." For those of us opposed to the continuum, the task becomes clearer: the notion of a "well-run institution" is just another king of France whose time has come and gone.

The History of the Continuum

The idea of arranging services for people with intellectual disabilities along this range of settings that we now call a continuum does have a history going back for about one hundred years, and it is the beginning of that story I want to explore now. Where did this hidden logic of the continuum come from? For many, the ubiquity of the arrangement makes it difficult to imagine a time without it. There seems to be something obvious and unavoidable about arranging people and services along a linear progression that mirrors a classification scheme based on degrees or levels of intellectual disability. It does seem almost instinctual in some sense to classify and organize—to impose an order on—an unruly disarray of differences. However, to foretell my argument, what happens in the early twentieth century is the merger of the taxonomic and the territorial. It is a time when the diagnostic and distributive impulses combine within a growing field of specialized medical and educational professionals to move from a statistical curve of normal distribution to a geographic mandate to move people along a chain of linked but separate service settings (P. Ferguson 1994). It is this merger that represents the birth of the continuum as we know it today, where intensity of support is fused with separateness of setting: the more intensive the support needed, the more segregated the placement required to provide that level of support.

The Continuum and the LRE

First, some more recent history should be reviewed. In a pair of influential articles, Steven J. Taylor (1988, 2001) explores the concept of the continuum and the framework for services that it has provided for people with intellectual disabilities. In his writings, he analyzes the intellectual and legal elements that have served to join the notion of a "continuum of services" to the legal concept of "least restrictive" settings or services. For Taylor and most others reviewing this concept, the story goes back to the 1960s and 1970s. It was during these decades of an emerging disability rights movement that a number of reformers presented a continuum of service options as a way of moving children and adults from more segregated to less segregated placements. In education, Maynard Reynolds (1962) used the idea to justify a call for "mainstreaming" children with disabilities back into neighborhood schools and classrooms. Just a few years later, Evelyn Deno (1970) developed a so-called cascade model of placements that remains influential today.

At the same time, a series of groundbreaking court decisions concerning residential services was building up a body of case law that laid out a "right to treatment" for people with intellectual and psychiatric disabilities who were being warehoused in the back wards of the large institutions of the era. Moreover, the treatment was to occur in the least restrictive setting possible (Taylor 2001). What the courts were saying in this era of reform was that you have to have a continuum of service settings that will allow people to move from more restrictive settings to less restrictive, more integrated settings. Referring to the 1960s and 1970s, Taylor notes the irony of how this legal argument evolved: "The concept of the continuum emerged in an era in which persons with developmental disability and their families were offered segregation or nothing at all. The early proponents of the concept were extremely forward-looking for their time. . . . The continuum was used to create opportunities for integration when few existed. It is ironic, therefore, that the continuum concept is used today to support institutionalization" (2001, 21).

The Origins of the Continuum

I am in complete agreement with Taylor's account of the events in the 1960s and 1970s whereby the legal principle of LRE and the organizational arrangement of the continuum of placement were linked. However, as indicated earlier, I think that the story of the continuum itself can be traced back even further to the beginning of the twentieth century, when both public schools and public institutions were focusing renewed attention on the need to separate and control the so-called menace of the "feeble-minded." In both residential services and special educational services, one finds in the period from roughly 1900 to 1920 several examples in which influential professionals worked with policymakers to use their newly refined tools of diagnosis (e.g., the Binet test) to create increasingly elaborate arrays of specialized service settings with the promise of improved training and control of people with disabilities.

Two examples support this view. First, I look at the work of Charles Bernstein at the Rome State School in upstate New York and his extension of the institution into communities throughout the state with a system of group homes and parole. Second, I look at the work of Wallace Wallin and his elaboration of a special education continuum for the city of St. Louis that went from total exclusion to what would today be called "resource rooms."

Bernstein and the Colony Plan

On a snowy April 1, 1906, just one year after Russell dispatched his bald French king, Charles Bernstein watched a small parade leave his institution outside of Rome, New York. Led by a horse-drawn sleigh holding members of the asylum band, a second sleigh of eight young men followed, with "two cows, one extra horse, a few cooking utensils, one month's supply of food and the eight patient's [sic] clothing and trunks" (Rome State School 1907, 31) pulling up the rear of the parade. The men were leaving their home at the Rome State School to take up residence in what was called a "farm colony" on some 177 acres adjacent to the institutional grounds. It was to be the first in a rapid series of expanded placements in both rural and town settings, for both men and women, that Bernstein would undertake as superintendent of the Rome facility. By 1935, under Bernstein's guidance, the Rome system of "extrainstitutional" care included some thirty separate farm and industrial colonies for 750 "boys" (as they were called regardless of age), with 250 of the boys going on to be paroled[1] and another 250 discharged. In addition, there were twenty-two domestic colonies for 450 "girls" (as the women were called regardless of age) (Riggs 1936, 50). In an article defending his program in 1927, Bernstein reported that more than 40 percent of the total population of people admitted to Rome were actually served in placements outside the "central institution." Even in this period situated at the height of the eugenics scare, Bernstein went on to proclaim his conviction that community placements worked well and saved money: "We are more firmly than ever of the opinion that from one-third to one-half of all the feeble-minded and mental defectives that must receive State care and training can well be cared for under a reasonable system of colony and parole care and supervision" (1927, 424).

Certainly, Bernstein was not the first to establish one of these so-called farm colonies. Walter Fernald at the Waverly, Massachusetts, asylum had started a farm colony in the late 1890s. In some ways, the Wisconsin system of specialized county asylums was a network of farm colonies. Moreover, at places in Belgium, Scotland, and elsewhere in Europe, a practice of placing out inmates from a central asylum to the homes of local families had been used with enough tradition and success to draw the notice of people such as Bernstein (1921) and Fernald (1907). However, Bernstein's system became by far the largest network of such settings, at one point with houses located all the way from upstate to New York City to Staten Island. Visiting officials from these same institutions in Europe would make the trek to upstate New York to learn more about Bernstein's system (Riggs 1936, 49).

Several other features of the Rome system can be noted. First, Bernstein clearly saw the colonies as part of a system of individualized placements that provided more flexibility in support than the institution offered. As Bernstein put it, one advantage of "colony care" was the "large variety

1. Parole in institutions of this era worked the same way as it did in prisons: a conditional release that could be revoked should certain behavioral or vocational outcomes not be met. After a given period of time, if a paroled inmate's behavior was deemed acceptable, then a complete discharge was allowed.

of environmental conditions" that could be created, with "small groups fitting the individual to the environment which seems to suit him best" (1927, 419). The less restrictive colonies were places where the smaller numbers allowed "individual attention" to be paid and consideration to be given to the residents' "individual likings" (419).

A second feature to be noticed is that Bernstein moved quickly from farm colonies (and a few "reforestation" camps) for young, able-bodied men to a network of houses for men and women in towns throughout the area. The first of these "domestic" colonies for "girls" opened in 1914 in the town of Rome, New York, with the following announcement:

> A working girls' home has been established at 209 West Thomas Street, telephone number, 172-J—where girls are available for domestic work, sewing, etc., by the day, week, or month. The girls going out from this place to work are capable of doing all kinds of domestic work, except special cooking. They are only able to do common cooking.
>
> Their services may be secured by telephone. The rate is fifty cents per day, and their services will be available for employment at any time on short notice. . . .
>
> This colony is carried on in a rented house in the city, which constitutes the girls' home and social center, presided over by a housekeeper or matron, with a social visitor to inspect their working places and their street deportment, to accompany them to moving-picture shows and other social diversions, and to assist them in purchasing their clothing. We hope in this way to have many of these girls learn through experience normal social reactions and family life, and thus to return the services of many of these willing and competent domestic workers to society. (Bernstein 1920, 7–8)

A third feature that makes Bernstein's case especially relevant is that he went beyond the system of colonies to develop an equally extensive system of parole and discharge. A New York State law passed in 1912 created the opportunity for inmates of various state institutions to be paroled as an intermediary step before full discharge. Bernstein ran with the opportunity that the new law provided. Indeed, the next step in the continuum of placements that Bernstein developed was to have men move from laboring on the farm colonies to working for neighboring farmers, often seasonal work at first, but subsequently full-time work and parole from Rome. Women in domestic colonies would be paroled to move on as live-in maids in private homes. Again, if judged successful in such placements, some of them would be discharged completely. Movement, of course, could go both ways. The parole status allowed Bernstein—in both threat and reality—to move individuals judged less successful on parole to the more restrictive setting of a colony or back to the state school itself.

Bernstein was aggressively expanding and defending this system at the height of the eugenics push for sterilization and segregation, especially of feeble-minded women of childbearing age. Bernstein's assessment of the situation shows that there were at least a few lonely voices among the institutional professionals who questioned the eugenicists' arguments:

> We are more thoroughly convinced with each succeeding year's experience in parole and discharge of cases that, with our limited knowledge of and [sic] the many more or less misleading theories pertaining to the eugenic aspect of work with the so-called mental defectives and borderline cases of feeble-minded, eugenic consideration should not constitute the principal or controlling factor or consideration when we come to pass on paroles and discharges, and even though marriage and reproduction ensue still we are not deterred in continuing this hopeful practice. (1921, 45–46)

Bernstein's continuum of residential placements stagnated and started to wither away in the late 1930s and 1940s. Under the economic pressures of the Depression, inmates competing with unemployed townspeople for scarce jobs in the community were not always favorably received. The Rome institution itself continued to grow, and with Bernstein's death in 1942, any sense of it as more than a custodial facility began to fade rapidly. By 1957, many of the colonies had been closed; others had been taken over by other institutions, leaving a total of only 266 residents still living in Rome State School colonies (Davies 1959, 124).

Nevertheless, the demonstration of a residential continuum for people with intellectual disabilities is a neglected legacy of Bernstein's tenure as superintendent. Instead of Bernstein's understanding of a "colony system" as a network of halfway houses or large group homes, the "colony plan" reverted to a definition that Fernald put forth in 1907: "[I]nstead of the conventional monastic structure housing the patients, the modern institution is likely to be constructed with widely detached departments allowing the specialization of the different classes and the utilization of their different capacity" (417). In essence, *colony* merely became another name for an institution with separate units or so-called cottages distributed around a common campus.

Wallin and the Special Education Continuum

At the same time that Bernstein was pursuing his plan for colonies and parole for "feeble-minded" adults, educators and psychologists in America's public schools were also busy elaborating a system of classification and alternative placements for "feeble-minded" children (and others). This emergence of special education has received its share of historical attention and analysis (among others, Giordano 2007; Lazerson 1983; Osgood 2008; Winzer 1993). However, I want to look at it briefly as yet another original source for what we now confront as the service continuum. In this case, I want to look at the work of J. E. Wallace Wallin and the school district of St. Louis, Missouri, from 1914 to 1921.

Special classes for so-called feeble-minded children in St. Louis were first begun in 1908. The plan was to create a network of totally separate schools rather than the "ungraded" classes that New York City and other large systems were adopting (Farrell 1914a, 1914b). The school superintendent in St. Louis, Frank Soldan, had apparently traveled to Europe and visited the systems of separate, "auxiliary" schools used for feeble-minded children in Germany and England (Maennel 1907; Wallin 1955, 64). For St. Louis, Soldan was specific about the size and accommodation needed for each school. Each of these separate schools was in actuality to be a house with two rooms used for classes of fifteen students each (compared to the fifty or more that a typical elementary school classroom might have), along with living space for one teacher, who would also be responsible for the maintenance of the property. In fact, after building the first such school from scratch, the district rented houses in various residential neighborhoods for the rest of its special schools well into the 1920s. The schools were officially called "Special Schools for Individual Training" to avoid "the stigma which the name 'Schools for Defectives' would carry" (St. Louis Public Schools 1905–1906, 208).

The schools' purpose was clear, at least to Superintendent Soldan. On the one hand, imbeciles belonged in asylums, not in public schools. On the other hand, "no child who can in any way profit sufficiently from instruction in the ordinary school should be transferred to the special room [i.e., separate school]" (St. Louis Public Schools 1905–1906, 209). However, the actual situation was apparently much more confused and ambiguous. Kate Cunningham, the original supervisor of the Special Schools, explained: "Our work is new to us, and we are not all agreed as to which is the defective and which the backward child; we are not sure as to what is exactly the proper treatment for the defective child when we have defined him. But we are convinced that opportunities for psychological research are present on every side" (St. Louis Public Schools 1907–1908, 238). Nevertheless, far be it for professionals to let a little uncertainty of diagnosis or treatment slow down the labeling and placement. By the time Wallin arrived in St. Louis in 1914, there were thirteen of these special schools, with 355 students and twenty-nine teachers.

Even though this system of separate schools had been in place in St. Louis for six years by the time the school board hired Wallin to establish the Psycho-Educational Clinic, the public perception was that little had been done for the type of pupil served in these schools. The newspaper headlines announcing Wallin's hiring proclaimed the promise of his arrival: "Abnormal Pupils of St. Louis to Be Specially Taught . . . [Wallin] Will Stop Wasted Work" (1914). And, in fact, Wallin was beginning something substantially new. He thought it was clear that the current options of regular class or separate school left far too many "abnormal pupils" wasting everybody's time in regular classrooms. "More than one-third of the public school pupils are behind in grade work. Children who prove a drag on their classes should be singled out and examined by scientists. . . .

To hitch a slow pupil with a bright pupil is like hitching a fast horse with a slow horse and expecting to win a race. This should have been seen long ago" (quoted in "Abnormal Pupils" 1914).

By 1921, when Wallin left St. Louis, the city's public-school system had twenty-five "special schools for individualized instruction" with more than 500 students enrolled (Wallin 1921, 58). More important for our purposes, another 3,260 students were enrolled in more than sixty ungraded classes located in schools throughout the city (Wallin 1921, 60). The district had taken responsibility for all instruction at the former House of Refuge, changing its name to "Industrial School." A teacher-training program designed to provide a steady flow of teachers (unmarried women only) specifically prepared as special educators was operated as part of the general "normal school" run by the school district. Administrators from other cities were visiting St. Louis to learn more about the breadth of special education services that Superintendent Soldan and then Wallin had created (Franklin 1994, 38).

The continuum of placements that Wallin established in St. Louis schools was based firmly on his belief in differential diagnosis by careful testing and evaluation of children by what we would now call "school psychologists." Differential diagnosis led to differential support, which led to differential placement in an increasingly elaborate array of specialized settings. One of Wallin's superintendents at St. Louis provided a rationale for this arrangement, which would—with contemporary labels—find widespread assent to this day.

> It is obvious that a type of education suited to the feeble-minded child would not be the best type of training to give to a backward child, or a normal child with specific pedagogical handicaps, or a speech defective who is not feeble-minded. And it is evident that if all types of misfit pupils are placed in the same class it will be difficult to do justice to any one type. It is therefore necessary in the interest of the individual child who cannot be reached by the ordinary curriculum, and in the interest of the economic administration of the schools, that the differentiations must be drawn as finely and accurately as possible, so that pupils subject to the same type of disability or degree of subnormality may be grouped together. (Withers 1917, xiii–xiv)

Of course, the system was also dealing with children with types of disabilities other than intellectual (deaf or blind or "paralytic" children, children with "word blindness," or "delinquent" children). However, even within the narrow category of mental ability, Wallin was able to identify what he thought were seven distinct levels of student. At the "low" end of the scale were three categories of feeble-mindedness: "idiots," "imbeciles," and "morons." These children had an incurable mental defect. All of those at the idiot level and most at the imbecile level, Wallin thought, should be excluded from any public school program; after Lewis Terman's version of the Binet test established the IQ over Mental Age as the appropriate score, the cut-off for school eligibility was usually put at a 50 IQ. Children tested at below that score were thought to be "custodial" cases. Above the three categories of feeble-mindedness, Wallin referred to four additional levels: "borderline," "backward," "retarded," and "normal." Then, of course, there were the cases of uncertain diagnosis: "I have employed [the term] 'potential moron' to designate a defective testing as an imbecile who, based on experience with similar cases, evidenced sufficient potential ability to ultimately develop to the status of a moron, while [the term] 'potential feeble-minded' has been applied to a type of child who could not be classed as feeble-minded at the time of examination but who . . . would probably prove eventually to be feeble-minded because of the slow rate at which he was developing" (1923, 170). Above the feeble-minded and properly placed in some version of ungraded class were the borderline, backward, and retarded children. All of these children were thought capable of dramatic progress and in some cases "restoration" to the regular grade. The slowness in learning in these cases was thought to be the result of ill health, chronic absence, moral debilitation, or simply bad teaching. Indeed, Wallin used the term *pedagogical retardation* for those students who through a mix of circumstances had simply not spent enough time with instruction that was appropriate for their age level.

In terms of placement options, all this categorization translated into a range that would seem familiar to many special educators today. The ungraded classes in the regular schools were themselves divided up into multiple groupings. Some children would use special classes as resource rooms, coming there for instruction in certain subjects and then returning to the regular class. For most, however, the ungraded placement was essentially a full-time placement in a self-contained classroom.

Just as with the current debates, the system of classification and placement became embroiled in an ongoing argument over where on the continuum a child should be placed, not over whether the continuum itself should exist. If children from the special schools for the feeble-minded ended up (as many did) successfully supporting themselves in the community after leaving school, then this was simply proof that they had been misdiagnosed as feeble-minded in the first place. If others failed to progress adequately after being placed in an ungraded class, then the potential moron became a "real" moron. For most of the children in the ungraded class, there was movement back to regular class, as predicted by the appropriate original diagnosis. Wallin claimed that in one year (1917), 42 percent of all the students "registered in ungraded classes on full-time or part-time were reported 'restored to grade'" (1923, 174–75).

For Wallin, one of the most important debates he had was with Henry H. Goddard and other prominent psychologists. Wallin challenged whether the "high-grade" moron should be classified as feeble-minded at all. In one article, he cites the work of Bernstein and the colonies at Rome as showing that the high end of the moron level of IQ should not be included among the feeble-minded. The evidence was simple. Bernstein's paroling of "middle and high grade morons," according to Wallin, "demonstrated beyond cavil that large numbers of these individuals have sufficient intelligence and discretion to earn their livelihood or to live an independent existence. They have proved that they are not feeble-minded as judged by the social or legal standard, which is the only decisive test of feeble-mindedness" (1923, 173–74).

To revert to Russell's scheme, the question becomes whether the king is bald or not, not whether the king exists. Even in this earlier era, then, the question created by the newly defended continuum of placements was a version of the hidden conjunction: there is an appropriately segregated placement for truly disabled persons. We are left, then, with the progressive's professional quandary. True or false: The present king of France is feeble-minded.

Of Kings and Continua: The Persistence of Separate Placements and Differentiated Support

The power of the continuum logic is easily seen in how relatively quickly the assumptions behind its assertions became unnoticed and largely unchallenged. If Bernstein's network of colonies faded away in the 1930s, it was because of the economic competition during the Great Depression rather than any increased skepticism about the soundness of the policy itself. Wallin lost his battle with Goddard and others over the location of the line separating the moron from the merely backward, but the assumption that children on either side of that line needed separate and special placements was one that he did not even have to defend. For the past one hundred years, the details of the continuum have shifted and evolved, but the assumptions have remained largely unchallenged to this day.

Yet if this review has shown that the continuum of placements for children and adults with intellectual disabilities has a beginning, then it may be easier to imagine its end. The beginning of the end is to understand the logic and to challenge the hidden claims being asserted. To move further, however, requires a deeper understanding of the durability of this arrangement of services and supports. In the remainder of this chapter, I speculate about some of the embedded reasons for the continuum's persistence and power. Hidden or not, why is the logic of the continuum so persuasive?

In some ways, this question would not have been asked until the past few decades. That is, it is only through the lens of disability studies that one can bring into focus the assumptions that otherwise lie blurry and indistinct behind the developmental policies of the deficit model of disability. Disability studies allows us to analyze critically how disability comes to be rationalized and governed by the power of professional knowledge. As Shelley Tremain has described the impact of disability studies, "Academics who conduct their work under the rubric of disability studies have begun to problematize the foundational assumptions of many disciplines and fields of inquiry, as well as the methodologies that they employ, the criteria of evaluation to which they appeal, and the epistemological and social positioning of the researchers and theorists invested in them" (2005, 2).

For this specific question about the enduring force of the continuum model of services, a disability studies perspective allows us to undertake that "problematization" of which Michel Foucault (1965, 1973) and Tremain speak by analyzing the formal and informal roles played in reinforcing the status quo. The continuum of placement serves the interests of different groups of people involved in the process in different ways. Indeed, this multiple utility is itself a part of the continuum's robust survival. I want to look at how the continuum serves the needs of three different groups who often control the lives of people with intellectual disabilities: administrators, professionals, and parents. Individuals in each of these groups, whether consciously or not, have specific needs met by the continuum's continued dominance.

Administrative Control: Territory Triumphs

Like most of the institutional superintendents of his era, Bernstein had a medical degree. Yet, as is even truer in today's institutions, his role as superintendent of the Rome State School was entirely administrative. Charles Bernstein, Walter Fernald, Martin Barr, Edward Johnstone, and the other institution superintendents were, almost by default, the main policymakers in terms of the day-to-day shape and structure of the state-sponsored programs for people with intellectual disabilities. Today that policymaker role—at least for adults with such disabilities—is more firmly lodged in the higher levels of the state bureaucracy. For children, the administrators of the special education systems in state and local school systems play that role.

What emerges from a review of Bernstein's creation and defense of his colony and parole system is that one key factor in how the continuum of placements serves the needs of disability administrators is territory. The more physical space one has charge over, the more power one has. It is, to a large degree, all about turf: a range of separate placements under a single administrative jurisdiction means, all things being equal, more money, more influence, more control. As Bernstein's colonies spread across the state of New York, his territory of influence also expanded.

A similar process can be viewed today in many special education bureaucracies. Many states have districts or regions whose special education services are spread out across classrooms, schools, and other buildings. In many states, a regionalized bureaucracy for students with more significant disabilities has control of self-contained schools. From there, in an arrangement reminiscent of Bernstein, the administrators colonize local schools with a network of self-contained classrooms whose faculty and students "belong" to the kingdom of special education rather than to the local principal or general education administrator. Having an array of placements in distinct locations, each with its own employees, clients, and supporters, creates an educational empire that inclusive approaches challenge. For many disability administrators, the power of the continuum, consciously or not, comes down to turf and who controls it.

Professionals: Involuntary Change

Historians sometimes talk about three broad types of change over time. Revolutionary changes are those rare occasions when there is a radical, fairly sudden (in historical terms) shift in social trends, cultural norms, economic arrangements, and so on. Of course, there are debates about whether a particular development or sequence of events constitutes a truly revolutionary change, but those involved in such times often have the sense that the ground is shifting under their feet. A second type of change is the much more common companion of historical analysis: evolutionary development. This is the type of incremental change wherein gradual alteration occurs. Instead of the cataclysmic change of revolution, evolutionary change is the slow emergence of amendments and mutations. In this process, it is only the clarity of hindsight that reveals what was murky and unclear for those in the midst of change. Finally, there is the type of change that is purely involutionary: superficial and often illusory. This type of change involves transition without transformation, or, to paraphrase Clifford Geertz, it is a process where things become more elaborately the same (1963, 63).

Professionals involved in the diagnosis and treatment of people with intellectual disabilities use the continuum of placements as a source of involutionary change. The continuum of placements has three essential features. First, there must be an array of alternative settings where people are placed. This is the process where taxonomy becomes territory and classification is linked to control. Second, to be a true continuum, these settings must be linked or tied together in some sort of logical or conceptual way. This geographic distribution unites territory under a centralized administrative dominion. Finally, there is the feature of movement. For professionals such as Wallin and the legions of school psychologists who followed him, it is the potential for movement of the individual student from one setting to another along the educational continuum that provides the power of professional discretion. It is important that the movement be largely illusory, but also that it occur often enough to maintain the illusion. The more intricate and elaborate the points along the continuum, then the more opportunities available for this illusion of change to occur. Despite the promise of progress, movement along today's continuum is largely an illusion maintained by individual exceptions to the immobility of the aggregate.

After one year in his position in St. Louis as the head of the Psycho-Educational Clinic, Wallin was glad to give an interview to a local newspaper about the early results of his work. The headline read "Feeble-Minded in Schools Reduced by Dr. Wallin" (1915). In the article, Wallin claimed to have found that up to 25 percent of the children had been misplaced in the separate schools for feeble-minded children, when they really belonged in one of the "higher" categories. Of course, these newly identified backward or pedagogically retarded students needed their own placements in the array of ungraded classrooms that Wallin was trying to establish. By establishing himself as the essential gatekeeper, Wallin was certainly working to legitimize the specialized knowledge that he claimed for himself and his newly emerging profession of school psychology. However, part of the gatekeeper's power comes from convincing the community and his administrative supervisors that he is keeping the gate open as much as closed. Another newspaper article on Wallin's work presented precisely this message to its general readers: "Few St. Louisans have known that almost a thousand children, previously thought mentally weak, have been shown to be of sound mind and have been reclaimed from the opprobrium of suspicion" ("City Has Hopper for Measuring Mentality" 1918).

The same prospect of movement back to society was held out for both families and inmates of the Rome asylum as one of the benefits of Bernstein's parole. Indeed, the continuum of placement and the possibility of movement that it created became tools of coercion for compliance and control: if you behave, you can get out. One member of the board of supervisors at Rome, James Riggs, used glowing terms to describe the change of attitude that the colonies and paroles had created among the residents at Rome: "[t]he new spirit of ambition that the installation of this system has given to the children [*sic*] remaining in the institution[;] [t]he possibility that good behavior and effort may result in a graduation to a freer life, and one more like that lived by other human beings has relieved and brightened the dead, dreary atmosphere of hopelessness which must of necessity pervade a merely custodial institution" (1936, 44).

Movement along the continuum can occur in both directions, of course. Not only must the professional use the intricacies of more integrative placement to hold forth the promise of success, but he or she also needs the more segregative placement as an explanation of failure. Thus, Wallin used his category of "potential moron" as a clearinghouse. If the child made progress, then clearly the child was never truly feeble-minded and could be moved up along the continuum. However, if the child did not succeed, then the true nature of the mental defect was just as clear, and the appropriate setting was ready and waiting in the schools for the feeble-minded.

Parents: The Security of Sameness

It must be acknowledged that one of the most persistent and effective voices in defense of the continuum of placement was and is that group of parents and other family members of individuals with intellectual disabilities who feel that the most segregated placement options must be maintained. Of course, many families have lobbied long and hard to undo the continuum (D. Ferguson 1995; Macartney 2011; Snow 2010). Their effectiveness must be acknowledged. However, it is the familial support for the full range of placements that is most notable. Whether defending the institution as the only setting that can adequately support their adult sons and daughters, testifying before legislatures on behalf of sheltered workshops and day activity programs, or arguing with professionals who want to move their children to less restrictive educational settings, these parents are often viewed by the general public as the most credible voice among all of those speaking about preserving the continuum.

Why do so many families find the continuum a laudable arrangement? The reasons, I think, are complex and go beyond the logical confusion that we have been discussing. Certainly, these parents have taken to heart the assertions by professionals and administrators that conjoin the intensity of support and the separateness of setting. However, I suspect that many parents who defend the continuum are expressing a choice. They are choosing the security of sameness over the risk of difference. To achieve that sameness, these families accede to the professional control that is at the heart of the continuum. In terms of visual rhetoric, this choice is what Rosemarie Garland-Thomson might call a choice of the "diagnostic gaze" over the "social stare" (2001, 346). Better to have my child corralled with others with similar appearance, behavior, and skills under the medical supervision of the doctor or psychologist or teacher than to allow him or her to be singled out by the stares of normal society as visibly different and defective.

The choice relies on the promise of success and the illusion of movement that professionals have used so well. If I give you control of my child to help him or her escape the stares of the masses, then I must see the road back to society that we will follow as improvement occurs. In other words, the continuum of placement and its obscured logical structure have been the mechanism through which professionals have persuaded parents to accede to dominance by professionals and parents in the lives of their children (whether as students or adults). For most parents, as we have seen, the movement is seldom realized—an illusion. Yet the promise of such movement is powerful enough to maintain many families' support for the continuum over the past one hundred years.

Conclusion

For those of us who feel that the continuum of placements is one of the major obstacles to truly restructuring schools and society for intellectually disabled people, discovering that its history goes back more than one hundred years can be discouraging. However, it may also be true that reviewing this history helps us to understand more fully why the logic of the continuum seems so irrefutable to many. The history of the continuum of placement complicates our opposition but should not overwhelm it.

Again, we may turn to Bertrand Russell for encouragement on this point. After all, embedded in his very involved argumentation analyzing the logical structure of sentences such as "The present king of France is bald" is his worry that some readers may reject his theory of description (or "denotation," as he put it) because of "excessive complication" (1905, 493). He begs forgiveness from the readers and urges them to try and come up with something better before writing off his own effort. Such an attempt, he said, will provide convincing evidence that "whatever the true theory may be, it cannot have such a simplicity as one might have expected beforehand" (493).

However, maybe a historical view is just what is needed to break through the continuum logic's obfuscation. Understanding the ways in which even the earliest professionals in special education and institutional administration could quickly blend the notions of support and placement into a single assertion of inevitability may provide a hard-won clarity of how important our continued opposition to the continuum is. When it comes to the disability continuum, we have been fighting over the king's baldness for one hundred years. Perhaps it is time to quit trying to grow hair and just concentrate on overthrowing the mythical monarch.

7

Disabling Racial Repetition

ZANITA E. FENTON

Because of institutionalized racism, combined with institutionalized able-ism, extreme numbers of black boys receive inadequate education. Black children, especially boys, are disciplined, suspended, and expelled when it is least likely that their parents will challenge the outcome and when their parents are in poverty (Voltz 1998, 63, 64–66). When the parents of a black child are more affluent and generally more engaged in their child's educational welfare—often by challenging disciplinary measures—there is an increased likelihood that the child will be diagnosed as intellectu-ally disabled (formerly known as "mental retardation") or emotionally disturbed (Garda 2005, 1084). The effect of this dynamic is that black children are expelled whenever feasible. When it is less than practicable, as when the parents are more affluent, the child is placed in an educa-tional category that permits segregation from the general population and thereby positioned to receive inferior services and education.

The causes of the disproportionate representation of black male stu-dents in the intellectually disabled and emotionally disturbed categories are "numerous and controversial" (Garda 2005, 1093) and, most pertinent,

This chapter is a modified version of Zanita E. Fenton, "Disabling Racial Repeti-tion," *Law & Inequality* 31 (2012): 77–115. I am grateful to Arlene Kanter and Beth Ferri for inviting me to submit this chapter based on the remarks I presented at the Second City Conference at Syracuse University in 2009 and for encouraging development of this work. I also appreciate the careful reading of and comments on an earlier draft by my col-league Osamudia James as well as the editorial suggestions from Rachel Sayers.

persistent (Losen and Gillespie 2012, 16–18). This disproportional representation provides the "justifications" for continuation in segregated class
placements (Dunn 1968; Jordan 2005, 128; US Department of Education
2005, 48; Weatherspoon 2006, 28). As Daniel Losen and Kevin Welner
describe the situation, "Despite remarkable legislative achievements over
the last thirty-seven years, minority students remain doubly vulnerable to
discrimination. First, they tend to receive inequitable treatment within
school systems that remain segregated and unequal. Second, they are put
disproportionately at risk of receiving inadequate or inappropriate special
education services because of systemic problems with special education
identification and placement" (2001, 408).

The artificial categories of race, gender, and disability converge in
the creation of this crisis. In spite of efforts at reform, social biases in the
administration of education, in concert with legal structures that enable
these biases in the system, produce extremely unjustifiable and disproportionate outcomes (Losen and Orfield 2002a, xv, xxiii). The frustration is
that this is not a new circumstance, but one that continues to resurface,
reinvent, and repeat itself.

Compounding this problem is a long history of educators using
"punishment" as the primary approach to educating children with learning disabilities: "All too often, schools treat children whose emotional
disabilities lead them to behave inappropriately as bad children who
deserve to be punished rather than as children who need to learn to
understand and control their own behavior" (Glennon 1993, 325–26). In
a corresponding manner, teachers discipline black children, especially
boys, more than they discipline nonminority children for similar or
lesser behaviors (Cole and Blair 2006). This overdisciplining of minority
children, in combination with their disproportionate representation in
special education, reinforces the segregation and inferior education of
minority students, in particular black males (Jordan 2005, 129). "That
students of color are shunted into the special education ranks for disciplinary or other reasons is by no means a new phenomenon; in fact the
history of the symbiotic relationship of black students and such labeling
is long and protracted" (Pauken and Daniel 2000, 772). With this relationship, one can only wonder whether the labeling of a disproportionate

number of black students as intellectually disabled is just another means of punishment.

Many education scholars credit Lloyd Dunn's 1968 study "Special Education for the Mildly Retarded—Is Much of It Justifiable?" as first identifying as an issue of concern the disproportionate placement of black boys in low tracks or ability groups that are labeled as intellectually disabled or emotionally disturbed (Semmel, Gerber, and MacMillan 1994, 487). Since Dunn's study, numerous others have reached the same conclusion, each at a different point in time (e.g., Connor and Ferri 2005, 111; Ferri and Connor 2005b, 453; Hosp and Reschly 2004, 185; Parrish 2002, 15). Although there have been studies, changes in statutes, directives from case law, and discussions of best practices, none of them seems to change this ultimate conclusion. Even though Dunn's 1968 article continues to be widely cited (McLeskey 2004, 81–82), the evils he pointed out remain largely unaddressed in the forty-five years since its publication (Losen and Gillespie 2012, 4).

The legal origin of the modern manifestation of this crisis in the landscape of education is located in the case *Brown v. Board of Education* (1954, *Brown I*). *Brown I*, which prohibited legalized segregation but did not require actual equality, exemplifies how the law appears to promote profound change yet simultaneously enables a migration back to the original state of affairs (D. Bell 1992, 5–9; Ogletree 2004). This paradox is the primary theme of this essay: that which is seemingly designed to address a problem is instead used as a tool to subordinate and maintain the status quo. Education in the United States on the whole continues to be segregated and differentially delivered (Minow 2010, 26–27). On a basic level, *Brown I* eschewed meaningful equality in educational opportunity for the empty pragmatics of desegregation. It was also less than definitive in its dictates of equality; it may have affirmatively disavowed segregation, but it did not then take the next step of affirming the principles of meaningful equality. In truth, the malleability of the legal doctrine arising from *Brown I* has been a significant means of facilitating retreat from the hope of equality that the case promised. Legislative acts and other legal options continue in the same manner, being so open to manipulation that the intended solution is instead used as a tool for subordination (Garda 2005,

1090–93, 1100). In effect, *Brown I* may have opened the door for equality in education, but it did nothing to prevent the undermining of its own basic principles.

Comprehension of the reoccurring yet indefensible disproportionate labeling of black boys as intellectually disabled can be found in the labyrinth of structures perpetuated by laws, policies, and institutions that operate to ensure the continued subordinated status of groups based on race and disability, each status used to reinforce the other. The repetition of the disproportionate labeling of black boys as intellectually disabled and emotionally disturbed is only symptomatic of a range of social repetitions related to education that operate to continue subordination of certain groups, most often defined by race, class, and disability status. Punishment for marginalized students is too often preferred over inclusion and needs-based education, thus preconditioning their entry into the criminal justice system (A. Ferguson 2000, 230). There are also repetitions in the differential delivery and inferior quality of education. Racial segregation continues both between school districts and within single schools (Weatherspoon 2006, 9–13).

This crisis in education is situated at the juncture of social bias, inert education policy, and malleable legislation. This essay seeks to illuminate the interaction of some relevant variables that routinely return things to the original status. Part I engages in basic logic and light economic analyses to gain an understanding of how, despite the fact that realization of universal education would maximize individual potential to the benefit of society, education has become a focus of social competition. It also describes the role of *Brown I* in both promising educational reform and simultaneously allowing restoration of the original predicament. Part II examines the exploitation of the interaction between socially subordinated categories to perpetuate those forms of subordination. It first focuses on the role of case law and legislation in this ecosystem. It then discusses forms of social bias that serve as the basis for relevant actors' discretion in the administration and delivery of education. Part III focuses on the No Child Left Behind Act and the manner in which it has intensified miseducation of all children and deepened levels of inequality in education. To conclude, part IV laments the inadequacy of reform efforts that are sometimes more harmful than the subject of those reforms. It also ties miseducation to the other prevalent social disproportions for both persons of color and individuals with intellectual disabilities. It ends with a plea that future reform efforts struggle more intensely and effectively to accomplish the goal of equality in education.

Part I: The Economics of Social Competition

Education: A Tragedy of the Commons

Education is essential to the success and sustainability of almost every area of social accomplishment and standing (Geib et al. 2011, 4; Weatherspoon 2006, 8). Therefore, education is a primary means of breaking barriers to achievement. If we control for logistical practicalities and resource differentials, education might be viewed as being a good of infinite supply. It is conceivable that all individuals can receive an appropriate education. If, in fact, there is a limitless supply of education, it would seem that the relevant actors would have no incentive to perpetuate differential distribution.

However, because education as a variable is a key to entry to or maintenance of the various forums for social power, its access is jealously coveted: "[A study by McKinsey & Co.], . . . estimated [that] closing the gap in the U.S. between White students and their Black and Latino peers could increase annual GDP by as much as an additional $525 billion, or about 4 percent. In its report, McKinsey said existing achievement gaps have 'created the equivalent of a permanent, deep recession in terms of the gap between actual and potential output in the economy'" (Tomsho 2009).

Even where the greatest overall benefit would be achieved without competition, education becomes a catalyst for generating that competition.[1] Thus, what would otherwise be a non-zero-sum game becomes zero sum with multiple stakes, giving actors the impression that education as

---

1. Here the meaning of the term *competition* is intended to be pejorative, consistent with theories of social Darwinism (T. Leonard 2009), as contrasted with the assumed ambition for the efficient allocation of resources (A. Smith [1776] 1902).

a good is scarce and is therefore one for which they must compete. The resulting perceptions of scarcity of goods gives incentives to the actors "at the top" of one hierarchy to cooperate with other actors "at the top" of another as a means of hoarding this scarce good and thus ensuring continuation of both positions. Other actors consequently have incentive to get to the top and then to maintain the relevant hierarchy. What results is a multiparty form of the prisoner's dilemma: a situation where the quest for individual benefit leads to the least desirable results overall. More accurately, this situation is best described as a variation on the "tragedy of the commons" (Hardin 1968). That is, even though the greatest good would be accomplished through a greater distribution of appropriate education, individuals generally perceive the good to be a limited resource and thus act in their own self-interest.

This description is consistent with current observations by scholars within education. For instance, Beth Harry and Janette Klinger state that

> what has come to be known as the disproportionate representation of minorities in special education programs is the result of a series of social processes that, once set in motion, are interpreted as the inevitable outcomes of real conditions with children. These social processes do not occur by happenstance, or by the good or evil intentions of a few individuals. Rather, they reflect a set of societal beliefs and values, political agendas, and historical events that combine to construct identities that will become the official version of who these children are. (2006, 7)

Recognizing the interaction of the relevant socially constructed hierarchies is essential to understanding the magnitude of the problem at issue here. Disability is often misunderstood and stigmatized; race has historically been a disabling factor in education and in most other areas of life (Jordan 2005, 136–40). Society emphasizes the medical nature of disability, understanding difference as "scientific, genetic, or inherent" (Jordan 2005, 136–40; see also A. Ferguson 2000, 43). Individuals have only recently come to understand disability as socially constructed—in other words, that disability is defined as a function of an individual's impairment in context (Glennon 1995, 1243, 1301–7). This definition also easily functions for understanding race, gender, and sexual identity (Glennon 1993, 313–16). Each of these categories has been understood as a "natural" difference, grounded in the "scientific" and "genetic," and considered "inherent" and "immutable" (Cooper 2006). The socially constructed variant of disability interplays with the "disabling" social identities of race and gender in ways we need to understand better. "All people have multiple identities," states Susan Peters, and "[t]hese identities take on different meanings and importance in different contexts" (2006, 418). Each socially constructed category—especially in the context of education—has an impact on the success of and the process by which the system of education should address its own failings.

We must also be mindful that there is overlap in labels and categories when we discuss the lives and realities of real people. Black males' position in public education, particularly in conjunction with their being labeled as learning disabled, is at the crossroads of understanding this overlap, the impact on socially understood realities, and especially the failings of the current system of education: "By bringing into line through special education those who comply with ideological mandates, as well as by excluding and containing those who insist on staking their claim for recognition as human beings, these policies become the most effective way of supporting the racialization of disability and the disabilization of race in the ghettoes of special education" (Erevelles 2006, 1341). Put another way, "The dramatic racial disparities and negative consequences of identification as disabled occur in a society that claims to stand for racial equality but has historically had difficulty recognizing and remedying pervasive racial discrimination. Special education has been used as a tool of racial discrimination" (Glennon 1995, 1242). That is to say, stratifications based on race and those based on disability are used to reinforce each other.

It may be that the structure of any given hierarchy is invested in its own affirmation and continuation. Some might suggest that this would not be true in a Marxist society because the intent of Marxist ideology is the elimination of hierarchy; at least as Marx and Engels ([1848] 1964) saw it, their economic philosophy aimed to eliminate both capitalism and the exploitation of workers. Nonetheless, societies that have attempted to follow Marxist ideals have most often replaced gaping economic and class disparities with other sorts of privileges, such as political ones (Djilas 1957). It is also the case that where there are multiple lines of hierarchy, each coordinates with the others to maintain the social status quo. Indeed, the dynamic described within this essay suggests not only that all black children are presumed to have an intellectual disability, but that nonminority children labeled intellectually disabled are implicitly tainted with "racial inferiority" (Glennon 1995, 1276).

When we ask policymakers and educators to eliminate the disparities in education, we must confront the question about how to educate the educators (Marx and Engels 1978, 144). In a system of mutually sustaining hierarchies, altering only one element rather than redesigning the entire system wholesale (without more direction) allows readjustment and return to the original order. Single-focus reforms instead of systemic solutions account for the repetition in outcomes (Jordan 2005, 136–40). The familiarity of repetition emulates what is natural, providing a level of comfort and excusing society from analytic engagement in the underlying issues. Legal structures and the subordinating systems of race and disability coordinate to ensure the continuation of the relevant hierarchies (Fenton 1998, 2003, 2007; Losen and Welner 2001). Repetition of subordination then becomes cathartic, even therapeutic, for those in positions of power.

Persistent Inequality Enabled by Brown's Paradox

Brown I is most often cited and hailed for ending legalized racial segregation (even though *Loving v. Virginia* [1967] was not decided for another thirteen years) and opening educational opportunities for nonwhite children.[2] Education advocates also understand *Brown I* as a case that paved the way for the educational rights of children with disabilities (Engel 1991, 194). The ideal of a right to education for students with disabilities was furthered by the requirement of a free and appropriate public education, as identified in *Pennsylvania Association for Retarded Citizens v. Pennsylvania* (1972) and

---

2. Also consider *Mendez v. Westminister School District* (1946), which preceded *Brown I* and paved the way for desegregation for Latino students.

in *Mills v. Board of Education of the District of Columbia* (1972), which together mandated that no child, even one with behavioral problems, be excluded from public education for the reason of a disability. It is no wonder that *Brown I*, given the credit for such monumental progressions, has taken on an iconic appeal in the field of education.

However, *Brown I* has another side that completes the paradox. The Supreme Court in *Brown I* made a choice to eliminate state-sponsored segregation in education, but it did not mandate implementation of meaningful equality. It did not require the implementation of any means designed to accomplish real equality when it overturned *Plessy v. Ferguson* (1896). The "separate but equal" doctrine created by *Plessy* proved to be followed only with respect to required separation. Court challenges seeking to enforce the equality side of the doctrine (for example, *Sweatt v. Painter* [1950] and *McLaurin v. Oklahoma* [1950]) eventually led to the decision in *Brown I*, which overruled *Plessy* and ended legal segregation but did not require or ensure formal equality. The unstated assumption that the elimination of legal segregation would be sufficient to foster equality was idealistic and naive at best, but more likely a deliberate move to allow self-preservation of the state.[3]

The aftermath of *Brown I*, in which attention focused on desegregation but without any priority given to equality, ended up providing neither equality nor desegregation (Garda 2005, 1072; Ogletree 2004; Rosenberg 1991). An opinion from the second phase of the *Brown v. Board of Education* case, known as *Brown II*, enabled the delay tactics of the opponents of desegregation by accepting compliance with the principles identified in *Brown I* only "with all deliberate speed" (at 300). The failure of busing as a remedy for segregation is represented by the outcomes after *Swann v. Charlotte-Mecklenburg Board of Education* (1970). In approving busing as one means to effectuate integration, the *Swann* Court severely

---

3. The need to improve the international image of the United States as a moral authority during the ideological battles of the Cold War was more influential in accomplishing the *Brown I* decision than genuine commitment to the educational needs of segregated minority students (D. Bell 2004, 60–68; Dudziak 2000, 107–9).

undermined the efficacy of school district rezoning as a means of desegregation by deferring to localities' judgments instead of demanding tangible results. Equality in education was further undermined by the Court's decision in *San Antonio v. Rodriguez* (1973), which refused to characterize education as a fundamental right. By failing to identify education as a fundamental right, the Court created system-wide hurdles—for democracy, for individual liberty and free speech, for work and self-sufficiency, and for equality (*Brown I*, at 493; *Rodriguez*, at 112 [Marshall, J., dissenting]; *Grutter v. Bollinger* 2003, at 332). These very hurdles have been instrumental in contributing to and perpetuating the homeostasis of inequality in the system that created them. In addition, although the Court focused on desegregation, it not only deferred to state control but went further in its deference to local financing schemes that relied only on the local tax base, ignoring the relevance of class or affluence. This deference enabled a system of differential education—in this instance having the greatest impact on children in impoverished communities. And *San Antonio v. Rodriguez* (1973) and *Milliken v. Bradley* (1974) are even credited with prompting one means of resegregation, "white flight," whereby whites flee urban concentrations of the black population by moving to suburban and commuter communities (Crowder 2000, 223). Indeed, because education and residential choices continue to be closely associated with each other (Lankford and Wyckoff 2006, 232), we continue to be profoundly racially segregated in both (Minow 2010, 5–9).

Thus, in the years after *Brown I*, subsequent court decisions have effectively made quality education a scarce good, intensified the competition over education, and undermined the original social objectives. *Brown I* itself, along with its progeny, provided the very means to undermine its own core principles.

Part II: Coordinated Subordination

Segregation Redux: Tracking

Specialized classes were originally created as a means of giving focused attention to students with a learning disability. Tracking emerged as a result of the practice of classifying and labeling students so that they could receive this benefit (Ferri and Connor 2005b, 457). That is, once a student was labeled—whether within the special education categories or the gifted student category—that student was placed in an academic "track" based on that label (Losen 1999, 517). Thus, tracking proceeded and helped labels to become permanent, often stigmatizing students during their academic careers and throughout life (Losen 1999, 522, 538). A secondary result in the aftermath of *Brown I* was that the same tracking intended to give greater attention to the needs of students with learning disabilities became an early means of racial resegregation within a school (Losen 1999, 521). Tracking not only resegregated students within a single school—accomplished through the overrepresentation of the students of color in the special education tracks and simultaneous underrepresentation in the gifted tracks—but also found a new way to stigmatize students as outside the mainstream, reinstituting effects that were supposed to be remedied by the decision in *Brown I*—a case that spent a significant portion of its opinion decrying the stigmatizing effects of racial segregation in education. The Court explained how separating students solely based on race makes the students feel inferior: "[Segregation] may affect their hearts and minds in a way unlikely ever to be undone" (at 494). The Court further emphasized that feelings of inferiority deprive students of the motivation to learn and thus impede their mental and educational progress (at 494).

Through tracking, ableism together with racism created a practice that systematically hurt black students labeled with potential disabilities. *Hobson v. Hansen* (1967), thirteen years after *Brown I*, was the first major case to raise questions about placement in special education. Judge Skelly Wright ruled that using test scores to group students into "tracks" was unconstitutional because it discriminated against blacks and the poor, extending the ruling in *Brown I* to both de facto and de jure segregation. Similarly, in *Diana v. State Board of Education* (1970) the plaintiffs were Spanish-speaking students who were placed in a class for mildly intellectually disabled students after they had scored low on an IQ test given to them in English. The Court ruled that Spanish-speaking children should be retested in their native language to avoid errors in placement. When the students retook the IQ test in Spanish, the scores of eight of the nine students resulted in a classification of nondisabled (Connor and Ferri 2005, 108). *Larry P. v. Riles* (1984) was an expansion of the ruling in *Diana*, holding that schools are responsible for providing tests that do not discriminate on the basis of race. However, less than a decade later, in the class-action case *Parents in Action on Special Education (PASE) v. Hannon* (1980), the Court interpreted a qualitatively similar test to that in *Larry P.* and found little evidence of bias in the test items.[4]

Though *Brown I* is viewed as opening the door of educational rights for children with disabilities, it was not until 1966 that Congress first addressed the education of students with disabilities when it amended the Elementary and Secondary Education Act of 1965 (ESEA) to establish grants to assist states in efforts to educate handicapped children. Cases such as *Hobson*, *Diana*, and *Larry P.*, which identified discriminatory practices in education affecting students in poverty and those with disabilities, were decided roughly at the same time as busing was attempted as a practical remedy for desegregation. Neither the discrimination cases nor the use of busing was ultimately effective in altering patterns of segregation. Resistance to racial integration was both intense and multifaceted. Disability classifications became one more means of effectuating the continuation of social hierarchy.

Also during this time, the Education for All Handicapped Children Act (EAHCA) was enacted in 1975, replacing the ESEA; it required placement of special education students in the "least restrictive environment" (LRE) and permitted educators to segregate students according to disability classification. By labeling and placing students in various special education classes or tracks, educators acted in accordance with the EAHCA's

---

4. One of the several tests used by the schools in *Larry P.* was the Wechsler test, and the test used in *PASE* was a revised version of the Wechsler. The unrevised version of the Wechsler test was standardized based only on white children, whereas the revised Wechsler was standardized based on a population that included 305 black children out of the 2,200 total children tested (Harry and Klinger 2006).

ambiguous LRE directive (Ware 2006b, 1053). An increase in the use of testing to determine students' IQs served to "justify the academic tracking of students according to 'abilities'" (Connor and Ferri 2005, 107). Tracking created a "'systematic form of racial segregation within schools,'" and labeling was "used to resegregate classrooms along race and class lines" (Ferri and Connor 2005b, 459, quoting Oakes et al. 1997, 492). The negative results simply doubled: the stigmatizing effects of a low IQ score and the resulting low-track classification are long lasting (Losen 1999, 522).

Then in the 1980s, in response to the tracking that had become pervasive, some parents and educators called for efforts to reintegrate the disabled students into general education classes. This effort is known as "mainstreaming" (Ware 2006b, 1053). Mainstreaming in many obvious ways mirrors desegregation efforts. *Pennsylvania Association for Retarded Children v. Pennsylvania* also expressed a preference for mainstreaming similar to Congress's preference in the EAHCA. Just as in desegregation, policymakers should be mindful that such efforts are empty if they are solely about physical location. In other words, mainstreaming has been another attempt to desegregate classrooms without substantive reform—again.

The subjectivity of the intellectual disability classifications perpetuates a vicious trend in which those with more mild classifications are still categorized together with the most severe cases. There are five types of retardation classifications: borderline, mild, moderate, severe, and profound (Field and Sanchez 1999, 31). The vast majority of those diagnosed with an intellectual disability, 89 percent, are lumped into the "mild" category, which is the most subjective and allows for the most discretion (Field and Sanchez 1999, 33). "What is more disturbing than the law's focus, or the number of cases devoted to one group or another, is that current rules often treat degrees of retardation together, as though differences become slight once the 'retardation' label is attached" (Field and Sanchez 1999, 33). If the goal of classification is to identify how to tailor education to each group's needs, this goal is not served by lumping most of the mentally handicapped into one group. Not only does this undermine the efficacy of special education, but it reinforces the stigmatizing effect of the intellectual disability label.

Another troubling fact is that minority students who are labeled with a disability are more likely to be placed into a more restrictive educational situation than their white peers with the same label (Ferri and Connor 2005b, 458). One article concludes, "Minority students deemed eligible for special education are significantly more likely than their white counterparts to wind up in substantially separate settings with a watered-down curriculum" (Losen and Welner 2001, 427). Another points out that "'increased time in the regular education classroom is largely attributable to a special needs student's race'" (Connor and Ferri 2005, 116, quoting Fierros and Conroy 2002, 53).

In the United States, students whose native language is not English and those from poor socioeconomic backgrounds tend to score lower on IQ tests, yet many of these children do not have a mental handicap (Field and Sanchez 1999, 23). The American Association on Intellectual and Developmental Disabilities (AAIDD, formerly the American Association on Mental Retardation) requires that a person have both a low IQ score and "significant[ly] limit[ed]" adaptive skills in order to qualify as intellectually disabled. Such skills include "communication, self-care, home living, social skills, community use, self-direction, health and safety, functional academics, leisure, and work" (Field and Sanchez 1999, 29). The adaptive skills requirement is a subjective one and is easily judged based on bias and subject to teacher discretion. Further, research shows that subjectivity makes its way into all aspects of the evaluation process, including which students to test, the test used, and how the results are interpreted (University of California at Los Angeles 2012). Thus, the AAIDD's attempt to make intellectual disability/mental retardation classifications dependent solely on IQ tests is in actuality ineffective because the subjective "social skill" criterion can be easily manipulated.

Tracking has become a means of stigmatizing children; it sends messages of inferiority, instills low self-esteem, and lowers expectations for specific children (Oakes 1985, 8). It reasserts segregation in a different form, replicating differential education and delivery of services based primarily on racial classification, but now enabling "inclusion" in these classifications of the poor and the learning disabled. Most significantly, however, it continues the legacy of stigma and miseducation.

Punishing Disability

In 1975, the EAHCA and the regulations implementing it provided for a free, appropriate public education (FAPE) for all handicapped children. In *Smith v. Robinson* (1984), the Supreme Court found that Congress intended the EAHCA to be the "exclusive avenue" for disabled students to claim their right to equal access in public education. In response to this ruling, Congress passed the Handicapped Children's Protection Act of 1986 (HCPA), which amended the EAHCA to allow for the granting of "reasonable attorneys' fees" under the law. In 1987, the Court in *Honig v. Doe* (1988) found that the expulsion of a learning disabled student violated the EAHCA's "stay-put" clause—which requires states to educate all handicapped children, including those whose disabilities cause disruptive behavior—by holding that students with disabilities may not be expelled without due process (Minnesota House of Representatives 2002). The earlier decision in *Mills v. D.C. Board of Education* (1972) laid the groundwork for the decision in *Honig*. The *Mills* Court's ruling extended the legal right to public education to all handicapped children in the DC area, and the "zero-reject policy," a core principle of the FAPE requirement in the EAHCA of 1975, prevented schools from expelling students with handicaps because of behavioral problems (Sailor and Stowe 2003). This ruling also requires school districts to provide adequate funding of special education services for handicapped children. Unfortunately, but perhaps predictably, "[i]n the years since the Supreme Court's decision in Honig, schools have continued to advocate for the authority to punish students with emotional disabilities rather than [to treat] their behavior as an issue to be addressed through an [Individualized Educational Program]" (Glennon 1993, 330). In 1990, Congress also passed the Americans with Disabilities Act (ADA), a civil rights law that prohibits discrimination based on disability. It is intended to provide protections for people with disabilities similar to those provided for reasons of race, religion, sex, national origin, and other characteristics under the Civil Rights Act of 1964. In 1997, the Individuals with Disabilities Education Act of 1990 (IDEA) received significant amendments, including a requirement that education agencies provide parents with the opportunity to use mediation to resolve disputes over their child's FAPE. Evaluating student behavior is complex and inherently subjective, and it is unfortunately apparent that these points of subjectivity are not resolved in the favor of black students often enough.[5] One must wonder whether these standards will ever have a meaningful effect.

In 2004, IDEA was once again amended by the Individuals with Disabilities Education Improvement Act of 2004 (IDEIA). This version revised the requirements for evaluating children with learning disabilities and added more concrete provisions relating to discipline of special education students. Unfortunately, Robert Garda notes, "[t]he IDEIA cannot effectively reduce minority overrepresentation because it does not limit the bias that accompanies highly subjective identification practices" (1995, 1100). Thus, even the most recent of reforms enable their own subversion. As Floyd Weatherspoon points out, "Unfortunately, the IDEA has been at times a double-edged sword. . . . It has been overly used to label and disproportionately place African-American males in special education programs and out of mainstream educational instruction. At the same time, African-American males with mental disabilities have been suspended and expelled from school in lieu of receiving services required by the IDEA" (2006, 29).

Out-of-school suspensions of black male students occur at nearly three times the rate for other students (Losen and Gillespie 2012, 6). These suspensions in many cases lead to students ending their school careers before graduation (Holzman 2010, 35). Even when engaging in similar behavior as other students, black students, especially males, are "disciplined at rates that far exceed" their numbers in the relevant population (Monroe 2006, 102). In fact, no convincing studies have been published to show that black males have higher rates of unruly behavior than other students (Monroe 2006, 104). Educators using discipline in the place of

5. These decisions are for the most part individually made by teachers, social workers, and psychologists. It is not possible to adequately study or understand the extent to which decision makers' judgments are conscious as opposed to subconsciously influenced. In either case, institutional structures, including legal frameworks, set the stage.

education locate responsibility for negative outcomes with the individual student rather than with the school or the system of education. "The disproportionate suspension of black males," argue Maurice Taylor and Gerald Foster, "falls in line with the other discriminatory practices protected, supported, and obfuscated by educational policies" (2007, 504).

Poor parents are less likely to be involved in their children's school-related matters than wealthier parents (Yan 1999, 7). Moreover, educators are aware that involvement by poor parents is less likely and that minorities are more likely to be poor and must spend more of their time on "basic survival needs." "[I]t seems reasonable that these parents may not always be physically, emotionally, or cognitively available to participate as vigorously in the education of their children as educators—and, perhaps, they themselves—would desire" (Voltz 1998, 65). Thus, children who are both from poverty and from minority backgrounds are the most likely to be expelled with little or no challenge from their parents, and educators can thus use this method to discipline children with impunity.

The wealthier the parents are, the more likely they are to be involved in their children's education (Yan 1999, 7). In this case, however, the focus on a "medical" problem ostensibly based in science deflects minority parents' attention away from the more familiar fight against racism. In addition, when educators identify the "problem" as a diagnosable disorder, they locate the problem in the student rather than with the system or in the overall approach to education (Jordan 2005, 140). Thus, even when the multilayered challenges of poverty do not predetermine the expulsion of minority students, racial stereotyping of the child as well as social realities make it more likely that minority parents will accept directives from authority figures, resulting in the acceptance of inferior education for a disproportionate number of their children. "Discrimination on the basis of ability doesn't receive the same amount of protection as discrimination based on race, religion, or ethnicity" (Sailor and Stowe 2003, 17), effectively allowing disability discrimination to be a proxy for continuing racial discrimination and perhaps also explaining why it lacks institutional priority.

The influence of race is apparently more significant than poverty in trends for labeling intellectually disabled students. "Recent studies show that overrepresentation [in special education] persists even when poverty is taken into account[,] and, alarmingly, African-American students are in fact more likely to be identified as eligible [for placement in special education] in upper- and high-income schools" (Garda 2005, 1088; see also Losen and Welner 2001, 415, and Oswald, Coutinho, and Best 2002, 8). As a school district's wealth increases, the more likely it is that black students, especially males, will be labeled intellectually disabled. One can only wonder if in fact labeling black males as having an intellectual disability is a form of punishment that furthers the tacit objective of educating as few black male children as possible. The influence of race is apparently distinct from the influence of poverty in trends for labeling mental retardation (Losen and Welner 2001, 415). To put a fine point on the confluence, "when race and gender are disaggregated for students with disabilities, we see the highest rates for male children of color with disabilities" (Losen and Gillespie 2012, 35).

Punishing Lessons

In educational settings, it seems that punishment is preferred over education, especially for black boys. This is the case even though it is proven that low levels of education have a high correlation to high-risk behaviors leading to delinquency or adult prison (Weatherspoon 2006, 5). Even though it has also been proven that education and opportunity are essential for lasting rehabilitation, educational instruction and opportunity, especially for individuals with disabilities, are limited or lacking in prison settings (Morrison and Epps 2002, 225). Catherine Geib and her colleagues point out that "because of the mismatch between the philosophies of punishment and education, correctional educational services often lack the sufficient tools and qualified staff to develop, implement, and sustain educational reforms consistent with the delivery of the special education and related services mandated by law under both the No Child Left Behind Act of 2001 (NCLB) and the IDEA. As a result, such well-intentioned legislative goals promoting high-quality educational services for all children often fail to reach the children behind bars" (2011, 4). Notably, it is cheaper to educate prisoners than to incarcerate them (Torre and Fine 2005, 591).

It has been pointed out often that "[p]oor educational opportunity leads to high-risk behaviors such as dropping out of school, abusing substances, and becoming involved in delinquent activities" (Young, Phillips, and Nasir 2010, 203). Given the high rates of disciplinary actions as well as the labeling of black male students as intellectually disabled, both of which lead to poor educational opportunities and outcomes, it is little surprise that the individuals incarcerated in juvenile correctional facilities are disproportionately male, African American, and poor and have an intellectual disability—often undiagnosed (Leone and Meisel 1997, 2; Leone et al. 1995; Morrison and Epps 2002; Osher, Woodruff, and Sims 2002; Winters 1997; Young, Phillips, and Nasir 2010, 203). Catherine Geib and her colleagues provide the startling statistic that "rates of disabilities among incarcerated youth are estimated at 30–70 percent, as compared to 10–13 percent in the general population" (2011, 4).

Individuals younger than twenty-one who are incarcerated are entitled to an education, as required first under the EAHCA (Lewis, Schwartz, and Ianacone 1988, 66) and currently under the IDEA. But despite the requirement that a FAPE be given to all children, "youth entering the juvenile justice system, . . . eligible for special education services, often do not receive these services while in detention[,] resulting in an unwarranted reduction of services" (Geib et al. 2011, 5). Juvenile justice practitioners often lack training and even awareness of the legal rights of juveniles with disabilities and are therefore ill equipped to provide proper services.

Rehabilitation is often understood as a key objective of incarceration, especially for juvenile and youth offenders. Effective education is a logical and proven means of accomplishing this goal. "Programs in juvenile corrections should promote the academic and social competence of their students and ensure that they reenter their communities better prepared to assume roles as students, workers and citizens" (Leone and Meisel 1997, 5). Unfortunately, the "policies of incapacitation, control, retribution, and punishment," their related practices, and the disparity between the philosophies of punishment and education undermine the implementation and realization of such objectives (Geib et al. 2011, 5; Young, Phillips, and Nasir 2010, 204). The structure and organization of prisons and the constant presence of prison staff mean that "a disciplinary presence [is] a part of classroom life" (Young, Phillips, and Nasir 2010, 209). The restrictions affect both basic and modern means of learning, from pencils to computers, in favor of concerns over safety and control (Young, Phillips, and Nasir 2010, 209).

Perhaps because of the transient nature of the prison population and the variable levels of the incarcerated students' academic ability and grade levels, the rigor of instruction is relatively low in prisons. The result is that schoolwork in prison is easier than schoolwork in schools, which enables incarcerated students to earn much-needed credits but does not prepare them for re-entry into more rigorous educational environments once released. "The inadequacies of educational programs in correctional facilities provide little hope for juveniles in transition back into the general population. Many are released, still lacking the necessary skills for success, only to return to juvenile or adult correctional facilities" (Young, Phillips, and Nasir 2010, 209).

Part III: Miseducation and Inequality

No Child Left Behind: The Emperor Has No Clothes

The NCLB is the current reauthorization of the ESEA, which Congress has reauthorized every five years since its enactment in 1965. It is the most far-reaching federal legislation affecting education ever passed by Congress, funding primary and secondary education, while explicitly forbidding a national curriculum. It emphasizes equal access to education, establishes high standards and accountability, and aims to reduce achievement gaps among students by providing fair and equal opportunities. The NCLB authorizes funds for professional development, instructional materials, and educational programs and encourages parental involvement initiatives. It applies to students with disabilities (Sailor and Stowe 2003, 9). In fact, Section 1421 requires a school district to provide a FAPE to each qualified child with a disability who is in the school district's jurisdiction regardless of the nature or severity of the child's disability.

NCLB requires all government-run schools receiving federal funding, through ESEA Title I, to administer an annual statewide standardized test to all students. It mandates that states use "the same academic assessments

. . . to measure the achievement of all children" (§1111 State Plans(b)3(C)(i)). The students' scores are used to determine whether the school has taught the students well. Schools that receive this federal funding must make adequate yearly progress in test scores (Karp 2004, 54–55). NCLB imposes sanctions, "corrective actions," "reconstitutions," and "restructurings" for when "targets" are missed and thus gradually requires student transfers to other schools (along with a loss of funding) and possible state takeover or private management (Karp 2004, 54–55).

This accountability structure requires the biggest gains from the lowest-performing schools, which have the students who need the most assistance. States with the "highest standards will have the most schools wanting" greater support to educate all of its children, even with high relative levels of performance, and states that use the most ambitious tests and high standards will experience the greatest failure rates (Darling-Hammond 2004, 10).

NCLB's complicated accountability structure is predicted to produce between 85 and 99 percent of the nations' "failing" public schools within the next few years (Darling-Hammond 2007, 11, 14). Added to this large problem, "there is growing evidence that the law's strategy for improving schools may, paradoxically, reduce access to education for the most vulnerable students" (Darling-Hammond 2007, 11, 14). This compounds the damage of existing structural inequalities that make it likely that minority students from impoverished backgrounds are punished and expelled, whereas those from more affluent backgrounds are labeled with an intellectual disability and provided inferior education. With the NCLB incentive structure, this pattern is intensified as schools that manage to raise test scores often "lose" large numbers of low-scoring students, mostly black and Latino students when "exclusionary policies [are] used to hold back, suspend, expel or counsel out students in order to boost test scores" (Darling-Hammond 2007, 11, 14).

Because not meeting test-score targets is tied to sanctioning of schools, NCLB gives schools incentives to punish and ultimately expel students who are struggling or on whom the system has already given up. Stan Karp summarizes the NCLB's fundamental problems: "Tests alone do very little to increase the capacity of schools to deliver better educational services. . . . The keys to school improvement are not standards and tests, but teachers and students. And while teachers and students need a complicated mix of support, resources, motivation, pressure, leadership, and professional skills to succeed, the idea that this mixture can be provided by test-driven sanctions is simply wrong and is not supported by any educational research or real world experience" (2004, 58). NCLB is destroying independent and innovative thought, agrees Linda Darling-Hammond, because "serious intellectual activities . . . are being driven out of many [US] schools by the tests [it] promote[s]" (2007, 14).

The NCLB's "one-size-fits-all" approach is not a legitimate means of providing meaningful education for any child. Diversity means strength for the United States in a competitive world. Maximizing individual talents ought to be the goal, not dwelling on differences or "deficiencies." "Yet," as Karp points out, "the goal of equality in test scores for all student groups, including special education and bilingual students, contrasts sharply with the widespread inequality that is tolerated or even promoted, by federal policy in many other areas. . . . A closer look at this contradiction sheds light on why critics see NCLB as part of a calculated political campaign to use achievement gaps to label schools as failures, without providing the resources and strategies needed to overcome them" (2004, 53–54).

The core of a democratic society ought to be education of its citizens and future citizens. "In such a society, teachers would not merely employ the curriculum, pedagogy, and assessments as determined by others but would become educative leaders engaged in deliberation with the community" (Hursh 2004, 515).

NCLB Vouchers, Funding, and Resources: "Papa's Got a Brand New Bag"

One of the many negative results of the NCLB is a constriction of funding.[6] As Darling-Hammond points out, "Where states have replaced

---

6. The reference in this section's title is of course to James Brown's "Papa's Got a Brand New Bag" (King Records, 1965).

investing with testing . . . students are forced to attend underresourced schools where they lack the texts, materials, qualified teachers, computers, and other necessities for learning. In lieu of resources, the state offers tests, which are used to hold students back if they do not reach benchmarks (a practice found to increase later dropout rates but not to improve achievement) and to deny them diplomas, which in today's economy is the equivalent of denying access to the economy and to a productive life" (2007, 22).

A further problem is that the NCLB authorizes the use of both public and private vouchers, which enables the depletion of public funds for general education as well as for special education, further ravaging those schools that serve students in the greatest need (Darling-Hammond 2007, 14).

According to Wayne Sailor and Matt Stowe, "Under Title I, section 1116(b)(E) of the NCLB, schools, beginning with the 2002–2003 school year[,] must offer public school choice to their students if those schools are in their first or second year of school improvement, in corrective action, or in a planning year for restructuring" (2003, 9). In addition, they say, "NCLB is the first federally supported (though not mandated) program that allows federal funds to purchase educational services from private entities" (2). However, the rights afforded by the IDEA as a general rule do not extend to children with disabilities who take advantage of voucher programs (2–3). Section 504 of the Rehabilitation Act of 1973 and the ADA still applies to the administration of the program, but not to the activities of private schools (Sailor and Stowe 2003). The inapplicability of the IDEA to voucher programs run through private schools is inconsistent when one considers that the IDEA allows the use of public funds to finance private-school education (1) in cases where parents find an appropriate private program in response to a public school's failure to provide a FAPE and (2) in cases where a private-school placement is identified as appropriate according to an Individualized Education Plan (IEP) as mandated by the IDEA (Sailor and Stowe 2003, 11). Regardless of how the placement occurs, private schools are not bound by the IDEA's requirements; private schools are free to abandon the LRE requirement "almost entirely" (Sailor and Stowe 2003, 24). Students with disabilities using a general education voucher will not rely upon the IDEA in private schools (Sailor and Stowe

2003, 14). "Because vouchers can only cover a portion of costs of special education over and above the cost of private school tuition in many cases, particularly for students with moderate, low-incidence, and severe disabilities, such programs may benefit only the affluent who can afford to supplement vouchers to cover actual costs" (Sailor and Stowe 2003, 9).

In addition to the issues of relative wealth, parental participation in a child's education becomes less likely as affluence decreases (Harry and Anderson 1994, 611; Voltz 1998). Parental participation is essential for the success of students legitimately identified as disabled, but even in cases where nonaffluent parents are able to get their disabled child into a private school through the use of vouchers, "marginalized groups . . . do not have sufficient market power to influence the school [regarding IDEA compliance]. Without expanded protections, individuals in a dissatisfied minority will have no recourse except to pull their students out of the private school" (Voltz 1998, 63), making it even less likely that these children will benefit from these programs.

Even worse, for children who cannot or do not seek to participate in the voucher programs, public-school districts now have depleted funds and looted coffers but are still obligated to provide a FAPE to all children (Voltz 1998, 63). This reality is in conjunction with the growing evidence that "a large-scale universal voucher program would not generate substantial gains in overall student achievement and that it could well be detrimental to many disadvantaged students" (Ladd 2002, 4).

Florida created an alternative to a general voucher program for students with disabilities: the John M. McKay Scholarship Program for Students with Disabilities. The McKay program is a statewide voucher program aimed at providing the resources necessary for disabled students to attend a different public school or even a private school if they so choose (Sailor and Stowe 2003, 3). McKay scholarships are available to any Florida public-school student who because of his or her disability was assigned an IEP during the prior year (Sailor and Stowe 2003, 10). The amount of the scholarship is equal to the amount the student would have received in the public school to which the student is assigned or the amount of the chosen private school's tuition and fees, whichever is less (Sailor and Stowe 2003, 3).

The McKay program appears to be successful, at least in that parents who choose to participate in the program, regardless of race, are well informed of their choices and make the effort to research the resources available (Weidner and Herrington 2006, 43). It also does not pose the same issues for disabled students that are structurally endemic in general voucher programs. Nevertheless, the program still has some major shortcomings. It seems to have provided motivation for the creation of new schools to serve the needs of disabled students (Sailor and Stowe 2003, 28). This trend proceeds in the face of scientific documentation supporting the provision of educational services to disabled students in the LRE and inclusive of other opportunities (Sailor and Stowe 2003, 29–30). "The end result of large-scale voucher extensions to students with disabilities could lead to a new kind of institutionalization at public expense" (Sailor and Stowe 2003, 29–30).

Furthermore, NCLB's authorization of funding for charter schools, "school choice," and voucher programs implicitly endorses private residential as well as educational racial segregation (Lankford and Wyckoff 2006, 232). The Supreme Court cases *Rodriguez* and *Milliken* were modes of retrenchment after *Brown I* and *II*, encouraging "white flight" and permitting the return or continuation of segregated residential patterns and, hence, geographically induced racial segregation in education.

The "bundling" of education and residential location is the continuing custom. NCLB supports and furthers this reality in several ways. "Choice" facilitates white parents' option to move away, further decimates funding for schools in urban areas, and enables the privatization of education by removing it from state and federal regulation (Ladd 2002, 8).

[E]stimates suggest that the school choices afforded to parents through private school choice and residential location importantly affect the racial segregation of schools. . . . Whites confronted with urban public schools with even moderate concentrations of African-Americans or Latinos are much more likely to opt for private schools or choose suburban public schools. When they do choose private schools they choose those with lower concentrations of nonwhites. In combination, the effect is to make schools more racially segregated. As a result of this sorting directly related to race, urban public schools, which already have substantially higher concentrations of nonwhites than their suburban counterparts, have become even more segregated. (Lankford and Wyckoff 2006, 232)

"Choice" is a means to return to social choice grounded in stereotype, endorsed by *Plessy v. Ferguson,* and maintained by the state through Jim Crow segregation (Alexander 2010).[7] Furthermore, the legislative move to prefer private choices over the public good and ultimately toward the privatization of schools further disenfranchises marginalized and subordinated populations.[8]

NCLB's rhetorical posture is difficult to disagree with; however, its operation and effects reaffirm and intensify differential delivery of educational services, racial segregation in education and residence, and the closure of schools in the neighborhoods where they are most needed (Darling-Hammond 2007, 12–14). The unfortunate effects of the focus on testing are the removal of marginal students from school altogether and an education lacking in broad substance or critical thinking for the rest (Darling-Hammond 2004, 18–19). The rhetoric and "ideals" that enabled the passage of NCLB also enable the state to avoid students' real problems and real educational needs (Darling-Hammond 2004, 25–26). We are shamefully in an era when the rhetoric of exclusion need only be thinly veiled and the structure of inequality so transparent as to confirm everything else stated in this essay.

7. Michelle Alexander (2010) makes a powerful case that Jim Crow continues to exist systematically through the operation of the criminal justice system. She states, however, that she is addressing only one aspect of the broader picture.

8. The federal government's direction in supporting some citizens' "social choices" over other citizens' civil rights is also part of a historical "repetition" reflected in cases such as *United States v. Cruikshank* (1876), *United States v. Harris* (1883), and the Slaughter-House cases (1873). However, elucidation of this point is better undertaken elsewhere.

Part IV: Reform

Solutions? Consequences

The harmful and destabilizing effects of NCLB are real and widespread. Perhaps because these effects are felt by more than the minority population of students or the population of students with disabilities, either independently or combined (Bell 1980), and perhaps because NCLB is a version of the ESEA that imposes more requirements on states, undermining their control in matters of education, it has encountered criticism from multiple sectors. Several states have recently sought waivers from the NCLB's harsh requirements (Bevins 2012; Burton 2012; Garrow 2011; McDaniel 2012; Slayton 2012), at least one suing in court for relief (Gordon 2005). As each of these waivers is granted, we can hope for the wholesale dismantling of NCLB in favor of a more effective act that encourages universal education. However, given the track record of miseducation and noneducation for boys of some communities, educators, policymakers, and the authors of legislation must be more vigilant in finding a means of honestly meeting educational objectives for all members of society.

We have seen judicial decisions that identify the problem and fashion solutions—from *Brown I* to *Mills* and beyond. We have seen legislation and amendments, from the EAHCA to the IDEA and NCLB, "intending" to identify the problem and create solutions. Despite these solutions, we continue to have disproportional representation of black male students in the categories of intellectually disabled and emotionally disturbed. No "solution" will work if we do not own up to the core of the problem—competition over the modes of success—as well as to the combining effects of the tools for maintaining the status quo, racism and ableism.

The approaches to which we look for solutions have several structural flaws. The continued results of litigation as well as the legislative attempts to fix the problem and to direct the focus onto the individual often deflect responsibility away from the system (Hahn 1988, 39–40). Education and civil rights cases have focused on remedying past discrimination, not on preventing future harm or inequities. In its backward-looking posture, the law seeks to form a rigid structure to provide consistency rather than providing useful flexibility or experimentation for good. Solutions intended to address students' needs have instead become additional tools for subordination. Policies that are intended, on their face, to assist students are instead used as additional tools for oppression (Garda 2005, 1081–85).

Pre-referral interventions, in which teachers implement intervention strategies for six weeks prior to the decision to place a student in special education (Garda 2005, 1127), as well as other efforts in making labels and eligibility determinations more objective can be successful in decreasing minority overrepresentation in special education programs. These approaches are ironically the direct result of a forty-six-year-old case, *Lee v. Macon County Board of Education* (1967), in Macon County, Alabama. The Supreme Court found that African American students in the state were three times more likely to be labeled intellectually disabled than white students, and in 2000 it ordered that a pre-referral process be initiated pursuant to the long-standing consent decree in the 1967 case (Garda 2005, 1126–27). By 2003, pre-referral intervention resulted in zero referrals of African American students (Garda 2005, 1127). Despite this success, the current IDEA does not require pre-referral interventions, nor does it provide real incentive for their use; they are purely voluntary, leaving the prevailing subjectivity in place. Ultimately, understanding the landscape of general education is an important backdrop for discussions of disability education, especially as it intersects with racial concerns. Alterations to education for disabled students as well as changes designed to provide integration in education seem only to be Band-Aids on a greater problem. Mainstreaming, just like desegregation, works only if it focuses on good teaching, not just on integration and assimilation as the magic salve (Weber 2009, 151). "It is through effective regular education, not special education, that we may begin to see the racial disparities reduced" (Glennon 1995, 1335). Studies show that all students, including those with learning disabilities, benefit from the same type of instruction and learning activities, broadly speaking, regardless of gender or race (Bowe 2000; Haycock 1998, 62–63). Perhaps if we were to focus on a good education for all children, minor differences or needs might be accommodated (Voltz, Brazil, and Ford 2001, 25–29). "[M]inor modifications to content, delivery, and instruction," says Robert Garda, "are not special education, but rather good pedagogy for all students. Good teaching requires adjustments to classroom instruction to meet the varying individual needs of all students" (1995, 1122). And Darling-Hammond notes that "NCLB contains some major breakthroughs. . . . The first-time-ever recognition of students' right to qualified teachers is historically significant" (2007, 11, 13). Of course, this breakthrough is undermined by an operational structure used to penalize schools and a remarkable lack of resources and accountability to students, parents, and teachers (Garda 1995, 1122). "Most centrally," says Darling-Hammond,

> the law does not address the profound educational inequalities that plague our nation. . . . School funding lawsuits brought in more than twenty-five states describe apartheid schools serving low-income students of color with crumbling facilities, overcrowded classrooms, out-of-date textbooks, no science labs, no art or music courses and a revolving door of untrained teachers, while their suburban counterparts, spending twice as much for students with fewer needs, offer expansive libraries, up-to-date labs and technology, small classes, well-qualified teachers and expert specialists, in luxurious facilities. (2007, 13)

Statistics regarding those who are labeled as intellectually disabled and those who are most likely to be punished correlate eerily and predictably with other social statistics imposing consequences on society. African American students are disproportionately represented in special education; according to one study, African American children accounted for only 17 percent of the total school population, but an astounding 35 percent of the special education for learning disabled students (Harry and Klinger 2006, 6). For classes for the emotionally disturbed, the same study found that "at least [80 percent] of the students in the program were Black" (Harry and Klinger 2006, 6). On average, black males are more likely to attend the most segregated and least resourced public schools (Lee and Wong 2004, 809). Minority students account for the highest percentage of high school dropouts in any given year. From 1987 to 2007, students of black and Hispanic origin—specifically male students—were consistently the highest percentage of dropouts (US Bureau of the Census 2008). In 2005,

7.5 percent of black males dropped out of high school, as compared to 3.4 percent of white males and 5.6 percent of Hispanic males (US Bureau of the Census 2008). Figures from the most recent United States Census (US Bureau of the Census 2012) indicate that black males have consistently low educational attainment levels. Only 16.4 percent of black males age twenty-five to twenty-nine years achieved four or more years of college (see also Institute of Education Sciences 2011; National Council on Disability 2011; Ryan and Siebens 2012). Blacks compose a disproportionately large percentage of the population that is in poverty; this group's unemployment rate is twice as high as the national average, with annual incomes at only three-quarters of that for white men (US Bureau of Labor Statistics n.d.). Black men live about seven years less than men in other racial groups (Arias 2007) and are also seven times more likely than other men to spend time in jail (Mauer and King 2007, 3; US Federal Bureau of Prisons 2012).

The social problems confronting individuals with some form of disability are not so dissimilar from the problems faced by African Americans.[9] People with disabilities experience low rates of educational attainment. In 2008 in the United States, approximately 24 percent of noninstitutionalized persons with a disability ages twenty-one to sixty-four had an educational attainment that was less than a high school degree (Cornell University 2010). This same percentage is found for those people with a disability who live below the poverty line (Cornell University 2012; Erickson, Lee, and von Schrader 2008, 6). The percentage of individuals with disabilities who achieve a college degree or higher depends on the nature of the disability and has generally been increasing over time, yet the achievement of those with mental retardation or an intellectual disability remains consistently low (Brault 2012). People with disabilities are more likely to be in poverty than almost any other group (Erickson, Lee, and von Schrader 2008, 43) and to have extremely high rates of unemployment. The percentage of noninstitutionalized people with a disability who were employed in the United States in 2008—male or female, from ages twenty-one to sixty-four,

9. The populations discussed are not exclusive of each other; neither are they coextensive.

of all races and ethnicities, and at all education levels—was approximately 39.5 (Erickson, Lee, and von Schrader 2008, 32). This group is also highly unlikely to carry health insurance (Erickson, Lee, and von Schrader 2008, 56). Finally, disproportional numbers of the mentally ill are represented in the prison population—to the point where it seems prison is the preferred form of treatment (Fellner 2006; Lamb and Weinberger 1998, 486). This statistic, along with those concerning black males, is very troubling not only because of the correlation with our choice to punish rather than to educate elementary-school-age children, but also because of society's apparent preference for warehousing people who are different rather than helping them to find meaningful assistance and solutions.

The correlation between low educational attainment and other social statistics relevant both to black males and to individuals with disabilities is evident. To the extent that education is central to achievement and status in life, focusing on the education of black male children is essential. This focus must include appropriately determining each child's needs. This process, in effect, will help all children and especially enable the proper resources to be directed to the education of those with real intellectual disability. The United States faces a crisis in its public-education system. The teaching techniques and structuring of school systems that are beneficial for the education of black males and students with genuine learning disabilities will ultimately also create a better system of education for all students. Finding ways to alter conceptualizations of effective teaching without inappropriate labeling, categorizing, or tracking may lessen the prevalence of inappropriate labeling, categorizing, or tracking in other areas of society. Thus, the repetitions indicated by this prevalence are not just chronic in a vertical sense, but also in a horizontal sense by means of their reach and consequences throughout all aspects of life and society. In essence, by not correcting the disparities early, especially in education, we are ensuring the perpetuation of disparities in all other areas of life.

Conclusions: Wanting . . . Something Different

Rather than educating all of our children, we use education as another means of subordination. We label many children, most often black males, as intellectually disabled to avoid fully educating them. The systematic overlabeling of students as intellectually disabled reduces resources for and attention to those students with genuine disabilities, reducing the quality of education for them. We use current laws and policies that promote racial segregation within schools and between school districts. These same laws and policies also encourage and permit differential delivery of educational services. We punish and expel large numbers of children, most often black males, rather than finding ways to reach and include them in their own education. Even though we understand that education is a major factor in solutions for crime and repeated incarceration, we not only prefer punishment and expulsion, leaving high-risk behaviors as the likely outcome, but also water down and create large barriers to education within incarceration facilities, further limiting opportunity and increasing the likelihood of recidivism. Where education could be the solution to many problems in our society and a path to prosperity for both individuals and the collective nation, it appears instead that educational settings use the promises of education to the detriment of some.

The system of (mis)education operates from a structure perpetuated by laws, policies, and institutions that ensure the continued subordinated status of groups based on race and disability—one used to reinforce the other. This is not unlike the manner in which the system of "mass incarceration" operates to ensure the subordinate status of a group defined largely by race. As Michelle Alexander puts it, "Rather than rely on race, we use our criminal justice system to label people of color 'criminals' and then engage in all the practices we supposedly left behind" (2010, 2). The connection between these two areas and their relative operation cannot be mistaken. Alexander notes that

> [i]n Chicago (as in other cities across the United States), young black men are more likely to go to prison than to go to college. . . . In fact, there were more black men in the state's correctional facilities . . . just on drug charges than the total number of black men enrolled in undergraduate degree programs in state universities. . . . The young men who go to prison rather than college face a lifetime of closed doors, discrimination, and ostracism. Their plight is not what we hear about

on the evening news, however. Sadly, like the racial caste systems that preceded it, the system of mass incarceration now seems normal and natural to most, a regrettable necessity. (2010, 185, emphasis omitted)

The system of education creates a situation wherein we punish those labeled as disabled to keep them from an education; we label those in prison as felons to create legal and social disabilities.

8

Children with Disabilities, Parents without Disabilities, and Lawyers

Issues of Life Experience, Affinity, and Agency

MARK C. WEBER

The role of parents without disabilities as proxies for children with disabilities in educational decision making is an insufficiently explored issue, as is the role of nondisabled attorneys as representatives of nondisabled parents of children with disabilities. This essay examines both the parents' role and that of the lawyer in decisions concerning the education of a child with a disability.

Parents' Role in Special Education Decision Making

Parents play a powerful role in the education of their disabled children. The Education of All Handicapped Children Act of 1975, which was renamed the Individuals with Disabilities Education Act in 1990 (IDEA), made a fundamental change in the American educational landscape by mandating participation and due process rights for parents of children with disabilities. Unlike parents of children in general education, parents

Thanks to Elizabeth Powell for her research assistance. Special thanks to Ani Satz and Arlene Kanter for their comments when the paper was originally presented at the Second City Conference at Syracuse University in May 2009.

of children with disabilities must be included in meetings that devise programs and services for their children. These parents can demand hearings on the appropriateness of the education offered their children by public schools, even taking the matter to court (20 U.S.C.A. §1415(f)–(i), 2011). They also may assert challenges to student discipline beyond the minimal due process rights guaranteed students in general education (*Honig v. Doe* 1988). In some instances, the parents may recover reimbursement for privately obtained schooling or obtain compensatory services for education wrongfully denied in the past (*Forest Grove School District v. T.A.* 2009). Though hearing officers and courts show deference toward school officials' decision making, parents quite frequently prevail in challenges to school district decisions (Archer 2002).

The Supreme Court underscored the importance of the parent as the bearer of legal rights in special education in its 2007 decision *Winkelman v. Parma City School District*. In that case, the lower courts had ruled that Mr. and Mrs. Winkelman, acting without an attorney, could not file an action in court to challenge the program that the public-school system had offered their son. The general rule is that nonlawyer parents may not represent minors in court; they may represent only themselves. The Supreme Court reversed the lower courts, holding that IDEA grants parents themselves rights that are enforceable in court, and those rights not only extend to parts of the law that refer directly to parents, such as the rights to procedural protections and tuition reimbursement, but also include the right of a free, appropriate public education of their child (at 528–33).

Children with Disabilities and Parents without Disabilities

Thus, the parents have power. Nevertheless, exercise of power by parents of children with disabilities is not the same thing as effective exercise of power by people with disabilities. One of the central ideas of the disability rights movement is the social model of disability: that physical or mental conditions do not necessarily disable, but instead that disability arises from a dynamic between those conditions and the social environment of physical space and mental attitudes (Fine and Asch 1988, 9). A person who uses a wheelchair for mobility is not disabled but for curbs, steps, and attitudes that operate literally or metaphorically as barriers. Close corollaries of this proposition are that attention should be paid to changing the environment rather than to the individual with the disability; that the individual who has a disability should be treated as an agent, not an object; and that people with disabilities are asserting rights rather than asking for charity (Erkulwater 2006, 30–31). Scholars have paid critical attention to all of these ideas (e.g., Minow 2008, 7), but the reorientation of disability thinking around the person with a disability, his or her lived experience, and the potential to exercise agency in the world remains central to contemporary disability studies (Bagenstos 2004, 12; Charlton 1998, 127; Malhotra 2008, 86). In the context being addressed here, the environment is education, and the disabled person is the child.

This is not to say that every child with a disability has what might be thought of as disability consciousness or a chosen identity as a person with a disability. Autobiographical writing frequently mentions an overriding desire on the part of young children and adolescents with disabling conditions to pass as nondisabled and describes how they eventually choose an identity as a disabled person (e.g., Michalko 2002, 9–10). More than half of children with disabilities who are identified as such for special education services have learning disabilities or emotional disturbance (US Department of Education 2007) and so will not in every context be conspicuous as persons with disabilities. These children may not even necessarily think of themselves as individuals with disabilities whose perspective is unique on that ground, even if they are designated by the public schools as "children with disabilities" for purposes of the law.

Moreover, it should be remembered that all children need others to act for them, whether the children have disabilities or not. Minors lack the capacity to file suit on their own, just as they lack the ability to make binding contracts, vote, or invoke other legal privileges and protections. Children are always in the custody of someone (*Schall v. Martin* 1984), and though children have limited rights to obtain abortions without parental consent (*Bellotti v. Baird* 1979) and some protections against parental decisions on psychiatric hospital admission (*Parham v. J.R.* 1979), these cases are exceptions to the general rule that parents are the ones in charge.

Moreover, simply because of their youth, children may lack the judgment and skills to determine, articulate, and pursue their own interests. Parents ordinarily have the responsibility and power to advance the well-being and proper development of their children.

Not only do parents in general have this role vis-à-vis their children, but nondisabled parents of children with disabilities have a unique experience and point of view that should be valued. Parents of children with disabilities may experience stigmatization and marginalization from both the world at large and the disability community, and in response they may develop special competencies and unique positions of alliance with their own children and other disabled persons (Ryan and Runswick-Cole 2008).

Nevertheless, it is the child who negotiates the world "from the vantage point of the atypical," an atypicality the dominant culture characterizes "as deficit and loss" (Linton 1998a, 5). Some sources describe the disconnection between children with disabilities and nondisabled parents in strong terms (Harrison and Freinberg 2005, reporting the view of Autistic Liberation Front members; Ortega 2009, 428), even as others explore the affinity between children and parents (Ryan and Runswick-Cole 2008). It is true that not all parents of disabled children are nondisabled, and those parents who are disabled may have greater or lesser degrees of awareness of the child's disability consciousness (as described in Michalko 2002). But the conflict in perspective is most acute when the child with a disability has a nondisabled parent.

Under US law, absent a conflict in the interests of parent and child or evidence of neglect or abuse of a child, the parents have the ultimate say on most of the child's life decisions, including those relating to education for a child with a disability. Are there conflicts of interest on education issues between parents and their children with disabilities? Problems may arise in at least two areas.

The first of these areas is decisions about placements and services in general. Few parents remember the acute vulnerability to embarrassment and fear of not fitting in during middle school and high school years, and so parents may favor placements that have the effect of stigmatizing children or separating them from their friends and siblings. The enforced separation of individuals with disabilities is strongly associated with their social degradation and devaluation (*City of Cleburne v. Cleburne Living Center* 1985), just as fear and repulsion stem from rarity of daily contact with disabled people functioning in the community (Field 1993, 117).

Parents choose isolated or stigmatizing settings for their children often in the hope of giving the child better educational services or sometimes in the hope of protecting the child from others or all too frequently because that is the only option the school system offers (Engel 1991, 185). In fact, a mainstreamed setting may be contrary to the child's real interests when the child will be afforded inadequate supports and adaptations or will be exposed to abuse or ridicule on the basis of disability but afforded no protection by the school. Thus, guarding against stigma, harassment, and mistreatment is key (Weber 2007a). Children frequently do not report harassment, even to their parents, because they think their parents will not understand or will think less of them for not handling the problem themselves. Rarely are school districts sufficiently diligent in establishing policies, training, and complaint-and-intervention procedures for dealing with disability harassment (Weber 2007a).

Moreover, an individual parent is at a disadvantage in finding a mainstreamed setting with adequate supports if the school district is unwilling to cooperate (Engel 1991, 187). Collective political action is needed to force school districts to expand the range of well-supported educational options and provide truly adaptive education in the mainstream. This pressure will not eliminate the problems that parents will have in aligning their views of what realistically is best for their children with the children's own perspectives, but it will at least cause school districts to serve children more effectively with less isolation and stigma.

In the second problem area, transition from secondary school to adult life may expose fault lines between parent and disabled child. Here the framers of the law have attempted to empower the child by mandating that the Individualized Education Plan (IEP) in effect when the child turns sixteen and for subsequent years has to include appropriate measurable postsecondary goals and provide for the transition services needed to assist the child in reaching those goals (20 U.S.C.A. §1414(d)(1)(A)(i)(VIII)(aa)–(bb), 2011). The regulations enforcing this provision go further by providing that the school district "must invite a child with a disability to attend the child's IEP Team meeting if a purpose of the meeting will be the consideration of the postsecondary goals for the child and the transition services needed to assist the child in reaching those goals" (34 C.F.R. §300.321(b)(1), 2011). This regulatory provision recognizes that as the child ages and life after high school looms, the child's interests may diverge from those the parents are able to identify or are willing to pursue with the same degree of intensity as the child. Requiring that the child be invited to IEP meetings gives the child a voice separate from that of the parent. Of course, the statute and regulation do nothing to change the fundamental fact that it is the parent who has the ability to consent to services or invoke the procedural protections in the law, something that does not change until the child reaches the age of majority. But the acknowledgment of potential conflict and the allowance for an independent voice for the student point up the complexity of the parent–child relationship in connection with special education rights and provide a role for the child.

IDEA's solution for the potential divergence of views on transition from secondary school is worthy of consideration as a means to mediate the tension between the vantage of the parent without the disability and that of the disabled child on other issues. Requiring that children with disabilities, particularly those who are older, be invited to participate in all meetings in which program or placement decisions are made would not dramatically shift the locus of power, but it would provide more of a role for the individual with the experience of disability itself. Current law provides for inclusion of the child in the IEP team "whenever appropriate" (20 U.S.C.A. §1414(d)(1)(B)(vii), 2011), but that obligation is much weaker than that which applies to meetings on transition, and it is difficult to imagine how the child could ever enforce it.

The potential for divergence of interest between parent and child is not unique to the situation of a disabled child and nondisabled parent in educational decision making. Medical decision making has some of the same potential for conflicts, and sources have suggested solutions such as application of trust law (Ouellette 2010, 991–1000) and consent and hearing requirements (Albright 2006, 190–94). Overlegalization of special education is a matter of public-policy concern (Neal and Kirp 1985, 85–86), however, and militates against extending similar law-focused regimes to the parent–child dynamic in special education cases. But a participation requirement of the type that now applies to transition may well prove beneficial.

Children with Disabilities, Parents without Disabilities, and Lawyers

Adding lawyers to the parent–child mix complicates matters still further because lawyers have their own professional interests and characteristics and are one step further removed from the child than is the parent. Disability studies writers have noted that professionals frequently serve their own agendas and may not share power with persons with disabilities, much less step back while people who have disabilities exercise their own agency. James Charlton's aptly titled work *Nothing about Us without Us* discusses at length the divergence of interests between care providers and people with disabilities (1998, 92–97). Michael Oliver notes that professionals dealing with people who have disabilities tend to stress independence of personal functioning in matters such as washing, dressing, toileting, and cooking on one's own; by contrast, many people with disabilities themselves are more interested in making decisions on their own and establishing control over their daily lives, even though that may entail using assistants for daily life activities (1990, 91).

There are mitigating considerations in the lawyer–client context, however. Perhaps to a degree that exceeds that of other professionals, lawyers are trained to defer to the decision making of the person they serve, and that training may moderate the worst of the conflict between professional and client interests. Under the *Model Rules of Professional Conduct*, a lawyer must abide by the client's decisions about the objectives of representation and has to consult with the client about the means of pursuing them (American Bar Association 2006, rule 1.2). The lawyer must obey the client regarding settlement of a case. The lawyer also has the duty to keep the client reasonably informed about his or her case and comply with reasonable requests for information. There is a duty to explain a matter to a client thoroughly enough to permit the client to make informed decisions about the representation (rule 1.4). Representation of a client is not to be taken as the lawyer's endorsement of the client's views or activities (rule 1.2). As a general matter, a lawyer is always advocating for someone else, and successful lawyers develop the ability to empathize with their clients and see the world from their perspectives.

It is also worth stressing that, for the client, having a lawyer is a form of power (the most apt reference here is Warren Zevon's song "Lawyers, Guns, and Money"). An Illinois study indicates that when parents have lawyers representing them in due process hearings, they win in 50.4 percent of cases, but when they represent themselves, they prevail only 16.8 percent of the time (Archer 2002). Of course, it is unknown to what degree a selection effect may be at work in this situation. Lawyers may take only the strongest cases or present the cases more effectively or both. But it appears to be far better to have a lawyer than to be without one. Moreover, despite serious concern about power imbalances between attorney and client that typically favor the attorney and may undermine the client's autonomy (Miller 1994, 503–5), the client selects and always remains able to fire the lawyer.

Nevertheless, several potential problems may arise in the instance when a lawyer—who is typically nondisabled—represents a nondisabled parent who is advocating for a child with a disability in a special education dispute.

First, there is the difficult question "Who is the client?" Lawyers sometimes say that they represent the family, as though the family were a corporate or governmental unit with a legal personality and a defined management structure. Families lack those characteristics, and even entities with them often place lawyers in situations of conflict when the lawyers try to fulfill duties to the corporation or governmental body itself that are not identical to the wishes identified by the individual members of management (American Bar Association 2006, rule 1.13(b)). What the lawyer actually needs for successful representation is someone who is able to set goals, evaluate risks, and make decisions. That person is the parent rather than the child, and the parent typically also is the one who is responsible for the bill. For this reason, it appears that most lawyers who have given the matter thorough consideration view the parent as the client in a special education case.

Second, and in some tension with the first point, there is the situation when the lawyer perceives the parent as irrational or acting with obvious disregard of the interests of the child. Lawyers' professional training, which emphasizes logic and detachment, leads to a general view of clients as overly emotional and incapable of clear thinking, of course. Not that the lawyerly characteristics are always or necessarily bad: detachment and logic are often critical to developing and presenting a case that a neutral— sometimes hostile—judge or hearing officer will accept, so the lawyer's cultivation of these traits is highly functional. The traits, however, may lead the lawyer to perceive parents as less than fully in touch with reality when it is the lawyer who is simply failing to appreciate the reality the client faces.

However, there are some instances in which the parent is, by anyone's assessment but the parent's, irrational or making decisions that are harmful to the child. The lawyer has the option to resign, but that may do more harm to the child than continuing a difficult relationship with the parent. Other options include making efforts to strengthen the parent's decision making, as by encouraging the parent to contact a disability organization or to obtain supportive therapy. Help for the lawyer may also be indicated, perhaps by consulting with other lawyers or with communications experts or possibly by working with relatives or individuals the parent trusts if the parent will authorize contact (Herr 1998–99, 642–50; Neely 1982, 1389–94).

One alternative possibility would be appointing a lawyer for the child in addition to the lawyer for the parent. Just as papers by researchers uniformly recommend further research, so articles by lawyers often advocate solutions that call for more lawyers. But it is less than clear what a lawyer representing the child, but not the parent, should do. Under professional standards, when representing a child or someone else of diminished capacity to make adequately considered decisions in connection with representation, "the lawyer shall, as far as reasonably possible, maintain a normal client–lawyer relationship with the client," but "maintaining the ordinary client–lawyer relationship may not be possible in all respects" (American Bar Association 2006, rule 1.14(b) and comment [1]). Although the lawyer should solicit opinions from the child, these views do not bind the lawyer.

This decision-making void raises the prospect of a lawyer who is accountable to no one but his or her own sense of the child's interests.

Even sources that are favorably disposed toward representation of children independently of their parents (e.g., Neely 1982) offer little guidance for the lawyer about how to determine the objectives of the representation, which means to pursue, and which risks or negotiated solutions to accept. Although some would advocate having lawyers pursue only the expressed wishes of the child-client (e.g., Hawkins 1996, 2110), the child's limited judgment and life experience make that position doubtful. In some situations, as in abuse and neglect proceedings or custody disputes, a separate attorney for the child may be a better course than any other and is generally authorized or required (Moore 1996, 1822n16), but special education disputes do not involve stakes quite as high or conflicts quite as acute as those cases. Availability of and compensation for the additional lawyer are further problems with independent representation of the child in a special education case.

Unlike the situation of meetings between school personnel and parents, where adding the child's voice may be beneficial, creating any formal role for a child who is not represented by an attorney to participate in administrative or court proceedings independently of the parent is not a good idea. Such a measure would provide an opportunity for the attorney for the public-school system to drive a wedge between child and parent. The child would not even have his or her own attorney to balance the influence of the lawyer representing the school system. In a contested case, a formal role for the child would undermine the fundamental plan of IDEA to assign legal rights to the parents and trust their judgment. Giving power to the parents may not be ideal in all instances, but it is superior to any other way of allocating it.

Third, lawyers are only too well aware that appeals to victimhood and disability stereotypes may be highly powerful tools, something that is tempting to exploit in pursuing a client's goals, but may be detrimental to the interests of persons with disabilities in general or to the desires of a specific client and the good of the individual child with a disability. Laura Rovner (2001) points out that lawyers are inclined to portray people with disabling conditions in ways that generate sympathy from decision makers, even when that sympathy is little more than condescension. Specifically in school cases, there is sometimes a strategic benefit to portraying the child as less academically successful than the child really is in order to make sure that the child is deemed eligible for services and receives the most intense services. Obtaining a private placement or more minutes of specialized services is how the lawyer measures success and, not coincidentally, how courts determine prevailing-party status in making attorney fee awards. Of course, it may be that the best the lawyer can do for the client is increased services or a private placement or some other remedy available only by showing that the child is sufficiently disabled to support a case for something more than what the school system is offering. But the unintended consequences of the portrayal of helplessness to the self-concept of the child and the general image of persons with disabilities should not be ignored. No legal solution to this difficulty is suggested here, merely a caution to lawyers about the potential problems with such a portrayal.

Conclusion

This discussion identifies more problems than solutions. Parents have power in the special education setting, and they have a unique and valuable perspective, but it is not the same perspective as that of a child with a disability. Enhanced participation rights for the child could bring the lived experience of disability into the discussion. Lawyers are twice removed from the child with a disability, but greater participation in formal proceedings for the child will not necessarily be beneficial. It will remain the responsibility of lawyers to be certain that the interests and perspectives of parents and of children with disabilities are honored.

9

The Tale of a Reluctant Expert Witness

ALICIA A. BRODERICK

In recent years, I have been involved as an "expert witness" in two different cases in two different states being litigated under the Individuals with Disabilities Education Improvement Act of 2004 (IDEIA). In one case, I reviewed the student's written records, conducted observations of and interviews with the child involved (which others conceptualize as "evaluations"), prepared a written summary and analysis of these activities, was verbally prepared by a team of lawyers, and testified before the presiding judicial officer. In the other case, I reviewed the student's written records, conducted a single observation/interview with the child involved (which, again, others conceptualized as conducting an "evaluation"), prepared a written summary and analysis of these activities, was verbally prepared by a team of lawyers, and had my scheduled testimony canceled at the last minute for reasons I explain later. One of these cases was being heard in federal district court; the other by a state administrative law judge. Both cases involved young people who were seeking to gain access to grade-level academic educations in proximity to their nondisabled peers in place of the segregated sites to which both students had been relegated (one to a segregated disability-specific classroom within a mainstream school, the other to a segregated disability-specific day school). Both involved young people who experienced a significant communication impairment and who were regarded by their teachers, therapists, school psychologists, administrators, and other professional representatives of the school district as intellectually disabled or cognitively impaired in addition to being labeled autistic.

In this essay, I treat these two experiences largely as a single composite experience for two reasons: (*a*) to protect the individual identities of the young people, families, and school districts involved; and (*b*) because my reflections upon the similarities of the two experiences led to the analysis that is this essay, and the differences of identifying detail are generally not germane to the points I endeavor to make herein, except as noted otherwise. The reader is advised of this approach at the outset because I wish to position the offered analysis as necessarily partial, specific, situated, and emergent. I do not position myself in any way as an "expert" expert witness (and if the reader does not immediately apprehend the irony in that statement, please read on). I present here a series of descriptive vignettes of salient experiences I had as an expert witness, interspersed with my analytic reflections upon those experiences and upon the implications of those reflections for the political project of endeavoring to "right educational wrongs" through the provisions of due process and litigation guaranteed to families under the IDEIA. Two key themes that I explore in this process are the dominance of the discourses of "expertism" and of the "capacity to benefit" from one's education.

Interrogating "Expertise"

A central and significant aspect of my experiences as an expert witness relates, perhaps not surprisingly, to the struggle over the discourse of expertism itself. This struggle manifested itself most obviously, perhaps, in the performative discursive moves by which each set of lawyers attempted to establish its own expert witness as a real, genuine, credible, and legitimate expert, while simultaneously attempting to discredit the other's expert witness as *not* an expert at all and therefore not to be heeded in his or her opinion on the points of law at hand. A second, less visible, though no less difficult struggle was the internal ethical dissonance I experienced over my own participation in the discourse of expertism throughout the process.

"What Do You Mean You're Not an Expert?"

Lawyers seem to find me frustrating. This fact might not be surprising to you until I clarify that I am referring not to the lawyers for the school district, known as the "opposing" counsel (though they undoubtedly also found me somewhat trying at times). Rather, I refer here to the lawyers for the children and the families who were soliciting my "expert" testimony in support of their cases. For one thing, being a qualitative researcher and disability studies scholar, I tend to write my observational reports (excerpts of which I include here verbatim as data drawn upon in my "expert" summary report) in the same format as I prepare qualitative field notes: in one column, I record my descriptive observations and documentations of dialogue, spatial layouts, nonverbal interactions, and other relevant descriptions of what I note happening around me, and in the other column I record my own reflections on and analysis of what I have documented in the first column, including self-reflection on my own actions and dialogue. Perhaps you begin to see where this is going.

In one observational report, I included the following data in the left column: "She [the district official escorting me to the classroom for my observation] then asks me if I am 'an expert in autism.' We are nearly at the classroom door at this point, and I hesitate before responding. 'Yes, I suppose so,' I respond, and we enter the classroom." True to form, qualitative researcher that I am, in the right-hand column I write that I was uncertain how to respond to her query, but, lacking the time and space for any substantive discussion or critique of the epistemological underpinnings of "expertism," it seemed simplest merely to respond in the affirmative, which seemed to be the expected response. I write further that I am aware that I am likely to be regarded by others as an "expert in autism" owing to the fact that I am a professor who has both conducted research on and taught courses on the topic of autism and who has been a special educator to students so labeled, despite the fact that I do not personally identify as an expert in autism owing to my own critique of the discourse of expertism. As a qualitative researcher, I was intrigued by the way in which I had slipped so quickly (albeit reluctantly) into the discourse of expertism, despite the fact that I would never represent myself as such to someone upon introduction.

You may imagine how the team of lawyers for the family responded to this portion of my "expert witness report." "What do you mean you're not an expert?!" they exhorted with more than some small measure of exasperation. "You *are* an expert; that is precisely why we sought out your testimony in this case, and you must represent yourself as such in your report and in your testimony." In my preparation, I was asked to replace tentative, interpretive language such as "the student seems to be" with the certainty and authority conveyed by "the student is" as well as to mark the basis of my opinions as being well grounded in "scientific" literature and in "data." During my testimony, the lawyers attempted to support me in this endeavor by posing questions during my testimony that I was obviously supposed to answer in the affirmative, confirming the status of my identity as expert and thereby bolstering the legitimacy of the opinions I rendered in that capacity. For example, I was gently prompted with queries such as "And is there a scientific basis for the recommendation that you just offered?" or "So it's fair to say that your report is well grounded in the scientific literature?" (The latter question earned my counsel a sustained objection that she was leading the witness.) I was asked, directed, encouraged, and led to adopt a positivist discourse on expertism—to draw upon language of certainty, objectivity, legitimacy, and validity. I was straightforward with the lawyers and the families from the beginning about my ethical qualms with so misrepresenting my own epistemological beliefs, and I steadfastly refused (or failed or both, depending on your perspective) throughout my reports and testimony to do so.

You may imagine how the family's team of lawyers cringed when, during my cross-examination, the opposing counsel asked me if I were an expert in the area of autism, and I responded by saying: "I don't typically bind to the language around expertise. I hold myself out as someone who has experience as an educator and a researcher related to autism, but I . . . I typically reject the label of expert for myself as well as for others because I . . . I find it more often a . . . a power play than a useful instructional status" (ellipses indicate pauses).[1]

---

1. I quote the case transcripts here and elsewhere, but a full citation to the cases would compromise the identity of the families involved.

The school district's counsel, by contrast, seemed delighted with my response and appeared not to notice or care that I was disavowing the status of expert not merely for myself, but for their expert psychologist as well. My attempts to provide honest responses in testimony were not intended to undermine, discredit, or sabotage my own expertise or the family's case, but rather to disrupt the discourse of expertism itself, a disruption that completely and utterly failed to be heard or understood. It would seem that the teams of lawyers were correct in their advisement to me—courts of law appear perhaps not to be receptive venues for epistemological critique. But I refuse to accept that the courts' not being a receptive venue translates to the conclusion that they are therefore not an appropriate or necessary venue for epistemological critique.

The school district's counsel began her questioning of me by asking me if I had a license to practice clinical psychology. I do not. She hammered home my repeated admissions that, no, I was not licensed in the state in question to practice clinical psychology. She apparently aimed to establish that I had no expertise at all because I was (admittedly) not a licensed clinical psychologist in the state in question (the implication being that this is the only professional role with expert purview as it relates to students labeled with autism). I was then asked repeatedly if I had a license or certification in the state in question to administer a variety of standardized, norm-referenced assessments of intellectual ability, to which I repeatedly responded "no." The judicial official finally interrupted this line of questioning to ask me if I were a psychologist at all (let alone one licensed in the state in question). I responded that I am not a psychologist; I am an educator. At this point, the judge concluded that questions as to my disciplinary background, state licensure, and experience with administering standardized, norm-referenced tests might have some bearing on what weight he might afford whatever testimony I might offer, but he nevertheless agreed to qualify me to testify as an expert witness. Hurdle number one crossed. I would be permitted to speak, though it remained to be seen what, if any, relevance would be accorded to what I had to say.

In reviewing the transcripts from the testimony, I see now that although both sets of attorneys objected (of course) to the recognition of the opposing side's witness as "expert," and notwithstanding the fact that

each of these objections was ultimately overridden and both of us certified as expert witnesses and permitted to testify, the discourse at work in
the process positioned each of us very differently in the courtroom. For
example, although both the opposing counsel's expert witness and I hold
PhD degrees (he in school psychology and I in education), the presiding
judicial official nonetheless addressed him as "Dr. Expert," whereas that
same official addressed me (without objection by counsel) as "Ms. Broderick." The judge was willing to certify me as an expert but noted that the
concerns that the opposing counsel raised might yet come into play in
his weighing of my expert opinion. By contrast, he appeared to be utterly
bewildered at the family counsel's attempts to present the school district's
PhD school psychologist as a factual rather than an expert witness: "I still
don't understand—the man is an expert. If you're not going to qualify
him as an expert, I'm not going to allow him to go into the definitions."
And thus, although I, as an educator—even a PhD teacher educator—
(rather than a psychologist) and a qualitative (rather than quantitative)
researcher was only reluctantly certified as an expert witness, the court
actually requested that counsel move to certify the school psychologist as
an expert because he was clearly, obviously, and unquestionably an expert
as far as the court was concerned. Throughout my cross-examination, the
opposing counsel repeatedly positioned me as an "advocate" rather than
as an "expert," an assertion that in the end the presiding judge explicitly
embraced in his ultimate decision to dismiss my testimony as neither
credible nor compelling. It was only the testimony of an advocate, not
an expert.

The Discursive Constitution of Expertise

The decision of who does and who does not constitute an expert is, of
course, an extremely powerful discursive act in the litigation process. In
the *Board of Education of the Hendrick Hudson Central School District,
Westchester County, et al., v. Amy Rowley* (1982) decision, the US Supreme
Court stated, "In assuring that the requirements of the Education for All
Handicapped Children Act of 1975 have been met, courts must be careful
to avoid imposing their view of preferable educational methods upon the

States" (at 208). The Court further noted, "In this case, for example, . . . [the courts were] presented with evidence as to the best method for educating the deaf, a question long debated among scholars. . . . The District Court accepted the testimony of respondents' experts" (at 207). Douglas Biklen (1992) points out that in matters of law related to the interpretation of the "appropriateness" of education (Individuals with Disabilities Education Act [IDEA]) or of treatment (the Developmentally Disabled Assistance and Bill of Rights Act of 1975) for disabled citizens, the judgment of experts will prevail, barring any procedural violation of provisions of the act in question. Biklen quotes the Supreme Court decision in *Youngberg v. Romeo* (1982), a decision he describes as *"Rowley's* twin": "'We emphasize that courts must show deference to the judgment exercised by a qualified professional. . . . Decisions made by the appropriate professional are entitled to a presumption of correctness' [at 322, 324–25]" (97). My experience would certainly concur with Biklen's conclusion: "Predictably then, if parents or people with disabilities disagree with a state's experts, the courts will nearly always defer to the official experts" (97).

There were three primary facets of expertism as discursively constituted by the counsel for the school districts in these experiences, each of which the court tacitly accepted and endorsed in its decision making in each case. The first facet was that the most appropriate person to exercise expert judgment regarding the education of a disabled student is not an educator, but rather a psychologist (to say nothing of the fact that the student and the parents are excluded entirely from expertise on this matter). That is, a disabled student's master status (Goffman 1963) is not "student," but rather "disabled." I testified at length as to "appropriate" pedagogical supports (i.e., supplementary supports and services) that should be put in place for disabled students with significant communication impairments to be "satisfactorily" educated in the least restrictive environment. Midway through this testimony, the court interrupted me, asking if I could please define "pedagogy" because he didn't know what I was talking about. Educational expertise was clearly not understood to be as relevant to these students' educational decision making as was expertise in classifying, labeling, and identifying "deficits" or in definitively quantifying a child's "capacity" and therefore the most appropriate "treatment" (rather than education) for him or her.

A second facet of the discursive constitution of expertise throughout these experiences was the default assumption that applied behavior analysis (ABA) is without question the most appropriate "treatment" methodology for autistic students, and therefore one cannot, by definition, be an expert if one does not embrace ABA as one's primary recommended methodology. In their cross-examination of my testimony, the counsel for the school district had asked me if my recommendations for a range of pedagogical supports were not necessarily based on a generalized stance I held as an advocate of inclusion rather than being grounded in the particularities of the needs of the student in question due to the limited length of time that I had spent in observing and interviewing the student. I responded that I had spent no less time with the student than had the district's expert psychologist and that his recommendations were likewise based on a generalized stance he held as an advocate for ABA instruction for students labeled with autism. I further noted that just as the expert psychologist could produce a generalized literature base in support of his argument that segregated ABA programs were most appropriate for autistic students, so, too, could I produce a literature base that supported my argument that such students could benefit from inclusive schooling. I was asked if the student in question had been a participant in any of the research studies in support of inclusive education to which I referred, and I responded that to the best of my knowledge, no, she had not. Nevertheless, despite the fact that the student had not been a participant in any of the research studies claiming that ABA is most appropriate for autistic students, these studies were cast as legitimate expert knowledge, whereas the literature in support of inclusive education was cast as irrelevant because it did not directly involve the student in question, thus constituting my position as an advocate, not an expert. In his final decision, the judge noted (apparently having attended to only half of my testimony) that in my testimony I had "admitted" that ABA is the best methodology for autistic students generally, and he further noted that "testimony clearly indicates that [the student] needs discrete trial instruction in a small classroom setting . . .

[and that] the District properly considered [the student's] *potential* and educational needs" (emphasis added).

If a court will not dispute issues of methodology with the state's representatives (in these cases, the local school districts), it is of course helpful if those recognized as experts happen already to espouse the methodology that the district already has in place programmatically. And if the erstwhile expert proposing an alternative methodology (that would require creativity, program development, and a different way of thinking about disability on the part of the school district) can conveniently be recast not as expert, but as an advocate for that particular pedagogical approach, then so much the better. Being an advocate of ABA as a methodology somehow constitutes one as an expert in autism rather than simply as an advocate of ABA as a methodology. I was asked if I routinely administered a number of behaviorally based assessments designed for autistic students. I responded that I do not do so. I was asked how many programs of discrete trial instruction I had developed for individual autistic students. I responded that although I have developed and added individual programs to students' ABA programs in previous years, I do not currently engage in such activities because it is not a methodology that I support. By contrast, the school officials who developed the curriculum for the ABA program offered to autistic students were cast as experts precisely because of their expertise in developing the very kinds of methodological programs that the program offers and advocates as most appropriate. Thus, despite being experienced with using ABA methodology, I was not an expert in special education as it relates to autistic students because I was not an expert *in ABA* (the methodology already espoused by the district and advocated by it as "appropriate" for the student in question and, indeed, for all autistic students within the district).

The third facet of expertise discursively constituted by the school districts in question throughout these proceedings was the notion that an expert would necessarily have as a central purpose, focus, and area of experience the determination (through standardized IQ testing) of the alleged cognitive "capacity" of the person at the center of a case—a notion I turn my attention to now.

Interrogating "Capacity"

My disavowal of any identity as an expert was not merely self-imposed. Upon being introduced to the court with a request to be certified as an expert witness for the family, the opposing counsel immediately objected to permitting my testimony, claiming I was not an expert after all: "Your Honor, we would object to her being called as an expert, on the basis of relevance. We believe that she does not have the qualifications that— to administer any of the—many tests that are utilized to determine the child's cognitive abilities." This constitution of the notion of the expert as one who has "qualifications . . . to determine the child's cognitive abilities" is unfortunately grounded in case law both preceding and subsequently interpreting the Education of All Handicapped Children Act of 1975 (subsequently reauthorized and renamed the Individuals with Disabilities Education Act of 1990 [IDEA] and then the Individuals with Disabilities Educational Improvement Act [IDEIA]). Indeed, the majority opinion in *Hendrick Hudson v. Rowley* (1982), to date the only Supreme Court interpretation of the 1975 act's substantive provisions, points out that "[i]mplicit in the congressional purpose of providing access to a 'free appropriate public education' is the requirement that the education to which access is provided be sufficient to confer some educational benefit upon the handicapped child" (at 201). The Court further observed that "the Act requires participating States to educate a wide spectrum of handicapped children . . . [and] it is clear that the *benefits obtainable* by children at one end of the spectrum will differ dramatically from those *obtainable* by children at the other end" (at 203, emphasis added). In offering the notion of "benefits obtainable," the *Rowley* decision explicitly invokes the history of this concept in both the *Mills v. Board of Education of District of Columbia* (1972) and *Pennsylvania Association for Retarded Citizens (PARC) v. Pennsylvania* (1972) decisions. The *Rowley* decision quotes *Mills* as requiring that "'no child is entirely excluded from a publicly supported education consistent with his needs and *ability to benefit* therefrom' [at 876]" (at 201, emphasis added). In addition, it quotes the *PARC* court's assertion that each "mentally retarded" child be provided a free, public program of education "*appropriate to the child's capacity*' [at 1260]," noting that "the right of access to free public education enunciated by these cases is significantly different from any notion of absolute equality of opportunity regardless of *capacity*" (at 201, emphasis added). Thus, although the exact phrase "capacity to benefit" never explicitly appears in the *Rowley* decision, the phrase "benefits obtainable" seems to be inextricably bound up with the cited history of the notions of "capacity" or "ability" to benefit. Appropriateness is thus conceptually constructed in the *Rowley* decision in relation to capacity to benefit—"consistent with . . . ability to benefit," "appropriate to . . . capacity," relative to "benefits obtainable."

Indeed, during my testimony the opposing counsel objected to my even voicing an expert opinion on the appropriateness of the student's education "due to the fact that [I had] no evaluative data to present in regards to the child's cognitive ability." Because I had not independently administered to the child a Stanford-Binet or Weschler or other standardized, norm-referenced purported assessment of intelligence, it was deemed inappropriate for me even to venture an opinion because any such opinion would be considered credible and relevant only if grounded in an expert evaluation of the student's capacity to benefit from the proposed education. And the only way to make an expert determination as to that capacity is clearly through the objective results of such standardized assessment instruments.

It seems clear to me, upon reading the transcripts of testimony coupled with the judgments handed down in each of these cases, that my credibility as an "expert" and therefore any weight that may have been afforded my testimony were undermined by my explicit critique of the discourse of intelligence testing. I was asked whether I believed I was "qualified" to interpret and evaluate the results of tests administered by a school psychologist. I responded that, yes, I believe I was reasonably well qualified to do so. I was asked whether I would agree that seven out of ten children on the autism spectrum have a moderate to severe cognitive deficit. I responded that I did not agree based on the inaccessibility of the testing instruments for people with significant motor and communication impairments as well as on recent research that calls this widely cited statistic into question (Dawson et al. 2007; Goldberg-Edelson 2006). I was asked if I was aware of the fact that instruments such as the Stanford-Binet and the Weschler intelligence scales have more than fifty years of scientific research behind them. I responded that I was aware of the existence of such research. I was asked if I then wished to maintain the opinion that such tests were inaccurate measures of a child's ability. I responded that for children with significant motor and communication impairments, yes, I did maintain that view (to say nothing of the eugenic history of IQ testing generally, but I limited my caveats to the particulars of these cases). I was asked if I wished to maintain that two different evaluating psychologists were somehow mistaken in their assessment of the student's cognitive abilities as being severely delayed. I responded that I considered those results to be invalid owing to the inaccessibility of the testing instruments to the student in question. The opposing counsel who was conducting my cross-examination looked at me with satisfied bemusement throughout this exchange (apparently enjoying the good fortune that I was playing directly into her hand). The judge asked me to restate my answers a couple of times, apparently to make sure that he hadn't misunderstood my (apparently, to him, incredulous) responses.

In writing up his judgment in the case, the judge cast me as an "advocate of inclusion" rather than a "compelling" expert (which is how the school psychologist was cast) based on my position regarding the student's capacity to benefit from education. As the judge noted in his summary of my testimony, I "presumed the competence of all children . . . and that this presumption should override the opinion of two psychologists' findings and evaluations, or a [sic] the very least calls [sic] their opinions into question." In further establishing my lack of credibility, he noted that I "testified that children in the lowest or first and second percentile . . . would still be capable of being educated in a regular education classroom." By contrast, his summary of the school's expert psychologist noted that "he concluded that [the student] had significant cognitive delays." He stated that one of "the purpose[s] of the evaluations was to . . . provide information as to whether or not any specific programs are likely to result in [the student] receiving a meaningful educational benefit. . . . The Stanford Binet Intelligence Test was administered, in which [the student] scored a 52. . . . This score indicates significant cognitive difficulties."

This determination was taken and recorded as fact despite the additional fact that this psychologist had also noted in his report that this nonverbal student "had problems with standardized tests."

Although in this case my explicit critique of the validity of standardized assessments of intelligence for the student in question rendered me an advocate in the eyes of the court (but most certainly not an expert), in the other case my submitted expert witness report raised red flags and alarm bells sufficient to set off a whole slew of additional litigative machinations even before I appeared in a courtroom to render my expert testimony. The school district in the second case deemed the student in question, as described at the outset, to be "mentally retarded" in addition to being autistic. Owing to her presumed diminished capacity to benefit from general education among nondisabled peers, she had been subjected to segregated educational placements with what can only be described as a vacuous curriculum (e.g., the school had spent numerous years trying to teach the student the letters of the alphabet, a goal that she by their account failed to achieve because she could not verbally name the letters when asked to do so). The family and their legal counsel asked me to meet with and interview the student because she currently had no access to any kind of system of expressive communication, and they wondered if the supports offered by facilitated communication might be a useful tool to enable her to access and participate in the general curriculum should they be successful in their suit to earn her entry to her neighborhood school.

I spent two hours with the student, and during that time she composed, with my facilitated support, a small number of sentences on a laptop computer equipped with voice output. I did not conduct anything approaching a full or comprehensive assessment of her language, cognitive, or academic skills. A portion of my submitted expert witness report reads:

> The most conservative interpretation of the assessment information gathered during my assessment interview . . . is that significant doubt must be cast upon the validity of the assessments of [the student's] academic achievement, assessments that do not adequately compensate for the inaccessibility of format caused by [the student's] noted difficulties

with spoken verbal language. If assessments of her academic achievement being "at best" at a "kindergarten level" are a significant component of a rationale for the school district's recommendation to restrict her access to nondisabled peers and to general academic curricula through placing her in a segregated educational setting, I believe that that recommendation must be revisited in light of the additional information that I present.

I also contended that "the acknowledged, yet not adequately accommodated for, inaccessibility of the format of many of the assessments of [the student's] academic achievement are tantamount to a discriminatory, rather than the striven-for nondiscriminatory, evaluation process."

Perhaps most interesting, I pointed out in my report that my assessment of the student, whose understanding and literacy skills had probably been vastly underestimated, was actually *consistent with* the results of the district's standardized measures of her intellectual ability. In this instance, in contrast to the student's experience in the other case, the school's Individualized Education Plan team had actually gone to some lengths to ensure that all the assessment instruments being used to assess the nonverbal student's intellectual ability were nonverbal assessment instruments, and the student successfully scored in the range of "average" intelligence on multiple assessment measures. Nevertheless, the student continued to be constructed throughout the school district's documentation of her academic achievement as severely cognitively impaired, a construction based almost entirely on the multiple curriculum-based measures of academic achievement she was subjected to (all of which required a verbal response and virtually none of which she was able to respond to). Even if I had not conducted an assessment interview with this student using facilitated conversation, I would still have been critical of the vast discrepancies between the district's own assessments of her cognitive potential, which were conducted nonverbally and judged to be average, and its assessments of her academic achievement (which were conducted verbally and judged to be at a kindergarten level "at best"). The court, by contrast, was not as critical.

Tellingly, though perhaps not surprisingly, in the first case the student was judged to be intellectually incompetent *because* of the fact that she made low scores on the standardized tests of intellectual ability that were administered to her by a licensed psychologist. This finding was made despite the fact that the instruments in question were neither normed upon a population of nonverbal people nor accessible to enable a non-verbal student to actively participate in the testing, thereby rendering the results invalid as well as discriminatory. Conversely, in the second case the student was judged to be intellectually incompetent *despite* the fact that she repeatedly scored in the average range of intelligence on non-verbal assessments of intellectual ability that were administered to her by a licensed psychologist. These intelligence test results were nevertheless quietly overlooked in favor of the narrative of intellectual incompetence that could be indirectly derived from the student's abysmal performance on multiple tests of academic achievement, all of which were verbal assess-ments administered to a nonverbal student, thereby also rendering them both invalid and discriminatory. Upon reflection, I cannot help but to understand these students and others like them as being damned if they do and damned if they don't. My legitimacy as an expert was undermined in part because I dared to challenge the dominant cultural narrative about "mental retardation" and autism and, further, to challenge the validity of psychological assessments of intellectual ability for students such as those whom I was attempting to support. Ethically, I felt that I could do no less. Pragmatically, I do not feel that my reports or testimony ultimately helped either student in question to secure the access to an education among their nondisabled peers to which they are entitled under the law.

Shortly after I submitted my report to the attorneys in the second case, and it was made available to the school district's legal team, I received a court order, signed by the officiating judge, to submit with the student to a filmed assessment of the student using the Facilitated Communica-tion Authorship Protocol designed by and in this case administered by Dr. Howard Shane. Included in the rationale for the district's motion for the assessment was the following admission and charge:

> If Dr. Broderick's assessment is correct, then [the student] can already read and write at a very high level, and she requires very different learn-ing objectives. Unfortunately, there is no reliable evidence that the

responses attributed to [the student] in Dr. Broderick's report were initi-ated by [the student] and not by Dr. Broderick. . . . If [the student] did indeed author the communications facilitated by Dr. Broderick, then she is actually functioning at or above grade level in language arts. If that is true, then [the student] can comprehend language at a much higher level than has been previously assessed, and learns at a much faster rate than we now believe, her abilities and skills are much differ-ent than previously understood, as are her educational needs.

Interestingly, the discrepancy between the literacy skills expressed in the few sentences that the student authored with me with the support of an augmentative communication device (a computer) and those that she had been able to demonstrate through the district's own (verbally adminis-tered) curriculum-based assessment caught the immediate and somewhat alarmed attention of the school district's counsel. Their proposed narra-tive for making sense of this discrepancy was the possibility that the report I had written was fraudulent, so until such time it could be adequately "validated," it would be regarded as such. As described in the court's order, "[T]he quality and consistency of [the student's] responses during the Authorship Protocol will be compared with the quality of her answers during the interview with Dr. Broderick. All of which will clarify which of the highly discrepant measures of [the student's] abilities is accurate." The Authorship Protocol's stated purpose was "to determine who, as between Student and her facilitator, Dr. Broderick, is the true originator of the responses cited in Dr. Broderick's report." Indeed, the order specified that the report would not be considered nor my testimony permitted until such time that the ordered "assessment" was conducted and validated. Interest-ingly, the district counsel didn't seem to need to "determine" which of the contradictory results in their own data might be more "accurate": the student's purportedly average ability as determined by the nonverbal tests of intellectual ability administered by the district's own psychologists or her purportedly severely delayed academic achievement administered by its teachers and learning specialists. Nor, notably, was the professional-ism of either the teachers or the psychologist derided through insinuation that one or the other of their sets of assessment results was potentially fraudulently derived. To my knowledge, there was no request for a court order to determine who was the "true originator" (the student or the psychologist administering it) of the student's responses on the nonverbal tests of intelligence in which she scored in the average range. There were only two possible outcomes of this ordered "assessment": (*a*) that the student might potentially not be as "mentally retarded" as the school district had thus far believed and that I might not be a fraud after all, which meant that she would be entitled to a very different sort of educational program than she had thus far been afforded, or (*b*) that the student was really, objectively, validly confirmed to be "mentally retarded" and that I was a fraud, thus justifying the "appropriateness" of the student's segregated and intellectually vacuous educational program. Except that there was actually only one possible outcome.

This was the point at which I uttered the words "over my dead body" to the team of lawyers. "What are you talking about?" they asked. They actually seemed excited by the prospect and eager for the student and me to submit to the proposed assessment protocol. The lawyers told me that it would be the perfect opportunity to "prove" definitively in court that the student was competent and therefore entitled to be freed from her segregated schooling experience. I explained to them that she would fail the assessment because if we had learned one thing from the literature around authorship and facilitated communication, it was how to design a validation protocol that students will fail and how to design a validation protocol that students can pass (Biklen and Cardinal 1997). The protocol to be used in the new assessment was not one the student would pass. I told the lawyers that I could design an authorship protocol that the student could pass, but that it would take a considerable amount of time for her to do so because it would need to be longitudinal, authentic, and portfolio based. Time was something that we unfortunately did not have.

Despite having in my hands a judicial order that such a meeting should be scheduled and the assessment conducted, I told the lawyers for the family that even if the court planned to subpoena my participation, cite me with contempt of court, and throw me in jail for failing to comply, I simply would not do it. I explained that the test would be very high stakes and extremely stressful and anxiety provoking for the student and that we could save her the time and trouble because the outcome of such an assessment was predictable in that the student had little experience or practice with communicating through facilitated communication. I also explained that I did not accept the premise that the results of this assessment would "prove" either the student's intellectual competence or incompetence. Rather, the assessment would show only that the student was (probably) unable to validate her communication under those particular conditions. I steadfastly refused to participate in subjecting the student to what I essentially understood to be a piece of performance art in which the student would be subjected to an official narrative that her "incompetence" was objectively and "legitimately" determined once and for all.

Lest it seem at this point that I am somehow demonizing the lawyers for the school district and valorizing those for the student and her family, allow me to share an additional layer of the complexity of this particular narrative. As excited as the lawyers momentarily were with the prospect of legally "proving" the student's competence and therefore the inappropriateness of her placement in the segregated school, they were simultaneously concerned with the legal conundrum this strategy posed to the family's case. Their argument thus far was that the segregated site was "inappropriate" because the student had failed to make any progress during the years she was there. For years, she had been working on the same education goals but failing to achieve them. Therefore, according to the family's lawyers, the placement was inappropriate to her needs. The counsel for the school district made it clear that if in fact the student had literacy and cognitive abilities that approximated those of her same-age peers, then she had clearly made great progress *while at the segregated site* because, after all, she came to them without those skills. Therefore, not only would the site be an appropriate setting for her to continue in, but the family's suit for compensatory damages would also fail. That is to say, in terms of legal strategy, the family's lawyers *needed the student to be incompetent* just as much as the school district's lawyers needed to refuse to recognize her competence. In the end, counsel met with counsel, various legal strategies were discussed, and concessions were offered, made, accepted. Despite the average scores in the student's record on nonverbal tests of intellectual ability, both parties agreed to accept the premise of her intellectual incompetence and proceed from there. The order for the assessment protocol was withdrawn, as was my report, and my testimony was canceled.

One of the families described in my combined narrative was successful in their suit; the other was not. I will not say which is which. Both cases are currently under appeal, so the ultimate outcomes for these particular students remain to be seen. I turn now to the question of what, if any, impact the epistemological critique levied by disability studies in education might potentially have on the agenda of righting educational wrongs through the process of litigation under IDEIA.

Epistemological Critique, Cultural Narrative, and Courts of Law (or, Poking Sticks at Sleeping Dragons)

Deborah Gallagher neatly synthesizes what she calls "the debates behind the debates" in special education. She argues that the literature in special education addresses four major problems or debates, each of which is ultimately unresolved (and potentially unresolvable). These four debates include: (*a*) how we understand disability, (*b*) research or knowledge production, (*c*) teacher preparation, and (*d*) place, or where students should receive instruction (2004, 4). Each of these unresolved debates, with the exception of the third (teacher preparation), was evident in the contradictory testimony and arguments presented by both sides in the cases described. The larger debate behind each of these topical debates, as Gallagher points out, is a fundamentally epistemological one: What is the nature of knowledge, and how do we know what we purport to know about the world? In these cases in particular, what do we know about the educational needs of two nonverbal autistic students? Gallagher reasonably posits that the fourth debate (the issue of place) is "intimately related to the first three" (2004, 4). In the two cases described, the decisions about where the students in question should most appropriately be educated were clearly bound up with disagreements both about how disability is understood generally and about the definitions of autism and intellectual competence specifically. It also involved a disagreement about research or knowledge production, specifically which knowledge counts as expert knowledge, who produces it, and what knowledge can be dismissed as nonlegitimate. According to Gallagher, "Because those opposed to full inclusion are generally disposed toward believing that disability is scientifically definable and identifiable (at least theoretically) and that specialized teaching practices can be derived through empiricist scientific research that teachers can and should be trained to use, they believe instruction often should take place in separate environments. In challenging all of these premises, others have countered that the question of full inclusion is fundamentally, and inevitably, a moral one" (2004, 4). That is, are questions of place moral or scientific? Within the dominant positivist worldview, which understands this situation as a binary construct, one's stance on this issue may discursively constitute one as either an advocate or an expert. As Douglas Biklen noted two decades ago, "Scientific investigation can provide information; it cannot tell society how to behave, who to value, or where its future lies" (1992, 105).

As an educational philosopher and disability studies scholar, Gallagher repeatedly (1998, 2001, 2004) brings us back to the central question of epistemology. She argues that in order to understand the nature of the topical debates, it is necessary first and foremost to understand the nature of the foundational assumptions underlying empiricism, the dominant epistemological framework in special education: "If the foundational assumptions of the empiricist framework can withstand scrutiny, those who side with the traditional arrangements of special education can safely maintain their positions. If these assumptions turn out to be inadequate, as the dissenters have submitted they are, whatever knowledge these assumptions produce must accordingly be called into question" (2004, 5). Indeed, a strong argument can be made that one of the greatest incursions that disabilities studies in education scholarship has made to date upon business as usual in special education practice has been its incisive epistemological critique of the education bureaucracy. Scholars such as Ellen Brantlinger (1997) and others have illustrated not only the ways in which epistemology shapes the kinds of decisions made in special education, but, perhaps more important, the ways in which ideological assumptions are at work throughout the enactment of special education.

These epistemological and ideological critiques make clear the central role that cultural narrative plays in the enactment of special education specifically and disability generally. *Rowley*'s holding that a court must defer to the judgment of "professionals" appears to have conferred, either wittingly or unwittingly, canonical status upon particular, dominant cultural narratives about disability while simultaneously marginalizing and delegitimizing alternative cultural narratives. Ample disability studies in education scholarship examines the ways in which particular cultural narratives about disability dominate spheres such as television, film, and other media representation, but comparatively little that examines the ways in which particular cultural narratives about disability are enacted in legislation and in subsequent interpretations by the courts.

Within the cultural narrative I witnessed as an "expert" witness, it seems to me that "legitimate" expert professionals appear to be those who faithfully reproduce and espouse the dominant cultural assumptions around autism and special education, including the notion that 50 to 70 percent of autistic students are "mentally retarded," that autistic students learn best through ABA, and that ABA instruction requires a small group (and therefore a segregated setting) to be administered properly. Once one is discursively established as a legitimate expert, it further appears that one can apparently administer as many invalid and discriminatory assessment instruments as one likes as long as the results conform to the dominant cultural narrative about disability. These "facts" are accepted as truth, and the students are labeled as "mentally retarded" despite fairly straightforward and obvious threats to the validity of those claims. When I presented an alternative narrative, it was acknowledged as intriguing but troublesome. Yet before it would even be considered, the "method" by which I came to "know" this narrative had to be "legitimated" through double-blind assessment of the assessment method itself. I had to prove from the outset that my report wasn't fraudulently derived before the court would even consent to consider it in the decision-making process. If the school district's rather extreme response to the submission of my report and testimony seems to be out of proportion to its significance, I would argue that it was not. This is what happens when one pokes sticks at sleeping dragons—they rear their heads with surprising ferocity. The sleeping dragons in this case were, first, the dominant cultural narratives about disability that were at risk of being exposed as narratives rather than as expert, objective fact or Truth and, second, the broader and deeper cultural narrative about the nature of truth itself.

Perversion of the Procedural over the Substantive

And so, one may reasonably ask, what has any of this to do with expert knowledge or truth or (dare I say it?) justice? With righting educational wrongs? Vanishingly little, in my humble opinion. Now, perhaps the most obvious lesson to take from this analysis would be never to ask me to be an expert witness in your lawsuit. Frankly, that would be just fine with me because a more reluctant expert witness you are not likely to find. Nevertheless, I would submit that there is a broader lesson to be derived. Expertism, empiricism, positivism, and the ways of thinking about knowledge, legitimacy of expertise, and power are intricately intertwined with dominant narratives about disability. Therefore, to challenge prevailing dominant narratives about disability is to further challenge deeply held and well–ingrained cultural beliefs about the very nature of reality and how we come to know and understand it. The challenge to special education as a bureaucratic system, which is resistant to having its foundational epistemological assumptions questioned, is just beginning. I would argue that the legal system is even more deeply rooted and invested in these ideas, and it will undoubtedly prove significantly more resistant to substantive change than the bureaucratic practices of special education.

One of the lawyers who spent some hours in preparing me for testimony made clear to me the purpose of my testimony. I had expressed my ongoing discomfort and intellectual and ethical dissonance with what I was being asked to do, explaining to her that I could not participate in a positivist discourse about disability and that I was very fearful that my testimony would actually do nothing to help the student in question and, indeed, might potentially hurt the family's case. "Your testimony will ultimately have very little to do with whether this family wins or loses their suit," she told me. This case, she said, would be decided (as many are) on procedural matters. She explained that the primary purpose of my testimony was to "educate the bench" and that even if the family were to lose the case at this level, there would be an appeal, and I nevertheless would have had the opportunity to expose the court to a different way of thinking about disability. So I guess it turned out to be performance art after all. The only thing I can say with any certainty as I offer my final reflections on these experiences is that I feel reasonably certain that my decision not to pursue a career as a lawyer, an idea I toyed with years ago, seems in retrospect to have been a sound one.

When I have elsewhere referenced my own painful and ongoing ethical struggles during these processes, which I shared openly and honestly with both families and their teams of counsel throughout those processes, colleagues have chided me that I erred and that what I should have done (and need to do in future, apparently) is to proudly and steadfastly claim positivist legitimacy and authority as an expert in order to "play the game by their rules" if I expect to win. They counseled me further "not to worry about" the fact that such a course of action would ultimately involve perjuring myself, which I am not willing to do. Although dismayed to read of others' similar experiences, I was nevertheless heartened to realize that I am not alone in my somewhat pessimistic outlook on the prospect of engaging courts in epistemological critique. Roger Slee conveys a similar tale wherein his "status as an expert witness was withdrawn" (2011, 114). He writes of encouraging a family to pursue legal redress for the educational discrimination their son was experiencing, and they did so, all the way to the High Court of Australia, where their appeals were ultimately denied. In hindsight tinged with regret and substantially dampened hope, he writes: "I felt culpable for putting them through such emotional and financial difficulty. How would I respond to them knowing what I now know about the pursuit of justice through law? The law and justice should not be conflated; they are altogether different propositions" (115). I cannot help but concur, and I can only hope that our colleagues within the legal profession are better able than I to withstand the profound ambivalence and even angst that appears to be inherent in the pursuit of justice through the practice of law, at least in the area of access to education for students with disabilities. I have come to understand the pursuit of justice to be a complex and multipronged activist agenda, which may or may not be advanced through litigation in any given case. There is certainly much work to be done toward righting educational wrongs, and I look forward to carving out spaces within which that work might take place and continuing to work with families and schools, to engage in critical teacher education, and to work with disabled activists in community political initiatives. Though others will undoubtedly persist in doing critical work within courtrooms and law offices, I'm not sure if I'll ever again personally pursue the righting of educational wrongs in those spaces. I concur, in closing, with Slee's observation that cases such as those described in this chapter and discussed in his text are "testimony to the truth in Touraine's stark observation that our juridical rules and educational programmes are the litmus test of the spirit of a society" (2011, 116). And I shall soldier on in my own fashion, alongside countless others, in pursuit of a society that doesn't merely rhetorically espouse but actually enacts a spirit of justice for all.

10

The Case for Inclusive Eligibility under the Individuals with Disabilities Education Act

WENDY F. HENSEL

The question of who is "disabled enough" to qualify for services and legal protection is a recurring theme in legislation relating to people with disabilities. Because disability is a social construct rather than an immutable characteristic, a change in the legal definition of the term *disability* or a shift in judicial interpretation of its meaning can significantly expand or contract the class protected by law (Eichhorn 1999, 1418–24; Hensel 2009, 641–43). This phenomenon has received significant attention in the context of the Americans with Disabilities Act of 1990 (ADA), which regulates the conduct of most employers, public entities, and public accommodations. Scholars have used both social disability theory and historical conceptions of stigma to explain how the ADA's statutory definition of disability has driven unfavorable outcomes and societal resistance to expansive rights (e.g., Mcgowan 2000). Legal scholars have paid scant attention, however, to the imagery of disability embraced by the Individuals with Disabilities Education Act (IDEA) and its impact on eligibility for special education.

To receive services under the IDEA, the child must first establish that he or she is a "child with a disability," defined in part as a child who, by

Portions of this chapter are excerpted with permission from Wendy F. Hensel, "Sharing the Short Bus: Eligibility and Identity under the IDEA," *Hastings Law Journal* 58 (2007): 1147–202.

reason of an impairment identified in the statute, "needs special education and related services" (§1401(3)(A)–(B) (2010)). The question of who should fall within this class has increasingly come under scrutiny by critics of special education. The percentage of children in public schools receiving services under the IDEA has increased dramatically since its initial passage as the Education for All Handicapped Children Act of 1975 (EAHCA) (Parrish et al. 2004, 5–8). Critics have offered a variety of explanations for this expansion, ranging from misdiagnosis by professionals and the failure of school systems generally to improved diagnostic techniques and rising incidence rates of certain impairments, such as autism (e.g., Berman et al. 2001, 183; Seligmann 2001, 761). Some have even speculated that highly educated and affluent parents are fueling the rise in numbers by aggressively seeking eligibility to secure expensive services and preferential treatment on standardized tests (Horn and Tynan 2001, 12). Despite the disparate nature of such explanations, a common theme among them is that eligibility under the IDEA is too expansive and no longer serves the "truly disabled" as Congress intended (e.g., Garda 2005, 1074). Because the majority of growth has occurred at the margin among students with more moderate disabilities, calls to restrict eligibility to the more substantially impaired are increasingly common.

Perhaps in response to this critique, many courts and administrative hearing officers have required evidence of serious academic failure before eligibility is deemed appropriate under the IDEA (Hensel 2007, 1162–78; Horn and Tynan 2001, 37). The fact that a child must work significantly harder than typical peers to achieve relative success is often ignored in assessing the need for special education and related services (Hensel 2007, 1177–78). The vagueness of the statutory terms allows the eligibility team's ideological and political motivations to play a potentially prominent role in eligibility determinations.

The trend toward restrictive eligibility under the IDEA stands in sharp contrast to the recent expansion of coverage under the ADA. The ADA Amendments Act of 2008 (ADAAA) broadened the definition of disability under the statute and directed courts to interpret this term "in favor of broad coverage of individuals . . . to the maximum extent permitted by this Act" (§12102(4)). Its passage calls into question whether the IDEA's trend toward narrow statutory coverage enhances the integration and advancement of children with disabilities as intended or actually reinforces the stigma of difference and inequality. A close look at this question reveals that the rising number of special education students is not entirely troublesome. Instead, it is a positive reflection of the IDEA's success in reducing the pervasive stigma attached to disability. By defining disability broadly and contextually, the IDEA will avoid the entrenched problems created by the original ADA's coverage of only "substantially limiting" impairments, restrictively defined. Because calls for limiting the IDEA's reach to the "truly disabled" would return the focus to the severity of a child's internal medical limitations rather than focus on the contextual need for assistance, they are ill advised and represent an undesirable return to the medical model of disability.

Severity as Proxy for Funding Entitlements

Throughout history, society has relegated people with disabilities to the margins of the community. The existence of any impairment, whether physical or mental, has been sufficient to place an individual into the category of "other" and well outside the normal social order. In the medical model of disability, there is no recognition of a continuum of human ability or the potential for changing status across time. To put it simply, either one is disabled, or one is not. Because disability arises from internally generated medical limitations that naturally separate people, society is neither responsible for the exclusion of people with disabilities from the mainstream nor concerned with this population outside of the benevolent desire to bestow charity on the less fortunate (Hensel 2005, 146–48).

The requirement in EAHCA and IDEA to educate children with disabilities in the least restrictive environment reflected a monumental shift toward a social model of disability, which acknowledges the role of cultural attitudes and environment in shaping the experience of impairment. Congress explicitly recognized that "[d]isability is a natural part of the human experience" rather than an aberrant state (IDEA 1990, §1400(c)(1) (2006)). In requiring educators to meet these children's individual needs,

Congress acknowledged that institutional arrangements and disability stigma may pose obstacles to their educational success greater than those posed by their internal medical limitations. Mandating the inclusion of children with disabilities into mainstream classrooms simultaneously expanded these children's educational opportunities and diminished the stigma of otherness and isolation that formerly served as the hallmarks of public education.

Calls to restrict the IDEA to the "truly disabled" and insistence on academic failure prior to eligibility represent subtle but distinct challenges to the normalization of disability in education and recognition of disability as a social construct. When the label is attached only to those children with the most severe impairments who are incapable of meaningful academic success, the view of disability as a medical state suffered only by unfortunate individuals outside of the norm is reinstated. Disability is no longer viewed as part of the natural variation in human functioning, but instead as a destination reserved for those unable to function alongside "normal" peers. The medical model of disability is resurrected, and the contextual experience of disability as a social construct is, at best, given secondary consideration. Under such circumstances, the stigma attached to disability will inevitably rise.

This change in the imagery of disability and the return to a medical model of disability represent more than a troublesome theoretical shift for scholars to ponder. Once this view becomes widespread, it may have a significant substantive impact on the inclusion of children with disabilities in general education classrooms and on typical peers' exposure to children with impairments. Children with less severe impairments are likely to have the best opportunity for meaningful integration into mainstream classrooms. Many children with learning disabilities, for example, can succeed in general education when provided with additional individualized instruction or alternative methods of delivery—methods that also often enhance the learning opportunities of the other children in the classroom. Limiting IDEA's reach to only those with serious impairments threatens to truly transform special education into a place rather than a set of services. Because children with more significant impairments may be less likely to secure an appropriate education in an integrated setting, the severity-linked identification of disability becomes irretrievably linked to a self-contained classroom separate and apart from the general school population. Whatever the cost savings generated by restricted eligibility, they come at a steep price to the community of people with disabilities and to society at large.

One need look no further than the ADA for a cautionary tale in this regard. When the statute was passed in 1990, disability advocates celebrated what they believed to be the beginning of the end of society's marginalization of millions of Americans with physical and mental impairments. Many believed that the ADA would facilitate the integration of people with disabilities into all facets of life. Today, however, most agree that the original legislation failed to achieve these goals, largely as a result of the narrow definition of *disability* adopted in the statute (e.g., Eichhorn 1999, 1408; Stefan 2000, 271). The ADA, unlike other civil rights litigation, requires all litigants to establish in the first instance that they are members of the class protected by law. The legislation's antidiscrimination and reasonable accommodation mandates do not arise unless and until an individual demonstrates that he or she has an impairment that substantially limits a major life activity (ADA 1990, §12102(A)).

The Supreme Court repeatedly endorsed a strict interpretation of these terms, and lower courts followed suit.[1] As a result, the focus of most ADA employment cases under the original statute was not on the defendant's allegedly discriminatory behavior or failure to accommodate a plaintiff with impairments, but instead on the severity of the plaintiff's internal limitations, which is consistent with a medical model of disability. The drive to limit the ADA to the "truly disabled" resulted in court findings that individuals with epilepsy, cancer, and diabetes were insufficiently

---

1. See, for example, *Toyota Motor Mfg., Ky., Inc. v. Williams* (2002), holding that an employee who could not perform repetitive manual tasks on the job was not disabled because she nevertheless could perform manual tasks at home, such as brushing her teeth; *Sutton v. United Airlines* (1999), holding that courts must take into account all mitigating measures employed by plaintiffs in determining whether the plaintiff is disabled within the meaning of the ADA; *Murphy v. United Parcel Serv., Inc.* (1999), same as for *Sutton*.

impaired to be disabled within the meaning of the statute.[2] Courts viewed an individual's ability to overcome difficulties posed by internal limitations as evidence that no disability existed in the first place instead of as a reflection of achievement and progress.

The ADA's original focus on the severity of medical limitations rather than on the contextual nature of disability and discrimination ignored the impact of disability stigma on employment opportunities and the barriers that institutional arrangements may pose to successful integration. Particularly troubling, it shifted society's focus from defendants' discriminatory behavior to an evaluation of the crippling nature of plaintiffs' internal impairments. The imagery of disability left in the original ADA's wake was pathetic and extreme, placing those sad individuals unfortunate enough to possess such characteristics squarely into the category of "other." The legislation's supporters hardly anticipated this result. In the ultimate irony, those individuals with disabilities who were most employable and likely to benefit from an antidiscrimination mandate were those least likely to receive assistance or protection from discrimination.

In late 2008, Congress rejected this approach by passing the ADAAA, making clear that the Supreme Court's grudging interpretation of disability had impermissibly "narrowed the broad scope of protection" that Congress had intended to afford through the ADA (§2(a)(4)–(5)). Although the requirement of class membership remains in the legislation, the ADAAA clarified that this inquiry "should not demand extensive analysis" and provided liberal guidance on the meaning of the components of the statutory definition (§2(a)(4)–(5)). In language sure to be repeatedly cited by courts, Congress made clear that "[t]he definition of disability . . . shall be construed in favor of broad coverage . . . to the maximum extent permitted by the terms of this Act" (§4(a)).

The legislative history of the amendments reflects that Congress intended to extend this logic to the treatment of learning disabilities under the ADA. Congress recognized that even students who perform

---

2. See, for example, *Orr v. Wal-Mart Stores, Inc.* (2002) (diabetes); *Pimental v. Dartmouth-Hitchcock Clinic* (2002) (cancer); *Todd v. Academy Corp.* (1999) (epilepsy).

well academically may nevertheless have a disability for purposes of the ADAAA if their method or manner of learning is substantially different than most people (Hensel 2009, 676–81). Such students are not excluded from coverage "simply because [they] managed their own adaptive strategies or received informal or undocumented accommodations that have the effect of lessening the deleterious impacts of their disability."[3] In short, under the revised legislation, even gifted students may fall within the class protected by law and be entitled to reasonable accommodations in an academic setting.

Restricting IDEA eligibility to those who are simply incapable of academic success is equivalent to imposing an exacting "substantial limitation" requirement on students akin to that rejected by Congress in the ADAAA. Students who look and act like typical peers in any meaningful respect are necessarily deemed not disabled enough to qualify for "charitable" intervention. No consideration is given to the challenges a student must overcome to secure academic competence or to his ability to succeed at other critical life skills and tasks routinely addressed in the school environment. In the absence of complete failure, this model acknowledges no need to reflect on the unstated assumptions of normalcy and attitudes of administrators that may have contributed to the impaired student's difficulties. Instead, the student's crippling internal limitations are deemed the source of the problem and the foundation for intervention, thus reinforcing a medical model of disability.

Although there are significant parallels between the IDEA and the ADA, critics might argue that the differences between them call into question the relevance of the comparison. ADA plaintiffs, unlike children seeking eligibility under the IDEA, are given the Herculean task of establishing a substantially limiting impairment while simultaneously demonstrating qualifications for the position in question, a tension that often derailed class membership under the original statute (§12112). The ADA's antidiscrimination focus, moreover, conceivably creates some distance from the IDEA. Because disability animus is not limited to impairments

3. 154 *Congressional Record* H8290-91 (daily ed., Sept. 17, 2008).

that are substantially limiting, scholars have argued that it makes little sense to restrict the ADA's protection to this category rather than to prohibit discrimination broadly based on any physical or mental limitation (e.g., Eichhorn 1999, 1474). Because the IDEA is focused largely on identifying eligibility for governmental services rather than on prohibiting bias on the basis of disability, strict class delineations in order to ensure legitimate service delivery may not only be defensible but necessary in the context of that statute.

Unlike other civil rights laws, however, the ADA not only proscribes discriminatory conduct but also imposes positive obligations of accommodation on private employers. Discrimination is defined in part in the statute as the failure to provide "reasonable accommodations" to members of the protected class (§12112(b)(5)(A)). It is this provision that is most akin to the IDEA. Both statutes require a third party, once an impairment is identified or suspected, to actively engage in an interactive process to determine how the adult or child can best function in an environment tailored to meet the needs of the "typical" worker or student. Because this determination can be interpreted as bestowing a benefit upon an individual rather than as simply withholding a negative, scrutiny of the protected class is likely to be intense to ensure that only the "truly disabled" are the recipients of benefits.

One might argue that Congress and the courts have paid more exacting scrutiny to the delineation of disability in Title I because the imposition of positive obligations on private industry is more problematic than bestowing unfunded mandates on school districts. As special education enrollment rises and schools are required to comply with the No Child Left Behind Act of 2001 (NCLB) without adequate funding, however, the competition for scarce education dollars and, with it, scrutiny of the class receiving services under the IDEA will increase. Such scrutiny may lead to a reduction in funds available for special education students generally, not just for those with more moderate impairments. Tying eligibility to the severity of impairment undermines the recognition of disability as a social problem for which the public is at least in part responsible. As calls to restrict the protected class rise, public debate and court scrutiny will increasingly focus on the characteristics of those receiving services rather than on the quality of the education extended to them, similar to the ADA context.

A narrow definition of disability is likely to generate heightened suspicion of and anger toward all individuals with disabilities, in particular those with hidden impairments. Few are likely to debate whether the child who has Down syndrome is eligible for services within the meaning of the statute or whether the child who is blind requires individualized attention within an educational setting. Even casual observers can appreciate the nature of such limitations, which comfortably fall within a medical understanding of disability. Children who look and act like typical peers, regardless of their academic struggles, are a different story altogether. Because these children are not easily cabined within the stereotypes of disability, their receipt of an individualized education and scarce educational resources appears suspect. The enhanced services and parental input deemed necessary to the education of the severely impaired is positioned as unfair advantage and largesse in the context of children with moderate impairments. Schools may be chastised for indiscriminately bestowing scarce resources reserved for "real" disabilities on typical children, leading to calls to reduce funding for special education generally in an attempt to force administrators to stop unnecessary spending.

Indeed, the seeds of this funding backlash are already present in public discourse. Massachusetts, convinced that schools were overidentifying students with disabilities and too lax in containing the costs associated with special education, changed its state funding formula in the early 1990s (Berman et al. 2001, 187–88). Rather than allocating funds based on actual enrollment of special needs students in a district, the state instead based funding "on a preset percentage of children in special education set lower than the state average" and allocated "less than half of what would be required to pay for services for these students" (Berman et al. 2001, 187, 189). In addition, children were required to demonstrate both the presence of a disability and the inability to make effective progress in regular education in order to establish eligibility. The legislature believed that these disincentives would cause districts to review eligibility and placement decisions more carefully.

Despite the financial disincentives imposed by the legislature, the number of children in special education in the state declined by less than one percent of the student population over the next decade (Berman et al. 2001, 190). The funding available to serve their educational needs, however, indisputably declined as a result of the revised formula (Berman et al. 2001, 206). A study evaluating the shift in funding concluded that the rise in special education eligibility experienced in the past and predicted for the future did not flow from lax enforcement of eligibility standards, but instead from a variety of social, medical, and economic sources outside the school districts' control (Berman et al. 2001, 205–6). Despite the study's finding, children in other states may face a similar reduction in resources if increased challenges to eligibility result in a restrictive definition of disability at the federal or state level. Challenges to the eligibility criteria for children on the margins thus have the potential to place at risk the funding needed for all children with disabilities in education.

As this trend progresses, moreover, the stigma associated with disability will rise. Tying assistance to academic failure and impaired functioning creates perverse incentives to emphasize the significance of a child's impairment in his life. Because eligibility is all or nothing, parents are encouraged to characterize their child's functioning as negatively as possible to the eligibility team. They may be reluctant to share the child's strengths and abilities with educators out of fear that doing so will result in a refusal of services. This characterization is damaging both to parents' perception of their child and the child's perception of himself to the extent that he is involved in the evaluation process. Children with disabilities will increasingly be viewed as a bundle of problems to solve rather than as individuals with strengths and weaknesses in need of educational redress. The moral foundation of supporting these children is no longer the educational system's failure to meet their needs, but instead the extent of the children's internal impairments. The resources and educational services schools allocated to this population look more like benevolent charity and less like the equitable distribution of resources to all children in society. The medical model of disability, eroded by the passage of EAHCA, is thus resurrected as the dominant paradigm in American special education.

The Problem of Resource Allocation

Regardless of the desirability of an inclusive definition of disability under the IDEA, it is indisputable that the world of education funding is limited and that the need to draw attention to difference as a funding mechanism may outweigh the harms of a restrictive definition. Some scholars have pointed out that relaxed eligibility guidelines will permit general education to absorb special education, with the result that children with disabilities would no longer be served as Congress intended (Weber 2006, 22). In contrast, other commentators argue that eligibility must be tightened to prevent special education from draining the resources available to general education students (Horn and Tynan 2001). Both positions make clear that a tight line must be drawn to secure funding from Congress in the first instance.

Drawing that line at academic failure or near failure as a precursor to eligibility, however, is misguided and inappropriate in light of the statutory eligibility requirements. The IDEA makes clear that the eligibility team must "use a variety of assessment tools and strategies" in evaluating whether a child qualifies for protection under the act (§1414(b)(2)(A)). There is little point to this requirement if even modest academic performance automatically trumps all other indicators of educational need. A child who as the result of an impairment is capable of securing a passing grade only with significant supports in place and only with the expenditure of significant effort is no less "adversely affected in educational performance" than a child who is ultimately unable to overcome such obstacles. In both cases, internal functional limitations impair the ability to learn and achieve commensurate with typical children. In both cases, internal functional limitations are exacerbated by the social imagery of disability that does not acknowledge or recognize that impairment need not be synonymous with failure.

Underlying pundits' complaints that special education is "taking away" dollars from general education, moreover, is the implicit assumption that typical children are presumptively entitled to all educational funding. Education is conceived of not as a public good to which every child is entitled, but instead as a privilege reserved for those fortunate enough to fall within the mainstream. Any shift from this starting point requires special justification and is immediately suspect (Minow 1985, 204). The designation "special" education itself is clearly reflective of this view and reinforces the lesser social standing of children with disabilities. The more justification that is required to secure funding, the more funding for all students becomes suspect.

If the purpose of restricting eligibility is merely to contain costs and transfer wealth to the general student population, moreover, such calls ignore a significant fact: students struggling academically as a result of moderate impairments will still be in the classroom whether they are officially labeled as "disabled" under the IDEA or not. These children have not been and are not likely in the future to be successful under the one-size-fits-all approach employed in general education. A disability label does not alter their educational needs or the level of funding necessary to meet such needs (Berman et al. 2001, 209). It may have a direct impact, however, on a school district's responsiveness to parental demands. In the absence of due process guarantees, a school district may with impunity ignore the parents of children with disabilities because the parents have no enforceable rights to the contrary. This is true even with respect to IDEA funding for pre-referral services because Congress made clear that children served in that program do "not have the same rights and protections as students that are identified as eligible for services" under Part B (H.R. Rep. 108-77, at 104 (2003)).

The extent of savings generated by restricting the definition of disability thus would depend significantly on the intentions of the school district in question. In those districts committed to meeting the needs of students with moderate impairments, the costs associated with this population are unlikely to change dramatically. Certainly, there would be fewer costs associated with eligibility determinations if certain students were clearly excluded from coverage. Moreover, such districts will conceivably save the administrative expenses attributable to due process challenges and the development of Individualized Education Plans (IEPs) otherwise associated with these students. The savings attributable to the former are unlikely to be substantial, however, because formal legal challenges under the IDEA are rare even in inferior school districts and represent less than

0.3 percent of all special education expenditures (Chambers, Harr, and Dhanani 2003, 5). In order to remediate the learning difficulties experienced by moderately impaired students who are not IDEA eligible, moreover, educators necessarily will be required to investigate the nature of academic failure and devise a plan for individualized remedial instruction not unlike an IEP.

Those school districts experiencing the largest savings would presumably be those that are the least sincere and capable of educating students with disabilities as well as those with the fewest resources. If students who are struggling receive educational intervention only if mandated by law under the IDEA, then clear cost savings will result from limiting the number of eligible students with disabilities. To the extent that hostility to individualized education can be generalized, these districts are also most likely to experience cost benefits as a result of being insulated from legal challenges.

The debate over the parameters of special education eligibility accordingly should not focus on whether the additional costs associated with educating the moderately impaired should be incurred; instead, the focus should be on who is going to bear these costs and when. To the extent school districts are granted permission to treat these students indifferently, costs are merely transferred from the district to society at large in that students who do not reach their potential ultimately will have a difficult time finding employment, resulting in dependence on government benefits and welfare programs. These principles motivated passage of EAHCA in 1975 in the first place and remain equally relevant today.[4]

One may nevertheless argue that restricting eligibility under the IDEA will result in a more equitable distribution of scarce resources because it will impair the ability of highly educated and affluent parents to manipulate the system by classifying academic failure as a medical problem. Although the diminished stigma attached to learning disabilities

---

4. "Improving educational results for children with disabilities is an essential element of our national policy of ensuring equality of opportunity, full participation, independent living, and economic self-sufficiency for individuals with disabilities" (IDEA 1990, §1400(c)(1) (2006)).

and moderate disorders is positive, some contend that it has simultaneously encouraged a subset of parents to seek eligibility as a way of securing entitlement to services not otherwise forthcoming. In this view, services under the IDEA are provided not to rectify disadvantage, but instead to create unfair advantage for the politically powerful. The laudability of the shift in the imagery of disability may be complicated by the regressive distributive consequences of focusing scarce resources on those with more marginal impairments.

There is little evidence, however, establishing that the number of children identified as IDEA eligible in wealthy districts reflects improper classification rather than a heightened awareness of rights and acceptance of disability in education. Disability stigma is often highest in communities that do not have access to professional support and informational services, which leads to "self-exclusion . . . at the early stages of identification" (Caruso 2005, 181). It is equally plausible that such numbers reflect administrators' unwillingness, for cost reasons or otherwise, to provide the supports or services mandated by law in the absence of genuine accountability, which is often lacking in poor districts. Parental input under the IDEA is desirable precisely because school systems, intent on the costs of services, may offer what they are willing to provide rather than what they are required to provide for a child with disabilities. In a recent study, for example, 14 percent of the parents seeking services for their children reported that school staff refused to test their child for disabilities because the staff did not believe the child needed the requested services (Leiter and Krauss 2004, 144). Parents living in poverty have reported even more difficulty in securing assistance from school districts (Leiter and Krauss 2004, 144). In the wake of Supreme Court decisions making it more difficult for poor and middle-class parents to pursue due process challenges, this trend is likely to be exacerbated in the future.[5]

---

5. See, for example, *Arlington Central Sch. Dist. v. Murphy* (2006), holding that expert witness fees are not recoverable by parents as "costs" under the IDEA's fee-shifting provision; *Schaffer ex rel. Schaffer v. Weast* (2005), holding that the party seeking relief has the burden of proof in due process hearings.

Scholars have demonstrated that treatment secured by affluent parents willing to force disputes into litigation has at least some beneficial effect on other children with disabilities in a school district (Palmaffy 2001, 15). School administrators intent on fairness between students and parents aware of districts' treatment of similarly situated students will work to ensure that one child's gain is replicated by others (Caruso 2005, 182). It may be, then, that the appropriate conclusion is not that affluent and educated parents are manipulating the system, but rather that their less affluent counterparts are insufficiently educated and empowered to ensure similar results. Greater education and outreach programs for parents who are less knowledgeable about the system of special education as well as greater access to professionals would permit parents without resources to secure the benefits extended by law.

It is equally important to note that many of the instances of alleged abuse of the system by wealthy parents noted in the popular press do not revolve around whether a student is sufficiently impaired to be eligible for assistance or not, but instead on the level of assistance to which he is entitled. One newspaper article, for example, criticized parents for seeking "extra-special" education in the form of private schools, summer camps, therapies, and personal aides (Asimov 2006). Because education funding is neither limitless nor elastic, a robust public debate should occur on the types of services and aids available to assist children with disabilities. Well-intentioned people must address whether cost is or should be a more relevant and explicit factor in administrative decision making. That is a distinct issue, however, from the question of who is eligible as a child with disability under the statute in the first instance.

The Problem of Stigmatization

Not all advocates of people with disabilities would support a call for liberal eligibility guidelines under the IDEA. Although identification as a child with a disability provides service entitlement, it may also stigmatize the child, lead to harassment by peers, and diminish self-esteem and expectations (Rice 2002, 172; Weber 2006, 22). A compelling argument accordingly can be made that children with moderate impairments are best served when they receive appropriate educational services without the label of special education. Indeed, many of the interventions and strategies that work best for children with moderate impairments are employed in general education classes, which may explain why courts and hearing officers have had a difficult time articulating distinctions between "special education" and regular interventions (Hensel 2007, 1174–78). If this position is correct, then children with moderate impairments may be better served by changing the delivery of instruction to general education classes and improving teaching generally than by requiring individuals to acquire a special education label. In this way, different learning styles become part of the norm, diminishing the stigma attached to such struggles.

The social difficulty and victimization that many children with disabilities experience is a very serious problem that requires serious contemplation by policymakers. The root of these problems does not reside, however, in the legal identification of impairment. Instead, it lies in the overt hostility and discomfort that many people continue to feel toward individuals who diverge from the norm in any meaningful respect, reflecting the continued significance of the social model of disability (Weber 2002, 1081). The harassment and stigmatization of these children did not begin with EAHCA and will not end with restricted eligibility criteria. Using that stigma to deny children with impairments the protection that the law extends to them is fundamentally unsound; it is precisely because of the stigma that the law was necessary in the first place. Neither adults nor children need official labels to identify and target difference, although labeling admittedly can facilitate their efforts (Riddick 2000, 657). This is true even with respect to "invisible" impairments that are not immediately identifiable, such as dyslexia. Children outside the norm will continue to be the victims of bullying and harassment unless and until school districts clearly communicate that such behavior will not be tolerated in any form. In addition, laws prohibiting bullying and providing real remedies when such conduct occurs are needed to ensure that schools will take these issues seriously (Weber 2002, 1159). Restricting eligibility rather than dealing with the underlying conduct is a shortsighted and ineffectual solution to this very troubling problem.

The argument that children referred to special education will unnecessarily suffer from diminished self-esteem likewise deserves serious consideration by policymakers. Any action that causes a child to be less motivated or confident in school should be scrutinized carefully. Nevertheless, it is inescapable that this problem, like harassment and bullying, derives in large part from the treatment children receive from society once they are identified as students with disabilities (Garda 2005, 1083). Children with moderate impairments presumably are referred for eligibility determinations at least in part because they are struggling in the general classroom, which itself is not conducive to high self-esteem. It is likely, moreover, that they are aware of negative labels attributed to them by teachers and fellow students prior to the eligibility referral and recognize that they are perceived as different from typical peers (Barga 1996, 415). If the labeling process results in automatic transfer into a self-contained classroom where teachers communicate the message of diminished status and expectations, there is little doubt that the student's self-image will suffer significantly from the eligibility determination (Arceneaux 2005, 243–44; Barga 1996, 415). If eligibility instead is the gateway to improved educational services and the identification of difficulty as intended by Congress, however, this outcome is neither predetermined nor inevitable. Studies have shown that in these circumstances identification can actually improve self-esteem for some students, in particular those with intangible impairments, because it pinpoints the source of difficulty as something other than poor motivation and lack of ability (Riddick 2000, 659).

It is important to recognize that the advancement of people with disabilities will not be achieved by conceding that the stigma attached to this status is so great that any reasonable person would do anything to avoid such a label, including foregoing services designed to foster educational success. It is in such concessions that the imagery of disability as an unnatural and pathetic state is reinforced and entrenched. It is only by normalizing the concept of impairment rather than by restricting the membership of people in the category of individuals with disabilities that the stigma of disability will be reduced. If students capable of even modest academic success are deemed insufficiently "special" to qualify for assistance, this reduction of stigma will not occur. It is not the legal identification process itself that harms the student, but rather the negative imagery of disability that teachers, administrators, and fellow students communicate in the wake of labeling.

Despite these limitations, it is important to acknowledge that the separation of special education and regular education does highlight the differences between students rather than the common ground among all learners (Rice 2002, 174). A commitment to serve all struggling students would reduce the administrative complexity of the current system of federal aid based on student characteristics. Parents would not be required to jump through legal eligibility hoops to ensure their child's educational needs are met, and the focus would positively shift from the recipient's characteristics to the level of educational services being provided. This approach also would address the objection by those who question whether there is a moral basis for concluding that students with disabilities deserve assistance while other struggling students do not (Kelman and Lester 1997, 6).

Few would disagree that each and every child is entitled to receive the services that he or she needs in order to become a successful and productive adult. It is questionable, however, whether it is possible for schools to effectively meet the needs of all learners without any type of labeling or identification process as this approach suggests. Some scholars have argued that this kind of generalized approach to academic difficulty is overly simplistic and "assumes that simply observing behavior is a reliable way of identifying children's disabilities" (Riddick 2000, 656). This fact, in combination with the reality that education has never and may never receive adequate funding to allow for the widespread individualization of instruction, negates the wisdom of restricting special education in order to individualize education generally, at least at this point in time.

To create a world where disability does not matter, educators and policymakers must begin with the recognition that it does. Schools have not demonstrated an impressive track record of providing services to children with impairments in the absence of federal mandates. Although much has changed since 1975, the stigma attached to this population still thrives and continues to present challenges to people with disabilities. Significantly, that stigma is disproportionately greater than that experienced by other minority groups in society, particularly in the context of mental disabilities (Campbell 1994, 137). In a world of equivalent educational dollars for each child, children with disabilities will inevitably lose. These children do not begin on a level playing field because of both societal attitudes and internal impairments, and a level playing field in education will only relegate them to perennial status in last place.

The Problem of Overidentification

Although scholars may legitimately argue over the boundaries of eligibility, few, if any, would argue that there is any positive aspect to the misidentification of children as disabled. Some scholars have argued, as has Congress, that many children in this category end up in special education because of poor regular classroom instruction rather than because of the existence of internal medical limitations (e.g., Horn and Tynan 2001, 42; Palmaffy 2001, 2). There is a great deal of concern in particular over the number of African American children who are being referred to special education. It is beyond dispute that children improperly identified as eligible can suffer "significant adverse consequences, particularly when these students are being removed from regular education settings and denied access to the core curriculum" (H.R. Rep. 108-77, at 84 (2003)).

The overidentification of children of color is of such significance to the special education system because it lies at the intersection of race, class, and disability prejudice. African American children in particular not only are statistically more likely to be identified as eligible for special education but are also more likely to be assigned to self-contained classrooms once eligibility is established (Glennon 1995, 1251–52). Most scholars and commentators agree that this identification occurs in large part because of racial discrimination and the poor expectations often held of people of color (Glennon 1995, 1317–18).

Although scholars are in agreement as to the seriousness of this issue, the tenor of the conversation here is revealing. Many commentators acknowledge but do not focus on districts' failure to strictly implement the least restrictive environment requirement so that eligibility is not an automatic referral to a self-contained classroom (Garda 2005, 1094). It is in the self-contained classroom that children are the most segregated from typical peers and least likely to follow the general curriculum. Instead, most commentators focus on the disability identification in the first instance, which suggests that at least some of the objection to eligibility springs from a rejection of association. There is a hierarchy of prejudice in the United States, and individuals with disabilities, in particular those identified as mentally impaired, are at the bottom of the pecking order. Although such prejudice does not transform improper eligibility determinations into positive accomplishments, it reveals that the heart of this debate once again is on the identity of disability in American education rather than on the quality of the services that children with disabilities receive once eligibility is established.

The fact that minorities are overrepresented in special education supports one thesis of this article: that loose guidelines enable eligibility determinations to be subject to political capture. The appropriate answer to this issue is not to restrict eligibility only to those with the most extreme impairments, but instead to adopt principled guidelines that minimize the effects of prejudice on the determination of eligibility and to enhance federal monitoring and enforcement mechanisms. There is some early evidence, for example, that the inclusion of children in special education under NCLB's reporting and accountability requirements may be improving educational outcomes, particularly for children of color and children who live in poverty (Koballa 2007). Despite the disability community's mixed reaction to standards-based expectations, early reports in at least some districts reflected significant gains for students with disabilities, in part as a result of increased placement in inclusive rather than self-contained settings (Losen and Welner 2001, 411). Moreover, at least some leaders in the advocacy community have voiced their support for NCLB (Commission on No Child Left Behind 2007, 66). To the extent that eligibility carries with it additional assistance and placement in inclusion classrooms, there are significantly fewer negative consequences attributable to the misdiagnosis and overidentification of disability.

If, in contrast, the only answer to the problem of overidentification is to reduce the number of children in special education, what goal is served thereby? Perhaps these children will more readily remain in general education classrooms and benefit from their teachers' higher expectations. If the source of the referral is at least in part attributable to race discrimination, however, it seems implausible to argue that the stigma attributed to these children simply disappears when the referral can no longer be made. The end result, moreover, is a child who no longer has any procedural protection or enforceable way to secure a free, appropriate education. Although special education programs are often inadequate, no account is taken of these children's failure to succeed in general education, and no explanation is offered as to how the status quo is likely to change outcomes for them.

In a very meaningful way, the problems of overidentification are at their zenith when special education is treated as a destination for problem students rather than as a set of services to assist children with impairments. This treatment is unacceptable regardless of the parameters of protected class. There will always be a need for thoughtful administrators to apply eligibility criteria rigorously. States must provide clarity and consistency so that the eligibility determination will not be subject to capture by politically driven and resource-strapped eligibility teams. Such insight, however, does not alter the fact that educational performance is broader than mere academic performance and that impairments may adversely impact a child's school performance in meaningful ways even when he or she is capable of achieving passing grades. However significant these issues, they do not mandate the conclusion that fewer children are entitled to services.

A distinction must be made between the children who are entitled to receive services and the quality of services they are entitled to receive. As the President's Commission on Excellence in Special Education has stated, eligibility for special education should be "a gateway to more effective instruction and strong intervention" rather than a dead end for children deemed dispensable (2002, 6). The early legislative debates surrounding EAHCA's passage acknowledged as much. Concerned with the mislabeling and overidentification of children with disabilities pursuant to the act, the Senate Committee on Labor and Public Welfare concluded:

> In the educational process, the appropriate identification of handicapping conditions must take place in order to assure that a child receives

appropriate services designed to meet his or her needs. Such identification must also take place in order that a State or local educational agency may plan for the provision of appropriate services to meet the child's unique needs.

In the absence of this process and without the provision of appropriate services, the educational process for a handicapped child is totally inadequate. There is nothing in this process, however, which justifies or necessitates the carrying over of these classification "labels" into the classroom educational process itself such that the child becomes thereby labelled [sic] as having a particular "handicap" which for that reason, sets the child apart as being "different." (S. Rep. 94–168, at 27)

Disability activists testifying before the committee confirmed this same point, making clear that "they recognized the need for the identification and labeling of their handicapping conditions, if that identification and label meant that appropriate educational services would be forthcoming" (President's Commission 2002, 6). The very purpose of the IDEA and other federal legislation is to remedy the discrimination and exclusionary treatment of people with disabilities. Legislators should not use the fact that such ideals are neither universally embraced nor fully implemented in American public schools as the basis for restricting eligibility rather than aggressively pursuing solutions to flaws in service delivery that follow. Congress has acknowledged that the IDEA has yet to reach its goal of "improving educational results for children with disabilities" because of the "low expectations" attached to these children. Such expectations will never alter if those impaired students who may be best able to maximize opportunity as a result of special education are routinely deemed insufficiently impaired to qualify for intervention.

Conclusion

As disability scholars have argued for several decades, disability is an inevitable and natural part of the continuum of human ability. There is no clear demarcation between the able and the disabled, particularly in the context of developing children. Calls to restrict IDEA benefits to the "truly disabled" would return disability to a classification reserved for those with severe and pervasive impairments clearly outside of the norm. This characterization both enhances the stigma of disability and reinforces a medical model wherein people with disabilities are largely the source of their own problems.

The rise in the number of special education students has created real challenges for school districts and policymakers. Creating clear eligibility standards will assist in insulating these important decisions from the political and ideological positions of the eligibility team. No line should be drawn, however, at academic failure on the pretense that children capable of any success necessarily cannot be disabled for purposes of the IDEA. To continue on a contrary path both enhances the stigma of disability and trivializes the struggles that many public-school children encounter as a result of their impairments.

The disability community must look beyond the obvious argument of restricting eligibility in order to protect the limited resources extended to the class. This argument exploits the natural divisions present in the community because of the divergent impairments experienced by group members. The most effective path to achieving social change and integration historically has been to insist on the rights of all people with disabilities. A collective commitment to the equitable treatment of all children with impairments has been and will continue to be the most effective way to achieve social acceptance of disability and integration into the public schools.

11

Disability, Vulnerability, and Fragmented Protections

Accessing Education, Work, and Health Care

A N I   B .   S A T Z

In many ways, the effectiveness of US disability law depends on the continued role of a targeted approach to disability discrimination. The Americans with Disabilities Act of 1990 (ADA) recognizes disability as a protected class and prohibits discrimination in the employment, service, transportation, and public accommodation contexts. Individuals who qualify as disabled may receive limited accommodations from employers, businesses, or covered government entities in statutorily protected environments, so long as accommodations or other modifications do not pose an undue hardship. Individuals who are not recognized as disabled or who are disabled but require material support outside statutorily designated areas have no entitlement to accommodations.

Restricted class membership and limited material support have constrained the ADA's reach as well as that of other related statutes, such as the Rehabilitation Act of 1973 (applying to institutions receiving federal funding) and the Individuals with Disabilities Education Improvement Act of 2004 (IDEIA) (pertaining to primary and secondary education and referred to as IDEA from this point forward). Many individuals with

Parts of this chapter are derived from an article entitled "Disability, Vulnerability, and the Limits of Antidiscrimination" that first appeared in 2008 in volume 83, issue 4, of the *Washington Law Review*.

functional impairments have difficulty qualifying as disabled for protections or benefits. The ADA Amendments Act of 2008 (ADAAA) seeks
to address class eligibility by broadening the definition of *disability* and
requiring courts to assess individuals for their disability in a premitigated state—that is, before the use of drugs, devices, or other measures
to improve functioning. The ADAAA, however, leaves a number of issues
unresolved. The US Supreme Court often looks to outcomes rather than
to methods of functioning to determine disability; thus, if an individual
functions atypically but effectively without legally recognized mitigating
measures, she may not be considered disabled (Satz 2006, 243–48). Further, the ADAAA does not address individuals who are vulnerable to disability given certain environmental changes, such as those affecting air
quality, office layout, or lighting. Although ADA jurisprudence influences
determinations of disability under the Rehabilitation Act, the IDEA has its
own eligibility requirements.

Even individuals who qualify as disabled may face barriers to accessing education, employment, health care, and other aspects of the social
realm. These barriers are interrelated. Lack of health care may influence
an individual's ability to have meaningful access to education or to enter
the workforce. Students who have difficulty qualifying for services under
the IDEA may not obtain the assistance they need to learn, denying them
the opportunity to form the educational foundation for further education
and employment. Postsecondary students with disabilities who are covered under the ADA bear unique financial burdens associated with disability testing and documentation as well as reduced course loads, which
may lengthen and increase the cost of degree programs (Carter et al. 2010,
195). Students who are able to obtain postsecondary education face barriers to entering the workforce. Students with disabilities often receive
greater accommodation in postsecondary education than in employment,
and transition programs are lacking (Carter et al. 2010, 195; Pacer Center
2010). Depending on which studies one finds compelling, employment
rates of individuals with disabilities are either unimproved (Acemoglu and
Angrist 2001, 929; Beegle and Stock 2003, 850; Stapleton, Burkhauser,
and Houtenville 2004, 1–4) or lower (Jolls and Prescott 2004, 5; cf. Donohue and Heckman 1991, 1713) than before the passage of the ADA.

For employed individuals with disabilities, accommodation is limited, resulting in barriers to retention. Title I of the ADA, which pertains to employment, requires that a worker who discloses a disability and requests an accommodation receive only "a" (meaning one) reasonable accommodation to facilitate her functioning in the workplace. The Equal Employment Opportunity Commission (EEOC, 2013) regulations do not require that the accommodation be one that an individual prefers or that best promotes her functioning, "so long as it is sufficient to meet the job-related needs of the individual" (29 C.F.R. §1630). There is no requirement, for example, that an accommodation support atypical modes of functioning (Satz 2006, 225–58). Further, accommodations are typically confined to the physical workspace or to modifications to the work day (Bagenstos 2004, 42) and do not include assistive devices that facilitate an individual's employment by supporting her functioning both at home and at work (Satz 2008, 2010, 2011). In addition, an interactive process during which employees and employers discuss a preferred accommodation is not federally mandated, so the law fails to afford uniform requirements for the employer–employee dialogue (Satz 2008, 2010).

Lack of sufficient supports—including health care and transportation—also may hinder education, work, and other social participation (Bagenstos 2004, 26–34). Wage and health benefits under Social Security are limited and may require a claimant to prove disability that prevents gainful employment. This means, with some exceptions (the Ticket to Work and Work Incentives Improvement Act of 1999), that one cannot both return to work (or pursue educational opportunities) and continue to receive the same level of Social Security benefits. For individuals with disabilities who are working, employee benefit plans may not cover medical services necessary to manage the effects of their disabilities because the ADA generally fails to apply to the content of health insurance policies (*Pegram v. Herdrich* 2000; ADA, §12201(c)). Although public transportation services are covered under the ADA (Titles II and III), limited routes and vehicles cause individuals with disabilities to compete with the growing elderly population over benefits such as Paratransit.

This chapter argues that targeted approaches to disability discrimination fragment disability protections both by including only certain impaired individuals in the protected class and by providing limited accommodations that do not allow for meaningful access to education, work, transportation, services, and places of public accommodation. Individuals with impairments that do not rise to the legal level of disability face barriers to accessing statutorily protected environments. For individuals recognized as part of the protected class, protections are interrupted when disability extends across public environments that are not statutorily protected or into the private realm.

One possible solution to fragmentation is the adoption of universal benefit programs, which do not require a certain degree of impairment for eligibility and provide the same level of benefits to all enrollees. In the education and health care contexts, universal approaches may be politically possible, and I advocate further research and legal development in those areas. A universal work program, however, poses formidable challenges. In the work context, I argue that individuals who qualify as disabled should be provided broader material supports through government subsidies to enable access to work. Universal design of buildings falls somewhere between work and education/health care in terms of political feasibility and should be encouraged through government assistance but not mandated. But universal design may prove the most efficient way to accommodate functioning within physical spaces and offer benefits to all individuals.

This chapter is divided into three sections. Section I discusses disability as an aspect of the human condition. This perspective provides a foundation for universal approaches to disability discrimination. Martha Fineman's theory of vulnerability lends support to my arguments that every human being is vulnerable to disability, and such vulnerability (and vulnerability to discrimination if disability is realized) is constant and exists across environments. Section II develops my theory of fragmentation. The first part of that section discusses the limitations of viewing disability in terms of protected class (an identity category) rather than as an element of the human condition. The second part demonstrates the detrimental effects of treating disability discrimination as situational or limited to a particular environment in the public realm rather than as extending across environments in both the public and private spheres. Section III proposes some solutions to the problems of fragmentation in the work, education, and health care contexts. The first part of that section addresses barriers to unemployment and accommodation and proposes a method to expand reasonable accommodation through government subsidies. Under that proposal, individuals will receive accommodations that facilitate employment by enabling them to function more fully across environments. This proposal exceeds the ADA's reasonable accommodation mandate but leaves the protected class status requirement intact. The second part of the section suggests that more research is required with regard to universal approaches within primary and secondary education and that transition programs should be developed to assist individuals moving from secondary education into postsecondary education or from school into the workforce. The last part of the section argues that universal vulnerability to disability supports a universal approach to health care.

I. Disability and Universal Vulnerability

Disability is an inherent aspect of the human condition. All individuals are vulnerable to disability, and most will experience disability during some part of their lives. Individuals with disabilities are universally vulnerable to further disability as well as to exclusion and discrimination. Martha Fineman's (2008) theory of vulnerability lends support to these arguments.

Fineman's vulnerability thesis is a critique of formal equality, or the view that equality means providing the same opportunities to both privileged and disadvantaged groups. A formal equality approach does not address substantive inequalities embedded within legal structures, but treats individuals in the same manner under existing structures. The ADA embraces formal equality by seeking to provide individuals with disabilities access to various parts of the social realm that are accessible to individuals without disabilities. The ADA, like other civil rights mandates, is a targeted approach that affords protections only to individuals who qualify for membership in the protected class.

Fineman's theory of vulnerability argues that disadvantage (which may give rise to discrimination) is best addressed by moving beyond social, cultural, and political identity categories, including protected classes, and focusing on common vulnerability (2008, 4n7, 16). To this effect, she argues that vulnerability is a "universal, inevitable, enduring aspect of the human condition" (8). All individuals are vulnerable in the sense that they have the potential to become impaired. (Although Fineman speaks of "dependency" rather than "impairment," I do not believe it is too much of a stretch to apply her theory to impairments that may not give rise to dependency.) The ontology of impairments may differ (Fineman 2008, 12). Fineman conceives of vulnerability as not situated in the body alone; that is, it may be the product of economic, institutional, and other social harm (2008, 9–10). Thus, Fineman's "vulnerable subject" may have social, economic, or biological limitations (11–12) that may give rise to discrimination or other disadvantage.

Current laws assume individuals are for the most part fully functioning over a lifetime. As a result, they are framed with reference to a subject whose vulnerability, owing to existing social supports or serendipity, never manifests as impairment or "dependency" (Fineman 2008, 15–16). Those who require additional health care, wage supports, or environmental adaptations to function are disadvantaged by a system that views their needs as exceptional and as requiring something akin to affirmative action (J. Leonard 2005, 43) rather than as a manifestation of the human condition (Fineman 2008, 17–18). Thus, the current legal scheme results in double jeopardy for some: individuals are disadvantaged by the realization of their vulnerability, and they are consequently denied assistance or provided only limited assistance because their needs are viewed as special (Satz 2008, 1483).

Fineman argues for a strong state with structures that support vulnerability as universal (2008, 19–22), contending that "[v]ulnerability . . . freed from its limited and negative associations is a powerful conceptual tool with the potential to define an obligation for the state to ensure a richer and more robust guarantee of equality than is currently afforded under the equal protection model" (8–9). The state's role is expanded beyond addressing specific dependencies of some protected groups to responding to the vulnerability of all individuals, regardless of whether financial, social, or physical impairments rise to dependency. The role of the state and its institutions is to provide support that enables vulnerable individuals to remain resilient (Fineman 2008, 13, citing Kirby 2006).

Fineman's theory has clear applications to the disability context, both in terms of thinking about the disabled subject and the state's response to vulnerability to impairment. A vulnerable subject may become a disabled subject based on biology or environment. Vulnerability to disability, like other impairments, is universal and constant. An individual becomes disabled when vulnerability is realized (Satz 2008, 2010, 2011). An individual with a disability remains vulnerable to further disability and may experience vulnerability more acutely: "[u]ndeniably universal, human vulnerability is . . . particular [and] is experienced uniquely by each of us" (Fineman 2008, 10). This experience of disability may give rise to disadvantage, including isolation and discrimination.

Fineman's conception of vulnerability underscores the harms of fragmentation, which I identify in section II. Individuals with impairments that do not qualify them for the protected class may experience discrimination. Even individuals who are entitled to legal protections experience disadvantage because their vulnerability is not limited to statutorily defined and protected public contexts. This disadvantage bears directly on the public/private distinction, or the question of when and under what constraints the state may act. Currently under US law and policy, the state is assumed to be noninterventionist; state intervention to address impairments to functioning outside the marketplace is considered an intrusion into the private realm. Fineman's view of vulnerability as universal and constant illuminates the difficulty with this distinction—namely, that vulnerability does not end when one leaves the public realm (or particular parts of the public arena).

Section II examines the limits of targeted approaches to disability discrimination, focusing on fragmentation resulting from the requirement of protected class membership and situational disability protections.

II. Theory of Fragmentation

The current targeted approaches to disability discrimination fragment protections and benefits for individuals with disabilities. Fragmentation occurs as a result of eligibility requirements for legal protection and to restrictions on disability accommodation under the ADA and IDEA.

The ADA recognizes individuals with disabilities as part of a protected class rather than viewing disability as an aspect of the human experience. Thus, as in the gender, race, and religion contexts, antidiscrimination protections for individuals with disabilities are contingent upon protected class membership. For individuals who are recognized as disabled, the ADA limits accommodation to certain statutorily designated environments. Protection for class members is fragmented when disability is viewed as arising within discrete environments—such as the workplace, the shopping mall, or the public library—rather than as existing continuously across environments. The IDEA similarly contains eligibility requirements and limits on accommodation.

In this section, I first demonstrate that the limitations on class membership for individuals with disabilities are inherent constraints of targeted approaches such as the ADA and IDEA rather than an issue of statutory implementation. Many scholars (C. Anderson 2000, 83; Feldblum 2000, 91; B. Tucker 2000, 321) and, indeed, the ADAAA's authors and supporters suggest that construing the definition of disability to include more persons with impairments will address substantially the barriers to disability protection.[1] I argue that identity categories pose limitations that cannot be remedied by judicial or legislative adjustments. However broadly the protected class is defined, it will necessarily exclude individuals with functional impairments that do not meet the disability threshold test.

Next, I assert that protections are fragmented for individuals who are legally recognized as disabled. The ADA assumes that the vulnerability associated with impairments may be addressed within particular environments in the public realm, such as the workplace, transportation vehicles, and places of public accommodation. This approach fails to account for the vulnerability of individuals with disabilities while moving between and outside these environments. Under current ADA case law, for example, a Deaf person must be able to enter a movie theater, but the law does

---

1. Statements of Representative Capps, a cosponsor of the ADAAA, 154 Cong. Rec. E1376 (daily ed., June 26, 2008), and Representative Jackson-Lee, 154 Cong. Rec. H6083-84 (daily ed., June 26, 2008).

not require that she be able to view a film with closed captioning. Further, the ADA does not address accommodation that facilitates entry from the private realm into the public domain. For instance, it does not provide for accommodation at home that is necessary for an employee to complete vital personal tasks required to maintain a routine work schedule, such as personal grooming, laundry, and meal preparation.

Fragmentation also occurs under the IDEA with respect to eligibility and accommodation. A child with an impairment may be excluded from IDEA coverage based on the restricted list of qualifying impairments, varying state standards, or subjective teacher assessment. Further, students removed from public school may not be entitled to the full benefits of an Individualized Education Plan (IEP). Accommodation also may depend on other environmental factors, such as the ability of a child's parents to advocate on her behalf as members of her IEP team and other students' competing interests (Wagner 1990, 6). Although the IDEA requires schools to place students with disabilities in the least restrictive environment, the No Child Left Behind Act of 2001 (NCLB) requires teachers to improve all student outcomes, which may be difficult without adequate support for an integrated classroom. Accommodation also is fragmented when students move from secondary to postsecondary school and then ultimately into the workforce; in fact, each step carries with it reduced eligibility for accommodation. As is the case under the ADA, the IDEA does not provide for accommodation at home, and individuals may be indirectly denied educational opportunities when they lack accommodation in the private sphere.

A. Exclusion from the Protected Class

Much is written in critical legal scholarship about the value of identity categories—groups of individuals based on social, cultural, or political affiliation—and their relation to legal rights (see Butler 1999, 2004; Crenshaw 1988; Minow 1990, 1997). I do not in this chapter intend to take a position in the debate about whether identity categories promote or hinder rights overall. My argument is simple: civil rights and other targeted approaches to disability discrimination are inherently limited because they require class membership. This requirement necessarily excludes some individuals with impairments from disability protections. Although expanding the definition of disability may protect more individuals with disabilities, it does not address adequately the vulnerability of individuals outside the protected class.

The ADA requires that an individual be "substantially limit[ed]" in "one or more major life activities," have "a record of such an impairment," or "be[] regarded as having such an impairment" (42 U.S.C. §12102(1)). The US Supreme Court historically limited class membership by imposing strict tests for "substantially" and "major life activities" as well as by assessing individuals for disability after they employed drugs and devices that mitigated the effects of impairments. Individuals "regarded as" disabled were required to show that their perceived disability, if actual, would substantially limit a major life activity.

The ADAAA clarifies that the disability threshold test is no longer meant to be overly restrictive. It states that "whether an individual's impairment is a disability . . . should not demand extensive analysis" (ADA, §12101, note (b)(5)), and the Rules of Construction indicate that "[t]he definition of disability in this Act shall be construed in favor of broad coverage of individuals . . . to the maximum extent permitted by the terms of this Act" (§12102(4)(A)). The ADAAA explicitly rejects the standard put forth in *Toyota Motor Manufacturing of Kentucky, Inc. v. Williams*, that an individual must be "severely restrict[ed] . . . from doing activities that are of central importance to most people's daily lives" (2002, at 185; ADA, §12101 note (b)(5)). Although the ADAAA leaves the task of reinterpreting the term *substantially* to the EEOC, it demonstrates how broadly major life activities are to be interpreted by providing an extensive, nonexhaustive list of relevant activities, including "working" and "major bodily functions" (ADA, §12102(2)). Further, the ADAAA includes episodic or in-remission impairments that would qualify as disabilities when active (§12102(4)(D)), thereby covering a large number of conditions that previously encountered mixed judicial treatment, such as epilepsy, cancer, and multiple sclerosis. In addition, the act states that an individual needs to be impaired in only one major life activity (§12102(4)(C)). Also, individuals "regarded as" disabled no longer must demonstrate that their perceived disability would "substantially limit" a major life activity (§12102(3)(a)).

Perhaps the most fundamental change to class membership after the ADAAA, however, is that an individual is assessed in an unmitigated state, or prior to using drugs, devices, or other tools to promote functioning (ADA, §12102(4)(E)). The ADAAA provides a nonexclusive list of ameliorative measures with effects that must not be considered when assessing an individual for class membership (ADA, §12102(4)(E)).

Although these changes greatly enhance individuals' ability to qualify as disabled, some people with impairments still are left unprotected. For example, individuals who are functional in their current environments but hypervulnerable to impairment from environmental alterations are not protected unless they have a qualifying episodic disability or one that is in remission (ADA, §12102(4)(D)). An individual with a disability is hypervulnerable to changes in her environment when she requires certain environmental supports to function, such as a break room with a refrigerator in which to store medicine or special meals, a quiet and unpopulated workspace, or a smoke-free common area in her place of residence. It is only after an environmental shift—an employer turning a break room into a gym and an employee becoming unable to function in her workplace— that an individual may be eligible for disability protection. Individuals who are mildly symptomatic or asymptomatic for disabling illnesses that they have not previously experienced also are not classified as disabled under the ADAAA. Although assessing individuals in a premitigated state will allow greater numbers to qualify as disabled, some factors such as individual fortitude and varied disease expression (severity) nevertheless may result in different outcomes for individuals with the same condition.

Further, membership in the protected class may be insufficient to establish a claim to a remedy. Although the US Supreme Court seems to combine the questions of whether an individual is disabled and whether she is entitled to a remedy, these inquiries are conceptually distinct (Satz 2006, 248–50). After the ADAAA, it is possible that the Court will separate these questions more clearly. The ADAAA in fact specifies that employers are not required to provide accommodations—such as workplace alterations or sensitivity training—for employees who are "regarded as" disabled, that is, who may have impairments that do not rise to the level of disability (ADA, §12201(h)). More generally, however, by including greater numbers of individuals in the protected class, the ADAAA likely will focus more attention on whether an accommodation is required or imposes an "undue hardship" on an employer. In other words, protected class membership may no longer serve as the gatekeeper doctrine for accommodating disability; thus, expanding class membership may mean that protected class status cannot be equated with a remedy, even in the narrow situational sense discussed in the next part of this section.

Similar issues arise under the IDEA. This act requires that students with disabilities in kindergarten through twelfth grade receive a "free and appropriate public education that emphasizes special education" (20 U.S.C. §1400(d)(1)(A) (2006)). In order to qualify for benefits under the IDEA, a student must have one of the thirteen categories of impairments listed in the statute, and, "by reason thereof, need[s] special education and related services" (§1401(3)(A)(ii)). With some exceptions, courts have interpreted the phrase "needs special education" to mean that the child cannot, without accommodation, pass her grade level. For example, the Ninth Circuit Court of Appeals held that a child with a qualifying disability was not entitled to benefits under the IDEA because she could progress to the next grade under the general curriculum (*Hood v. Encinitas Union Sch. Dist.* 2007).

A child with an impairment also may be excluded from IDEA coverage in a number of other circumstances. A highly intelligent child with a statutorily listed disability who by reason of her disability performs at an average level but below her academic potential may be ineligible for coverage. A child with a statutorily listed impairment who receives consistently low grades may not receive IDEA benefits if her poor academic performance is attributable to something other than her disability. For example, a district court in Texas held that a student with attention deficit hyperactivity disorder who had violent outbursts and poor academic performance was ineligible for IDEA coverage because his academic difficulties were owing to his behavior rather than to his disability (*M.P. v. Nebraska. Independent School District* 2007). In addition, students with emotional issues who are considered gifted and students who are considered socially maladjusted rather than emotionally disturbed may be ineligible for services (*J.D. v. Pawlett School District* 2000; 34 C.F.R. §300.8; *Springer v. Fairfax County School Board* 1998). Eligibility also may depend on serendipity. If a lenient teacher documents that a student with a disability receives mediocre but passing grades, that student will not receive services under the IDEA. Meanwhile, a student with the same disability and level of performance may receive failing grades from a stricter teacher and consequently be eligible for services under the IDEA. Furthermore, fragmentation of benefits occurs based on age; once a student graduates secondary school, IDEA coverage ends.

In addition, states have interpreted differently the requirement that a student have a listed disability that "adversely affects educational performance" (34 C.F.R. §300.8(c)(9)(ii) (2007)), and these inconsistencies further fragment benefits. For example, "emotional disturbance" may be a disability, but some courts have interpreted it narrowly to exclude depression, and others broadly to include drug abuse (cf. *Tracy v. Beaufort County Board of Education* 2004; *New Paltz Central School District v. St. Pierre* 2004). Some courts have interpreted "adverse effect" to mean "more than a minimal impact," whereas others construe it as "significantly below age or grade norms" (Hensel 2007, 1170). In some states, mitigating measures have undermined findings of adverse effects, whereas in other states they have not (Hensel 2007, 1172). Different states also treat the ability to engage in extracurricular activities varyingly in terms of demonstrating the impact of an impairment: a child in one state who receives passing grades but is unable to participate in extracurricular activities may receive benefits under the IDEA, whereas that same child in another state may not (cf. *Mr. I. v. Maine School Administrative District* 2007 and *Dale M. v. Board of Education of Bradley-Bourbonnais High School* 2001). Courts have interpreted "educational performance" in divergent ways as well, with some including only academic performance and others considering additional life skills ranging from "'communication skills, social skills, and personality'" to "'all forms of human experience'" (Hensel 2007, 1168n136, 1169).

In sum, a targeted approach to disability necessarily excludes some individuals with impairments from the protected class. Further, class membership does not guarantee a remedy. In the next subsection, I argue that the scope of accommodation or other modification for class members may be limited by fragmented protections.

B. Limited Accommodation

Disability law currently responds to vulnerability to discrimination as if it is situational. That is, federal and parallel state laws address vulnerability within isolated contexts for certain individuals rather than more generally. The ADA covers the workplace, public services, places of public accommodation, and transportation. The Rehabilitation Act similarly applies to recipients of federal grants and programs, and litigation under this law focuses on contexts similar to those under the ADA's public-service and employment titles. The Fair Housing Act of 1968 and the IDEA also address discrete contexts.

Because each of these laws provides accommodation only in statutorily defined contexts, protections for individuals with disabilities are often interrupted, denying them meaningful social participation. For example, under the ADA, one may be able to enter a building but not partake in the services offered within. Workers with disabilities are entitled to accommodation at the worksite or with regard to work schedules to assist them in completing the essential functions of their jobs, but the ADA does not address barriers to employment outside the workplace, such as lack of transportation to work, inability to complete vital household tasks in order to get to work, and limited or no health insurance. Even within the workplace, accommodation may be limited if courts assess an individual's functioning within a small environment. An employee will likely be viewed as able to function in a smaller environment (such as a cubicle), even if she is unable to function throughout the larger workplace environment (building).

Under the IDEA, fragmentation similarly occurs with respect to the level of services provided in the classroom, under IEPs, in transition plans between education programs, in education programs, and in the workforce. Service levels under individualized plans may vary depending on the school and the classroom environment. Compounding the effects

of fragmentation experienced under the IDEA, once a student graduates from secondary school, the level of services provided under the ADA
(within postsecondary education and in the workforce) will differ altogether from those provided under the IDEA.

Before I turn to a detailed discussion of the limitations of mainstream
classrooms and transition programs, it is necessary to note that students
also may receive varying levels of IDEA services based on circumstances
unrelated to their disabilities. If a student's parents move her from public
to private school, she may not be entitled to an IEP. Instead, she may
receive a "services plan," which offers a lower level of benefits and affords
her parents weaker rights (34 C.F.R. §300.138(a)(2) (2010); Hensel 2010,
316–18). Under a services plan, "parents can exercise due process hearing
rights only with respect to complaints about failure to identify, locate, and
evaluate their children, not complaints about failure to serve them or to
serve them as fully as the parents would like" (Weber 2006, 24).

In addition, fragmentation in services may occur when parents' knowledge of the law or of their child's disability is lacking. Parents are required
to be part of their child's IEP team, which means that they attend the IEP
team meetings along with their child's teachers, school psychologist, and
other team members (20 U.S.C. §1414(d)(1)(B)). Unlike representatives
from the school district (Huss 2003, 361–62), parents often do not have
knowledge of the IEP process and of their rights under the IDEA (Nietsch
et al. 2008, 19). Further, parents may not be able to relay critical information about their child's disability during IEP team meetings, especially if
the student has a single parent without a high school education (Wagner
1990).

With respect to the limits of mainstream classrooms, the education of
students with disabilities may be fragmented as competition over scarce
classroom resources increases. More than 6.4 million students nationwide
qualify for IDEA benefits (National Center for Education Statistics 2013).
As the number of IDEA students grows within regular classrooms, the
basic goals of the IDEA (to educate children with disabilities in the least
restrictive environment in accordance with individualized plans) and
NCLB (to standardize assessment and improve outcomes for all students)
may increasingly conflict (Roberts 2008, 1044). This is true even though

the IDEA was amended in 2004 to require performance goals as well as methods of assessment and reporting for students with disabilities that parallel those of NCLB.

NCLB and the amended IDEA require a report documenting Adequate Yearly Progress (AYP) based on grade-level standardized test scores for all students. Under NCLB, schools may exclude only 3 percent of their student body from AYP (an estimated 30 percent of all students with disabilities [Daniel 2008, 356]) based on an inability to achieve grade-level standards (34 C.F.R. §200.13(c)(2)(i), (C)(3) (2007)). AYP determines schools' eligibility for continued funding and may give rise to sanctions if schools fail to meet certain standards (20 U.S.C. §6316(b)(1)–(3) (2002)). Thus, if classroom resources are limited, teachers and schools may be forced to choose between improving the education of most students (i.e., those without disabilities) and accommodating students with disabilities. The latter group of students may be removed from regular classrooms or have their IEPs implemented in an inadequate fashion (Banchero and Little 2004; Roberts 2008, 1045; Schemo 2004).

Fragmentation also exists when students move from secondary to postsecondary education and from secondary or postsecondary education to the workforce. Though the IDEA charges a student's IEP team with documenting needed transition services, these documentation efforts may be minimal. According to one commentator, "It is not uncommon for a student heading to college to simply have the word 'college' written on his or her IEP as the full extent of the transition process" (Yellin 2009, 326).

Although students with disabilities in postsecondary education are eligible for support under the ADA, Section 504 of the Rehabilitation Act, and individual college and university policies, students and their families often incur financial expenses to avail themselves of these resources (Learning Disabilities Association of America 2010). A report by the US Government Accountability Office found that students with disabilities frequently must pay for testing to document their disabilities and for assistive devices (2009, 17). It also found that some students with disabilities may not be able to take a full course load, and a reduced load may both render them ineligible for the maximum amount of federal aid per term and result in extra room-and-board expenses to complete their degrees.

In addition, fragmentation affects individuals with disabilities when they move from education to the workforce. Many state plans to assist students moving from high school to vocation are inadequate because they focus primarily on student and family involvement in planning rather than on skills training of students with disabilities (Carter et al. 2010, 195; Pearman, Elliott, and Aborn 2004, 27). Although federal funding is available for secondary education to work-transition programs, the IDEA does not require schools to coordinate with local or state agencies to offer any particular service or level of services. For example, a study of twenty-nine high schools found that special-education teachers engage in fewer than four of nine possible career-preparation activities (Carter et al. 2010, 197).

When transition programs are provided to high school students, they often lack the infrastructure and coordination needed to deliver services effectively (Benz and Lindstrom 1999, 56). Students and their parents frequently are unaware of or are unable to navigate opportunities (Wittenburg, Golden, and Fishman 2002, 204). Federal coordination of benefits is also lacking, resulting in conflicting eligibility requirements. For example, Supplemental Security Income, which offers financial benefits to minors with disabilities, provides strong work disincentives for adults that conflict with the work-experience emphasis of federally supported vocational rehabilitation programs. Workplace (and postsecondary education) opportunities also correlate strongly with high school credentials, and graduation policies vary dramatically across states (Pacer Center 2010).

Students moving from postsecondary education to the workforce face other challenges. Although most colleges and universities have disability services offices, career counseling may not be provided (National Collaborative on Workforce and Workforce Strategy Center 2009, 6). Further, individuals receive more extensive accommodations in secondary and postsecondary school than in the workplace, which creates significant barriers to entry into the workforce and to job retention.

Some states have passed legislation to improve IEP transition planning in high school, but approaches vary. The Massachusetts Department of Elementary and Secondary Education requires a Transition Planning Form, which includes a student's postsecondary education vision, a disability-related needs section that describes her skills and the transition services required, recommendations for postsecondary preparation, and the roles of interested parties, including school personnel, family members, and service providers (Bouchard and Thompson 2010, 14.3). In response to the issue that colleges and workplaces often do not recognize nontraditional degrees, Tennessee's "one path" program requires that schools include students with disabilities in regular curricula where possible and allow them to earn a traditional diploma (Foster-Spence 2009, 464). Students with the requisite IEP may be provided more avenues than other students for demonstrating knowledge under the regular curriculum and may receive that curriculum until age twenty-two (Foster-Spence 2009, 464).

At least two states offer successful transition programs from secondary school to work. In California, a partnership between the Special Education Local Plan Area and El Camino College provides individualized transition services for individuals with disabilities after high school. The program offers training, evaluation of progress toward transition goals, and support at job sites (Pearman, Elliott, and Aborn 2004, 27, 29). Oregon offers a state and federally supported vocational training Youth Transition Program in which 75 percent of its school districts participate (Benz and Lindstrom 1999). The program provides students support for up to three years after graduation by creating and managing IEPs, providing educational materials, facilitating job placement, and supervising work (Benz and Lindstrom 1999). Specific support services include: developing a student's "person-centered" plan; instructing her on social and academic skills, independent living, and money management; and assisting her with living situations, court visits, and transportation (Benz and Lindstrom 1999, 58). The program offers follow-up services for up to two years after job placement to assess progress and to identify and address problems (Benz and Lindstrom 1999, 59). The California and Oregon transition programs could be extended to all high school students who require additional skills training.

In the following section, I argue for a mixed civil rights/social welfare approach to disability law reform to resolve the problems of fragmentation. I assert that protected class status should continue to govern workplace entitlements, but accommodations must be broader to enable work. Susceptibility to disability discrimination is not situational, requiring material supports within limited public environments, but instead extends throughout one's daily environment. Yet some shared vulnerability of individuals with and without disabilities, including interruptions of education and medical care, may be addressed better through universal programs that do not require protected class membership.

III. Addressing Fragmentation

Individuals with disabilities continue to experience barriers to education, work, and material support such as health care. The vulnerability thesis supports a move toward social welfare programs in these areas. This move would entail a departure from targeted approaches to disability issues to an approach that would respond to universal vulnerability, which would require the restructuring of legal and social institutions. In the employment context, for example, institutions would need to address the shared vulnerability of workers with and without disabilities to barriers to entry and to accommodation. As William Johnson argues, workers disabled as adults face barriers to reentry into the workforce similar to those unemployed by workforce cutbacks or factory closings: "low skills, intermittent or marginal employment, [and] the relative ease with which an employer can find replacement workers" (1997, 168–69).

My proposal to address fragmentation in disability law is a compromise between a targeted/civil rights approach and a universal benefits/social welfare approach. Vulnerability theory reveals that the ADA's goals of increasing employment and reducing social isolation are not fulfilled by equal protection or sameness treatment. The IDEA's mission of a "free and appropriate public education" for students with disabilities similarly is not realized by a targeted approach.

In the first part of this section, I advocate a mixed civil rights/social welfare approach to employment. Although class membership will be restricted in accordance with a civil rights approach, accommodation will be more broadly available and subsidized by the state as a matter of social welfare. I also discuss the role of reasonable accommodation in addressing barriers to employment. I argue that the reasonable accommodation mandate must be given a broader social purpose that extends beyond what formal equality requires.

In the next two parts of this section, I propose universal approaches to education and health care, respectively. First, I advocate further research regarding and development of existing universal approaches to primary and secondary education. Then I argue that the state should adopt a social welfare approach to health care to address universal vulnerability.

The difference in my approaches to employment and education/ health care stems largely from practical considerations. In the employment context, I do not believe that a radical departure from the formal equality approach to disability discrimination to a system addressing workers' universal vulnerability is politically feasible at this time. Historical resistance to expanding most social welfare programs (see Somers and Block 2005), the declining benefits of existing programs (Moffitt, Ribar, and Wilhelm 1998, 423–24), and sustained periods of low unemployment during solid financial times (Blank 2000, 7; US Department of Labor 2008) provide support for this view. In addition, the history of oppression of individuals with disabilities and the staggering numbers of such persons who are denied entry into the workplace bolster an approach that focuses on disability as a protected class in this context. I do not mean to suggest that law reformers should abandon the push for greater equity in employment irrespective of identity categories. Women, racial minorities, unskilled laborers, workers with disabilities whose impairments limit their productivity, and individuals whose impairments do not rise to legally cognizable disabilities also face barriers to employment owing to fragmented protections. The state ideally would respond to all such vulnerability.

Meanwhile, universal approaches to education and health care may be politically and practically possible. Primary and secondary education is compulsory and publicly available, and the question is only how such education should be provided. In the health care context, large-scale government health care programs already operate and are expanding; public spending on health care before the 2010 reforms was at 60 percent of total health care expenditures (Woolhandler and Himmelstein 2002, 91, 94).

A. Rethinking Reasonable Accommodation under the ADA

I argue that the reasonable accommodation mandate must have a broader social or redistributive purpose than that embodied in the ADA. Broadening the scope of reasonable accommodation entails a mixed civil rights/ social welfare approach to modification. Eligibility for accommodation would remain tied to membership in the protected class, though the vulnerability of individuals with disabilities would be viewed as extending across contexts. As a result, individuals with disabilities would be entitled to greater material resources enabled by government support. Although expanding the reasonable accommodation mandate does not reflect the ADA drafters' intent (Stein 2004, 637–40), it supports congressional goals of decreasing barriers to entry for workers with disabilities and lessening isolation more generally (42 U.S.C. §12101(a)(3), (5), (8), (b), note (a)(1)– (2), (b)(1)). Such an expansion substantially addresses employment barriers for individuals with disabilities that occur outside the workplace, including the lack of reliable transportation and accommodation that benefits an employee at work as well as at home. The focus here is on employment, but I also discuss how my concept of reasonable accommodation might facilitate multiple ways of functioning for people utilizing public services or places of public accommodation.

Addressing Barriers to Employment. Under the mixed civil rights/ social welfare approach I advocate, protected class members would receive accommodation at work that exceeds the scope of the current civil rights mandate of Title I of the ADA and formal equality. The reasonable accommodation mandate would be expanded with more government supports for workers with disabilities. Employees with disabilities would receive accommodation throughout their daily environments. For example, they might have accommodation for transportation to work or tools that facilitate their functioning at home as well as at the workplace.

This expansion of the reasonable accommodation mandate would require law reform on two fronts. First, it would be necessary to create funding structures to relieve employers of the financial burden of providing all reasonable accommodations. The legislature could determine a ceiling for the percentage of annual earnings it would require employers to spend on accommodations for employees with disabilities. Affected employers, as defined currently by the ADA, would not be required to fund accommodations outside this amount. Government subsidies would begin where employer subsidization ends. This approach would allow employer responsibility for accommodations to be capped while expanding disability protections beyond discrete environments.

Second, the interactive process recommended by the EEOC, a process by which an employer engages an employee in a dialogue about the requested accommodation that would best facilitate her functioning, would be federally mandated and refined. During this process, an employee would identify an accommodation she needs to function in the workplace as well as what is required to assist her indirectly with her employment by enabling her to function at home. The law would require that adaptive tools benefitting an individual in her workplace as well as at home and in other environments be given preference over tools assisting an individual only in her workplace. In addition, priority would be given to accommodation that supports an employee's desired mode of functioning, whether it is typical (for example, walking upright with braces) or atypical (sitting and wheeling). The undue hardship test would remain a defense for failing to make an accommodation, though an employer's burden would be measured taking into account government subsidies for which she is eligible, even if she fails to apply for them.

Supporting Atypical Modes of Functioning. In addition to addressing barriers to employment, the mixed civil rights/social welfare approach to reasonable accommodation better supports atypical ways of functioning for employees than a pure civil rights approach. The proposed approach recognizes that although the vulnerability associated with disability is part of the human condition, each individual experiences it uniquely. The ultimate choice of reasonable accommodation would remain with the employer, but the mandated interactive process would give preference to an employee's preferred mode of functioning. An employee with a disability may favor typing with her feet instead of with her upper-arm prosthetics, working in a dark office space rather than wearing shaded glasses to address light sensitivity, or working from the floor rather than from a cushioned chair to avoid back pain. The employer's preference for typical as opposed to atypical modes of functioning is not relevant, so long as the employee is able to fulfill the essential functions of her job.

Supporting atypical functioning under Title II (public services) and Title III (public accommodations) is more complex than under Title I. It would require facilitating meaningful access to key areas of social and civic participation; enabling access into various physical spaces is insufficient. For example, an individual should be able to experience a film as well as enter a movie theater, signal for a stop and board a commuter train, and appreciate a public library's collection as well as enter that library. Given the number of people partaking in these experiences, the variety of ways in which people function, and current social infrastructure, reasonable accommodation in these contexts will require a more radical departure from current practices than in the employment context. Government funds should be available to improve the provision of transportation and other services.

For physical structures, most efficient change will likely not occur through renovation, but with new construction that aims to support more ways of functioning. Universal design, "the design of products and environments to be usable by all people, to the greatest extent possible, without the need for adaptation or specialized design" (Center for Universal Design 2008; see also Erlandson 2008, 17), may ultimately prove to be the best way to address the vulnerability of individuals with disabilities that arises from physical spaces. Universal design relies on seven principles: "equitable use," "flexibility in use," "simple and intuitive" use, "perceptible information," "tolerance for error," "low physical effort," and "size and space" appropriate for use (Center for Universal Design 2008). But universal design responds to impairments that may not be considered disabilities under law and supports functioning more generally (Erlandson 2008, 6). As a result, it extends beyond what my framework (or the ADA) requires for reasonable accommodation, and individuals would implement universal design principles on a voluntary basis.

Two areas where universal programs may be politically and practically feasible are education and health care. I next argue that the issues facing individuals with disabilities with regard to education and health care access are likely best addressed by moving away from targeted approaches to disability discrimination and benefits toward universal approaches to access.

B. Universal Approaches to Primary and Secondary Education

As both the IDEA and the NCLB statutes indicate, targeted approaches to improving student outcomes pit vulnerable students against each other in a fight for limited resources. Increasing the number of students included in disability-specific programs would not address this problem (Rosenbaum 2008). Competition for resources would continue, and parents might be forced to characterize their children as more impaired than they actually are to ensure they receive a basic level of education (Rosenbaum 2008, 380). Several scholars and commentators support individualizing education for all students (Hensel 2007, 1197n268; Kelman and Lester 1997, 157). Alternatively, further research about and development of universal models to education could be pursued. These models might operate on a macrolevel (school or classroom organization) or a microlevel (classroom instruction). I offer some suggestions about approaches that warrant further study.

At the macrolevel, research should be conducted about the benefits of "inclusive schools," which adopt a form of school governance aimed at assisting educators in working with all students regardless of perceived or diagnosed disabilities (Weishaar, Weishaar, and Borsa 2007, 17–18). More modest approaches also should be studied. The IDEA itself contains some provisions that recognize universal vulnerability to learning impairment that warrant further inquiry. These provisions offer a level of benefits and services to students who might not otherwise meet the threshold for "child with a disability" under the act. In addition, the IDEA allows school districts to spend up to 15 percent of the special education funds they receive from the federal government to "develop and implement coordinated, early intervening services." These services target any student who begins to show signs of slipping grades or other indicators of poor educational performance, regardless of potential eligibility under the IDEA (20 U.S.C. §1413(f) (2006)).

The federal Response to Intervention (RTI) program provides a more inclusive method than traditional IDEA assessment to determine a student's eligibility for disability services under the act (US Department of Education 2009). The traditional testing model relies on referrals from teachers and uses IQ testing to determine whether a gap exists between a student's intellectual abilities and academic performance (Gresham 2002). Under the RTI model, a student believed to be disabled is referred for testing, often after she begins to perform poorly in class (Weber 2009, 128–29). The school psychologist or social worker assesses the results of the student's IQ test, and a multidisciplinary team determines whether she requires special education services (Weber 2009, 128–29). RTI in its current form has limitations, however. It may underserve students who have learning disabilities but perform well on initial screening tests (Hensel 2009, 695; Weber 2009, 142). Further, some students who require the most intensive services may remain in the early phases of RTI for longer periods (Weber 2009, 142).

At a microlevel, universal design in learning (UDL) is a universal approach to education that could be developed to help equalize classroom benefits. UDL involves altering the style of teaching or presentation of material to allow students "multiple means . . . to access and respond to the content [of the curriculum]" (Lee et al. 2010, 213). It thus may involve a combination of lectures, PowerPoint and other visual media, and classroom participation (Lee et al. 2010, 214). Classroom materials themselves may be universally designed; some textbooks are available in alternative formats for students with visual impairments (Harrison 2009, 39). Although UDL still is confined predominantly to special education settings, it would enable many students with disabilities to function in general classrooms and may enhance student outcomes overall (Lee et al. 2010, 229). Some scholars argue that this should be the point of special education—that it is "not so much special as part and parcel of the educational enterprise as a whole" (Weber 2006, 9).

A more universal approach also could be taken with respect to transition programs facilitating movement from secondary to postsecondary education, or from education to work. Most students struggle when making these transitions, though individuals with disabilities may experience the difficulty more acutely. Further study should be conducted regarding Tennessee's "one path" high school curriculum approach and similar approaches that offer individualized services while making education (and work) more universally available. The possibility of expanding successful education-to-work transition programs—such as those in California and Oregon—to all students should be explored. Generally speaking, such transition programs would require collaboration between schools and funding agencies about program criteria and implementation as well as in the training of instructors. Schools must facilitate student and parent involvement where possible. Transition programs also must be routinely evaluated through the collection of state or even nationwide surveys to track changes in education or employment for different cohorts (Wittenburg, Golden, and Fishman 2002, 204).

C. Disability and Health Care Justice

Vulnerability analysis also provides strong support for a universal approach to health care. Universal vulnerability to illness encourages a move away from government insurance programs that target particular groups of individuals to a more comprehensive state response to medical needs. Restructuring current health care institutions to support health care as a public good may be the best way to address vulnerability to illness and the vulnerability that results from illness.

First and foremost, disability does not equate with illness. Thus, the population of individuals who are ill or medically fragile exceeds the disability class. Illness may give rise to disability, but it does not presuppose it (Silvers, Wasserman, and Mahowald 1998, 79; Wendell 1996, 20). All individuals are vulnerable to illness. When such vulnerability is realized, it results in dependency on care and impairment that may or may not be disabling. Without health, individuals cannot work or socially integrate. Indeed, philosophers argue that for this reason health care is a vital social good (see Daniels 1985; Pogge 1989, 181–96; Rawls 1999, 50).

Second, current legal structures that impede access to health care for individuals with disabilities also disadvantage individuals without disabilities. Access to care may be understood in part as the ability both to obtain health insurance and to have necessary services under a health plan. Government programs have historically targeted only particular segments of the population based on income, age, health status, and military or government employment, including individuals with disabilities who are eligible for Social Security benefits. Although voluntary state expansion of Medicaid programs is possible under the Patient Protection and Affordable Care Act of 2010, and the federal government will create health insurance exchanges accessible to a segment of the population directly or through employers of a certain size, coverage is not universal. Most health insurance in the United States has been and likely will remain provided through private employee benefit plans (Centers for Medicare & Medicaid Services 2008, table 4; Kaiser Family Foundation 2007, 1). Even after health care reform, employers with fewer than fifty employees will not face penalties for failing to offer health insurance plans, nor are employers required to offer a particular level of benefits beyond those defined as "essential," so long as all employees are treated in the same manner. Individuals with disabilities who receive Social Security benefits may in fact receive more support through federal programs than those without disabilities.

Any individual with health insurance may not receive coverage for all of the services she needs. So long as plans provide contracted-for benefits and do not make disability-based distinctions, they are allowed to employ cost-containment mechanisms that may result in the denial of certain services (ADA, §12201(c); *Pegram v. Herdrich* 2000, at 200–222). Until fairly recently, complete parity between mental and physical health care benefits was not required, under the views that mental health care services are provided to individuals who have statutorily recognized disabilities as well as to those who do not and that mental health care covers a range of dissimilar conditions (Mental Health Parity and Addiction Equity Act of 2008).

Thus, individuals who are disabled face the same barriers as other patients in accessing health care in terms of obtaining health insurance and having coverage for the particular services they need. Complicating factors for individuals with disabilities include high rates of unemployment if they do not qualify for Social Security benefits based on permanent disability, a possible higher consumption of health care resources, health care rationing schemes that disfavor those with existing medical impairments, and difficulty moving between assistance programs that include health care and the workforce. But individuals who are not disabled are also vulnerable in similar terms. Unskilled workers and at-will employees are vulnerable to unemployment; unskilled workers have a smaller range of employment opportunities than skilled workers, and at-will employees are vulnerable to discharge. Individuals who are not disabled also may require significant health care services. For example, premature infants and elderly persons are the greatest consumers of health care resources, with high costs for care during the first and last months of life (Centers for Disease Control and Prevention 2009).

Further, elderly as well as disabled individuals may be disproportionately impacted by the metrics used to ration care and to segregate risk. In Oregon, for example, care for the indigent through Medicaid is rationed based on predicted health outcomes and cost (Oregon Health Services Commission 2008). Disabled, elderly, and medically fragile individuals may face double jeopardy if they are medically needy but not entitled to health care resources based on their perceived health status or length of life. Temporarily unemployed disabled and other individuals may experience difficulty moving between social welfare programs for the unemployed that include health care and the workforce. William Johnson notes that health insurance is vital in order for individuals with disabilities to forego Social Security disability benefits, and their wages must be significantly higher to fund health care for a chronic condition (1997, 171). Although the Ticket to Work and Work Incentives Improvement Act of 1999 remedies the benefits-to-work transition issue to some extent, it leaves eligible workers uninsured after eight and a half years (§202(a)).

Conclusion

Current targeted approaches to disability fragment protections and benefits by excluding certain individuals with impairments from the protected class and treating disability as if it arises in discrete situations. To address the vulnerability associated with disability and to prevent fragmented protections under the ADA, the reasonable accommodation mandate must be given a broader social purpose. Government subsidies should facilitate access across daily environments to promote work and other civic and social participation. In the workplace, the interactive process must be federally mandated and developed. Broader universal approaches should be adopted in the education and health care contexts. Under the IDEA, resources must be devoted to exploring universal approaches to the structure and content of primary and secondary education. With regard to health care, a universal approach should be adopted whereby every citizen would have access to the same benefits. These steps more fully advance the ability of individuals with impairments to participate in society.

12

Inclusion in K–12 and Higher Education

WENDY S. HARBOUR

Like my colleagues in this anthology, I also look to disability studies to critique special education law and policy and simultaneously to provide a foundation for inclusive theory and practice. I have worked in both K–12 special education and postsecondary disability services. My primary interest, however, is in creating a more inclusive higher education system. At Syracuse University, I teach courses in inclusive K–12 education, disability studies, and higher education. I write this chapter to open up a dialogue about the potential connections between K–12, higher education law, and disability studies; to present possible reasons for the dichotomy that exists between them; and to offer suggestions for future directions in disability legal studies in education.

Differences between Special Education and Disability Services

As several authors in this volume note, at first glance K–12 and higher education are radically different. Most critically, the Individuals with Disabilities Education Act of 1990 (IDEA, most recently reauthorized in 2004) ceases to apply after a student leaves high school, when the comprehensive and cumulative Individual Education Plan (IEP) traditionally becomes no more than a large file of papers. In more than twenty years of working in higher education, I have yet to meet a disability services provider who regularly reads IEPs for incoming students and relies heavily on them to determine disability accommodations. However, this situation may change soon, with the 2012 publication of new documentation guidelines from the Association on Higher Education and Disability (AHEAD), which references legal decisions; the United Nations Convention on the Rights of Persons with Disabilities of 2006; and the social constructions of disability in justifying the legitimacy of *all* forms of postsecondary educational disability documentation (including student self-reports and IEPs) (AHEAD 2012).

More students with disabilities are pursuing higher education options than ever before. According to the second National Longitudinal Transition Study (best known by its abbreviation NLTS2), 60 percent of students with disabilities in the United States will pursue some form of postsecondary education within eight years of high school graduation (compared to 67 percent of the general population) (Newman et al. 2011). But whereas 52 percent of all students will complete some type of degree or certificate program, only 41 percent of students with disabilities will graduate (Newman et al. 2011).

Arriving on campus, all students face a situation that is very different from high school. If they received special education services in K–12, they may struggle with assumption of nearly all responsibility for negotiating disability services because they no longer have an interdisciplinary team of parents, special educators, and service providers to help them. Students must self-identify as disabled and find the disability services provider on campus. Offices may have a variety of titles, and some may not even be official offices (e.g., disability services may be provided by counseling centers, TRIO offices, or individual faculty) (Harbour 2008). Students may be surprised to learn that they and their families must now bear the costs of getting medical or psychological documentation of their disabilities, though many insurance companies will not cover necessary assessments and testing. A student may also discover that even though disability services providers will be evaluating medical documentation and making final decisions about the student's disability status and reasonable accommodations, those professionals may not have any experience with the student's particular disability or diagnostic label (professionals may even be new to the field and not have any background in disability at all).

There are no degrees or licensure systems to judge which campuses have "good" disability services offices, and the college or disability services rating systems that do exist are often focused on one type of disability only (see, e.g., Tiedemann 2012; Wells 2010). Modifications to coursework are generally nonexistent, and many professors do not take kindly to anything perceived as "special" assistance, especially when it may infringe upon what they perceive to be their right to academic freedom in the classroom. Courses may differ radically from each other, and each type of course (lab, discussion, lecture, field experience) may require different types of accommodations and negotiations with disability services providers. Colleges may be within their legal rights to balk at providing things that were freely offered in high school, such as tutoring, and may not provide any other services at all (such as physical therapy or speech therapy) (Shaw, Madaus, and Dukes 2010). Students with disabilities may find that discussions about accommodations are moot because they don't even meet criteria for having a disability; for instance, their depression is considered a "condition," or their learning disability documentation does not prove they have a "disability." Some students have Section 504 plans from high school, developed to comply with the Rehabilitation Act of 1973. Section 504 plans provide services, adjustments, or accommodations to students with disabilities, illnesses, or conditions that do not meet strict criteria of a "disability" under special education law. However, in higher education some campuses may view 504 plans as proof a student is not really disabled enough to get college services rather than as proof of the need for accommodations. (For more information about policies for higher education, see Ben-Moshe 2005; Getzel and Wehman 2005; Harbour and Madaus 2011; Shaw, Madaus, and Dukes 2010; Steele and Wolanin 2004.)

To prevent these issues from becoming barriers, IDEA mandates transition planning for students age sixteen or older. Transition services should include obtaining disability documentation, planning for college, arranging accommodations for standardized tests such as the SAT, and creating a transition statement to help the student summarize his or her disability and its impact (i.e., the "Summary of Performance"). However, as Mark Weber (chapter 8) and Ani Satz (chapter 11) note, transition out of high school exposes all of the problems, fragmentations, and fault lines of the special education system. Even this separate "transition" system for students with disabilities implies that students with disabilities must follow a path out of high school that is different from the one taken by their peers, who are simply graduating and moving on with their lives (Tashie, Malloy, and Lichtenstein 1998). Indeed, the transition process may expect students with disabilities to plan out their entire postsecondary education and career immediately upon graduation from high school, whereas non-disabled students are expected to explore options and make choices while in college (Caton and Kagan 2007). And, of course, the transition process may be a distant memory for those students who did not enter higher education immediately after high school. Older college students may have graduated before the idea of IDEA-mandated transition planning even existed, and others may acquire a disability before or during college, when the IDEA would not apply to them (e.g., disabled veterans from Iraq and Afghanistan returning to college).

Students arrive at college often feeling as if they have entered a different world. They encounter many policies designed to support students' development by allowing them to succeed or fail on their own terms. (Higher education disability services professionals often quote the mantra "We focus on access, not success," thus distancing themselves from perceptions that they are "helping" students as in special education.) Likewise, college disability services is supposed to be preparing the student for fields of employment, where disability determinations and decisions about reasonable accommodations can be even more stringent or complicated, with even fewer supports than in higher education (Fuecker and Harbour 2011). Some students, however, may relish the freedom that disability services provides. They may refuse accommodations, experiment with accommodations, or deliberately decide not to disclose in order to forego disability labeling or stigma (Cory 2011; Shaw, Madaus, and Dukes 2010). Nearly two-thirds (63 percent) of students with disabilities receive services in high school, but those who go on to college do not consider themselves "disabled" or in need of services when they get there; an additional 9 percent believe they do have a disability but choose not to disclose it (Newman et al. 2011). Even anthologies and narratives about undergraduates and graduate students with disabilities do not typically discuss disability services or accommodations, or they do so in a very peripheral way (see, e.g., Mooney and Cole 2000; Prince-Hughes 2002, 2004; Rodis, Garrod, and Boscardin 2001; Saks 2008; Vance 2007a; Wurtzel 2002).

Connections between Special Education and Disability Services

Although the differences between K–12 and higher education levels of disability law, services, and policy are clear, disability studies offers additional perspective and specific points for comparative critique: first, higher education's roots in a medical model services orientation and the field of special education; second, how larger issues of interest to disability studies and education (normality, expertise, gate keeping, inclusion, self-advocacy, and academic standards) are consistent across fields and simply take on different forms in higher education; and, third, how applicable laws and legislation overlap, with similar subjectivity in their interpretation. The following sections discuss each of these points.

History of Disability Services

Around the time of World War II, as Scot Danforth and Theodoto Ressa note in chapter 5, intelligence testing and other psychometrics were becoming increasingly popular. As a result, educational psychologists, learning specialists, and counselors were earning the respect of rehabilitation specialists, health care professionals, and remedial educators (including those working in institutions with students who had disabilities). These fields were also creating nascent degree programs at colleges and universities to train the next generation of practitioners, scholars, and researchers.

When World War II ended, the GI Bill allowed disabled veterans to go to colleges and universities and earn a degree. For the first time, larger universities were forced to accommodate these students in a systematic way. Many campuses looked to psychology, counseling, remedial education, and rehabilitation programs for help. Specialists in disability and education were especially useful because even many of the seemingly nondisabled veterans had nonvisible disabilities, such as post-traumatic stress disorder (i.e., "shell shock"), brain injuries, and undiagnosed learning disabilities (for further discussion, see Fleischer and Zames 2001; Jarrow 1993; Madaus 1998, 2000, 2011). These professionals working with veterans were the first generation of special education, counseling, and rehabilitation providers, but they were also the first generation of disability services professionals. As such, they set standards that continue in disability services today: individualized services, a reliance on disability documentation and labeling, an orientation toward "service" and "helping," and a role as gatekeeper for determining how people with disabilities get an education and enter professions.

After the 1960s and 1970s, disability services in K–12 and higher education diverged in important ways. Special education was codified into federal law, which led to the establishment of licensure and certification systems for teachers working in the field, a free public education guaranteed for all students with disabilities, and billions of federal dollars to maintain the special education system and document its effectiveness. Although Section 504, the Americans with Disabilities Act of 1990 (ADA), and the ADA Amendments Act of 2008 (ADAAA) apply in higher education, disability never appeared in higher education law until the Higher Education Opportunity Act of 2008 (HEOA) (with the notable exception of Gallaudet University, which requires federal oversight by Congress). There are no degree programs or licensure programs for anyone working in disability services, and postsecondary learning remains a privilege rather than an entitlement. Most notable, systems for tracking students with disabilities or their services are practically nonexistent (although the HEOA does require schools to begin reporting numbers of students with disabilities on campus, which are posted on the College Navigator website for the National Center for Education Statistics). Federal funding and research on disability in higher education are also scarce, and, as of 2012, some HEOA disability-related provisions remain unfunded with no significant protestations from the disability community or disability studies. In some ways, this lack of funding is to be expected: public education is universal, whereas higher education is considered a privilege; each campus guards its right to its own individual way of providing an education and educational services without federal intervention; and students with disabilities who have traditionally been excluded from K–12 are likely to have low expectations for going to college.

The number of disability services offices increased dramatically after Section 504 was enacted and increased again after the ADA was passed in 1990 (Blosser 1984; Jarrow 1993). Even today, disability services professionals continue to come from special education, rehabilitation, and counseling fields, and others join them from higher education fields related to student affairs (Harbour 2004, 2008). This means that current practices and underlying assumptions for disability services subsume all the strengths and problems of each of these fields. Most critically, many of special education's historical philosophies (examined in chapters 5, 6, and 7) and theoretical models have influenced higher education. The two fields may appear to be different, but they are two branches of the same tree.

Terms and Concepts from a Disability Studies Perspective

A disability legal studies framework can make clear that distinctions between K–12 and higher education look more like a Venn diagram with overlapping circles. One area where this overlap occurs is with the discourse of service provision and inclusion movements.

The language of special education and the language of disability services in higher education are quite different. The meanings of terms such as *accommodations, modifications,* and *adaptations* are distinct from each other in higher education, whereas they are often used interchangeably in special education literature (see the discussion of terminology in Shaw, Madaus, and Dukes 2010). In many cases, however, the underlying concepts are remarkably similar at the two levels. "Expert" professionals use medical and scientific evidence and evaluations ("documentation") in both fields to determine who is "truly disabled." The professionals then serve as gatekeepers who ply a continuum of individualized services ("individualized reasonable accommodations and services") that are centered on the student and disability instead of on courses and schools. Segregating or excluding those who are "most disabled" is common practice (especially through "transition," "special" programs, or "remedial" services and courses). Services are reserved for those who are eligible or "otherwise qualified"—as if concepts such as "disabled" and "qualified" are readily quantifiable and objective. "General" education teachers (a term that assumes "general" students are nondisabled) and "special" education teachers (those who teach the "special students" who have disabilities) often work separately in K–12; likewise, in higher education "general" faculty are not expected to know about disability services and are not generally involved in initial decisions about accommodations in their courses. Even "tracking" in K–12 has a parallel in the higher education system itself, with two-year community, vocational, and technical colleges viewed as a different track than four-year research universities and liberal arts colleges.

Another place where the overlap occurs is in movements toward greater inclusion for students with disabilities and in the spread of universal design. With disability studies on the rise in K–12 and higher education, special-interest groups and conferences on the topic have been held by the American Educational Research Association, the American College Personnel Association, and AHEAD. Disability studies programs are increasing, especially at the undergraduate level (Taylor 2011), and there has been a marked increase in books about disability studies in education—this book included (see also, e.g., Danforth and Gabel 2006; Gabel and Danforth 2008). Disability studies promotes inclusion in a number of ways, but as Susan Baglieri and Linda Ware note in chapter 4, it infuses disability into the curriculum while questioning why the study of disability is traditionally seen as the domain of medicine and service professions. It asks why special education and disability services are the only fields discussing disability and why disability awareness days are the only opportunity to learn about disability (for further discussion about this in the context of higher education, see Johnstone, Lubet, and Goldfine 2008 and Linton 1998a). Why not learn about disability in math, literature courses, foreign-language courses, and history?

Another inclusive movement that crosses educational levels is the spread of universal design, which shifts from a focus on access to general education *learning environments* to a focus on access to *learning itself* (Hehir 2009). Universal design in many ways embodies sociopolitical models of disability as a social and political construction because it seeks ways of changing the design of courses and communities for a "universe" of users, including those with (and without) disabilities. Universal design is now written into the IDEA and the HEOA, especially with regard to improved access to digitized texts. It is forging new strategies for pedagogy in K–12 (e.g., Rose and Meyer 2002) and higher education (e.g., Burgstahler and Cory 2008). In chapter 2 of this volume, Martha Minow discusses how disability law has "mainstreamed" disability into society but has not necessarily created an inclusive society or educational environment; universal design is one step toward true "inclusion" for all levels of education.

Finally, disability legal studies can also critique the term *inclusion* itself. Until the movement to include students with intellectual disabilities in higher education gained momentum (culminating in HEOA provisions for programs and research related to this population), the progressive term *inclusion* was not common in higher education. (For more information about this inclusive education movement, see Grigal and Hart 2009 and Katovitch 2009.) The term not only carries baggage and associations from K–12 but is also problematic in that it implies a norm (i.e., able-ness) and that a minority or oppressed group is being included into that larger normative population, thus unintentionally reinforcing the traditional status quo (Graham and Slee 2008). Perhaps these are some of the reasons the term *inclusion* has not been as common as terms such as *integration*, *access*, and *diversity* when discussing disability in higher education.

Recent lawsuits such as *Fialka-Feldman v. Oakland University Board of Trustees* (2011) test the limits of "inclusive" practices in higher education institutions, where individuals are routinely denied access to some campus features (e.g., NCAA athletes have access to and privileges at specialized athletics facilities, honors programs are not required to accept everyone, and housing is typically only for full-time matriculated undergraduate students). These internal hierarchies and exclusionary policies test what *full inclusion* might mean in higher education and whether the term is applicable.

Likewise, whereas any type of segregation is generally anathema in K–12, some college students may choose to segregate themselves as they explore identity, community, and cultural issues related to their disabilities; Santiago Solis (2009) refers to this choice as one of either "coming out" about a disability or "choosing to stay in." Segregation and finding a community can be an important part of identity development, especially in students with multiple intersecting identities (see, e.g., Hadley 2011; Harley et al. 2002; S. Harris 1995; Hockman 2010; Leake and Cholymay 2004; Vance 2007b). Likewise, students with disabilities may play with the language of disability (*dis/ability, DisAbility, impairment,* [*dis*]*ability*) while they decide on a label to use for themselves (Linton 1998a; P. Smith 2010). How can K–12 and disability legal studies take this chosen segregation into account when discussing inclusion? Both K–12 and higher education also use the term *inclusion* to focus on students, but a school or campus is not inclusive unless there are instructors and staff with disabilities (Anderson, Keller, and Karp 1998; Henderson 2011; Michalko 2001; Vance 2007a, 2007b). Are disability policies and law also fostering "inclusion" for these groups, or is there a "compulsory able-bodiedness" (McRuer 2006, 2) and compulsory "inclusion" inferred for nonstudents, to the point where their disabilities and experiences of ableism are minimized? Disability legal studies may answer these questions, especially as additional cases involving teachers, faculty, and staff go before the courts.

Law

In chapter 6, Philip Ferguson argues that much of inclusive education or special education in K–12 is framed by unacknowledged and unexamined assumptions. In special education and higher education, many of these assumptions relate to the law, making it excellent fodder for disability legal studies.

In K–12, the IDEA governs all aspects of special education, with thousands of pages in regulations to provide a blueprint for states and schools. There is even a federal website (www.idea.gov) to search regulations for specific topics related to IDEA implementation. States and school districts have some latitude in funding formulas or the overall organization of special education services, but other issues (such as whether students have IEPs) are mandated. Yet, as many authors in this volume note, interpretation of concepts such as "inclusion," a "continuum of services," and the "least restrictive environment" remain open for debate. For example, the IDEA includes phrasing about "individualized services" and "least restrictive environment," but it never uses the word "inclusion." The law is also continuing to evolve, reflecting current understandings of disability even when those understandings are rooted in sciences of exclusion (see, e.g., the discussions in chapters 5, 6, and 7).

Although the ADA, the ADAAA, and Section 504 of the Rehabilitation Act apply to both K–12 and higher education, the IDEA does not apply to college campuses. Furthermore, compared to thousands of pages of regulations for the IDEA, there are virtually no regulations to guide implementation of the ADA, the ADAAA, and Section 504 on college and university campuses. Instead, postsecondary institutions must rely on case law for deciding how to provide disability services (Rothstein 2002; Simon 2000). This reliance on case law is complicated for several reasons: most disability services providers are not lawyers, but they are trying to interpret the law; most legal decisions do not apply at every institution of higher education; and case law is constantly evolving. The US Office of Civil Rights has taken a lead in trying to interpret case law for disability services providers, but even its efforts falter with a lack of federal coordination related to higher education services (US Government Accountability Office 2009).

As a result, for decades both K–12 and higher education have ultimately had what Richard Weatherly and Michael Lipsky (1977) refer to as "street-level bureaucrats," who must make constant everyday decisions based on their personal and professional experiences and in consultation with colleagues. Thomas Skrtic (2005) has called this bureaucracy an "adhocracy," where decisions are made in an ad hoc fashion. From a legal and political perspective, this approach to decision making is actually good policymaking because it allows for flexibility within the constraints of the law. From the perspective of disability legal studies or the perspectives of teachers, families, and students fighting for inclusion in education, however, it can be bureaucratic chaos when professionals maintain the letter of the law instead of the spirit of the law. Indeed, disability services offices often see themselves as first and foremost a department for legal compliance, when a "beyond compliance" attitude is not yet the norm (Ben-Moshe et al. 2005; Cory 2011).

With passage of the ADAAA, there is some question about how it will affect "inclusion," with AHEAD and its affiliates creating resources for disability services professionals and looking at issues ranging from architecture to service animals to documentation of disabilities (e.g, AHEAD 2012; Dyer 2011). Some groups also suspect that the ADAAA's expanded definition of disability will result in more students qualifying for 504 plans in K–12 (see, e.g., Kaloi and Stanberry 2012), which will potentially expand the number of students seeking accommodations in higher education (and push the limits of who is "disabled" and who has "conditions"). As educational institutions and the courts determine exactly how the ADAAA will be implemented, there is a place for disability legal studies to examine intersections of law, policy, discourse, and practice and to apply that work to practice and policy.

Next Steps for Disability Legal Studies

This chapter provides a cursory comparison and contrast of special education in K–12 and disability services in higher education, with implications for disability legal studies. Delving too deeply into any of these issues is beyond the scope of this chapter. There are numerous other areas where overlap or intersections occur between the two levels: the experiences of English-language learners and students of color, resource allocation economics, and due process procedures with federal entities, to name a few. The purpose of this chapter, however, is simply to provoke conversation among disability legal scholars about how education is being defined and whether inclusive education debates can and should include higher education.

Indeed, it is critical to remember that the more inclusive K–12 becomes, the more expectations will rise for higher education to be inclusive as well. It also logically follows that as higher education becomes more inclusive, there will be a similar trend in the workforce and academia as well. Likewise, a more universally designed "beyond compliance" approach in higher education will also influence and enhance K–12's definitions of inclusion. As noted earlier, I am optimistic that "inclusion" will soon not only be about students, but also about parents with disabilities as well as about disabled administrators, staff, teachers, and professors. The fate of inclusion in K–12 is inextricably linked to the fate of inclusion in higher education.

Special education and higher education law share a common history and, as a result, share many similarities in theory and practice, even though the two fields have grown in distinctly different ways. The differences are readily apparent and easy to see; the subtle nexus and "unexamined assumptions" (Ferguson, chapter 6) between the two are where disability legal studies may have the most impact.

Epilogue

BETH A. FERRI

As Arlene Kanter explains in chapter 1, disability studies is not a singular discipline, but rather an interdisciplinary field of study drawing from a range of disciplines and intellectual traditions. The typical origin story of disability studies as a field emerging over the past several decades is generally related as a series of models of disability, which over time have competed for the ability to speak to and for disability experience and expertise.

The more or less official history of disability studies arises in the context of disability rights and in direct contestation of the medical model of disability, which locates the "problem" of disability in individual bodies and minds. From a medical model perspective, disability is considered a medical predicament, an inherent deficit, and a diminished state of being in comparison to normative, able-bodied lived experience. And whereas the problem of disability is firmly rooted in the individual, expertise *about* disability is situated in the clinician or other medical professionals, who retain authoritative control over the discourse of disability. Thus, the social model emerges as a counter discourse to the medical or deficit model of disability.

Yet the history of disability precedes the medical model. The medical model might be said to have arisen out of the charity model of disability within many of the major world religions. Within a charity model, individuals demonstrate their concern for humanity and their spiritual worthiness by caring for or giving alms to those deemed less fortunate, including the poor and the disabled. The charity model, far from being outmoded, continues to provide the impetus and justification for contemporary telethons, such as the Muscular Dystrophy Association Labor Day telethon, as well as for so-called advocacy organizations, such as Autism Speaks—both of which propagate pity in order to raise money for medical research aimed at finding a cure for a particular disability. In fact, in many ways the medical model did not overtake the charity model but rather co-opted it—enlisting charities to help bolster the medical model by raising money for medical research aimed ultimately at curing disability. In this way, the discourses of medical "cure" simply replaced those of religious "healing."

Initially, however, the charity model was the impetus for poorhouses and almshouses, which over time transitioned to asylums and institutions for individuals with disabilities. No history of disability would be complete without at least some mention of asylums (P. Ferguson 1994), monsters (Garland-Thomson 1997), freak shows (Bogdan 1988; Garland-Thompson 1997), and ugly laws (Schweik 2009)—all coinciding with the move from the charity model to the medical model. Moreover, a visit to an art museum often illustrates visually the history of disability, where the paintings of old-world masters are replete with visible disabilities—brought carefully and purposely into the frame for the value of their metaphoric and symbolic weight (Sandell, Dodd, and Garland-Thomson 2010). Whether disability comes to stand in for "social or individual collapse," limitation, deviance, or excess (Mitchell and Snyder 2000, 47), what the history of disability in art, literature, and film illustrates most clearly is the ways that disability has always been a constructed category and an occasion for interpretation and meaning making.

Thus, although the medical model was not actually the first model of disability, because disability studies is generally thought of as a counterdeficit, counterdiagnostic model, this model is typically where we start the story of disability studies as an academic field—cutting its teeth, if you will, against the grain of the medical model of disability. Borrowing from the ubiquitous wave version for retelling the history of a discipline or field of study, we might call the *first wave* of disability studies the *social model* (particularly if we start the story in the United Kingdom) or the *civil rights model* (if we start in the United States). Although there are subtle differences between these, it is not uncommon to think of the social model and the civil rights model as complementary (or even interchangeable) and to refer to them collectively as the "social model of disability." This first wave of disability studies was dominated by the social sciences, and some of this work was taking place, as Steve Taylor writes, "before [disability studies] had a name" (2006, xiii).

The social model coincided with the emergence of the *disability rights movement*—punctuated by bus boycotts, the independent living movement, deinstitutionalization, communication rights, and educational rights. Syracuse University was at the epicenter of several of these civil rights struggles and continues much of this work today. A major scholarly contribution of the social model of disability was to locate the "problem" of disability not in the bodies and minds of individuals with impairments, but in the structures of society, thereby disentangling impairment (as a biological fact) from *disability* (a socially produced system of barriers and negative values ascribed to impairment). This move proved to be quite useful politically, allowing disabled people to highlight the systems of oppression operating as a result of impairment. Thus, the inhumane conditions and degrading treatment in state institutions did not arise because of the individuals' impairments, but rather from the socially sanctioned, ableist attitudes and perceptions that afforded individuals with impairments less than human status. Moreover, if disability was located in structures of society, it was society that was in need of remediation, not the individuals with disabilities. In terms of legal studies and educational studies, this shift clearly provided a very different set of concerns. Rather than attempting to fix the individual according to the logic of the medical model, social modelists took aim at the structures of society that could be addressed by legal protections and equal access. In terms of educational reform, for instance, the social model helped to shift the object of remediation from individual students to inaccessible educational contexts. In other words, the problem of disability was not inherent in particular students but was ultimately an issue of access and inclusion. Of course, this shift is certainly incomplete given that the Individuals with Disabilities Act of 1990 (IDEA), even in its amendments, still focuses entirely on the services for the individual child, not on changing education to include all learners.

Once the social model of disability got a bit of traction, both in the academy and within the disability rights movement, the emergence of a *second wave* of disability studies scholarship followed. In this second wave, scholars in fields such as literature, philosophy, art history, and the like employed a humanities-focused set of methods and a new set of discourses to the study of disability. A major contribution in the second wave was to illustrate disability as a discursively produced system of oppressive relations of power. Scholars drew on textual and cultural studies to focus on disability representation in art (Sandell, Dodd, and Garland-Thomson 2010; Siebers 2010), literature (Mitchell and Snyder 1997, 2001; Garland-Thomson 1997), and film (Darke 1998; Norden 1994; Safran 1998). Scholars in the second wave also took aim at ableist metaphors (Danforth 2007; May and Ferri 2005; Vidali 2010; Wilson and Lewiecki-Wilson 2001) and at the overreliance on stereotypical tropes of disability, which functioned as a sort of "narrative prosthesis," according to David Mitchell and Sharon Snyder (2001).

Although less talked about, a *third wave* of disability studies scholarship now aims to address the intersections of gender, race, sexuality, nation, and social class. Here scholars are taking cues from other interdisciplinary fields such as women and gender studies, African American studies, queer studies, LatCrit, postcolonial and indigenous studies, and human rights jurisprudence in order to examine the interconnectedness of disability and other interlocking systems of oppression (see, e.g., Annamma, Connor, and Ferri 2013; C. Bell 2011; Erevelles 2011; Hall 2011; May and Ferri 2002; McRuer 2006; Meekosha 2011; Parekh 2007). This third wave also gave rise to some insightful and nuanced critiques not only of the medical model, but of the social model as well—interrogating gaps and rough spots that refuse to align with a one-size-fits-all theoretical model of disability. Some of these resistant voices have come from people of color (such as the late Chris Bell), but also from experiences of disability that have been underrepresented within disability studies. These critiques of the social model encompass an ever-expanding range of topics, including the need to account for neurodiversity (Biklen 2005; M. Price 2011), chronic illness (Morris 1996; Wendell 1996), and cognitive or intellectual disability (Carlson 2001), to name a few.

There is something to be said for this version of disability studies history—the waves are neat and tidy, and who doesn't like conjuring up the ocean? And yet it is also a problematic origin story for the field. First, the most obvious problem with this version of our collective history is that it implies that the work of the social sciences is stuck in the first wave—historically important, sure, but not as relevant or vibrant as more contemporary work. In actuality, as the contributors of this book demonstrate, there is no shortage of excellent work in the social sciences and in professional fields (such as education and legal studies), as well as ongoing work in humanities and area studies—which collectively have contributed to reimagining disability in productive ways.

But there is a larger problem with this kind of origin story. If I take this version of disability studies literally, the work of any number of scholars and activists cannot fit neatly into any of these waves; these scholars create riptides in and through these waves—pulling us sideways across disciplinary divides and across multiple and sometimes conflicting alliances. I like this messy work—I teach it, and it teaches me. Books such as Kenny Fries's *The History of My Shoes* (2007) and Anne Finger's *Elegy for a Disease* (2006), which blur the lines between social history and memoir, or the collective works of Nancy Mairs, whose memoirs are an early articulation of feminist disability studies, or of Lennard Davis, who refuses to settle into any singular genre—each of these scholars, like the field itself, has blurred disciplinary divides in the service of their unique intellectual contribution to the field. The same can be said of some of the earliest works in the field, such as Burton Blatt and Fred Kaplan's *Christmas in Purgatory* (1974), which is as much a sociological critique as it is investigative photo journalism, as well as more contemporary texts, such as Steven Taylor's (2009) study of the courageous activism of conscientious objector whistle-blowers in state-run institutions for the disabled or Susan Schweik's (2009) theoretically grounded social and political history of so-called unsightly begging ordinances or ugly laws. Maybe disability studies scholars have been floating among and between the waves of our disciplines all along—maybe we are just undisciplined, our bodies and our minds refusing to mind.

There is also no clear place in these waves of disability studies to place theory, artistic production, or even activism because those who do these things have been here all along—poets, artists, philosophers, dancers, disability performance artists, creative writers, comedians, and scholars who write memoirs that read like poetry and breathe light and sound and touch into theory. I am thinking here of the lyrical prose of Stephen Kuusisto and his ruminations on sight (1998) and hearing (2006), Georgina Kleege's (2006) impassioned letters to Helen Keller, Christoph Keller's (2009) interwoven narrative of love and loss, and Lynn Manning's (2005) moving performance of poetry and prose.

Yet when disability studies scholars, as informed by the social model, locate disabilities within the structures of society rather than within the biology or essence of individuals, they can inadvertently set up a false dichotomy not only between social sciences and humanities, but also between the social and the personal—mirroring other binary distinctions such as mind/body, public/private, ability/disability, legally protected/unprotected. When the personal is positioned in opposition to the social, autobiographical works in particular can inevitably be seen as too personal, too individualistic (Davis 1997a), or too confessional (Mitchell and Snyder 1997). Yet I have argued elsewhere that to read disability life writing or even fiction in this way is to miss the theory at work in these works (Ferri 2011). Rather than seeing these texts in opposition to theory or to social or political critique, we should read disability in creative works, as we do in scholarly texts, as an important site of intellectual and political resistance (McKay 1998). Writing specifically about the intellectual tradition of black women's autobiography, for instance, Nellie McKay writes that it is never politically insignificant for individuals who have been denied subjectivity and selfhood to "write themselves into being" (1998, 97). Thus, life writing deserves a prominent place on the bookshelf we call "disability studies" "by the same logic that has made it essential to other area studies," such as women's and ethnic studies (Couser 2002, 109). Thus, I would argue that disability life writing also represents another one of the riptides in disability studies scholarship, which blur distinctions between the social, the personal, and the political—talking back to oppressive ideologies and stirring in us a certain "recognition" of our self in an other.

I find autobiographical works particularly useful in teaching disability studies, not because I want to give my students some unobstructed or authentic view of disability, but rather because these works demand a reckoning with: the simultaneous and dialogic play of power between social structures and individual agency (Sherry 2005); the politics of language and naming; and the irreducibility of identity into discrete, unitary, or static categories.

As you might imagine, the history of disability studies that a tour of my bookshelf tells is one in which theory touches poetry and sociology bumps up against law, where disability studies in education speaks to disability film studies. My bookshelf will not be ordered—it is defiant in its dis/order. It is a messy bookshelf, but the way I think of it, disability resists order, which is why I call disability studies home.

In closing, my coeditor and I must say that bringing the various voices and perspectives together in this volume has been a privilege and a pleasure. We need more dialogic encounters across our disciplinary locations. Thinking of the field of disability studies as rooted in all of its disciplinary divides has not served those of us in this field all that well. Instead, we aimed in this volume to begin to bridge our various differences in method, discourse communities, and style guides in order to bring all our best efforts to the task ahead. We hope that we can continue this conversation because as long as there remain so many educational wrongs to put right, we have more work to do.

References

Secondary Sources

"Abnormal Pupils of St. Louis to Be Specially Taught." 1914. *St. Louis Post-Dispatch*, Apr. 19.

Abrams, Kathryn. 1997. "The Constitution of Women." *Alabama Law Review* 48:861–84.

Acemoglu, Daron, and Joshua D. Angrist. 2001. "Consequences of Employment Protection? The Case of the Americans with Disabilities Act." *Journal of Political Economy* 109:915–57.

Addams, Jane. 1902. *Democracy and Social Ethics*. New York: Macmillan.

Ahearn, Eileen. 2006. *Standards-Based IEPs: Implementation in Selected States*. Alexandria, VA: National Association of State Directors of Special Education.

———. 2010. *Standards-Based IEPs: Implementation Update*. Alexandria, VA: National Association of State Directors of Special Education.

Albrecht, Gary L. 2006. *Encyclopedia of Disability*. Thousand Oaks, CA: Sage.

Albright, Jennifer. 2006. "Free Your Mind: The Right of Minors in New York to Choose Whether or Not to Be Treated with Psychotropic Drugs." *Albany Law Journal of Science and Technology* 16:169–94.

Alexander, Michelle. 2010. *The New Jim Crow: Mass Incarceration in the Age of Colorblindness*. New York: New Press.

Altman, Andrew. 1993. *Critical Legal Studies*. Princeton, NJ: Princeton Univ. Press.

American Association of Intellectual and Developmental Disability. 2012. "Definition of Intellectual Disability." Available at http://www.aamr.org /content_100.cfm?navID=21. Accessed Sept. 17, 2012.

American Bar Association. 2006. *Model Rules of Professional Conduct*. Washington, DC: American Bar Association.

American Bar Association Commission on Mental and Physical Disability. 2010. *Disability Statistics Report, 2010*. Washington, DC: American Bar Association.

Available at http://www.americanbar.org/content/dam/aba/migrated/disability
/PublicDocuments/ABADisabilityStatisticsReport.authcheckdam.pdf.

―――. 2011. *Disability Statistics Report, 2011*. Washington, DC: American Bar Association. Available at http://www.americanbar.org/content/dam/aba /migrated/disability/PublicDocuments/ABADisabilityStatisticsReport.auth checkdam.pdf.

Anderson, Cheryl L. 2000. "'Deserving Disabilities': Why the Definition of Disability under the Americans with Disabilities Act Should Be Revised to Eliminate the Substantial Limitation Requirement." *Missouri Law Review* 65:83–150.

Anderson, James D. 1988. *The Education of Blacks in the South, 1860–1935*. Chapel Hill: Univ. of North Carolina Press.

Anderson, Ronald J., Clayton E. Keller, and Joan M. Karp, eds. 1998. *Enhancing Diversity: Educators with Disabilities*. Washington, DC: Gallaudet Univ. Press.

Angelou, Maya. [1983] 1994. "Caged Bird." In *The Complete Collected Poems of Maya Angelou*, 194–95. New York: Random House.

Annamma, Subini A., David J. Connor, and Beth A. Ferri. 2013. "Dis/ability Critical Race Studies (Dis/Crit): Theorizing at the Intersections of Race and Dis/ability." *Race, Ethnicity, and Education* 16, no. 1: 1–31.

Arceneaux, Marcia C. 2005. "The System and Label of Special Education: Is It a Constitutional Issue?" *Southern University Law Review* 32:225–46.

Archer, Melanie. 2002. "Access and Equity in the Due Process System: Attorney Representation and Hearing Outcomes in Illinois, 1997–2002." Available at http://www.dueprocessillinois.org/AccessDP.htm.

Arias, Elizabeth. 2007. "United States Life Tables." *National Vital Statistics Reports* 56, no. 9: 1–40. Available at http://www.cdc.gov/nchs/data/nvsr/nvsr 56/nvsr56_09.pdf.

Aristotle. 1987. *Politics*. Translated by W. E. Bolland. Whitefish, MT: Kessinger.

Artiles, Alfredo J., Robert Rueda, Jesús José Salazar, and Ignacio Higareda. 2005. "Within-Group Diversity in Minority Disproportionate Representation: English Language Learners in Urban School Districts." *Exceptional Children* 71:283–300.

Ash, Mitchel G. 1995. *Gestalt Psychology in German Culture, 1890–1967: Holism and the Quest for Objectivity*. Cambridge, UK: Cambridge Univ. Press.

Ashton, Jennifer R. 2011. "The CEC Professional Standards: A Foucauldian Genealogy of the Re/Construction of Special Education." *International Journal of Inclusive Education* 15, no. 8: 775–95.

Asimov, Nanette. 2006. "Extra-special Education at Public Expense." *San Francisco Chronicle*, Feb. 19. Available at http://www.sfgate.com/cgi-bin/article.cgi?file=/c/a/2006/02/19/MNG8THBH4V1.DTL.

Association on Higher Education and Disability (AHEAD). 2012. *Supporting Accommodation Requests: Guidance on Documentation Practices*. Huntersville, NC: AHEAD.

Bagenstos, Samuel R. 2004. "The Future of Disability Law." *Yale Law Journal* 114:1–83.

———. 2007. "Abolish the Integration Presumption? Not Yet." *Pennsylvania Law Review* 156: 157–64.

———. 2009. *Law & the Contradictions of the Disability Rights Movement*. New Haven, CT: Yale Univ. Press.

Baglieri, Susan, and Akintoye Moses. 2010. "'My Name Is Jay': On Teachers' Roles in the Overrepresentation of Minorities in Special Education and What Teacher Education Can Do." *Disability Studies Quarterly* 30, no. 2. Available at http://www.dsq-sds.org/article/view/1243/1287.

Baizley, Doris and Victoria Ann Lewis. 1997. "P.H.*reaks" (adaptation). In *Staring Back: The Disability Experience from the Inside Out*, edited by Kenny Fries, 303–32. New York: Plume.

Ball, Stephen. 1990. *Foucault and Education*. London: Routledge.

Banchero, Stephanie, and Darnell Little. 2004. "New Rules Help Raise Test Scores: Schools Learning How to Navigate Federal Reforms." *Chicago Tribune*, Dec. 15.

Barboza, David. 2009. "Still Dancing in Her Dreams." *New York Times*, Apr. 19. Available at http://www.nytimes.com/2009/04/19/arts/dance/19barb.html?pagewanted=all&_r=0.

Barga, Nancy K. 1996. "Students with Learning Disabilities: Managing a Disability." *Journal of Learning Disabilities* 29:413–21.

Barnes, Colin. 1997. "A Legacy of Oppression: A History of Disability in Western Culture." In *Disability Studies: Past, Present, and Future*, edited by Len Barton and Mike Oliver, 3–24. Leeds, UK: Disability Press, University of Leeds. Available at http://www.leeds.ac.uk/disability-studies/archiveuk/index.

———. 1999. *Exploring Disability: A Sociological Introduction*. Malden, MA: Blackwell.

———. 2003. "Rehabilitation for Disabled People: A 'Sick' Joke?" *Scandinavian Journal of Disability Research* 5: 7–24. Available at http://www.independentliving.org/docs6/barnes2003a.html.

Barnes, Colin, and Geof Mercer. 2010. *Exploring Disability*. 2d ed. Boston: Polity Press.

Barnes, Colin, Geof Mercer, and Tom Shakespeare. 2005. *Exploring Disability: A Sociological Introduction*. 2d ed. Boston: Polity Press.

Barsch, Ray H. 1965. *Movigenic Curriculum: An Experimental Approach to Children with Special Learning Disabilities Conducted at the Longfellow School, Madison, Wis., during the 1964–65 School Year*. Madison, WI: State Department of Public Instruction, Bureau for Handicapped Children.

———. 1968. *Enriching Perception and Cognition: Techniques for Teachers*. Seattle: Special Child Publications.

Basnett, Ian. 2001. "Health Care Professionals and Their Attitudes toward Decisions Affecting Disabled People." In *Handbook of Disability Studies*, edited by Gary Albrecht, Katherine D. Seelman, and Michael Bury, 450–67. Thousand Oaks, CA: Sage.

Bauman, Richard W. 2002. *Ideology and Community in the First Wave of Critical Legal Studies*. Toronto: Univ. of Toronto Press.

Baylies, Carolyn. 2002. "Disability and the Notion of Human Development: Questions of Rights and Capabilities." *Disability & Society* 17: 725–39.

Baynton, Douglas C. 2001. "Disability and the Justification of Inequality in American History." In *The New Disability History: American Perspectives*, edited by Paul K. Longmore and Laura Umansky, 33–57. New York: New York Univ. Press.

Beegle, Kathleen, and Wendy A. Stock. 2003. "The Labor Market Effects of Disability Discrimination Laws." *Journal of Human Resources* 38:806–59.

Bell, Christopher M. 2011. Blackness and Disability: Critical Examinations and Cultural Interventions. East Lansing: Michigan State Univ. Press.

Bell, Derrick A. 1980a. "*Brown vs. Board of Education* and the Interest-Convergence Principle." *Harvard Law Review* 93:518–33.

———. 1980b. *Race, Racism, and American Law*. New York: Little, Brown.

———. 1987. *And We Are Not Saved: The Elusive Quest for Racial Justice*. New York: Basic Books.

———. 1992. *Faces at the Bottom of the Well: The Permanence of Racism*. New York: Basic Books.

———. 1995. "Who's Afraid of Critical Race Theory?" *University of Illinois Law Review*. 1995:893–910.

———. 2004. *Silent Covenants: Brown v. Board of Education and the Unfulfilled Hopes for Racial Reform*. New York: Oxford Univ. Press.

Benjamin, Ludy T., Jr. 2007. *A Brief History of Modern Psychology*. Malden, MA: Wiley.

Ben-Moshe, Liat. 2005. "Lame Idea: Disabling Language in the Classroom." In *Building Pedagogical Curbcuts: Incorporating Disability into the University Curriculum*, edited by Liat Ben-Moshe, Rebecca C. Cory, Mia Feldblum, and Ken Sagendorf, 107–15. Syracuse, NY: Syracuse Univ. Available at http://disabilitystudies.syr.edu/docs/buildingpedagogicalcurbcuts.pdf.

Ben-Moshe, Liat, Rebecca C. Cory, Mia Feldbaum, and Ken Sagendorf, eds. 2005. *Building Pedagogical Curb Cuts: Incorporating Disability in the University Classroom and Curriculum*. Syracuse, NY: Graduate School, Syracuse Univ.

Benz, Michael, and Lauren Lindstrom. 1999. "Improving Collaboration between Schools and Vocational Rehabilitation: The Youth Transition Program Model." *Journal of Vocational Rehabilitation* 13:55–63.

Berman, Sheldon, Perry Davis, Ann Koufman-Frederick, and David Urion. 2001. "Rising Costs of Special Education in Massachusetts: Causes and Effects." In *Rethinking Special Education for a New Century*, edited by Chester E. Finn Jr., Andrew J. Rotherham, and Charles R. Hokanson Jr., 183–211. Washington, DC: Thomas B. Fordham Institute.

Bernstein, Charles. 1920. "Colony and Extra-institutional Care for the Feeble-minded." *Mental Hygiene* 4:1–28.

———. 1921. "Colony Care for Isolation, Defective, and Dependent Cases." *Journal of Psycho-Asthenics* 26:43–59.

———. 1927. "Advantages of Colony Care for Mental Defectives." *Psychiatric Quarterly* 1:419–25.

Bérubé, Michael. 1996. *Life As We Know It: A Father, a Family, and an Exceptional Child*. New York: Pantheon.

———. 2002. "Afterword: If I Should Live so Long." In *Disability Studies: Enabling the Humanities*, edited by Sharon L. Snyder, Brenda Jo Brueggemann, and Rosemarie Garland-Thomson, 337–43. New York: Modern Language Association of America.

———. 2003. "Citizenship and Disability." *Dissent*, Spring:52–57.

———. 2005. "College Makeover." *Slate*, Nov.

Bevins, Evan. 2012. "States Looks for Waivers of 'No Child Left Behind.'" *Marietta Times*, Feb. 26. Available at http://www.newsandsentinel.com/page/content.detail/id/557949/States-looks-for-waivers-of-No-Child-Left-Behind-.html?nav=5061.

Biklen, Douglas. 1992. *Schooling without Labels*. Philadelphia: Temple Univ. Press.

———. 2005. *Autism and the Myth of the Person Alone*. New York: New York Univ. Press.

Biklen, Douglas, and Donald Cardinal, eds. 1997. *Contested Words, Contested Science: Unraveling the Facilitated Communication Controversy*. New York: Teachers College Press.

Blank, Rebecca M. 2000. "Fighting Poverty: Lessons from Recent U.S. History." *Journal of Economic Perspectives* 14, no. 2: 3–19.

Blatt, Burton. 1983. "The Next Hundred Years." *Journal of Special Educators* 16:16–22.

Blatt, Burton, and Fred Kaplan. 1974. *Christmas in Purgatory: Photographic Essay on Mental Retardation*. Syracuse, NY: Syracuse Univ. Center on Human Policy, Law, and Disability Studies.

Blosser, Ron E. 1984. "The Roles and Functions and the Preparation of Disabled Student Service Directors in Higher Education." PhD diss., Southern Illinois Univ., Carbondale.

Bogdan, Robert. 1988. *Freak Show: Presenting Human Oddities for Amusement and Profit*. Chicago: Univ. of Chicago Press.

Bos, Sharon C., and Sharon Vaughn. 1998. *Strategies for Teaching Students with Learning and Behavior Problems*. 4th ed. Needham Heights, MA: Allyn & Bacon.

Bouchard, Rebecca, and Claire Thompson. 2010. "Special Education: Advocating on Behalf of School Districts." In *School Law in Massachusetts*, 14.1–14.4. Springfield, MA: Doherty, Wallace, Pillsbury & Murchy.

Bowe, Frank. 2000. *Universal Design in Education: Teaching Nontraditional Students*. Westport, CN: Greenwood.

Brantlinger, Ellen. 1997. "Using Ideology: Cases of Nonrecognition of the Politics of Research and Practice in Special Education." *Review of Educational Research* 67:425–59.

———. 2006. "Geometries of Inequality: Teaching and Researching Critical Mathematics in a Low-Income Urban High School." PhD diss., Northwestern Univ.

Brault, Matthew W. 2012. *Americans with Disabilities: 2010*. Washington, DC: US Census Bureau. Available at http://www.census.gov/prod/2012pubs/p70-131.pdf.

Brewer, Mary. 2005. *Staging Whiteness*. Middletown, CT: Wesleyan Univ. Press.

Broderick, Alicia A., D. Kim Reid, and Jan W. Valle. 2006. "Disability Studies in Education and the Practical Concerns of Teachers." In *Vital Questions Facing Disability Studies in Education*, edited by Scot Danforth and Susan L. Gabel, 133–60. New York: Peter Lang.

Brown, Wendy, ed. 2003. *Left Legalism/Left Critique*. Richmond, VA: Duke Univ. Press.

Bruder, Mary Beth, and Cristina Mogro-Wilson. 2010. "Student and Faculty Awareness and Attitudes about Students with Disabilities." *Review of Disability Studies* 6, no. 2: 3–13.

Bryen, D. N., and Sieglinde A. Shapiro. 1996. "Disability Studies: What It Is and Why It Is Needed." *Temple University Faculty Herald*, Feb. 12.

Burgstahler, Sheryl E., and Rebecca C. Cory, eds. 2008. *Universal Design in Higher Education: From Principles to Practice*. Cambridge, MA: Harvard Education Press.

Burleigh, Michael. 1995. *Death and Deliverance Euthanasia in Germany 1900–1945*. Cambridge: Cambridge Univ. Press.

Burton, Kailey. 2012. "Local Educators React to 'No Child Left Behind' Waiver." WJFW television, Feb. 24. Available at http://www.wjfw.com/print_story.html?SKU=20120224174440.

Bury, Mike. 1996. "Defining and Researching Disability: Challenges and Responses." In *Exploring the Divide: Illness and Disability*, edited by Colin Barnes and Geof Mercer, 17–38. Leeds, UK: Disability Press.

Butler, Judith. 1999. *Gender Trouble: Feminism and the Subversion of Identity*. New York: Routledge.

———. 2004. *Undoing Gender*. New York: Routledge.

Campbell, Jean. 1994. "Unintended Consequences in Public Policy: Persons with Psychiatric Disabilities and the Americans with Disabilities Act." *Policy Studies Journal* 22: 133–45.

Carlson, Licia. 2001. "Cognitive Ableism and Disability Studies: Feminist Reflections on the History of Mental Retardation." *Hypatia* 16, no. 4: 124–46.

Carrier, James G. 1983. "Masking the Social in Educational Knowledge: The Case of Learning Disability Theory." *American Journal of Sociology* 88, no. 5: 948–74.

Carter, Erik W., Nicole Ditchman, Ye Sun, Audrey A. Trainor, Beth Swedeen, and Laura Owns. 2010. "Summer Employment and Community Experiences of Transition-Age Youth with Severe Disabilities." *Exceptional Children* 76:194–212.

Caruso, Daniela. 2005. "Bargaining and Distribution in Special Education." *Cornell Journal of Law and Public Policy* 14:171–498.

Caton, Sue, and Carolyn Kagan. 2007. "Comparing Transition Expectations of Young People with Moderate Learning Disabilities with Other Vulnerable Youth and with Their Non-disabled Counterparts." *Disability and Society* 22, no. 5: 473–88.

Causton-Theoharis, Julie, and George Theoharis. 2008. "Creating Inclusive Schools for All Students." *School Administrator* 65. Available at http://www .aasa.org/schooladministratorarticle.aspx?id=4936.

Center for Applied Special Technology (CAST). 2010. "Policy, Property, and Permissions: A Discussion of Accessible Curriculum Materials." Oct. Available at http://aim.cast.org/learn/historyarchive/backgroundpapers/policy_property _permissions1.

Center for Universal Design. 2008. "About UD." At http://www.ncsu.edu/ncsu /design/cud/about_ud/about_ud.htm.

Centers for Disease Control and Prevention (CDC). 2009. "Premature Births." *CDC Features*. Available at http://www.cdc.gov/Features/PrematureBirth. Last updated Feb. 2013.

Centers for Medicare & Medicaid Services (CMMS). 2008. "Sponsors of Health Care Costs, Businesses, Households, and Governments, 1987–2008." Available at http://www.cms.hhs.gov/NationalHealthExpendData/downloads/bhg 08.pdf.

Chambers, Jay G., Jennifer J. Harr, and Amynah Dhanani. 2003. *What Are We Spending on Procedural Safeguards in Special Education, 1999–2000? Special Education Expenditure Project.* Palo Alto, CA: Center for Special Education Finance.

Charlton, James I. 1998. *Nothing about Us without Us: Disability Oppression and Empowerment.* Berkeley: Univ. of California Press.

Chen, Lung-chu. 1987. "Aging: A New Human Rights Concern—a Policy-Oriented Perspective." With remarks by Philip Alston. *American Society International Proceedings* 81:169–75.

"City Has Hopper for Measuring Mentality of Children." 1918. *St. Louis Globe-Democrat*, Apr. 28.

Clotfelter, Charles. 2004. *After Brown: The Rise and Retreat of School Desegregation.* Princeton, NJ: Princeton Univ. Press.

Clune, William H., and Mark H. Van Pelt. 1985. "A Political Method for Evaluating the Education for All Handicapped Children Act of 1975 and the Several Gaps of Gap Analysis." *Law and Contemporary Problems* 48, no. 1: 7–62.

Cohen, Felix. 1954. "The Reconstruction of Hidden Value Choices: Word Choices as Value Indicators." In *Symbols and Values*, edited by Lyman Bryson and Louis Finkelstein, 545–61. Whitefish, MT: Literary Licensing.

Cole, Mike, and Maude Blair. 2006. "Racism and Education: The Imperial Legacy." In *Education, Equality, and Human Rights: Issues of Gender, "Race," Sexuality, Special Needs, and Social Class*, edited by Mike Cole, 70–88. New York: Routledge, Palmer.

Coleman, James, et al. 1966. *Equality of Educational Opportunity*. Washington, DC: US Department of Health.

Colker, Ruth. 2006. "The Disability Integration Presumption: Thirty Years Later." *University of Pennsylvania Law Review* 154:789–862.

Commission on No Child Left Behind. 2007. *Beyond NCLB: Fulfilling the Promise to Our Nation's Children*. Washington, DC: Aspen Institute.

Connor, David J. 2008. *Urban Narratives: Portraits in Progress: Life at the Intersection of Learning Disability, Race, & Social Class*. New York: Lang.

Connor, David J., and Beth A. Ferri. 2005. "Integration and Inclusion—a Troubling Nexus: Race, Disability, and Special Education." *Journal of African American History* 90, nos. 1–2: 107–27.

Converge Staff. 2009. "Stimulus Package: Education's Raw Figures." Center for Digital Education, Feb. 9. Available at http://www.convergemag.com /economicstimulus/Stimulus-Package-Educations-Raw-Figures.html.

Cooper, Frank Rudy. 2006. "Against Bipolar Black Masculinity: Intersectionality, Assimilation, Identity Performance, and Hierarchy." *University of California Davis Law Review* 39:853–904.

Cornell University. 2010. *Disability Statistics: Online Resource for U.S. Disability Statistics*. Available at http://www.disabilitystatistics.org/reports/acs.cfm ?statistic=9. Accessed Nov. 5, 2012.

Corner, Jancy. 2002. "Are Inclusionary Practices Meeting the Needs of All Involved Parties (i.e., Children with Special Needs, Other Children, Teachers Etc.)?" *Journal of Physical Education, Recreation & Dance* 73:12–13.

Cory, Rebecca C. 2011. "Disability Services Offices for Students with Disabilities: A Campus Resource." *New Directions for Higher Education* 154 (Summer): 27–36.

Council for Exceptional Children. 2005. *Universal Design for Learning*. Boston: Pearson.

Couser, G. Thomas. 2002. "Signifying Bodies: Life Writing and Disability Studies." In *Disability Studies: Enabling the Humanities*, edited by Sharon L. Snyder, Brenda Jo Brueggemann, and Rosemarie Garland-Thompson, 109–17. New York: Modern Language Association.

Cover, Robert. 1986. "Violence and the Word." *Yale Law Journal* 95:1601–29.

Crenshaw, Kimberlé Williams. 1988. "Race, Reform, and Retrenchment: Transformation and Legitimation in Antidiscrimination Law." *Harvard Law Review* 101:1331–87.

Crenshaw, Kimberlé, Neil Gotanda, Gary Peller, and Kendall Thomas. 1996. *Critical Race Theory: The Key Writings That Formed the Movement*. New York: New Press.

Crocker, David A. 2008. *Ethics of Global Development: Agency, Capability, and Deliberative Democracy*. Cambridge: Cambridge Univ. Press.

Croly, Herbert. [1909] 1965. *The Promise of America*. Indianapolis: Bobbs-Merril.

Crossley, Mary. 2004. "Reasonable Accommodation as Part and Parcel of the Antidiscrimination Project." *University of Pennsylvania Law Review* 35:861–957.

Crowder, Kyle. 2000. "The Racial Context of White Mobility: An Individual-Level Assessment of the White Flight Hypothesis." *Social Science Research* 29, no. 2: 223–57.

Cruickshank, William M., and Daniel P. Hallahan. 1973. "Alfred A. Strauss: Pioneer in Learning Disabilities." *Exceptional Children* 39, no. 4: 321–27.

Danforth, Scot. 2007. "Disability as Metaphor: Examining the Conceptual Framing of Emotional Behavioral Disorder in American Public Education." *Educational Studies* 42, no. 1: 8–27.

———. 2009. *The Incomplete Child: An Intellectual History of Learning Disabilities*. New York: Lang.

Danforth, Scot, and Susan L. Gabel, eds. 2006. *Vital Questions Facing Disability Studies in Education*. New York: Lang.

Danforth, Scot, and William C. Rhodes. 1997. "Deconstructing Disability: A Philosophy for Inclusion." *Remedial and Special Education* 18:357–66.

Danforth, Scot, Laura Slocum, and Jennifer Dunkle. 2010. "Turning the Educability Narrative: Samuel A. Kirk at the Intersection of Learning Disability and 'Mental Retardation.'" *Intellectual and Developmental Disabilities* 48, no. 3: 180–94.

Daniel, Phillip. 2008. "'Some Benefit or Maximum Benefit': Does the No Child Left Behind Act Render Greater Educational Entitlement to Students with Disabilities?" *Journal of Law and Education* 37:347–65.

Daniels, Norman. 1985. *Just Health Care.* Cambridge: Cambridge Univ. Press.

Darke, Paul. 1998. "Understanding Cinematic Representations of Disability." In *The Disability Reader: Social Science Perspectives*, edited by Tom Shakespeare, 181–98. New York: Cassell.

Darling-Hammond, Linda. 2004. "From 'Separate but Equal' to 'No Child Left Behind': The Collision of New Standard and Old Inequalities." In *Many Children Left Behind: How the No Child Left Behind Act Is Damaging Our Children and Our Schools*, edited by Deborah Meier and George Wood, 3–32. Boston: Beacon Press.

———. 2007. "Evaluating 'No Child Left Behind.'" *The Nation*, May 21: 11–18.

Davies, Stanley P. 1959. *The Mentally Retarded in Society.* New York: Columbia Univ. Press.

Davis, Lennard J., ed. 1997a. *The Disability Studies Reader.* London: Routledge.

———. 1997b. "Introduction." In *The Disability Studies Reader*, edited by Lennard J. Davis, 1–6. London: Routledge.

———. 2002. *Bending Over Backwards: Disability, Dismodernity, and Other Difficult Positions.* New York: New York Univ. Press.

———. 2006. "Constructing Normalcy: The Bell Curve, the Novel, and the Invention of the Disabled Body in the Nineteenth Century." In *Disability Studies Reader*, 2d ed., edited by Lennard J. Davis, 3–16. New York: Routledge.

Dawson, Michelle, Isabelle Soulières, Morton Ann Gernsbacher, and Laurent Mottron. 2007. "The Level and Nature of Autistic Intelligence." *Psychological Science* 18:657–62.

Delgado, Richard, ed. 1995. *Critical Race Theory: The Cutting Edge.* Philadelphia: Temple Univ. Press.

Delgado, Richard, and Jean Stefencic. 1993. "Critical Race Theory: An Annotated Bibliography." *Virginia Law Review* 79, no. 2: 461–516.

———. 2001. *Critical Race Theory: An Introduction.* New York: New York Univ. Press.

Deno, Evelyn. 1970. "Special Education as Developmental Capital." *Exceptional Children* 37:229–306.

Dewey, John. [1927] 1988. "The Public and Its Problems." In *John Dewey: The Later Works, 1925–1953*, vol. 2, edited by J. A. Boydston, 235–372. Carbondale: Southern Illinois Univ. Press.

———. [1939] 1991a. "Creative Democracy: The Task before Us." In *John Dewey: The Later Works, 1925–1953*, vol. 14, edited by J. A. Boydston, 224–30. Carbondale: Southern Illinois Univ. Press.

———. [1935] 1991b. "Liberalism and Social Action." In *John Dewey: The Later Works, 1925–1953*, vol. 11, edited by J. A. Boydston, 1–65. Carbondale: Southern Illinois Univ. Press.

Diller, Matthew. 2000. "Judicial Backlash, the ADA, and the Civil Rights Model." *Berkeley Journal of Employment and Labor Law* 21:19–52.

DiMaggio, Paul J. 1988. "Interest and Agency in Institutional Theory." In *Institutional Patterns and Organizations: Culture and Environment*, edited by Lynne G. Zucker, 3–22. Cambridge, MA: Ballinger.

DiMaggio, Paul J., and Walter W. Powell. 1983. "The Iron Cage Revisited: Institutional Isomorphism and Collective Rationality in Organizational Fields." *American Sociological Review* 48:147–60.

Djilas, Milovan. 1957. *The New Class: An Analysis of the Communist System*. San Diego: Harcourt Brace Jovanovich.

Donohue, John J., III, and James J. Heckman. 1991. "The Law and Economics of Racial Discrimination in Employment: Re-evaluating Federal Civil Rights Policy." *Georgetown Law Journal* 79:1713–35.

Dowd, Nancy, and Michelle Jacobs. 2003. *Feminist Legal Theory: An Anti-Essentialist Reader*. New York: New York Univ. Press.

Drimmer, Jonathan C. 1993. "Cripples, Overcomers, and Civil Rights: Tracing the Evolution of Federal Legislation and Social Policy for People with Disabilities." *UCLA Law Review* 40:1341–1410.

Dudziak, Mary. 2000. *Cold War Civil Rights: Race and the Image of American Democracy*. Princeton, NJ: Princeton Univ. Press.

Dunn, Lloyd M. 1968. "Special Education for the Mildly Retarded—Is Much of It Justifiable?" *Exceptional Children* 35, no. 1: 5–22.

Dyer, Suzette. 2011. *An Overview of ADAAA and Other Disability Legislation Compliance Issues. A White Paper*. Oklahoma City: Association on Higher Education and Disability, May. Available at http://www.ok-ahead.org/ADAAA whitepaper.pdf.

Dzur, Albert W. 2008. *Democratic Professionalism: Citizen Participation and the Reconstruction of Professional Ethics, Identity, and Practice*. University Park: Pennsylvania State Univ. Press.

Education Law Center. 2010–11. "Improving 'Alternative Education for Disruptive Youth' in Pennsylvania." Mar. At http://www.elc-pa.org/pubs/downloads 2010/ELC_AltEdPA_FullReport.pdf.

Eichhorn, Lisa. 1999. "Major Litigation Activities Regarding Major Life Activities: The Failure of the 'Disability' Definition in the Americans with Disabilities Act of 1990." *North Carolina Law Review* 77:1405–77.

Elmore, Richard F., Charles H. Abelmann, and Susan H. Fuhrman. 1996. "The New Accountability in State Education Reform: From Process to Performance." In *Holding Schools Accountable: Performance-Based Reform in Education*, edited by Helen F. Ladd, 65–98. Washington, DC: Brookings Institution.

Emens, Elizabeth. 2006. "The Sympathetic Discriminator: Mental Illness, Hedonic Costs, and the ADA." *Georgia Law Review* 94:399–488.

———. 2008. "Integrating Accommodation." *University of Pennsylvania Law Review* 156:839–982.

Engel, David M. 1991. "Law, Culture, and Children with Disabilities: Educational Rights and the Construction of Difference." *Duke Law Journal* 1991:166–205.

Erevelles, Nirmala. 2006. "Race and Ethnicity." In *Encyclopedia of Disability*, edited by Gary L. Albrecht, 1335–441. Thousand Oaks, CA: Sage.

———. 2011. *Disability and Difference in Global Contexts: Enabling a Transformative Body Politic*. New York: Palgrave Macmillan.

Erickson, William C., Camille G. Lee, and Sarah von Schrader. 2008. *Disability Statistics from the American Community Survey (ACS)*. Ithaca, NY: Cornell Univ. Rehabilitation Research and Training Center on Disability Demographics and Statistics. Available at http://www.disabilitystatistics.org.

Erkulwater, Jennifer L. 2006. *Disability Rights and the American Social Safety Net*. Ithaca, NY: Cornell Univ. Press.

Erlandson, Robert F. 2008. *Universal and Accessible Design for Products, Services, and Processes*. Boca Raton, FL: CRC Press.

Fagan, Aimee R. 2002. "An Analysis of the Convention on the International Protection of Adults." *Elder Law Journal* 10:329–59.

Farrell, Elizabeth E. 1914a. "A Study of the School Inquiry Report on Ungraded Classes." *The Psychological Clinic* 8, no. 3: 57–74.

———. 1914b. "A Study of the School Inquiry Report on Ungraded Classes; Concluded." *The Psychological Clinic* 8, no. 4: 99–106.

"Feeble-Minded in Schools Reduced by Dr. Wallin." 1915. *St. Louis Post-Dispatch*, Sept. 20.

Feldblum, Chai R. 2000. "Definition of Disability under Federal Antidiscrimination Law: What Happened? Why? And What Can We Do about It?" *Berkeley Journal of Employment and Labor Law* 21:91–165.

Fellner, Jamie. 2006. "A Corrections Quandary: Mental Illness and Prison Rules." *Harvard Civil Rights–Civil Liberties Law Review* 41:391–412.

Fenton, Zanita E. 1998. "Domestic Violence in Black and White: Racialized Gender Stereotypes in Gender Violence." *Columbia Journal of Gender and Law* 8:1–65.

———. 2003. "Silence Compounded—the Conjunction of Race and Gender Violence." *American University Journal of Gender, Social Policy & Law* 11:271–85.

———. 2007. "The Paradox of Hierarchy—or Why We Always Choose the Tools of the Master's House." *New York University Review of Law & Social Change* 31:627–37.

———. 2009. "Sleight of Hand or the Old Bait & Switch? Article III and the Politics of Self-Policing by the Court in Parents Involved." *University of Miami Law Review* 63:561–75.

Ferguson, Ann Arnett. 2000. *Bad Boys: Public Schools in the Making of Black Masculinity.* Ann Arbor: Univ. of Michigan Press.

Ferguson, Dianne L. 1995. "The Real Challenge of Inclusion: Confessions of a 'Rabid Inclusionist.'" *Phi Delta Kappan* 77:281–87.

Ferguson, Philip M. 1994. *Abandoned to Their Fate: Social Policy and Practices toward Severely Retarded People in America, 1820–1920.* Philadelphia: Temple Univ. Press.

Fernald, Walter E. 1907. "Possibilities of the Colony." *Proceedings of the National Conference of Charities and Corrections* 34:411–18.

Ferri, Beth A. 2006. "Teaching to Trouble." In *Vital Questions Facing Disability Studies in Education,* edited by Scot Danforth and Susan L. Gabel, 289–306. New York: Lang.

———. 2008. "Changing the Script: Race and Disability in Lynn Manning's Weights." *International Journal of Inclusive Education* 12, nos. 5–6: 497–509.

———. 2011. "Disability Life Writing and the Politics of Knowing." *Teachers College Record* 113, no. 10: 2267–82.

Ferri, Beth A., and David J. Connor. 2005a. "In the Shadow of *Brown*: Special Education and Overrepresentation of Students of Color." *Remedial and Special Education* 26:93–100.

———. 2005b. "Tools of Exclusion: Race, Disability, and (Re)segregated Education." *Teachers College Record* 107:453–74.

Ferris, Jim. 2007. "Crip Poetry, or How I Learned to Love the Limp." *Wordgathering* 2. Available at http://www.wordgathering.com/past_issues/issue2/essay/ferris.html.

Field, Martha A. 1993. "Killing the 'Handicapped'—before and after Birth." *Harvard Women's Law Journal* 16:79–138.

Field, Martha A., and Valerie A. Sanchez. 1999. *Equal Treatment for People with Mental Retardation: Having and Raising Children.* Cambridge, MA: Harvard Univ. Press.

Fierros, Edward Garcia, and James W. Conroy. 2002. "Double Jeopardy: An Exploration of Restrictiveness and Race in Special Education." In *Racial Inequity in Special Education,* edited by Daniel J. Losen and Gary Orfield, 39–70. Cambridge, MA: Harvard Education.

Fine, Michelle, and Adrienne Asch. 1988. "Disability beyond Stigma: Social Interaction, Discrimination, and Activism." *Journal of Social Issues* 44:3–21.

Fineman, Martha Albertson. 2008. "The Vulnerable Subject: Anchoring Equality in the Human Condition." *Yale Journal of Law and Feminism* 20:1–23.

Finger, Anne. 2006. *Elegy for a Disease: A Personal and Cultural History of Polio.* New York: St. Martin's Press.

Finnis, John. 1985. "On the Critical Legal Studies Movement." *American Journal of Jurisprudence* 30:21–42.

Fleischer, Doris Z., and Frieda Zames. 2001. *The Disability Rights Movement: From Charity to Confrontation.* Philadelphia: Temple Univ. Press.

Foner, Eric. 1998. *The Story of American Freedom.* New York: Norton.

Formisano, Ronald. 1991. *Boston against Busing: Race, Class, and Ethnicity in the 1960s and 1970s.* Chapel Hill: Univ. of North Carolina Press.

Foster-Spence, Kenlyn. 2009. "Adding It Up: Implications of Tennessee's New High School Transition and Graduation Requirements for Students with Disabilities." *Tennessee Law Review* 76:447–70.

Foucault, Michel. 1965. *Madness and Civilization: A History of Insanity in the Age of Reason.* London: Tavistock.

———. 1973. *Birth of the Clinic: An Archaeology of Medical Perception.* New York: Vintage.

Fox, Ann. 2002. "'But, Mother—I'm—Crippled!' Tennessee Williams, Queering Disability, and Dis/Membered Bodies in Performance." In *Gendering Disability,* edited by Bonnie G. Smith and Beth Hutchison, 233–50. New Brunswick, NJ: Rutgers Univ. Press.

Franklin, Barry M. 1994. *From "Backwardness" to "At-Risk": Childhood Learning Difficulties and Contradictions of School Reform.* Albany: State Univ. of New York Press.

Fraser, Nancy. 1989a. "Struggle over Needs: Outline of a Socialist–Feminist Critical Theory of Late Capitalist Political Culture." In *Unruly Practices: Power, Discourse, and Gender in Contemporary Social Theory*, 161–87. Minneapolis: Univ. of Minnesota Press.

———. 1989b. *Unruly Practices: Power, Discourse, and Gender in Contemporary Social Theory.* Minneapolis: Univ. of Minnesota Press.

———. 1995. "Recognition or Redistribution? A Critical Reading of Iris Young's *Justice and the Politics of Difference.*" *Journal of Political Philosophy* 3, no. 2: 166–80.

———. 1997. *Justice Interruptus: Critical Reflections on the "Postsocialist" Condition.* New York: Routledge.

———. 2008. "Prioritizing Justice as Participatory Parity: A Reply to Kompridis and Forst." In *Adding Insult to Injury: Nancy Fraser Debates Her Critics*, edited by Kevin Olson, 327–46. London: Verso.

———. 2009. *Scales of Justice: Reimagining Political Space in a Globalizing World.* New York: Columbia Univ. Press.

Fraser, Nancy, and Axel Honneth. 2003. *Redistribution or Recognition: A Political–Philosophical Exchange.* London: Verso.

Fries, Kenny, ed. 1997. *Staring Back: The Disability Experience from the Inside Out.* New York: Plume.

———. 2007. *The History of My Shoes and the Evolution of Darwin's Theory.* New York: Carol & Graf.

Frug, Mary Jo. 1992. "A Postmodern Feminist Legal Manifesto" (An Unfinished Draft). *Harvard Law Review* 105:1045–75.

Fuecker, David, and Wendy S. Harbour. 2011. "UReturn: University of Minnesota Services for Faculty and Staff with Disabilities." *New Directions for Higher Education* 154 (Summer): 45–54.

Furner, Mary O. 1993. "The Republican Tradition and the New Liberalism: Social Investigation, State Building, and Social Learning in the Gilded Age." In *The State and Social Investigation in Britain and the United States*, edited by Michael J. Lacy and Mary O. Furner, 171–241. New York: Woodrow Wilson Center Press.

Gabel, Susan L., and Scot Danforth, eds. 2008. *Disability Studies and the Politics of Education: An International Reader.* New York: Lang.

Gallagher, Deborah J. 1998. "The Scientific Knowledge Base of Special Education: Do We Know What We Think We Know?" *Exceptional Children* 64:493–502.

———. 2001. "Neutrality as a Moral Standpoint, Conceptual Confusion and the Full Inclusion Debate." *Disability & Society* 16:637–54.

———. 2004. "Entering the Conversation: The Debate behind the Debates in Special Education." In *Challenging Orthodoxy in Special Education: Dissenting Voices*, by Deborah J. Gallagher, Lous Heshusius, Richard P. Iano, and Thomas M. Skrtic, 3–26. Denver: Love.

———. 2005. "Searching for Something Outside of Ourselves: The Contradiction between Technical Rationality and the Achievement of Inclusive Pedagogy." In *Disability Studies in Education: Readings in Theory and Method*, edited by Susan L. Gabel, 139–54. New York: Lang.

Gallagher, James J. 1998. "The Public Policy Legacy of Samuel A. Kirk." *Learning Disabilities Research and Practice* 13, no. 1: 11–14.

Garda, Robert A., Jr. 2005. "The New IDEA: Shifting Educational Paradigms to Achieve Racial Equality in Special Education." *Alabama Law Review* 56:1071–134.

Garland-Thomson, Rosemarie. 1997. *Extraordinary Bodies: Figuring Physical Disability in American Culture and Literature*. New York: Columbia Univ. Press.

———. 2001. "Seeing the Disabled: Visual Rhetorics of Disability in Popular Photography." In *The New Disability History: American Perspectives*, edited by Paul K. Longmore and Laura Umansky, 335–74. New York: New York Univ. Press.

———. 2002. "The Politics of Staring: Visual Rhetorics of Disability." In *Disability Studies: Enabling the Humanities*, edited by Sharon L. Snyder, Brenda Jo Brueggemann, and Rosemarie Garland-Thomson, 56–75. New York: Modern Language Association of America.

———. 2009. *Staring: How We Look*. Oxford: Oxford Univ. Press.

Garrow, Hattie Brown. 2011. "Va. to Pursue No Child Left Behind Waiver, Official Says." *Virginian-Pilot*, Sept. 24. Available at http://hamptonroads.com/2011/09/obama-rolling-back-no-child-left-behind.

Geertz, Clifford. 1963. *Agrarian Involution*. Berkeley: Univ. of California Press.

Geib, Catherine Foley, John F. Chapman, Amy D'Amaddio, and Elena L. Grigorenko. 2011. "The Education of Juveniles in Detention: Policy Considerations and Infrastructure Development." *Learning and Individual Differences* 21:3–11.

Gelb, Adhemar, and Kurt Goldstein. [1918] 1997. "Zur psychologie des optischen Wahrnehmungs—und Erkennungsvorganges." In *Source Book of Gestalt*

Psychology, translated and edited by Willis D. Ellis, 315–25. Highland, NY: Gestalt Journal Press.

Gerald, Debra E., and William J. Hussar. 2002. *Projections of Education Statistics to 2012*. Washington, DC: National Center for Education Statistics.

Gesell, Arnold, Frances L. Ilg, Glenna E. Bullis, Vivienne Ilg, and Gerald N. Getman. 1949. *Vision: Its Development in Infant and Child*. New York: Hoeber.

Getman, Gerald N. 1976. "Autobiography." In *Teaching Children with Learning Disabilities: Personal Perspectives*, edited by James M. Kauffman and Daniel P. Hallahan, 211–37. Columbus, OH: Merrill.

Getman, Gerald N., and Newell C. Kephart. 1956. *Perceptual Development of Retarded Children*. Lafayette, IN: Purdue Univ.

Getzel, Elizabeth E., and Paul Wehman, 2005. *Going to College: Expanding Opportunities for People with Disabilities*. Baltimore: Brookes.

Ginsburg, Faye, and Rayna Rapp. 2010. "The Social Distribution of Moxie: The Legacy of Christine Sleeter." *Disability Studies Quarterly* 30, no. 2: 1239–84. Available at http://dsq-sds.org/article/view/1239/1284.

Giordano, Gerard. 2007. *American Special Education: A History of Early Political Advocacy*. New York: Lang.

Glen, William J. 2006. "Separate but Not Yet Equal: The Relation between School Finance Adequacy Litigation and African American Student Achievement." *Peabody Journal of Education* 81:63–93.

Glennon, Theresa. 1993. "Disabling Ambiguities: Confronting Barriers to Education of Students with Emotional Disabilities." *Tennessee Law Review* 60:295–364.

———. 1995. "Race, Education, and the Construction of a Disabled Class." *Wisconsin Law Review* 1995:1237–338.

Godfrey, Barbara B., and Newell C. Kephart. 1969. *Movement Patterns and Motor Education*. New York: Appleton-Century-Crofts.

Goffman, Erving. 1963. *Stigma: Notes on the Management of Spoiled Identity*. Englewood Cliffs, NJ: Prentice Hall.

Goldberg-Edelson, Meredyth. 2006. "Are the Majority of Children with Autism Mentally Retarded? A Systematic Evaluation of the Data." *Focus on Autism and Other Developmental Disabilities* 21:66–83.

Goldstein, Kurt. [1934] 1939. *The Organism: A Holistic Approach to Biology Derived from Pathological Data in Man*. New York: American.

———. 1940. *Human Nature in the Light of Psychopathology.* New York: Schocken Books.

———. 1967. "Autobiography." In *A History of Psychology in Autobiography,* vol. 5, edited by Edwin G. Boring and Gardner Lindzey, 147–67. New York: American Psychological Association.

Golfus, Billy, and Doug Simpson, producers. 1994. *When Billy Broke His Head . . . and Other Tales of Wonder* (documentary). Brooklyn, NY: Fanlight Productions. Available at http://www.fanlight.com.

Gordon, Ed. 2005. "Connecticut Sues over 'No Child Left Behind.'" NPR, Aug. 24. Available at http://www.npr.org/templates/story/story.php?storyId=4813502.

Gould, Stephen J. [1981] 1996. *The Mismeasure of Man.* New York: Norton.

Graham, Linda J., and Roger Slee, 2008. "Inclusion?" In *Disability and the Politics of Education: An International Reader,* edited by Susan L. Gabel and Scot Danforth, 81–100. New York: Lang.

Gresham, Frank M. 2002. "Responsiveness to Intervention: An Alternative Approach to Identification of Learning Disabilities." In *Identification of Learning Disabilities: Research to Practice,* edited by Renee Bradley, Louis Danielson, and Daniel P. Hallahan, 467–520. Mahwah, NJ: Lawrence Erlbaum Associates.

Grigal, Meg, and Debra Hart. 2009. *Think College: Postsecondary Education Options for Students with Intellectual Disabilities.* Baltimore: Brookes.

Hadley, Wanda M. 2011. "College Students with Disabilities: A Student Development Perspective." *New Directions for Higher Education* 154 (Summer): 77–82.

Hahn, Harlan. 1985. "Towards a Politics of Disability: Definitions, Disciplines and Policies." *Social Science Journal* 22, no. 4: 87–105.

———. 1988. "The Politics of Physical Differences: Disability and Discrimination." *Journal of Social Issues* 44:39–47.

Hall, Kim Q. 2011. *Feminist Disability Studies.* Bloomington: Indiana Univ. Press.

Halley, Jane E. 2001. "Revised Version Entitled 'Like-Race Arguments.'" In *What's Left of Theory?* 40–74. New York: Routledge Press.

Haney Lopez, Ian F. 1996. *White by Law: The Legal Construction of Race.* New York: New York Univ. Press.

Hanson, Russell L. 1985. *The Democratic Imagination in America: Conversations with Our Past.* Princeton, NJ: Princeton Univ. Press.

Harbour, Wendy S. 2004. *Final Report: The 2004 AHEAD Survey of Higher Education Disability Services Providers.* Waltham, MA: Association on Higher Education and Disability.

———. 2008. *Final Report: The 2008 Biennial AHEAD Survey of Disability Services and Resource Professionals in Higher Education.* Huntersville, NC: Association on Higher Education and Disability.

Harbour, Wendy S., and Joseph W. Madaus, eds. 2011. "Disability Services and Campus Dynamics" (issue title). *New Directions for Higher Education* 154 (Summer).

Hardin, Garrett. 1968. "The Tragedy of the Commons." *Science,* Dec. 13.

Harley, Debra A., Theresa M. Nowak, Linda J. Gassaway, and Todd A. Savage. 2002. "Lesbian, Gay, Bisexual, and Transgender College Students with Disabilities: A Look at Multiple Cultural Minorities." *Psychology in the Schools* 39, no. 5: 525–38.

Harrington, Anne. 1996. *Reenchanted Science: Holism in German Culture from Wilhelm II to Hitler.* Princeton, NJ: Princeton Univ. Press.

Harris, Angela P. 1994. "Foreword: The Jurisprudence of Reconstruction." *California Law Review* 82, no. 4: 741–85.

Harris, Stacey. 1995. "Twice Oppressed and the Right Brain Exit." In *A Closer Look: Perspectives and Reflections on College Students with Learning Disabilities,* edited by Jane Utley Adelizzi and Diane B. Goss, 110–20. Milton, MA: Curry College.

Harrison, Anne. 2009. "Bookshare.org: Accessible Texts for Students with Print Disabilities." *Journal of Special Education Technology* 24:38–41.

Harrison, David, and Tony Freinberg. 2005. "Autistic Liberation Front Fights the 'Oppressors Searching for a Cure.'" *The Telegraph,* Jan. 20. Available at http://www.autisticsociety.org/News/article/sid=778.html.

Harr-Robins, Jenifer, Mengli Song, Steven Hurlburt, Cheryl Pruce, Louis Danielson, Michael Garet, and James Taylor. 2012. *The Inclusion of Students with Disabilities in School Accountability Systems.* NCEE 2012-4056. Washington, DC: National Center for Education Evaluation and Regional Assistance, Institute of Education Sciences, US Department of Education.

Harry, Beth. 1992. *Cultural Diversity, Families, and the Special Education System: Communication and Empowerment.* New York: Teachers College Press.

Harry, Beth, and Mary G. Anderson. 1994. "The Disproportionate Placement of African American Males in Special Education Programs: A Critique of Process." *Journal of Negro Education* 63:602–19.

Harry, Beth, and Janette Klinger. 2006. *Why Are So Many Minority Students in Special Education? Understanding Race and Disability in Schools.* New York: Teachers College Press.

Harvey, David. 2005. *A Brief History of Neoliberalism.* Oxford: Oxford Univ. Press.

Hawkins, Susan D. 1996. "Protecting the Rights and Interests of Competent Minors in Litigated Medical Treatment Disputes." *Fordham Law Review* 64:2075–132.

Haycock, Kati. 1998. "Good Teaching Matters . . . a Lot." *OAH Magazine of History* 13:61–63.

Hegge, Thorleif G. 1934. "Special Reading Disability with Particular Reference to the Mentally Deficient." *Proceedings of the American Association for the Study of Feeblemindedness* 39: 297–340.

Hegge, Thorlief Gruner, Richard Sears, and Samuel A. Kirk. 1932. "Reading Cases in an Institution for Mentally-Retarded Problem Children." *Proceedings of the Fifty-Sixth Annual Session of the American Association for the Study of the Feeble-Minded* 37: 149–212.

Hehir, Thomas. 1994. "Improving the Individuals with Disabilities Education Act: IDEA Reauthorization." Unpublished manuscript produced for the US Department of Education, Office of Special Education Programs.

———. 2009. "Policy Foundations of Universal Design for Learning." In *A Policy Reader in Universal Design for Learning,* edited by David T. Gordon, Jenna W. Gravel, and Laura A. Schifter, 35–46. Cambridge, MA: Harvard Education Press.

Heise, Michael. 2005. *Educational Adequacy as Legal Theory: Implications from Equal Educational Opportunity Doctrine.* Cornell Legal Studies Research Paper no. 05-028. Ithaca, NY: Cornell Univ., Sept. 23.

Held, David. 1996. *Models of Democracy.* 2nd ed. Stanford, CA: Stanford Univ. Press.

Henderson, Bill. 2011. *The Blind Advantage: How Going Blind Made Me a Stronger Principal and How Including Children with Disabilities Made Our School Better for Everyone.* Cambridge, MA: Harvard Education Press.

Hensel, Wendy F. 2002. "Interacting with Others: A Major Life Activity under the Americans with Disabilities Act?" *Wisconsin Law Review* 2002:1139–96.

———. 2005. "The Disabling Impact of Wrongful Birth and Wrongful Life." *Harvard Civil Rights–Civil Liberties Law Review* 40:141–95.

———. 2007. "Sharing the Short Bus: Eligibility & Identity under the IDEA." *Hastings Law Journal* 58:1147–202.

———. 2009. "Rights Resurgence: The Impact of the ADA Amendments Act on Schools and Universities." *Georgia State University Law Review* 25:641–98.

———. 2010. "Vouchers for Students with Disabilities: The Future of Special Education?" *Journal of Law and Education* 39:291–349.

Herr, Stanley S. 1989–90. "Representation of Clients with Disabilities: Issues of Ethics and Control." *NYU Review of Law & Social Change* 17:609–50.

Higbee, Jeanne, Rachel Katz, and Jennifer Schultz. 2010. "Disability in Higher Education: Redefining Mainstreaming." *Journal of Diversity Management* 5:7–16.

Hitchcock, Chuck, Anne Meyer, David Rose, and Richard Jackson. 2002. *Technical Brief: Access, Participation, and Progress in the General Curriculum.* Washington, DC: National Center on Accessing the General Curriculum. Available at http://cte.jhu.edu/accessibility/primer/resources/data/universal design/ncact_tech_brief_5_14_02.pdf.

Hochschild, Jennifer, and Nathan Scovronick. 2003. *The American Dream and the Public Schools.* New York: Oxford Univ. Press.

Hockman, Laura. 2010. "A Longer Journey of Reflexivity: Becoming a Domesticated Academic." In *Living the Edges: A Disabled Women's Reader,* edited by Diane Driedger, 16–28. Toronto: Innana Publications and Education.

Holzman, Michael. 2010. *Yes We Can: The 2010 Schott Fifty State Report on Public Education and Black Males.* Cambridge, MA: Schott Foundation for Public Education. Available at http://www.blackboysreport.org/bbreport.pdf.

Horn, Wade F., and Douglas Tynan. 2001. "Time to Make Education Special Again." In *Rethinking Special Education for a New Century,* edited by Chester E. Finn Jr., Andrew J. Rotherham, and Charles R. Hokanson Jr., 23–52. Washington, DC: Thomas B. Fordham Institute.

Hosp, John L., and David J. Reschly. 2004. "Disproportionate Representation of Minority Students in Special Education: Academic, Demographic, and Economic Predictors." *Exceptional Children* 70:185–99.

Hughes, Langston. [1951] 1990. "Theme for English B." In *Selected Poems of Langston Hughes,* 247–48. New York: Vintage Books.

Hursh, David. 2004. *Education Policy: Globalization, Citizenship, and Democracy.* Thousand Oaks, CA: Sage.

Huss, Damon. 2003. "Comment, Balancing Acts: Dispute Resolution in U.S. and English Special Education Law." *Loyola of Los Angeles International and Comparative Law Review* 25:347–68.

Institute of Education Sciences. 2011. "National Center for Education Statistics Tbl. 8." Available at http://nces.ed.gov/programs/digest/d11/tables/dt11_008 .asp.

Jarraway, David R. 1996. "Montage of an Otherness Deferred: Dreaming Subjectivity in Langston Hughes." *American Literature* 68, no. 4: 819–47.

Jarrow, J. 1993. "Beyond Ramps: New Ways of Viewing Access." *New Directions for Student Services*, no. 64 (Winter): 5–16.

Johnson, Mary. 2003. *Make Them Go Away: Clint Eastwood, Christopher Reeves, and the Case against Disability Rights*. Louisville, KY: Avocado Press.

Johnson, William G. 1997. "The Future of Disability Policy: Benefit Payments or Civil Rights?" *Annals of the American Academy of Political and Social Science* 549:160–72.

Johnstone, Christopher, Alex Lubet, and Leonard Goldfine. 2008. "Disability Narratives, Social Models, and Rights Perspectives as Higher Education Imperatives." In *Disability Studies and the Politics of Education: An International Reader*, edited by Susan L. Gabel and Scot Danforth, 599–618. New York: Lang.

Jolls, Christine. 2004. "Identifying the Effects of the Americans with Disabilities Act Using State-Law Variation: Preliminary Evidence on Educational Participation Effects." *American Economic Review* 94:447–53.

Jolls, Christine, and J. J. Prescott. 2004. *Disaggregating Employment Protection: The Case of Disability Discrimination*. Working paper. Cambridge, MA: National Bureau of Economic Research. Available at http://www.nber.org /papers/w10740.

Jones, Melinda, and Lee Ann Basser Marks. 2000a. "Approaching Law and Disability." In "Explorations on Law and Disability in Australia," special issue of *Law in Context* 17, no. 2: 1–7.

———. 2000b. "Valuing People through Law: Whatever Happened to Marion?" In "Law in Context," edited by M. Jones and L. Basser Marks. In "Explorations on Law and Disability in Australia," special issue of *Law in Context* 17, no. 2: 147–80. Available at http://search.informit.com.au/documentSummary ;dn=145908518945995;res=IELHSS. ISSN: 0811-5796.

Jordan, Kathy-Anne. 2005. "Discourses of Difference and the Overrepresentation of Black Students in Special Education." *Journal of African American History* 90, nos. 1–2: 128–50.

Kairys, David. 1998. *The Politics of Law: A Progressive Critique*. 3rd ed. New York: Basic Books.

Kaiser Family Foundation. 2007. *Employer Health Benefits: 2007 Summary of Findings*. Menlo Park, CA: Kaiser Family Foundation. Available at http://www.kff.org/insurance/7672/upload/Summary-of-Findings-EHBS-2007.pdf.

Kallenberg, Richard. 2001. *All Together Now: Creating Middle-Class Schools through Public School Choice*. Washington, DC: Brookings Institution Press.

Kaloi, Laura, and Kristin Stanberry. 2012. "Section 504." In *2009: Broader Eligibility, More Accommodations*. New York: National Center on Learning Disabilities, Mar. 28. Available at http://www.ncld.org/on-capitol-hill/federal-laws-aamp-ld/adaaa-a-section-504/section-504-in-2009.

Kalyanpur, Maya, Beth Harry, and Thomas M. Skrtic. 2000. "Equity and Advocacy Expectations of Culturally Diverse Families' Participation in Special Education." *International Journal of Disability, Development, and Education* 47, no. 2: 119–36.

Kanter, Arlene S. 2003. "The Globalization of Disability Rights Law." *Syracuse Journal of International Law and Commerce* 30:243–71.

———. 2007. "The Promise and Challenge of the United Nations Convention on the Rights of Persons with Disabilities." *Syracuse Journal of International Law and Commerce* 34:287–321.

———. 2009. "The United Nations Convention on the Rights of Persons with Disabilities and Its Implications for the Rights of Elderly Persons under International Law." *Georgia State Law Review* 25:527–73.

———. 2011. "The Law: What's Disability Studies Got to Do with It, or An Introduction to Disability Legal Studies." *Columbia Human Rights Law Review* 42, no. 2: 403–79.

Karp, Stan. 2004. "NCLB's Selective Vision of Equality: Some Gaps Count More Than Others." In *Many Children Left Behind: How the No Child Left Behind Act Is Damaging Our Children and Our Schools*, edited by Deborah Meier and George Wood, 53–65. Boston: Beacon Press.

Karst, Kenneth L. 1984. "Woman's Constitution." *Duke Law Journal* 33:447–508.

Katovitch, Diana M. 2009. *The Power to Spring Up: Postsecondary Education Opportunities for Students with Significant Disabilities*. Bethesda, MD: Woodbine House.

Keller, Christoph. 2009. *The Best Dancer*. Portland, OR: Ooligan Press.

Kelman, Mark. 1987. *A Guide to Critical Legal Studies*. Cambridge, MA: Harvard Univ. Press.

Kelman, Mark, and Gillian Lester. 1997. *Jumping the Queue: An Inquiry into the Legal Treatment of Students with Learning Disabilities*. Cambridge, MA: Harvard Univ. Press.

Kennedy, David W., and William Fisher, eds. 2006. *The Canon of American Legal Thought*. Princeton, NJ: Princeton Univ. Press.

Kennedy, Duncan. 1997. *A Critique of Adjudication [fin de siècle]*. Cambridge, MA: Harvard Univ. Press.

———. 2004. *Legal Education and the Reproduction of Hierarchy: A Polemic against the System: A Critical Edition*. New York: New York Univ. Press.

Kent, J. Robert. 2007. "Review Essay: Is American Liberalism Singular or Plural?" *American Studies* 48, no. 4: 129–45.

Kephart, Newell C. 1947. "The Importance of Phoria Measurements in Industrial Vision." *Optometric Weekly* 38:45–50.

———. 1948. "Visual Skills and Labor Turnover." *Journal of Applied Psychology* 32, no. 1: 51–55.

———. 1951. "Visual Correction and School Achievement." *American Journal of Optometry* 28, no. 8: 421–23.

———. 1953. "Visual Skills and Their Relation to School Achievement." *American Journal of Ophthalmology* 36: 794–99.

———. 1968. *Learning Disability: An Educational Adventure*. West Lafayette, IN: Kappa Delta Pi Press.

Kephart, Newell C., and Alfred A. Strauss. 1940. "A Clinical Factor Influencing Variations in IQ." *American Journal of Orthopsychiatry* 10:343–51.

Kevles, Daniel. 1985. *In the Name of Eugenics and the Uses of Human Heredity*. New York: Knopf.

Kingsbury, Forrest A. 1946. "A History of the Department of Psychology at the University of Chicago." *Psychological Bulletin* 43:259–71.

Kirby, Peadar. 2006. *Vulnerability and Violence: The Impact of Globalisation*. London: Pluto.

Kirk, Samuel A. 1936. *Manual of Directions for Use with the Hegge-Kirk Remedial Reading Drills*. Ann Arbor, MI: G. Wahr.

———. 1940. *Teaching Reading to the Slow-Learning Child*. Boston: Houghton Mifflin.

———. 1952. "Experiments in the Early Training of the Mentally Retarded." *American Journal of Mental Deficiency* 56:692–700.

———. 1962. "Effects of Educational Treatment." *Research Publications—Association for Research in Nervous and Mental Disease* 39:289–94.

———. 1963a. "A Behavioral Approach to Learning Disabilities." In *Samuel A. Kirk Conference on Children with Minimal Brain Impairment*, edited by Samuel Kirk and Walter Becker, 41–52. Chicago: National Society for Crippled Children and Adults.

———. 1963b. "Behavioral Diagnosis and Remediation of Learning Disabilities." In *Proceedings of the Conference on the Exploration into the Problems of the Perceptually Handicapped Child*, 1–23. Evanston, IL: Fund for Perceptually Handicapped Children.

———. 1966. *The Diagnosis and Remediation of Psycholinguistic Disabilities*. Urbana: Univ. of Illinois.

———. 1976. "Autobiography." In *Teaching Children with Learning Disabilities: Personal Perspectives*, edited by James M. Kauffman and Daniel P. Hallahan, 238–69. Columbus, OH: Merrill.

———. 1984. "Introspection and Prophecy." In *Perspectives in Special Education: Personal Orientations*, edited by Burton Blatt and Richard J. Morris, 25–55. Glenview, IL: Scott Foresman.

Kirk, Samuel A., and Merle B. Karnes. 1958. *Early Education of the Mentally Retarded, an Experimental Study*. Urbana: Univ. of Illinois Press.

Kirk, Samuel A., and Winifred D. Kirk. 1971. *Psycholinguistic Learning Disabilities: Diagnosis and Remediation*. Urbana: Univ. of Illinois Press.

———. 1978. "Uses and Abuses of the ITPA." *Journal of Speech and Hearing Disorders* 43, no. 1: 58–75.

———. 1983. "On Defining Learning Disabilities." *Journal of Learning Disabilities* 16, no. 1: 20–21.

Kirk, Samuel A., and James J. McCarthy. 1961. "The Illinois Test of Psycholinguistic Abilities—an Approach to Differential Diagnosis." *American Journal of Mental Deficiency* 66:399–412.

Kirp, David, William Buss, and Peter Kuriloff. 1974. "Legal Reform of Special Education: Empirical Studies and Procedural Proposals." *California Law Review* 62: 40–155.

Kittay, Eva F. 1999. *Love's Labor: Essays on Women, Equality, and Dependency*. London: Routledge.

Klarman, Michael. 2007. *Unfinished Business: Racial Equality in American History*. New York: Oxford Univ. Press.

Kleege, Georgina. 2006. *Blind Rage: Letters to Helen Keller*. Washington, DC: Gallaudet Univ. Press.

Kleinhammer-Tramill, Jeannie, and Karen Gallagher. 2002. "The Implications of Goals 2000 for Inclusive Education." In *Whole-School Success and Inclusive Education: Building Partnerships for Learning, Achievement, and Accountability*, edited by Wayne Sailor, 26–41. New York: Teachers College Press.

Koballa, Joyce. 2007. "Test Scores for Special Education Students on Rise." *Herald Standard* (Uniontown, PA), Jan. 2. Available at http://www.heraldstandard.com/site/news.cfm?newsid=17656765&BRD=2280&PAG=461&dept_id=480247&rfi=6.

Kudlick, C. J. 2003. "Disability History: Why We Need Another 'Other.'" *American Historical Review* 108:763–93. Available at http://www.historycooperative.org/journals/ahr/108.3/kudlick.html.

Kuusisto, Stephen. 1998. *Planet of the Blind*. New York: Delta.

———. 2006. *Eavesdropping: A Memoir of Blindness and Listening*. New York: Norton.

Ladd, Helen F. 2002. "School Vouchers: A Critical View." *Journal of Economic Perspectives* 16, no. 4: 3–24.

Lakin, K. Charlie, Sheryl Larson, Patricia Salmi, and Armanda Webster. 2010. *Residential Services for Persons with Developmental Disabilities: Status and Trends through 2009*. Minneapolis: Research and Training Center on Community Living, Institute on Community Integration, Univ. of Minnesota.

Lamb, Richard H., and Linda E. Weinberger. 1998. "Persons with Severe Mental Illness in Jails and Prisons: A Review." *Psychiatric Service* 49:483–92.

Lankford, Hamilton, and James Wyckoff. 2006. "The Effect of School Choice and Residential Location on the Racial Segregation of Students." *Advances in Applied Microeconomics* 14:185–239.

Lareau, Annette. 2003. *Unequal Childhoods: Class, Race, and Family Life*. Berkeley: Univ. of California Press.

Lazerson, Marvin. 1983. "The Origins of Special Education." In *Special Education Policies: Their History, Implementation, and Finance*, edited by Jay G. Chambers and William T. Hartman, 15–47. Philadelphia: Temple Univ. Press.

Leake, David W., and Margarita Cholymay, 2004. "Addressing the Needs of Culturally and Linguistically Diverse Students with Disabilities in Postsecondary Education." In *Information Brief: Addressing Trends and Developments in Secondary Education and Transition*, vol. 3, no. 1, n.p. Minneapolis: National Center on Secondary Education and Transition, Univ. of Minnesota.

Learning Disabilities Association of America (LDAA). 2010. *Learning Disabilities & the Law: After High School: An Overview for Students*. Pittsburgh: LDAA. Available at http://www.ldanatl.org/aboutld/adults/civil_rights/law.asp.

Lee, Jaekyung, and Kenneth K. Wong. 2004. "The Impact of Accountability on Racial and Socioeconomic Equity: Considering Both School Resources and Achievement Outcomes." *American Educational Research Journal* 41:797–832.

Lee, Suk-Hyang, Michael L. Wehmeyer, Jane H. Soukup, and Susan B. Palmer. 2010. "Impact of Curriculum Modifications on Access to the General Education Curriculum for Students with Disabilities." *Exceptional Children* 76:213–33.

Lehtinen, Laura E., and Alfred A. Strauss. 1944. "Arithmetic Fundamentals for the Brain-Crippled Child." *American Journal of Mental Deficiency* 49:149–54.

Leiter, Valerie, and Marty Wyngaarden Krauss. 2005. "Claims, Barriers, and Satisfaction: Parents' Requests for Additional Special Education Services." *Journal of Disability Policy Studies* 15:135–46.

Leonard, James. 2005. "The Equality Trap: How Reliance on Traditional Civil Rights Concepts Has Rendered Title I of the ADA Ineffective." *Case Western Reserve Law Review* 56:1–63.

Leonard, Thomas C. 2009. "Origins of the Myth of Social Darwinism: The Ambiguous Legacy of Richard Hofstadter's Social Darwinism in American Thought." *Journal of Economic Behavior and Organization* 71:37–51.

Leone, Peter E., and Sheri Meisel. 1997. "Improving Education Services for Students in Detention and Confinement Facilities." *Children's Legal Rights Journal* 17:2–11.

Leone, Peter E., Barbara A. Zaremba, Michelle S. Chapin, and Curt Iseli. 1995. "Understanding the Overrepresentation of Youths with Disabilities in Juvenile Detention." *District of Columbia Law Review* 3:389–403.

Levit, Nancy, and Robert Verchik. 2006. *Feminist Legal Theory: A Primer.* New York: New York Univ. Press.

Lewis, Kathleen A., Gail M. Schwartz, and Robert N. Ianacone. 1988. "Service Coordination between Correctional and Public School Systems for Handicapped Juvenile Offenders." *Exceptional Children* 55, no. 1: 66–70.

Linton, Simi. 1998a. *Claiming Disability : Knowledge and Identity.* New York: New York Univ. Press.

———. 1998b. "Disability Studies/Not Disability Studies." *Disability & Society* 13, no. 4: 525–40.

Linton, Simi, Susan Mello, and John O'Neill. 1995. "Disability Studies: Expanding the Parameters of Diversity." *Radical Teacher* 47:4–10.

Litvak, S. 1994. "Disability Studies v. Disability Policy Studies." *Disability Studies Quarterly* 14, no. 3: 23–26.

Longman, Jere. 2007. "An Amputee Sprinter: Is He Disabled or Too-Abled?" *New York Times*, Mar. 15. Available at http://www.nytimes.com/2007/05/15/sports/othersports/15runner.html.

Longmore, Paul, and David Goldberger. 2000. "The League of the Physically Handicapped and the Great Depression: A Case Study in the New Disability History." *Journal of American History* 97, no. 3: 888–922.

Longmore, Paul K., and Lauri Umansky. 2001. "Introduction." In *The New Disability History: American Perspectives*, edited by Paul Longmore and Lauri Umansky, 1–32. New York: New York Univ. Press.

Losen, Daniel J. 1999. "Silent Segregation in Our Nation's Schools." *Harvard Civil Rights–Civil Liberties Law Review* 34:516–45.

Losen, Daniel J., and Jonathan Gillespie. 2012. *Opportunities Suspended: The Disparate Impact of Disciplinary Exclusion from School*. Los Angeles: Civil Rights Project. Available at http://civilrightsproject.ucla.edu/resources /projects/center-for-civil-rights-remedies/school-to-prison-folder/federal -reports/upcoming-ccrr-research.

Losen, Daniel, and Gary Orfield. 2002a. "Introduction." In *Racial Inequity in Special Education*, edited by Daniel Losen and Gary Orfield, xv–xxxvii. Cambridge, MA: Harvard Univ. Press.

———. 2002b. *Racial Inequity in Special Education*. Cambridge, MA: Harvard Univ. Press.

Losen, Daniel J., and Kevin G. Welner. 2001. "Disabling Discrimination in Our Public Schools: Comprehensive Legal Challenges to Inappropriate and Inadequate Special Education Services for Minority Children." *Harvard Civil Rights–Civil Liberties Law Review* 36:407–60.

Macartney, Bernadette C. 2011. "Disabled by the Discourse: Two Families' Narratives of Inclusion, Exclusion, and Resistance in Education." PhD diss., Univ. of Canterbury, Christchurch, New Zealand.

Macpherson, C. B. 1977. *The Life and Times of Liberal Democracy*. Oxford: Oxford Univ. Press.

Macurdy, Alan H. 1995. "Commentary: Disability Ideology and the Law School Curriculum." *Boston University Public Interest Law Journal* 4:443–57.

Madaus, Joseph W. 1998. "The Effect of Demographic Characteristics on OSD Administrators' Perceptions of Essential Job Functions." *Journal of Postsecondary Education and Disability* 13, no. 1: 3–22.

———. 2000. "Services for College and University Students with Disabilities: A Historical Perspective." *Journal of Postsecondary Education and Disability* 14, no. 1: 4–21.

———. 2011. "The History of Disability Services in Higher Education." *New Directions for Higher Education* 154 (Summer): 5–16.

Maennel, Bruno. 1907. *The Auxiliary Schools of Germany: Six Lectures by B. Maennel*. Translated by F. B. Dreslar. Bulletin no. 3. Washington, DC: US Bureau of Education.

Malhotra, Ravi. 2008. "Expanding the Frontiers of Justice: Reflections on the Theory of Capabilities, Disability Rights, and the Politics of Global Inequality." *Socialism and Democracy* 22:83–100.

Manning, Lynn. 1994. *Clarity of Vision* (album). Cambridge, MA: New Alliance Audio Productions.

———. 1997. "The Magic Wand." In *Staring Back: The Disability Experience from the Inside Out*, edited by Kenny Fries, 165–66. New York: Plume.

———. 2005. *Weights: One Blind Man's Journey* (CD-ROM). New York: Bridge Multimedia.

Marcus, Neil. 1996. *Storm Reading*. Directed by Rod Latham. Performances by Neil Marcus, Matthew Ingersoll, and Kathrin Voice. Santa Barbara, CA: Access Theatre Productions. Available at http://www.newsun.com/StormRead.html.

Markus, Hazel. 2008. "Cultural Responsiveness and Feeling at Home: Models of Equality in America." In *Just Schools: Pursuing Equality in Societies of Difference*, edited by Martha Minow, Richard Shweder, and Hazel Markus, 63–100. New York: Russell Sage Foundation.

Marx, Karl. [1845] 1978. "Theses on Feurbach." In *The Marx–Engels Reader*, 2d. ed., edited by Robert C. Tucker, 143–45. New York: Norton.

Marx, Karl, and Frederich Engels. [1848] 1964. *The Communist Manifesto*. Edited by Joseph Katz. Translated by Samuel Moore. New York: Washington Square Press.

Mather, Nancy. 1998. "Dr. Samuel A. Kirk: The Complete Professor." *Learning Disabilities Research & Practice* 13:35–42.

Matsuda, Mari J. 1991. "Voices of America: Accent, Antidiscrimination Law, and Jurisprudence for the Last Reconstruction." *Yale Law Journal* 100:1329–407.

Mauer, Marc, and Ryan S. King. 2007. "The Sentencing Project." In *Uneven Justice: State Rates of Incarceration by Race and Ethnicity*. Washington, DC: Sentencing Project. Available at http://www.sentencingproject.org.

May, Vivian M., and Beth A. Ferri, 2002. "'I'm a Wheelchair Girl Now': Abjection, Intersectionality, and Subjectivity in Atom Egoyan's 'The Sweet Hereafter.'" *Women's Studies Quarterly* 30, nos. 1–2: 131–50.

———. 2005. "Fixated on Ability: Questioning Ableist Metaphors in Feminist Theories of Resistance." *Prose Studies* 27, nos. 1–2: 120–40.

Mazumdar, Pauline. 2006. *The Eugenics Movement: An International Perspective*. London: Routledge Press.

McBryde Johnson, Harriet. 2003. "Unspeakable Conversations." *New York Times Magazine*, Feb. 16.

McCall, Zach, and Thomas M. Skrtic. 2009. "Intersectional Needs Politics: A Policy Frame for the Wicked Problem of Disproportionality." *Multiple Voices for Ethnically Diverse Exceptional Learners* 11, no. 2: 3–23.

McCann, Michael. 2006. "Law and Social Movements: Contemporary Perspectives." *Annual Review of Law and Social Change* 18, no. 2: 17–38.

McDaniel, Leah. 2012. "Arkansas Looks to Waiver No Child Left Behind." *Arkansas State University Herald*, Feb. 23. Available at http://www.asuherald.com/mobile/news/ark-looks-to-waiver-no-child-left-behind-1.2705830.

Mcgowan, Miranda Oshige. 2000. "Reconsidering the Americans with Disabilities Act." *Georgia Law Review* 35:27–160.

McIntosh, Peggy. 1988. "White Privilege and Male Privilege: A Personal Account of Coming to See Correspondences through Work in Women's Studies." Working paper from the Wellesley College Center for Research on Women, Wellsley, MA.

McKay, Nellie Y. 1998. "The Narrative Self: Race, Politics, and Culture in Black American Women's Autobiography." In *Women, Autobiography, Theory: A Reader*, edited by Sidonie Smith and Julia Watson, 96–107. Madison: Univ. of Wisconsin Press.

McKinney, Fred. 1978. "Functionalism at Chicago—Memories of a Graduate Student: 1929–1931." *Journal of the History of the Behavioral Sciences* 14, no. 2: 142–48.

McLaughlin, Margaret J., and Christina Tilstone. 2000. "Standards and Curriculum: The Cornerstone of Educational Reform." In *Special Education and School Reform in the United States and Britain*, edited by Margaret McLaughlin and Martyn Rouse, 38–65. London: Routledge.

McLeskey, James. 2004. "Classic Articles in Special Education: Articles That Shaped the Field, 1960 to 1996." *Remedial and Special Education* 25:79–87.

McLesky, James, Nancy L. Waldron, and Steven A. Wornhoff. 1990. "Factors Influencing the Identification of Black and White Students with Learning Disabilities." *Journal of Learning Disabilities* 23, no. 6: 362–66.

McNicoll, Tracy. 2009. "Aging Crisis Will Soon Hit Developing World." *Newsweek Wealth of Nations Blog*, Sept. 10. Available at http://www.newsweek.com

/blogs/wealth-of-nations/2009/09/10/aging-crisis-will-soon-hit-developing world.html.

McRuer, Robert. 2002. "Compulsory Able-Bodiedness and Queer/Disabled Existence." In *Disability Studies: Enabling the Humanities*, edited by Sharon L. Snyder, Brenda Jo Brueggemann, and Rosemarie Garland-Thomson, 88–99. New York: Modern Language Association of America.

———. 2006. *Crip Theory: Cultural Signs of Queerness and Disability*. New York: New York Univ. Press.

Meekosha, Helen. 2011. "Decolonising Disability: Thinking and Acting Globally." *Disability & Society* 26, no. 6: 667–82.

Mehan, Hugh, Alma Hertweck, and J. Lee Meihls. 1986. *Handicapping the Handicapped: Decision Making in Students' Educational Careers*. Stanford, CA: Stanford Univ. Press.

Mercer, Jane. 1973. *Labeling the Mentally Retarded: Clinical and Social System Perspectives on Mental Retardation*. Berkeley, CA: Univ. of California Press.

Meyer, Anne, and David H. Rose. 1998. *Learning to Read in the Digital Age*. Cambridge, MA: Brookline Books.

Meyer, John W., and Brian Rowan. 1977. "Institutionalized Organizations: Formal Structure as Myth and Ceremony." *American Journal of Sociology* 83:340–63.

———. 1978. "The Structure of Educational Organizations." In *Environments and Organizations*, edited by Marshall W. Meyer, 78–109. San Francisco: Jossey-Bass.

———. 1983. "The Structure of Educational Organizations." In *Organizational Environments: Ritual and Rationality*, edited by John W. Meyer and W. Richard Scott, 71–97. Beverly Hills, CA: Sage.

Meyer, Marshall W. 1979. "Organizational Structure as Signaling." *Pacific Sociological Review* 22, no. 4: 481–500.

Michalko, Rod. 2001. "Blindness Enters the Classroom." *Disability and Society* 16, no. 3: 349–59.

———. 2002. *The Difference That Disability Makes*. Philadelphia: Temple Univ. Press.

Miller, Binny. 1994. "Give Them Back Their Lives: Recognizing Client Narrative in Case Theory." *Michigan Law Review* 93:485–576.

Miller, Paul Steven, and Paul Longmore. 2006. "'A Philosophy of Handicap': The Origins of Randolph Bourne's Radicalism." *Radical History Review* 94:58–83.

Millet, Ann. 2008. "Staring Back and Forth: The Photographs of Kevin Connolly." *Disability Studies Quarterly* 28, no. 3. Available at http://www.dsq-sds.org.

Minnesota House of Representatives. 2002. "Special Education Terms and Student Discipline." House Research, Oct. 9. Available at http://www.house.leg.state.mn.us/hrd/issinfo/specedterms.htm.

Minow, Martha. 1985. "Learning to Live with the Dilemma of Difference: Bilingual and Special Education." *Law and Contemporary Problems* 48:157–211.

———. 1990. *Making All the Difference: Inclusion, Exclusion, and American Law.* Ithaca, NY: Cornell Univ. Press.

———. 1997. *Not Only for Myself: Identity, Politics, and the Law.* New York: New Press.

———. 2008. "Accommodating Integration." *University of Pennsylvania Law Review,* 57, no. 1: 1–10.

———. 2010. *In Brown's Wake: Legacies of America's Educational Landmark.* New York: Oxford Univ. Press.

Minskoff, Esther H. 1998. "Sam Kirk: The Man Who Made Special Education Special." *Learning Disabilities Research and Practice* 13, no. 1: 15–21.

Mirowski, Philip, and Dieter Plehwe. 2009. *The Road from Mont Pèlerin: The Making of the Neoliberal Thought Collective.* Cambridge, MA: Harvard Univ. Press.

Mitchell, David T., and Sharon L. Snyder. 1997. *The Body and Physical Difference: Discourses of Disability in the Humanities.* Ann Arbor, MI: Univ. of Michigan Press.

———. 2000. *Narrative Prosthesis: Disability and the Dependencies of Discourse.* Ann Arbor: Univ. of Michigan Press.

Moffitt, Robert, David Ribar, and Mark Wilhelm. 1998. "The Decline of Welfare Benefits in the U.S.: The Role of Wage Inequality." *Journal of Public Economics* 68:421–52.

Monroe, Carla R. 2006. "African American Boys and the Discipline Gap: Balancing Educators' Uneven Hand." *Educational Horizons* 48, no. 2: 102–11.

Mooney, Jonathan, and David Cole. 2000. *Learning Outside the Lines: Two Ivy League Students with Learning Disabilities and ADHD Give You the Tools for Academic Success and Educational Revolution.* New York: Fireside.

Moore, Nancy J. 1996. "Conflicts of Interests in the Representation of Children." *Fordham Law Review* 64:1819–56.

Mor, Sagit. 2006. "Between Charity, Welfare, and Warfare: A Disability Legal Studies Analysis of Privilege and Neglect in Israeli Disability Policy." *Yale Journal of Law and Humanities* 18:63–137.

Morris, Jenny. 1996. *Encounters with Strangers: Feminism and Disability*. London: Women's Press.

Morrison, Elspeth, and Vic Finkelstein. 1991. "Culture as Struggle: Access to Power." In *Disability Arts and Culture Papers: Transcripts of a Disability Arts and Culture Seminar*, edited by Sarah Leeds. London: Shape. Available at http://disability-studies.leeds.ac.uk/files/library/Lees-arts-and-culture.pdf.

Morrison, Harriet R., and Beverly D. Epps. 2002. "Warehousing or Rehabilitation? Public Schooling in the Juvenile Justice System." *Journal of Negro Education* 71, no. 3: 218–32.

Muncy, Robin. 1991. *Creating a Female Dominion in American Reform: 1890–1935*. Oxford: Oxford Univ. Press.

Murphy, Mary, Claude M. Steele, and James J. Gross. 2007. "Signaling Threat: How Situational Cues Affect Women in Math, Science, and Engineering Settings." *Psychological Science* 18:879–85.

National Center for Education Statistics, US Department of Education. 2006. *Profile of Undergraduates in U.S. Postsecondary Education Institutions: 2003–04*. Washington, DC: US Department of Education. Available at http://nces.ed.gov/pubsearch/pubsinfo.asp?pubid=2006184.

———. 2013. "The Condition of Education: Children and Youth with Disabilities." Available at http://nces.ed.gov/programs/coe/indicator_cgg.asp.

National Center on Accessible Instructional Materials. n.d. Website. Available at http://aim.cast.org. Last updated June 6, 2013.

National Collaborative on Workforce & Disability for Youth and the Workforce Strategy Center. 2009. *Career-Focused Services for Students with Disabilities at Community Colleges*. Washington, DC: Institute for Educational Leadership.

National Council on Disability. 2011. *National Disability Policy: A Progress Report—October 2011, Postsecondary Education*. Washington, DC: National Council on Education. Available at http://www.ncd.gov/progress_reports/Oct312011.

National Organization on Disability. 2004. "2004 NOD/Harris Survey 22." Available at http://www.nod.org/assets/downloads/NODHarris-Results-2004.pdf.

National Research Council. 1982. *Placing Children in Special Education: A Strategy for Equity.* Edited by Kirby A. Heller, Wayne H. Holtzman, and Samuel Messick. Washington, DC: National Academy Press.

———. 2002. *Minority Students in Special and Gifted Education.* Edited by M. Susan Donovan and Christopher T. Cross. Washington, DC: National Academy Press.

Neal, David, and David L. Kirp. 1985. "The Allure of Legalization Reconsidered: The Case of Special Education." *Law and Contemporary Problems* 48:63–87.

Neely, David H. 1982. "Handicapped Advocacy: Inherent Barriers and Partial Solutions in the Representation of Disabled Children." *Hastings Law Journal* 33:1359–406.

Newman, Lynn, Mary Wagner, Anne-Marie Knokey, Camille Marder, Katherine Nagle, Debra Shaver, Xin Wei, with Renée Cameto, Elidia Contreras, Kate Ferguson, Sarah Greene, and Meredith Schwarting. 2011. *The Post–High School Outcomes of Young Adults with Disabilities up to 8 Years after High School. A Report from the National Longitudinal Transition Study-2 (NLTS-2) (NCSER 2011-3005).* Menlo Park, CA: SRI International.

Nietsch, Patti, Christine Siegel, Cindy Keefe, and Krista Horn. 2008. "Partnering with Parents of Special Needs Students: Barriers to Collaboration." *National Association of School Psychologists Communiqué* 37, no. 1: 16–19.

Noppeney, Uta. 2001. "Kurt Goldstein—a Philosophical Scientist." *Journal of the History of Neuroscience* 10, no. 1:67–78.

Norden, Martin F. 1994. *The Cinema of Isolation: A History of Physical Disability in the Movies.* New Brunswick, NJ: Rutgers Univ. Press.

Not Dead Yet.org. 2013. Website. Available at http://www.notdeadyet.org/.

Nussbaum, Martha C. 1988. "Nature, Function, and Capability: Aristotle on Political Distribution." *Oxford Studies in Ancient Thought*, Supplement 1, edited by Julia Annas: 145–84.

———. 1990. "Aristotelian Social Democracy." In *Liberalism and the Good*, edited by Gerald M. Mara, Henry S. Richardson, and R. Bruce Douglass, 203–52. New York: Routledge.

———. 2000a. "Aristotle, Politics, and Human Capabilities: A Response to Antony, Arneson, Charlesworth, and Mulgan." *Ethics* 111:102–40.

———. 2000b. *Women and Human Development: The Capabilities Approach.* Cambridge: Cambridge Univ. Press.

———. 2001. "Disabled Lives: Who Cares?" *New York Review of Books*, Jan. 11: 1–9.

———. 2003. "Capabilities as Fundamental Entitlements: Sen and Social Justice." *Feminist Economics* 9, nos. 2–3: 33–59.

———. 2006a. *Frontiers of Justice: Disability, Nationality, Species Membership.* Cambridge, MA: Belknap Press of Harvard Univ. Press.

———. 2006b. "Replies." *Journal of Ethics* 10, no. 4: 463–506.

———. 2009. "The Capabilities of People with Cognitive Disabilities." *Metaphilosophy* 40: 331–51.

———. 2011. *Creating Capabilities: The Human Development Approach.* Cambridge, MA: Belknap Press of Harvard Univ. Press.

Oakes, Jeannie. 1985. *Keeping Track: How Schools Structure Inequality.* New Haven, CT: Yale Univ. Press.

Oakes, Jeannie, Amy Stuart Wells, Makeba Jones, and Amanda Datnow. 1997. "Detracking: The Social Construction of Ability, Cultural Politics, and Resistance to Reform." *Teachers College Record* 98, no. 3: 482–510.

O'Connell, Rory. 2008. "The Role of Dignity in Equality Law: Lessons from Canada and South Africa." *International Journal of Constitutional Law* 6: 267–86. doi:10.1093/icon/mon004.

O'Day, Jennifer A. 2002. "Complexity, Accountability, and School Improvement." *Harvard Educational Review* 72: 293–329.

Ogletree, Charles J., Jr. 2004. *All Deliberate Speed: Reflections on the First Half Century of Brown v. Board of Education.* New York: Norton.

Olin, Tom. 1990. "ADA Demonstration" (photograph). Available through the Disability History Museum at http://www.disabilitymuseum.org.

Oliver, Michael. 1990. *The Politics of Disablement: A Sociological Approach.* London: Macmillan.

———. 1996. *Understanding Disability: From Theory to Practice.* New York: St. Martin's Press.

———. 1997. "Research: Realistic Goal or Impossible Dream?" In *Doing Disability Research*, edited by Colin Barnes & Geof Mercer, 15–31. Leeds: Univ. of Leeds, Disability Press.

Ong-Dean, Colin. 2009. *Distinguishing Disability: Parents, Privilege, and Special Education.* Chicago: Univ. of Chicago Press.

Oregon Health Services Commission. 2008. "Current Prioritized List." Available at http://www.oregon.gov/ OHPPR/HSC/current_prior.html.

Ortega, Francisco. 2009. "The Cerebral Subject and the Challenge of Neurodiversity." *Biosocieties* 4:425–45.

Osgood, Robert L. 2008. *The History of Special Education: A Struggle for Equality in American Public Schools.* Westport, CT: Praeger.

Osher, David, Darren Woodruff, and Anthony E. Sims. 2002. "Schools Make a Difference: The Overrepresentation of African American Youth in Special Education and the Juvenile Justice System." In *Racial Inequity in Special Education,* edited by Daniel J. Losen and Gary Orfield, 93–116. Cambridge, MA: Harvard Education Press.

Oswald, Donald P., Martha J. Coutinho, and Al M. Best. 2002. "Community and School Predictors of Overrepresentation of Minority Children in Special Education." In *Racial Inequity in Special Education,* edited by Daniel J. Losen and Gary Orfield, 1–13. Cambridge, MA: Harvard Education Press.

Ouellette, Alicia. 2010. "Shaping Parental Authority over Children's Bodies." *Indiana Law Journal* 85:955–1002.

Pacer Center. 2010. "Transition to the Next Steps after High School: The Individuals with Disabilities Education Act of 1997." Available at http://www.pacer.org/tatra/legislation/IDEAtransition.asp.

Palfrey, John. 2008. *Born Digital: Understanding the First Generation of Digital Natives.* New York: Basic Books.

Palmaffy, Tyce. 2001. "The Evolution of the Federal Role." In *Rethinking Special Education for a New Century,* edited by Chester E. Finn Jr., Andrew J. Rotherham, and Charles R. Hokanson Jr., 1–21. Washington, DC: Thomas B. Fordham Institute.

Parekh, Pushpa N. 2007. "Gender, Disability, and the Post-colonial Nexus." *Wagadu* 4. Available at http://appweb.cortland.edu/ojs/index.php/Wagadu/article/viewArticle/333.

Parrish, Thomas. 2002. "Racial Disparities in the Identification, Funding, and Provision of Special Education." In *Racial Inequity in Special Education,* edited by Daniel J. Losen and Gary Orfield, 15–37. Cambridge, MA: Harvard Education Press.

Parrish, Thomas, Jenifer Harr, Jean Wolman, Jennifer Anthony, Amy Merickel, and Phil Esra. 2004. *State Special Education Finance Systems, 1999–2000, Part II: Special Education Revenues and Expenditures.* Palo Alto, CA: Center for Special Education Finance.

Pauken, Patrick, and Philip T. K. Daniel. 2000. "Race Discrimination and Disability Discrimination in School Discipline: A Legal and Statistical Analysis." *Education Law Reporter* 139:759–90.

Pearman, Elizabeth, Twila Elliott, and Lucinda Aborn. 2004. "Transition Services Model: Partnership for Student Success." *Education and Training in Developmental Disabilities* 39:26–34.

Perl, Erica S. 2003. *NCAC Policy Group White Paper for Policy, Property, & Permissions: A Discussion of Accessible Curriculum Materials on Ordering, Producing, and Obtaining Accessible Versions of Curriculum Materials for K–12 Students with Print Disabilities.* Wakefield, MA: National Center on Accessing the General Curriculum. Available at http://aim.cast.org/learn /historyarchive/backgroundpapers/ncac_policy_white_paper. Last updated Nov. 1, 2012.

Perles, Keren. 2012. "Mainstreaming and Inclusion: How Are They Different?" Bright Hub Education. Available at http://www.brighthubeducation.com /special-ed-inclusion-strategies/66813-the-differences-between-mainstreaming-and-inclusion/.

Peters, Susan J. 2006. "Disability Culture." In *Encyclopedia of Disability*, edited by Gary L. Albrecht, 412–20. Thousand Oaks, CA: Sage.

Pogge, Thomas W. 1989. *Realizing Rawls*. Ithaca, NY: Cornell Univ. Press.

Powell, John A. 2005. "A New Theory of Integrated Education." In *School Resegregation: Must the South Turn Back?* edited by John Charles Boger and Gary Orfield, 281–304. Chapel Hill: Univ. of North Carolina Press.

Powell, Walter W., and Paul J. DiMaggio. 1991. *The New Institutionalism in Organizational Analysis*. Chicago: Univ. of Chicago Press.

Preiser, Wolfgang F. E., and Korydon H. Smith. 2011. *Universal Design Handbook*. 2d ed. New York: McGraw-Hill.

President's Commission on Excellence in Special Education. 2002. *A New Era: Revitalizing Special Education for Children and Their Families*. Washington, DC: US Government Printing Office.

Pretti-Frontczak, Kristi, and Diane Bricker. 2000. "Enhancing the Quality of Individualized Education Plan (IEP) Goals and Objectives." *Journal of Early Intervention* 23, no. 2: 92–105.

Price, David F. 1974. "Community and Control: Critical Democratic Theory in the Progressive Period." *American Political Science Review* 68: 1663–78.

Price, Margaret. 2011. *Mad at School: Rhetorics of Mental Disability and Academic Life*. Ann Arbor: Univ. of Michigan Press.

Prince-Hughes, Dawn, ed. 2002. *Aquamarine Blue 5: Personal Stories of College Students with Autism.* Athens: Ohio Univ. Press.

———. 2004. *Songs of the Gorilla Nation: My Journey through Autism.* New York: Harmony Books.

Radler, Don H., and Newell C. Kephart. 1960. *Success through Play: How to Prepare Your Child for School Achievement—and Enjoy It.* New York: Harper.

Rawls, John. 1971. *A Theory of Justice.* Cambridge, MA: Belknap Press of Harvard Univ. Press.

———. [1993] 1996. *Political Liberalism.* New York: Columbia Univ. Press.

———. 1999. *The Law of Peoples.* Cambridge, MA: Harvard Univ. Press.

Reaume, Denise G. 2003. "Discrimination and Dignity." *Louisiana Law Review* 63: 1–51.

Reid, D. Kim, and Jan W. Valle. 2004. "The Discursive Practice of Learning Disability: Implications for Instruction and Parent–School Relations." *Journal of Learning Disabilities* 37, no. 6: 466–81.

Reynolds, Maynard. 1962. "A Framework for Considering Some Issues in Special Education." *Exceptional Children* 28:367–70.

Rice, Suzanne. 2002. "The Social Construction of Disabilities." *Educational Studies* 33:169–80.

Riddick, Barbara. 2000. "An Examination of the Relationship between Labeling and Stigmatisation with Special Reference to Dyslexia." *Disability and Society* 15:653–67.

Riggs, James G. 1936. *Hello Doctor: A Brief Biography of Charles Bernstein, M.D.* East Aurora, NY: Roycroft.

Riley, Richard W. 1995. "Reflections on Goals 2000." *Teachers College Record* 96, no. 3: 380–88.

Roberts, Megan. 2008. "Comment. The Individuals with Disabilities Education Act: Why Considering Individuals One at a Time Creates Untenable Situations for Students and Educators." *UCLA Law Review* 55:1041–94.

Rodis, Pano, Andrew Garrod, and Mary Lynn Boscardin, eds. 2001. *Learning Disabilities and Life Stories.* Needham Heights, MA: Allyn and Bacon.

Rome State School. 1907. *Annual Report.* Albany, NY: Rome State School.

Rose, David H., and Anne Meyer, 2002. *Teaching Every Student in the Digital Age: Universal Design for Learning.* Alexandria, VA: Association for Supervision and Curriculum Development.

———. 2006. *A Practical Reader in Universal Design for Learning.* Cambridge, MA: Harvard Education Press.

Rose, David H., Anne Meyer, and Chuck Hitchcock. 2005. *The Universally Designed Classroom: Accessible Curriculum and Digital Technologies*. Cambridge, MA: Harvard Education Press.

Rosenbaum, Stephen A. 2008. "Full Sp[]Ed Ahead: Expanding the IDEA Idea to Let All Students Ride the Same Bus." *Stanford Journal of Civil Rights and Civil Liberties* 4:373–92.

Rosenberg, Gerald N. 1991. *The Hollow Hope: Can Courts Bring About Social Change?* Chicago: Univ. of Chicago Press.

Rothstein, Laura F. 2002. "Judicial Intent and Legal Precedents." In *Postsecondary Education and Transition for Students with Learning Disabilities*, edited by Loring C. Brinckerhoff, Joan M. McGuire, and Stan F. Shaw, 71–108. Austin, TX: PRO-ED.

Rovner, Laura. 2001. "Perpetuating Stigma: Client Identity in Disability Rights Litigation." *Utah Law Review* 2001:247–318.

Rowan, Brian. 1982. "Organizational Structure and the Institutional Environment: The Case of Public Schools." *Administrative Science Quarterly* 40:604–11.

Rubenstein, Grace. 2007. "Thwarting Stereotype: What Educators Can Do." *Edutopia*, Mar. 28. Available at http://www.edutopia.org/thwarting-stereotype -threat.

Russell, Bertrand. 1905. "On Denoting." *Mind*, New Series, no. 56: 479–93.

Russell, Marta. 1998. *Beyond Ramps: Disability at the End of the Social Contract*. Monroe, LA: Common Courage Press.

Ryan, Alan. 1972. "Two Concepts of Politics and Democracy: James & John Stuart Mill." In *Machiavelli and the Nature of Political Thought*, edited by Martin Fleisher, 76–113. New York: Athenaeum.

Ryan, Camille L., and Julie Siebens (US Bureau of the Census). 2012. *Educational Attainment in the United States: 2009*. Washington, DC: US Bureau of the Census, US Department of Commerce. Available at http://www .census.gov/prod/2012pubs/p20-566.pdf.

Ryan, Sara, and Katherine Runswick-Cole. 2008. "Repositioning Mothers: Mothers, Disabled Children, and Disability Studies." *Disability & Society* 23:199–210.

Safran, Stephen P. 1998. "The First Century of Disability Portrayal in Film: An Analysis of the Literature." *Journal of Special Education* 31, no. 4: 467–79.

Sailor, Wayne, and Matt Stowe. 2003. *School Vouchers and Students with Disabilities*. Washington, DC: National Council on Disability. Available at http://www.ncd.gov/publications/2003/April152003.

Saks, Elyn R. 2008. *The Center Cannot Hold: My Journey through Madness.* New York: Hyperion.

Sandahl, Carrie, and Phillip Auslander, eds. 2005. *Bodies in Commotion: Disability and Performance.* Ann Arbor: Univ. of Michigan Press.

Sandell, Richard, Jocelyn Dodd, and Rosemarie Garland-Thomson, eds. 2010. *Re-presenting Disability: Museums and the Politics of Display.* London: Routledge.

Satz, Ani B. 2006. "A Jurisprudence of Dysfunction: On the Role of 'Normal Species Functioning' in Disability Analysis." *Yale Journal of Health Policy, Law, and Ethics* 6:221–67.

———. 2008. "The Limits of Health Care Reform." *Alabama Law Review* 59:1451–99.

———. 2010. "Fragmented Lives: Disability Discrimination and the Role of 'Environment-Framing.'" *Washington and Lee Law Review* 68:187–252.

———. 2011. "Overcoming Fragmentation in Health and Disability Law." *Emory Law Journal* 60:277–323.

Schemo, Diana J. 2004. "School Achievement Reports Often Exclude the Disabled." *New York Times,* Aug. 30.

Schumaker, Jean B., Donald D. Deshler, Janis A. Bulgren, Betsy Davis, B. Keith Lenz, and Bonnie Grossen. 2002. "Access of Adolescents with Disabilities to General Education Curriculum: Myth or Reality?" *Focus on Exceptional Children* 35, no. 3: 1–16.

Schweik, Susan M. 2009. *The Ugly Laws: Disability in Public.* New York: New York Univ. Press.

Scott, W. Richard. 1987a. "The Adolescence of Institutional Theory." *Administrative Science Quarterly* 32:493–511.

———. 1987b. *Organizations: Rational Natural and Open Systems.* Englewood Cliffs, NJ: Prentice-Hall.

Selden, Steven. 2000. "Eugenics and the Social Construction of Merit, Race, and Disability." *Journal of Curriculum Studies* 32:235–52.

Seligmann, Terry Jean. 2001. "An IDEA Schools Can Use: Lessons from Special Education Legislation." *Fordham Urban Law Journal* 29:759–90.

Semmel, Melvyn I., Michael M. Gerber, and Donald L. MacMillan. 1994. "Twenty-Five Years after Dunn's Article: A Legacy of Policy Analysis Research in Special Education." *Journal of Special Education* 27:481–95.

Sen, Amartya. 1992. *Inequality Reexamined.* Oxford: Oxford Univ. Press.

———. 1999. *Development as Freedom.* Oxford: Oxford Univ. Press.

Shakespeare, Tom. 1996. "Disability, Identity, and Difference." In *Exploring the Divide: Illness and Disability*, edited by Colin Barnes and Geof Mercer, 94–115. London: Disability Press. Available at http://www.leeds.ac.uk/disability-studies/archiveuk/Shakespeare/Chap6.pdf.

Shapiro, Ian. 1999. *Democratic Justice*. New Haven, CT: Yale Univ. Press.

Shaw, Stan F., Joseph W. Madaus, and Lyman L. Dukes III. 2010. *Preparing Students with Disabilities for College Success: A Practical Guide to Transition Planning*. Baltimore: Brookes.

Sheppard, S. 1999. *The History of Legal Education in the United States: Commentaries and Primary Sources*. Salem, MA: Salem Press.

Sherry, Mark. 2005. "Reading Me/Me Reading Disability." *Prose Studies* 27, nos. 1–2: 163–75.

———. 2008. *Disability and Diversity: A Sociological Perspective*. Hauppauge, NY: Nova Science.

Siebers, Tobin. 2008. *Disability Theory*. Ann Arbor: Univ. of Michigan Press.

———. 2010. *Disability Aesthetics*. Ann Arbor: Univ. of Michigan Press.

Siegel, Reva. 2004. "Equality Talk: Antisubordination and Anticlassification Values in Constitutional Struggles over *Brown*." *Harvard Law Review* 117:1470–547.

Silvers, Anita. 1998. "Reprising Women's Disability: Feminist Identity Strategy and Disability Rights." *Berkeley Women's Law Journal* 13:81–116.

Silvers, Anita, David Wasserman, and Mary B. Mahowald. 1998. *Disability, Difference, Discrimination: Perspectives of Justices in Bioethics and Public Policy*. Lanham, MD: Rowman and Littlefield.

Simon, Jo Anne. 2000. "Legal Issues in Serving Students with Disabilities in Postsecondary Education." In *Dimensions of Managing Academic Affairs in the Community College: New Directions for Community Colleges*, edited by Douglas Robillard Jr., 69–81. San Francisco: Jossey-Bass.

Singer, Joseph William. 2006. *Property Law: Rules, Practices, and Policies*. New York: Aspen.

Skeels, Harold M. 1938. "Mental Development of Children in Foster Homes." *Journal of Consulting Psychology* 2, no. 2: 33–43.

———. 1940. "Some Iowa Studies of Mental Growth in Children in Relation to Differentials of the Environment: A Summary." In *The Thirty-Ninth Yearbook of the National Society for the Study of Education. Intelligence: Its Nature and Nurture, Part 1, Comparative and Critical Exposition*, edited by Guy Montrose Whipple, 281–308. Bloomington, IL: Public School.

Skeels, Harold M., and Harold B. Dye. 1939. "A Study of the Effects of Differential Stimulation on Mentally Retarded Children." *Proceedings and Addresses of the American Association on Mental Deficiency* 44:114–36.

Skiba, Russell J., Lori Poloni-Staudinger, Sarah Gallini, Ada B. Simmons, and Renae Feggins-Azziz. 2006. "Disparate Access: The Disproportionality of African American Students with Disabilities across Educational Environments." *Exceptional Children* 72:411–24.

Skiba, Russell J., Ada B. Simmons, Shana Ritter, Ashley C. Gibb, M. Karega Rausch, Jason Cuadrado, and Choong-Geun Chung. 2008. "Achieving Equity in Special Education: History, Status, and Current Challenges." *Exceptional Children* 74:264–88.

Skrtic, Thomas M. 1991a. *Behind Special Education: A Critical Analysis of Professional Culture and School Organization.* Denver: Love.

———. 1991b. "The Special Education Paradox: Equity as the Way to Excellence." *Harvard Educational Review* 61, no. 2: 148–206.

———. 1995. "Special Education and Student Disability as Organizational Pathologies: Toward a Metatheory of School Organization and Change." In *Disability and Democracy: Reconstructing (Special) Education for Postmodernity,* edited by Thomas M. Skrtic, 190–232. New York: Teachers College Press.

———. 2000. "Civic Professionalism and the Struggle over Needs." Paper presented at the Annual Leadership Project Directors' Conference, Office of Special Education Programs, US Department of Education, July 11–12, Washington, DC.

———. 2003. "An Organizational Analysis of the Overrepresentation of Poor and Minority Students in Special Education." *Multiple Voices* 6, no. 1: 41–57.

———. 2005. "A Political Economy of Learning Disabilities." *Learning Disabilities Quarterly* 28, no. 2: 149–55.

———. 2010. Review of *Distinguishing Disability: Parents, Privilege, and Special Education* by Colin Ong-Dean. *Contemporary Sociology* 39, no. 2: 188–90.

———. 2012. "Disability, Difference, and Justice: Strong Democratic Leadership for Undemocratic Times." In *Handbook of Leadership and Administration for Special Education,* edited by Jean Crockett, Bonnie Billingsley, and Mary Lynn Boscardin, 129–50. New York: Routledge.

Skrtic, Thomas M., Karen R. Harris, and James G. Shriner. 2005. *Special Education Policy and Practice: Accountability, Instruction, and Social Challenges.* Denver: Love.

Skrtic, Thomas M., and Zach McCall. 2010. "Ideology, Institutions, and Equity: Comments on Christine Sleeter's *Why Is There Learning Disabilities?*" *Disability Studies Quarterly* 30, no. 2: 1230–77. Available at http://www.dsq-sds .org/article/view/1230/1277.

Slayton, Jeremy. 2012. "No Child Left Behind Act: Virginia Finalizes Waiver Request." *Star Exponent* (Culpepper, VA), Feb. 24. Available at http:// www2.starexponent.com/news/2012/feb/24/no-child-left-behind-act-virginia -finalizes-waiver-ar-1712797/.

Slee, Roger. 2011. *The Irregular School: Exclusion, Schooling, and Inclusive Education.* London: Routledge.

Sleeter, Christine E. 1986. "Learning Disabilities: The Social Construction of a Special Education Category." *Exceptional Children* 53:46–54.

Smith, Adam. [1776] 1902. *The Wealth of Nations.* New York: Collier.

Smith, Kevin. 1999. "Disabilities, Law Schools, and Law Students: A Proactive and Holistic Approach." *Akron Law Review* 32:1–106.

Smith, Phil. 2010. "Split——ting the ROCK of {speci[ES]al} e.ducat.ion: FLOWers of Lang[ue]age in >DIS<ability studies." In *Vital Questions in Disability Studies in Education*, edited by Scot Danforth and Susan Gabel, 31–58. New York: Peter Lang.

Smith, Stephen W. 1990. "Individualized Education Programs (IEPs) in Special Education: From Intent to Acquiescence." *Exceptional Children* 57, no. 1: 6–14.

Smith, Stephen W., and Larry J. Kotering. 1996. "Using Computers to Generate IEPs: Rethinking the Process." *Journal of Special Education Technology* 13: 81–90.

Snyder, Sharon L., Brenda Jo Brueggemann, and Rosemarie Garland-Thomson, eds. 2002. *Disability Studies: Enabling the Humanities.* New York: Modern Language Association of America.

Snyder, Sharon L., and David T. Mitchell, dirs. 2001. *A World without Bodies* (documentary). Chicago: Brace Yourself Productions.

———. 2006. *Cultural Locations of Disability.* Ann Arbor: Univ. of Michigan Press.

Solis, Santiago. 2009. "I'm 'Coming Out' as Disabled but I'm 'Staying In' to Rest: Reflecting on Elected and Imposed Segregation." *Equity and Excellence in Education* 39, no. 2: 146–53.

Somers, Margaret R., and Fred Block. 2005. "From Poverty to Perversity: Ideas, Markets, and Institutions over 200 Years of Welfare Debate." *American Sociological Review* 70:260–87.

"Special Education." 2004. *Education Week*, Aug. Available at http://www.ed week.org/ew/issues/special-education/.

Spring, Joel. 2012. *Deculturalization and the Struggle for Equality: A Brief History of the Education of Dominated Cultures in the United States*. 7th ed. Columbus, OH: McGraw-Hill.

Stahl, Skip. 2002. "A Discussion of Accessible Curriculum Materials." Oct. Available at http://aim.cast.org/learn/historyarchive/backgroundpapers/policy _property_permissions1#b1.

Stapleton, David C., Richard V. Burkhauser, and Andrew J. Houtenville. 2004. "Has the Employment Rate of People with Disabilities Declined?" Policy Brief, Rehabilitation Research and Training Center for Economic Research on Employment Policy for Persons with Disabilities, Cornell Univ. Available at http://digitalcommons.ilr.cornell.edu/edicollect/92/.

Steele, Claude. 1997. "A Threat in the Air: How Stereotypes Shape Intellectual Identity and Performance." *The American Psychologist* 52:613–29.

———. 2010. *Whistling Vivaldi: And Other Clues to How Stereotypes Affect Us*. New York: Norton.

Steele, Patricia E., and Thomas R. Wolanin. 2004. *Higher Education Opportunities for Students with Disabilities: A Primer for Policymakers*. Washington, DC: Institute for Higher Education Policy.

Stefan, Susan. 2000. "Delusions of Rights: Americans with Psychiatric Disabilities, Employment Discrimination, and the Americans with Disabilities Act." *Alabama Law Review* 52:271–319.

Stein, Michael Ashley. 2004. "Same Struggle, Different Difference: ADA Accommodations as Antidiscrimination." *University Pennsylvania Law Review* 153:579–673.

———. 2007. "Disability Human Rights." *California Law Review* 95:75–121.

St. Louis Public Schools. 1905–1906. *52nd Annual Report of the Board of Education for the St. Louis Public Schools*. St. Louis: St. Louis Public Schools.

———. 1907–1908. *54th Annual Report of the Board of Education for the St. Louis Public Schools*. St. Louis: St. Louis Public Schools.

Stone, Deborah A. 1984. *The Disabled State*. Philadelphia: Temple Univ. Press.

Stone, Donald H. 2000. "What Law Schools Are Doing to Accommodate Students with Learning Disabilities." *South Texas Law Review* 42:19–57.

Strauss, Alfred A. 1944. "Ways of Thinking in Brain-Crippled Deficient Children." *American Journal of Psychiatry* 100: 639–47.

Strauss, Alfred A., and Newell C. Kephart. 1939. "Rate of Mental Growth in a Constant Environment among Higher Grade Moron and Borderline Children." *Proceedings of the American Association on Mental Deficiency* 44, no. 1: 137–42.

———. 1940. "Behavior Differences in Mentally Retarded Children Measured by a New Behavior Rating Scale." *American Journal of Psychiatry* 96: 1117–24.

Strauss, Alfred A., Laura E. Lehtinen, and Newell C. Kephart. 1947. *Psychopathology and Education of the Brain-Injured Child.* New York: Grune & Stratton.

Strauss, Alfred A., and Heinz Werner. 1938. "Deficiency in the Finger Schema in Relation to Arithmetic Disability." *American Journal of Orthopsychiatry* 8:719–25.

———. 1939. "Finger Agnosia in Children with Brief Discussion on the Defect and Retardation in Mentally Handicapped Children." *American Journal of Psychiatry* 95:1215–25.

———. 1941. "The Mental Organization of the Brain-Injured Mentally Defective Child." *American Journal of Psychiatry* 97:1194–203.

Sullivan, William M. 2005. *Work and Integrity: The Crisis and Promise of Professionalism in America.* 2nd ed. San Francisco: Jossey-Bass.

Swain, John. 2003. *Controversial Issues in a Disabling Society.* Buckingham, UK: Open Univ. Press.

Switzer, Jacqueline Vaughn. 2003. *Disabled Rights: American Disability Policy and the Fight for Equality.* Washington, DC: Georgetown Univ. Press.

Syracuse University Center on Human Policy, Law, and Disability Studies. 2004. Disability Studies for Teachers (website). Available at http://www.disabilitystudiesforteachers.org/index.php.

Tashie, Carol, Joanne M. Malloy, and Stephen J. Lichtenstein. 1998. "Transition or Graduation? Supporting All Students to Plan for the Future." In *Restructuring High Schools for All Learners: Taking Inclusion to the Next Level,* edited by Cheryl M. Jorgensen, 233–60. Baltimore: Brookes.

Tatum, Beverly Daniel. 2007. *Can We Talk about Race? And Other Conversations in an Era of School Resegregation.* Boston: Beacon Press.

Taylor, Maurice C., and Gerald A. Foster. 2007. "Bad Boys and School Suspensions: Public Policy Implications for Black Males." *Sociological Inquiry* 56:498–506.

Taylor, Steven J. 1988. "Caught in the Continuum: A Critical Analysis of the Principle of the Least Restrictive Environment." *Journal of the Association for Persons with Severe Handicaps* 13, no. 1: 45–53.

———. 2001. "The Continuum and Current Controversies in the USA." *Journal of Intellectual and Developmental Disability* 26, no. 1: 15–33.

———. 2006. "Foreword. Before It Had a Name: Exploring the Historical Roots of Disability Studies in Education." In *Vital Questions Facing Disability Studies in Education*, edited by Scot Danforth and Susan L. Gabel, xiii–xxiii. New York: Lang.

———. 2009. *Acts of Conscience: World War II, Mental Institutions, and Religious Objectors*. Syracuse, NY: Syracuse Univ. Press.

———. 2011. "Disability Studies in Higher Education." *New Directions for Higher Education* 154 (Summer): 93–98.

Tiedemann, Chris Wise. 2012. *College Success for Students with Physical Disabilities*. Austin, TX: Prufrock Press.

Tolbert, Pamela S., and Lynne G. Zucker. 1983. "Institutional Sources of Change in the Formal Structure of Organizations: The Diffusion of Civil Service Reforms." *Administrative Science Quarterly* 23:22–39.

Tomsho, Robert. 2009. "Study Tallies Education Gap's Effect on GDP." *Wall Street Journal*, Apr. 22. Available at http://online.wsj.com/article/SB124040 633530943487.html.

Torre, María Elena, and Michele Fine. 2005. "Bar None: Extending Affirmative Action to Higher Education in Prison." *Journal of Social Issues* 61, no. 3: 569–94.

Tremain, Shelley. 2005. "Foucault, Governmentality, and Critical Disability Theory." In *Foucault and the Government of Disability*, edited by Shelley Tremain, 1–24. Ann Arbor: Univ. of Michigan Press.

Tucker, Bonnie Poitras. 2000. "The Supreme Court's Definition of Disability under the ADA: A Return to the Dark Ages." *Alabama Law Review* 52:321–74.

Tucker, James. 1980. "Ethnic Proportions in Classes for the Learning Disabled: Issues in Nonbiased Assessment." *Journal of Special Education* 14, no. 1: 93–105.

Turnbull, H. Rutherford. 1993. *Free Appropriate Public Education: The Law and Children with Disabilities*. Denver: Love.

Turnbull, H. Rutherford, Mathew J. Stowe, and Nancy E. Huerta. 2007. *Free Appropriate Public Education: The Law and Children with Disabilities*. 7th ed. Denver: Love.

Udehn, Lars. 2002. "The Changing Face of Methodological Individualism." *Annual Review of Sociology* 28:479–507.

Unger, Roberto M. 1983. *The Critical Legal Studies Movement.* Cambridge, MA: Harvard Univ. Press.

University of California at Los Angeles Civil Rights Project. 2012. "Racial Inequity in Special Education: Executive Summary for Federal Policy Makers." Available at http://wrenchproject.com/linked/racial%20inequity%20in%20 special%20.pdf. Accessed June 25.

US Bureau of the Census. 2008. "High School Dropouts by Race and Hispanic Origin: 1980 to 2007" (table 262). Available at http://www.census.gov /compendia/statab/2010/tables/10s0262.pdf.

———. 2010. "Americans with Disabilities: 2010." Available at http://www .census.gov/compendia/statab/2010/tables/10s0262.pdf.

———. 2012. *United States Census.* Washington, DC: U.S. Bureau of the Census. Available at http://www.census.gov/population/www/pop-profile/disabil .html.

US Bureau of Labor Statistics, US Department of Labor. 2012. "Special Education Teachers." In *Occupational Outlook Handbook, 2012–2013 Edition.* Washington, DC: US Department of Labor. Available at http://www.bls.gov /ooh/education-training-and-library/special-education-teachers.htm.

———. n.d. "Economic News Release." Available at http://data.bls.gov/cgi-bin /print.pl/news.release/empsiy.t02.htm. Accessed May 10, 2010.

US Bureau of Prisons. 2012. *Quick Facts about the Bureau of Prisons.* Available at http://www.bop.gov/news/quick.jsp. Last updated Sept. 29, 2012.

US Department of Education. 2005. *Twenty-Seventh Annual Report to Congress on the Implementation of the Individuals with Disabilities Education Act.* Washington, DC: US Department of Education. Available at http://www .ed.gov/about/reports/annual/osep/2005/parts-b-c/27th-vol-1.pdf.

———. 2007. *Students Ages 6 through 21 Served under IDEA, Part B, by Disability Category and State.* Washington, DC: US Department of Education. Available at https://www.ideadata.org/TABLES31ST/AR_1-3.xls.

———. 2009. *Implementing RTI Using Title I, Title III, and CEIS Funds.* Washington, DC: US Department of Education. Available at http://www2.ed.gov /programs/titleiparta/rti.html.

———. 2010. *29th Annual Report to Congress on the Implementation of the Individuals with Disabilities Education Act, 2007.* 3 vols. Washington, DC: Office of Special Education and Rehabilitation Services, US Department of Education.

US Department of Labor. 2008. *Labor Force Statistics from the Current Population Survey.* Washington, DC: US Department of Labor. Available at http://data.bls.gov/PDQ/servlet/SurveyOutputServlet?data_tool=latest_numbers&series_id=LNS14000000.

US Federal Bureau of Prisons. 2012. "Quick Facts about the Bureau of Prisons." Available at http://www.bop.gov/news/quick.jsp. Last updated Sept. 29, 2012.

US Government Accountability Office (GAO). 2009. *Higher Education and Disability: Education Needs a Coordinated Approach to Improve Its Assistance to Schools in Supporting Students.* Report to the Chairman, Committee on Education and Labor, House of Representatives. Washington, DC: US GAO, Oct. Available at http://www.gao.gov/new.items/d1033.pdf.

Valle, Jan W., and David J. Connor. 2010. *Rethinking Difference: A Disability Studies Approach to Inclusive Practices.* New York: McGraw Hill.

Vance, Mary Lee, ed. 2007a. *Disabled Faculty and Staff in a Disabling Society: Multiple Identities in Higher Education.* Huntersville, NC: Association on Higher Education and Disability.

———. 2007b. "Taking Risks." In *Disabled Faculty and Staff in a Disabling Society: Multiple Identities in Higher Education,* edited by Mary Lee Vance, 11–21. Huntersville, NC: Association on Higher Education and Disability.

Vidali, Amy. 2010. "Seeing What We Know: Disability and Theories of Metaphor." *Journal of Literary & Cultural Disability Studies* 4, no. 1: 33–54.

Voltz, Deborah L. 1998. "Cultural Diversity and Special Education Teacher Preparation: Critical Issues Confronting the Field." *Teacher Education and Special Education* 21, no. 1: 63–70.

Voltz, Deborah L., Nettye Brazil, and Alison Ford. 2001. "What Matters Most in Inclusive Education: A Practical Guide for Moving Forward." *Intervention in School and Clinic* 37:23–30. Available at http://www.sagepublications.com.

Vonnegut, Kurt, Jr. [1961] 1998. "Harrison Bergeron." In *Welcome to the Monkey House,* 7–14. New York: Random House.

Wade, Cheryl M. 1995. "I Am Not One of the." *Ms.* 12, no. 3: 77.

Wagner, Mary. 1990. "The School Programs and School Performance of Secondary Students Classified as Learning Disabled Findings from the National Longitudinal Transition Study of Special Education Students." Paper presented to Division G at the American Educational Research Association annual meeting, Boston, Apr.

Wagner, Mary, Lynn Newman, Renée Cameto, Nicolle Garza, and Phyllis Levine. 2005. *After High School: A First Look at the Post School Experiences of Youth with Disabilities.* A report from the National Longitudinal Transition Study-2 (NLTS2). Menlo Park, CA: SRI International. Available at http://www.nlts2.org/reports/2005_04/nlts2_report_2005_04_complete.pdf.

Walker, Venessa Siddle. 1996. *Their Highest Potential: An African American School Community in the Segregated South.* Chapel Hill: Univ. of North Carolina Press.

Wallin, J. E. Wallace. 1921. "Progress in the Field of Mental Hygiene in Missouri." *Monthly Bulletin, Missouri State Board of Charities and Corrections* 23:48–61.

———. 1923. "The Diagnostic Findings from Seven Years of Examining in the Same School Clinic." *Journal of Delinquency* 8:169–95.

———. 1955. *The Odyssey of a Psychologist: Pioneering Special Education, Clinical Psychology, and Mental Hygiene with a Comprehensive Bibliography of the Author's Publications.* Wilmington, DE: J. E. Wallace Wallin.

Wapner, Seymour, and Bernard Kaplan. 1964. "Heinz Werner: 1890–1964." *American Journal of Psychology* 77, no. 3: 513–17.

Ward, Ian. 2004. *An Introduction to Critical Legal Theory.* 2d ed. London: Routledge.

Ware, Linda. 2001. "Writing, Identity, and the Other: Dare We Do Disability Studies?" *Journal of Teacher Education* 52, no. 2: 107–23.

———. 2003a. "Understanding Disability and Transforming Schools." In *Developing Inclusive Teacher Education,* edited by Tony Booth, Kari Nes, and Marit Stromstad, 146–65. London: Routledge.

———. 2003b. "Working Past Pity: What We Make of Disability in Schools." In *Inclusion, Participation, and Democracy: What Is the Purpose?* edited by Julie Allan, 117–37. The Hague: Kluwer Academic.

———. 2006a. "A Look at the Way We Look at Disability." In *Vital Questions Facing Disability Studies in Education,* edited by Scot Danforth and Susan L. Gabel, 242–64. New York: Lang.

———. 2006b. "Mainstreaming." In *Encyclopedia of Disability,* edited by Gary L. Albrecht, 3:1052–55. Thousand Oaks, CA: Sage.

———. 2006c. "Urban Educators, Disability Studies, and Education: Excavation in Schools and Society." *International Journal of Inclusive Education* 10, nos. 2–3: 149–68.

———. 2008. "Worlds Remade: Inclusion through Engagement with Disability Arts." *International Journal of Inclusive Education* 12, nos. 5–6: 563–83.

———. 2009. "The Hegemonic Impulse for Health and Well-Being: A Saga of the Less Well and the Less Worthy." In *Diversity and Multiculturalism: A Reader*, edited by Shirley R. Steinberg, 363–76. New York: Lang.

———. 2010. "Disability Studies in Education." In *The Handbook of Research in the Social Foundations of Education*, edited by Steven Tozer, Annette Henry, Bernardo Gallegos, Mary Bushnell Greiner, and Paula Groves Price, 244–59. New York: Routledge.

———. 2011. "When Art Informs: Inviting Ways to See the Unexpected." *Learning Disability Quarterly* 34, no. 3: 194–202.

Ware, Linda, and Jan W. Valle. 2010. "How Do We Begin a Conversation on Disability in Urban Education?" In *19 Urban Questions*, edited by Shirley R. Steinberg, 113–30. New York: Lang.

Waterstone, Michael E. 2005. "Lane, Fundamental Rights, and Voting." *Alabama Law Review* 56:793–825.

Weatherly, Richard, and Michael Lipsky, 1977. "Street-Level Bureaucrats and Institutional Innovation: Implementing Special-Education Reform." *Harvard Educational Review* 47, no. 2: 171–97.

Weatherspoon, Floyd. 2006. "Racial Justice and Equity for African-American Males in the American Educational System: A Dream Forever Deferred." *North Carolina Law Journal* 29:1–34.

Weber, Mark C. 2002. "Disability Harassment in the Public Schools." *William and Mary Law Review* 43:1079–158.

———. 2006. "Reflections on the New Individuals with Disabilities Education Improvement Act." *Florida Law Review* 58:7–52.

———. 2007a. *Disability Harassment.* New York: New York Univ. Press.

———. 2007b. "A Nuanced Approach to the Disability Integration Presumption." *University of Pennsylvania Law Review* 156:174–87.

———. 2009. "The IDEA Eligibility Mess." *Buffalo Law Review* 57:83–160.

Wehmeyer, Michael L., and Robert L. Schalock. 2001. "Self-Determination and Quality of Life: Implications for Special Education Services and Supports." *Focus on Exceptional Children* 33, no. 6: 1–16.

Weidner, Virginia R., and Carolyn D. Herrington. 2006. "Are Parents Informed Consumers? Evidence from Florida McKay Scholarship Program." *Peabody Journal of Education* 81, no. 1: 27–56.

Weis, Andrew. 1998. "Jumping to Conclusions in *Jumping the Queue*." Review of *Jumping the Queue: An Inquiry into the Legal Treatment of Students with Learning Disabilities* by Mark Kelman and Gillian Lester. *Stanford Law Review* 51:183–219.

Weishaar, Mary Konya, Mary Ellen Weishaar, and John Borsa. 2007. *Inclusive Educational Administration: A Case Study Approach*. 2nd ed. Long Grove, IL: Waveland Press.

Wells, Jett. 2010. "Colleges with the BEST Learning Disability Programs." *Huffington Post*, June 7. Available at http://www.huffingtonpost.com/2010/06/07/best-ld-programs_n_603369.html#s96857&title=Landmark_College.

Wendell, Susan. 1996. *The Rejected Body: Feminist Philosophical Reflections on Disability*. New York: Routledge.

Werner, Heinz. 1937. "Process and Achievement—a Basic Problem of Education and Developmental Psychology." *Harvard Educational Review* 7:353–68.

———. 1948. *Comparative Psychology of Mental Development*. New York: International Universities Press.

Werner, Heinz, and Alfred A. Strauss. 1938. "Approaches to a Functional Analysis of Mentally Handicapped Problem Children with Illustrations in the Field of Arithmetic Disability." *Proceedings of the American Association on Mental Deficiency* 43, no. 2: 105–38.

———. 1939. "Problems and Methods of Functional Analysis in Mentally Deficient Children." *Journal of Abnormal and Social Psychology* 34, no. 1: 37–62.

———. 1941. "Pathology of Figure–Background Relation in the Child." *Journal of Abnormal and Social Psychology* 36, no. 2: 236–48.

———. 1943. "Impairment in Thought Processes of Brain-Injured Children." *American Journal of Mental Deficiency* 47: 291–95.

Wernicke, Carl. [1874] 1977. "The Aphasia Symptom Complex: A Psychological Study on an Anatomic Basis." In *Wernicke's Works on Aphasia: A Sourcebook and Review*, edited by Gertrude H. Eggert, 91–145. The Hague: Mouton.

Williams, Patricia J. 1991. *The Alchemy of Race and Rights: Diary of a Law Professor*. Cambridge, MA: Harvard Univ. Press.

Wilson, James C., and Cynthia Lewiecki-Wilson. 2001. *Embodied Rhetorics: Disability in Language and Culture*. Carbondale: Southern Illinois Univ. Press.

Winters, Clyde A. 1997. "Learning Disabilities, Crime, Delinquency, and Special Education Placement." *Adolescence* 32, no. 126: 451–62.

Winzer, Margaret A. 1993. *The History of Special Education: From Isolation to Integration*. Washington, DC: Gallaudet Univ. Press.

Wittenburg, David C., Thomas Golden, and Michael Fishman. 2002. "Transition Options for Youth with Disabilities: An Overview of the Programs and Policies That Affect the Transition from School." *Journal of Vocational Rehabilitation* 17:195–206.

Withers, John W. 1917. "Introduction." In J. E. Wallin, *Problems of Subnormality*, xiii–xv. Yonkers-on-Hudson, NY: World Book.

Wollenberg, Charles. 1976. *All Deliberate Speed: Segregation and Exclusion in California Schools, 1855–1975*. Berkeley: Univ. of California Press.

Woolhandler, Steffie, and David U. Himmelstein. 2002. "Paying for National Health Insurance—and Not Getting It." *Health Affairs* 21:88–98.

World Health Organization. 1980. *International Classification of Impairments, Disabilities, and Handicaps: A Manual of Classification Relating to the Consequences of Disease*. Geneva: World Health Organization.

———. 2001. *International Classification of Functioning, Disability, and Health: ICF*. Geneva: World Health Organization.

———. 2011. *World Report on Disability*. Geneva: World Health Organization. Available at http://whqlibdoc.who.int/publications/2011/9789240685215_eng .pdf.

Wurtzel, Elizabeth. 2002. *Prozac Nation: Young and Depressed in America*. New York: Penguin Books.

Yan, Wenfan. 1999. "Successful African American Students: The Role of Parental Involvement." *Journal of Negro Education* 68:5–22.

Yell, Mitchell L. 2006. *The Law and Special Education*. 2nd ed. Columbus, OH: Pearson, Merrill.

Yellin, Susan. 2009. "Post Secondary Transition under the IDEA." *Practicing Law Institute: New York Practice Skills Course Handbook Series* 188:321–28.

Young, Iris Marion. 1990. *Justice and the Politics of Difference*. Princeton, NJ: Princeton Univ. Press.

———. 2000. *Inclusion and Democracy*. Oxford: Oxford Univ. Press.

———. 2008. "Unruly Categories: A Critique of Nancy Fraser's Dual Systems Theory." In *Adding Insult to Injury: Nancy Fraser Debates Her Critics*, edited by Kevin Olson, 327–46. London: Verso.

Young, Katherine. 2008. "'I Don't Think I'm the Right Person for That': Theoretical and Institutional Questions about a Combined Credential Program." *Disability Studies Quarterly* 28, no. 4. Available at http://www.dsq -sds.org.

Young, Morghan Vélez, Rachel Sophia Phillips, and Na'ilah Suad Nasir. 2010. "Schooling in a Youth Prison." *Journal of Correctional Education* 61, no. 3: 203–22.

Ysseldyke, James E., Martha L. Thurlow, Janet L. Graden, Caren Wesson, Bob Algozzine, and Stanley L. Deno. 1983. "Generalizations from Five Years of Research on Assessment and Decision Making." *Exceptional Education Quarterly* 4, no. 1: 75–93.

Zucker, Lynne G. 1981. "Institutional Structure and Organizational Processes: The Role of Evaluation Units in Schools." In *Evaluation and Decision Making*, edited by Adrianne Bank and Richard C. Williams, 69–89, CSE Monograph Series no. 10. Los Angeles: UCLA Center for the Study of Evaluation.

Legal Cases, Statutes, and Regulations

Albertson's, Inc. v. Kirkinburg. 1999. 527 U.S. 555.

Americans with Disabilities Act. 1990. Pub. L. No. 101-336, 104 Stat. 327 (codified as amended in section 42 U.S.C. §12101 et seq.).

Americans with Disabilities Amendments Act. 2008. Pub. L. No. 110-325, 122 Stat. 3553.

Arlington Central Sch. Dist. v. Murphy. 2006. 126 S.Ct. 2455, 2458.

Atkins v. Virginia. 2002. 536 U.S. 304.

Bellotti v. Baird. 1979. 443 U.S. 622, 643.

Board of Education of the Hendrick Hudson Central School District, Westchester County, et al., v. Amy Rowley. 1982. 458 U.S. 176.

Board of Trustees of University of Alabama v. Garrett. 2001. 531 U.S. 356.

Brown v. Board of Education (I). 1954. 347 U.S. 483, 74 S. Ct. 686, 98 L. Ed. 873.

Brown v. Board of Education (II). 1955. 349 U.S. 294.

Buck v. Bell. 1927. 274 U.S. 200.

City of Cleburne v. Cleburne Living Center. 1985. 473 U.S. 432, 461–63.

Civil Rights Act. 1964. 42 U.S. Code, chap. 21.

Columbus Board of Education v. Penick. 1979. 443 U.S. 449, 489.

Dale M. v. Board of Education of Bradley-Bourbonnais High School. 2001. 237 F.3d 813 (7th Cir.).

Developmentally Disabled Assistance and Bill of Rights Act. 1975. 42 U.S.C.

Diana v. State Board of Education. 1970. CA 70 RFT (N.D. Cal.).

Education for All Handicapped Children Act. 1975. Pub. L. No. 94-142, 89 Stat. 773 (codified as amended at 20 U.S.C §1400 et seq. (2006)).

Education of Mentally Retarded Children Act. 1958. Pub. Law 85-926.

Elementary and Secondary Education Act. 1966. Pub. L. 89-750.

Equal Employment Opportunity Commission. 2013. ADA Title I Regulations. 29 C.F.R. §1630.

Fair Housing Amendments Act. 1988. Pub. L. No. 100-430, 102 Stat. 1619 (codified as amended at 42 U.S.C. §§3601–31).

Fialka-Feldman v. Oakland University Board of Trustees, et al. 2011. 639 F.3d 711 (6th Cir.).

Forest Grove School District v. T.A. 2009. 129 S. Ct. 2484, 2496.

Goldberg v. Kelly. 1970. 397 U.S. 254, 90 S. Ct. 1011, 25 L. Ed. 2d 287.

Grutter v. Bollinger. 2003. 539 U.S. 306.

Handicapped Children's Protection Act. 1986. 20 U.S.C. §1415.

Higher Education Opportunity Act. 2008. Pub. L.110-315, Aug. 14; 122 STAT. 3078.

Hobson v. Hansen. 1967. 269 F. Supp. 401, 515 (D.D.C.), *aff'd. sub nom.*, Smuck v. Hobson, 408 F. 2d 175 (D.C. Cir. 1969).

Homer A. Plessy v. John H. Ferguson. 1896. 163 U.S. 537.

Honig v. Doe. 1988. 484 U.S. 305.

Hood v. Encinitas Union School District. 2007. 486 F.3d 1099 (9th Cir.).

Individuals with Disabilities Education Act. 1990. 20 U.S.C.A. §§1400–1482. West 2011.

Individuals with Disabilities Education Improvement Act. 2004. Pub. L. No. 108-446, 118 Stat. 2647 (codified as amended in 20 U.S.C. §§1400–1482 (2006)).

Individuals with Disabilities Education Regulation. 2012. 34 C.F.R. §§300.303.

J.D. v. Pawlett School District. 2000. 224 F.3d 60 (2d Cir.).

Larry P. v. Riles. 1984. 793 F.2d 969 (9th Cir.).

Lee v. Macon County Board of Education. 1967. 267 F. Supp. 458 (M.D. Ala.).

Loving v. Virginia. 1967. 388 U.S. 1.

McLaurin v. Oklahoma. 1950. 339 U.S. 637.

Mendez v. Westminister School District. 1946. 64 F. Supp. 544 (S.D. Cal.), aff'd. 161 F.2d 774 (9th Cir. 1947).

Mental Health Parity and Addiction Equity Act. 2008. Pub. L. No. 110-343, 122 Stat. 3881.

Mental Retardation Facilities and Community Health Centers Construction Act. 1963. Pub. L. 88-164.

Milliken v. Bradley. 1974. 418 U.S. 787.

Mills v. Board of Education of District of Columbia. 1972. 348 F. Supp. 866 (D.D.C.); contempt proceedings, EHLR 551:643 (D.D.C. 1980).

Missouri v. Jenkins. 1995. 515 U.S. 70, 114.

Moose Lodge No. 107 v. Irvis. 1972. 407 U.S. 163.

M.P. v. Nebraska Independent School District. 2007. U.S. Dist. Lexis 82739 *2–4 (W.D. Tex.).

Mr. I. v. Maine School Administrative District. 2007. 480 F.3d 1, 6–7, 12 (1st Cir.).

Murphy v. United Parcel Service, Inc. 1999. 527 U.S. 516.

New Paltz Central School District v. St. Pierre. 2004. 307 F. Supp. 2d 394 (N.D. N.Y.).

No Child Left Behind Act. 2001. 20 U.S.C. §§6301–304.

O'Connor v. Donaldson. 1975. 422 U.S. 563.

Olmstead v. L.C. 1999. 527 U.S. 581.

Orr v. Wal-Mart Stores, Inc. 2002. 297 F.3d 720, 725 (8th Cir.).

Parents in Action on Special Education (PASE) v. Hannon. 1980. 506 F. Supp. 831.

Parham v. J.R. 1979. 442 U.S. 584, 606–7.

Patient Protection and Affordable Care Act. 2010. Pub. L. No. 111-148, 124 Stat. 119.

Pegram v. Herdrich. 2000. 530 U.S. 211.

Pennsylvania Association for Retarded Citizens (PARC) v. Commonwealth of Pennsylvania. 1972. 334 F. Supp. 1257 (E.D. PA) (consent decree 1972).

Pimental v. Dartmouth-Hitchcock Clinic. 2002. 236 F. Supp.2d 177, 184 (D. N.H.).

Rehabilitation Act. 1973. Pub. L. No. 93-112, 87 Stat. 355 (codified as amended in 29 U.S.C. §§705.08 (2000)).

San Antonio Independent School District v. Rodriguez. 1973. 411 U.S. 1.

Schaffer ex rel. Schaffer v. Weast. 2005. 546 U.S. 49.

Schall v. Martin. 1984. 467 U.S. 253, 265.

Schiavo ex rel. Schindler v. Schiavo. 2005. 544 U.S. 915.

Slaughter-House Cases. 1873. 83 U.S. 36.

Smith v. Robinson. 1984. 468 U.S. 992.

Springer v. Fairfax County School Board. 1998. 134 F.3d 659 (4th Cir.).

Sutton v. United Air Lines, Inc. 1999. 527 U.S. 471.

Swann v. Charlotte-Mecklenburg Board of Education. 1970. 402 U.S. 1.

Sweatt v. Painter. 1950. 339 U.S. 629.

Tennessee v. Lane. 2004. 541 U.S. 509.

Ticket to Work and Work Incentives Improvement Act. 1999. Pub. L. No. 106-170, 113 Stat. 1860.

Todd v. Academy Corp. 1999. 77 F. Supp.2d 448, 452-53 (S.D. Tx.).

Toyota Motor Mfg., Ky., Inc. v. Williams. 2002. 534 U.S. 184, 185.

Tracy v. Beaufort County Board of Education. 2004. 335 F. Supp. 2d 675, 689 (D. S.C.).

United Nations Convention on the Rights of Persons with Disabilities. 2007. G.A. Res. 61/106, adopted Dec. 13, 2006, with Optional Protocol. Available at http://www.un.org/esa/socdev/enable/rights/convtexte.htm.

United States v. Cruikshank. 1876. 92 U.S. 542.

United States v. Georgia. 2006. 546 U.S. 151.

United States v. Harris. 1883. 106 U.S. 629.

Winkelman v. Parma City School District. 2007. 550 U.S. 516.

Youngberg v. Romeo. 1982. 457 U.S. 307.

About the Editors

Arlene S. Kanter is the Bond, Schoeneck & King Distinguished Professor of Law at Syracuse University College of Law and the Laura J. and L. Douglas Meredith Professor of Teaching Excellence at Syracuse University, where she also holds a courtesy appointment in the School of Education. She founded and directs the College of Law's Disability Law and Policy Program and codirects the Syracuse University Center on Human Policy, Law, and Disability Studies. Professor Kanter publishes and lectures extensively on US, comparative, and international disability laws and policies. She is the coauthor of the first casebook on international and comparative disability law, *Cases and Materials on International and Comparative Mental Disability Law* (2006), and author of the upcoming book *From Charity to Human Rights: The Development of Disability Rights under International Law* (2014). She is the coeditor of Syracuse University Press's Critical Disability Studies series and founder and coeditor of the Social Science Research Network *Journal on Disability Law*. She is also a founder of the American Association of Law Schools' Disability Law Section and the Law and Society Association's Disability Legal Studies Collaborative Research Network. She was a Fulbright Scholar in 2009–10, and she was selected as the 2010–11 Distinguished Switzer Fellow by the National Association of Disability Rehabilitation Research of the US Department of Education.

Beth A. Ferri is an associate professor in teaching, leadership, and disability studies at Syracuse University, where she also coordinates the doctoral program in special education. Professor Ferri has published widely on the intersection of gender, race, and disability. Her previous book, *Reading Resistance: Discourses of Exclusion in Desegregation and Inclusion Debates* (2006), written with David J. Connor, chronicles how problematic rhetorics of race and dis/ability were used to maintain and justify segregated education after the historic

Brown v. Board of Education decision. She is the coeditor of Syracuse University Press's Critical Disability Studies series. She was recognized in 2003 as an Outstanding Young Scholar by the organizers of the Disability Studies in Education conference.

About the Contributors

Susan Baglieri is a professor of adolescent special education at Long Island University–Brooklyn and the coauthor of the 2012 book *Disability Studies and the Inclusive Classroom: Critical Practices for Creating Least Restrictive Attitudes.* She is assistant editor for *Disability Studies Quarterly* and has served on the board of directors of the Society for Disability Studies. Baglieri is a member of the American Educational Research Association's special-interest group in disability studies in education and received the Junior Scholar Award at the group's Eighth Annual Second City Conference in 2008.

Alicia A. Broderick is an associate professor of education in the inclusive-education graduate program at Montclair State University. Her program of research aims to explore the implications of disability studies in education (DSE) work for teacher education and to engage in DSE scholarship through a specific exploration of the workings of ableism in media and cultural representations of autism. In 2002, she was recognized by the DSE special-interest group of the American Educational Research Association as its first Outstanding Young Scholar in Disability Studies.

Scot Danforth is professor and director of the School of Teacher Education at San Diego State University. He is a well-known leader in the field of disability studies in education. He has written many articles and books, including *The Incomplete Child: An Intellectual History of Learning Disabilities* (2009). He also served for six years as coeditor of *Disability Studies Quarterly*, the journal of the Society for Disability Studies.

Zanita E. Fenton is a professor of law at the University of Miami School of Law. Her scholarship addresses issues of structural inequality and forms of social subordination. Her focus has been on the intersection of race and gender subordination in a range of contexts where other categories of subordination are present, including class, sexuality, and disability. Her interests are incorporated in her teaching and in her advocacy for victims of domestic abuse.

Philip M. Ferguson is a professor at the College of Educational Studies of Chapman University. For more than thirty years, he has pursued an interest in the field of disability studies with a focus on issues affecting people with intellectual disabilities. Ferguson is a former president of the Society for Disability Studies. He is author of *Abandoned to Their Fate: Social Policy and Practice toward Severely Disabled Persons, 1820–1920* (1994) and coeditor of *Interpreting Disability: A Qualitative Reader* (1992).

Wendy S. Harbour is the Lawrence B. Taishoff Professor for Inclusive Education and executive director of the Taishoff Center for Inclusive Higher Education at Syracuse University. She teaches courses in disability studies, inclusive K–12 education, and disability in higher education. Harbour's areas of expertise include disability studies in education, universal design for learning, postsecondary disability services and accommodations, and transition from secondary to postsecondary settings.

Wendy F. Hensel is an associate dean for research and faculty development and professor of law at Georgia State University College of Law. She teaches and writes about disability discrimination in American society and its intersection with education, employment, and tort law. Hensel has authored numerous articles on the legal treatment of disability under the Individuals with Disabilities Education Act and the American with Disabilities Act.

J. Robert Kent is a research associate in American studies at the University of Kansas and a retired firefighter. He has been a lecturer in American studies and special education and is on the editorial board of *American Studies*. Kent has published essays in *Social Thought & Research* and *American Studies*.

Martha Minow is the Morgan and Helen Chu Dean and Professor of Law at Harvard Law School. She is an expert in human rights and advocacy for persons with disabilities, women, and people from racial and religious minorities. Minow's five-year partnership with the US Department of Education and the Center for Applied Special Technology has increased access to the general curriculum for students with disabilities. In addition to her many scholarly articles published in journals of law, history, and philosophy, her books include *In Brown's Wake: Legacies of America's Constitutional Landmark* (2010), *Just Schools: Pursuing Equality in Societies of Difference* (2008), coedited with Richard Shweder and Hazel Markus; *Not Only for Myself: Identity, Politics, and Law* (1997); and *Making All the Difference: Inclusion, Exclusion, and American Law* (1990).

Theodoto Ressa is the recipient of the 2006 Ford Foundation International Fellowship and a doctoral student in the School of Teaching and Learning at Ohio State University in Columbus.

Ani B. Satz is an associate professor at Emory University School of Law, Rollins School of Public Health, and Emory Center for Ethics. She is a regulatory health lawyer and philosopher who teaches courses at the intersection of disability and health law and ethics. Her research focuses on the legal response to vulnerability and governmental obligations to those who are vulnerable. Satz's most recent scholarship addresses disability discrimination, access to health care, and the well-being of nonhuman animals from a law and ethics perspective. Her book *Disability and Discrimination: Cases and Materials* is forthcoming. Satz served as 2009–10 chair of the Association of American Law Schools' Section on Disability Law.

Thomas M. Skrtic is a professor of education in the Department of Special Education at the University of Kansas. His academic interests include classical pragmatism, institutional theory, and democratic social reform, which inform several of his published works, including *Behind Special Education: A Critical Analysis of Professional Culture and School Organization* (1991) and *Disability and Democracy: Reconstructing (Special) Education for Postmodernity* (1995). His work also has appeared in journals such as *Harvard Educational Review, Exceptional Children*, and *Disability Studies Quarterly*. In 2009, he received the Senior Scholar Award of the Disability Studies in Education interest group of the American Educational Research Association.

Linda Ware is an associate professor and faculty member in the Ella Cline Shear School of Education, State University of New York–Geneseo. She teaches courses in curriculum, women's studies, disability in America, and interdisciplinary disability studies. Ware is recognized internationally for her research in the field of disability studies. She has published widely in humanities, education, and social science journals and has authored numerous book chapters on disability and education. She edited the international collection of scholarship on inclusion and disability studies *Ideology and the Politics of (In)Exclusion* (2004).

Mark C. Weber is the Vincent de Paul professor of law at DePaul University's College of Law. His professional interests are disability rights and complex tort litigation. He is the author of several books, including *Special Education Law and Litigation Treatise* (2008), *Disability Harassment* (2007), *Understanding Disability Law* (2007), and *Special Education Law Cases and Material* (2007), coauthored with Ralph Mawdsley and Sarah Redfield. Weber frequently speaks on disability law issues at national and international programs and has presented testimony on the implementation of the Americans with Disabilities Act to the US Civil Rights Commission.

Index